The Asbury Theological Seminary Series in Christian Revitalization Studies

This volume is published in collaboration with the Center for the Study of World Christian Revitalization Movements, a cooperative initiative of Asbury Theological Seminary faculty. Building on the work of the previous Wesleyan/Holiness Studies Center at the Seminary, the Center provides a focus for research in the Wesleyan Holiness and other related Christian renewal movements, including Pietism and Pentecostal movements, which have had a world impact. The research seeks to develop analytical models of these movements, including their biblical and theological assessment. Using an interdisciplinary approach, the Center bridges relevant discourses in several areas in order to gain insights for effective Christian mission globally. It recognizes the need for conducting research that combines insights from the history of evangelical renewal and revival movements with anthropological and religious studies literature on revitalization movements. It also networks with similar or related research and study centers around the world, in addition to sponsoring its own research projects.

    Christopher Anderson, Director of the Methodist Library and Coordinator of Special Collections at Drew University, offers a fresh collection of papers from a turning point Methodist conference that assessed the role of Methodism in dealing with a range of early twentieth century public issues. Presented with authoritative comment and interpretation, this study opens a window on the condition of Methodist life and thought at a critical juncture in its development within the crucible of the American culture. Being the largest denomination, its positions also represent views that were prominent in the American public debate of the day. Here is an in-depth study demonstrating how a revivalist denomination was struggling to live out its vocation as a transformative agent in a society that was shedding its international isolationism in the early twentieth century. As such, it is a study that has appeal for students of American history as well as the history of revitalization movements.

J. Steven O'Malley, PhD
Editor, The Pietist and Wesleyan Studies Series in the Asbury Theological Seminary Studies in Christian Revitalization

Voices from the Fair

*Race, Gender, and the
American Nation at a
Methodist Missionary Exposition*

Asbury Theological Seminary Series:
The Study of World Christian Revitalization Movements in
Pietist/Wesleyan Studies, No. 8

Christopher J. Anderson

EMETH PRESS
www.emethpress.com

Voices from the Fair: Race, Gender, and the American Nation at a Methodist Missionary Exposition

Copyright © 2012 Chris Anderson

Printed in the United States of America on acid-free paper
All rights reserved. No part of this book may be reproduced, or stored in a retrieval system or transmitted in any form or by any means, electronic, mechanical, photocopying, recording, scanning or otherwise, except as permitted by the 1976 United States Copyright Act, or with the prior written permission of Emeth Press. Requests for permission should be addressed to: Emeth Press, P. O. Box 23961, Lexington, KY 40523-3961.
http://www.emethpress.com.

Library of Congress Cataloging-in-Publication Data

Voices from the fair : race, gender, and the American nation at a Methodist missionary exposition / [compiled by] Christopher J. Anderson.
  p. cm. -- (The Asbury Theological Seminary series in world Christian revitalization movements in Pietist/Wesleyan studies ; no. 8)
 Includes bibliographical references and index.
 ISBN 978-1-60947-032-6 (alk. paper)
 1. United Methodist Church (U.S.)--Missions--Congresses. 2. Methodist Church--Missions--Congresses. I. Anderson, Christopher J. (Christopher Jay), 1969-
 BV2550.V65 2012
 266'.76--dc23
                              2012015081

Dedication

This edited collection is dedicated to the librarians, archivists, and private collectors who value primary sources. Voices from the past are available to us through several forms of media including the written word. Transcripts of speeches, sermons, meetings, and everyday conversations allow contemporary readers glimpses into the past with all its racial, cultural, and ideological complexities. Reading historical primary sources bring delight, insight, and outrage to contemporary audiences. Historians value the historical record as adjuncts to their historiographical and theoretical work. This manuscript joins other edited collections by providing a voice for those who made significant and unknown contributions to world history, particularly American Methodist history.

My parents, my siblings, and their families have given me encouragement to write and to explore the past. The many trips to museums and the dozens of books read during childhood helped shape my appreciation for those voices often lost to history. Growing up Methodist informed me of the rich tradition that helped shape my understanding of U.S. Christianity. My hope is that this collection brings awareness to those familiar and unfamiliar voices from history. Finally, I am especially grateful for Deb, Brett, and Trenton who heard me discuss the material found in the following pages. They encourage me every day.

Contents

Acknowledgments / ix

1. Missions and Missionary Expositions / 1

2. Methodist Missions and Racial Identities / 13

   Introduction / 13
   African Day Program, Afternoon Session / 16
   Negro Day Program, Morning Session / 31
   Negro Day Program, Afternoon Session / 41
   Southern Day Program, Morning Session / 59

3. Women's Missionary Societies and the Methodist Minute Men / 71

   Introduction / 71
   Woman's Day Program, Afternoon Session / 71
   Woman's Day Program, Afternoon Session / 93
   Meeting of National Woman's Party, Afternoon
      Session / 100
   Minute Men Day Program, Morning Session / 105
   Minute Men Convention, Afternoon Session / 121

4. Methodists, Prohibition and Universal Suffrage / 141

   Introduction / 141
   Woman's Christian Temperance Union Program,
      Afternoon Session / 144
   Temperance Rally, Morning Session / 163
   Prohibition Day Program, Afternoon Session / 187

5. Methodists, the U.S. Armed Forces, and the American Nation / 213
        Introduction   213
        Peace Signing Celebration, Morning Session / 216
        Americanization Day Program, Afternoon Session / 226
        Victory Day Program, Afternoon Session / 239
        Navy Day Program, Afternoon Session / 259
        Army Day Exercises, Morning Session / 268
        Program Honoring Lieutenant Commander A.C. Read &
            Sergeant Alvin C. York, Morning Session / 277

Appendix: Images and Photos of Participants in the 1919 Methodist
        Missionary Fair, A Centenary Celebration of American
        Methodist Missions / 287

Index / 325

Acknowledgments

The addresses and commentary found on these pages are the direct result of hours spent transcribing four leather bound volumes of primary source material located at the General Commission on Archives and History for The United Methodist Church in Madison, New Jersey, USA. The entire collection includes more than 1,700 pages of typescript along with a 400-page report on the Centenary Celebration of American Methodist Missions. The staff at the General Commission has been helpful both with access to these documents and with encouragement toward its completion. I'm especially grateful to Associate Archivist Mark Shenise who has helped me think through these materials since the earliest stages of the project and more recently Robert Williams, General Secretary of GCAH. Without their encouragement this project may have taken much longer than it did.

The staff of the Drew University Library has been gracious in their gentle critique of the introduction and the chapter transcripts. Special encouragement from Matthew Beland, Cory Fick, Lucy Marks, Lisa Miller, Masato Okinaka, Ernest Rubenstein, and Jocelyne Rubinetti helped me gain editorial momentum in order to complete what has been a six-year project. Andrew Scrimgeour, Dean of Libraries at Drew University, has been especially encouraging as we've discussed our book projects together and wished for more time to investigate and write about the past. Steven O'Malley, editor of the Wesleyan/Pietist Series for Emeth Press, has been a mentor and friend to me for nearly two decades. As a historian of Christianity he found research value in the addresses and commentary in this volume. He has been helpful during the process of moving the project from typescript to book. I am also grateful to Larry Wood for assisting me during the final stages of the project and for the staff of Emeth Press for publishing this collection.

Chapter One

Missions and Missionary Expositions

Introduction

A book published in 1919 by Methodist bishop and author Francis J. McConnell[1] proclaimed that American Methodists were on the front lines of an aggressive endeavor to redeem a world "open to successful cultivation." Imagining how Methodist missionaries might assist with the construction of a "World-Wide Church," McConnell proclaimed this global parish would include persons from every part of the world "standing together as one body before the throne."[2] Early twentieth century American Methodists, hoping to adopt and adapt John Wesley's notion of the "world as my parish," sought to craft an approach to mission that would initiate and ultimately help form locations of "Christian civilization" at home and abroad. As a result, American Methodists took ownership of the missionary impulse of earlier Wesleyans by attempting to establish a world-wide civilization centered upon Christian teachings and informed by American cultural expectations. This resulted in Methodist missionaries taking their own interpretations of the gospel of Christ to both mission stations and to the people who were the recipients of Methodist missionary work.

The same year that Bishop McConnell published *Democratic Christianity* Methodists from around the world traveled to Columbus, Ohio to experience a carefully planned missionary exposition marketed by church leaders as the "Centenary Celebration of American Methodist Missions." The three-week event attracted over one million visitors, each paying fifty cents to enter the Columbus fairgrounds complex to investigate ways in which American Methodists were positioning themselves to convert the world to Christ. The Centenary Celebration pointed Methodists toward the future by challenging fairgoers to imagine what Methodist missions at home and throughout the world might look like in the months and years following the completion of the exposition.

This book is a product of the 1919 Methodist missionary fair. The speeches and addresses found within this edited collection function as textual sound bites to help readers better understand the ideas, language, and motives of early twentieth century American Methodists. The hundreds of thousands of Methodists that gathered at the Columbus fairgrounds were ministers and laity from all over the world. Many worked as missionaries, government leaders and social activists. Their collective "voices" challenged listeners to think carefully about Christian missions as cultural and religious transformation in order to advance certain expressions of Christianity and the American nation at home and abroad.

These addresses also remind contemporary readers of how far (and not so far) Christian denominations and the political harbingers of the United States have come in broadcasting the language of mission, nation-building and empire. The language used throughout the following documents will sound both archaic and contemporary while challenging readers to think about how the work of missionaries and the motives of the U.S. government have changed throughout history and, yet, in some ways remain the same.

The structure and contents of the book reflect an attempt to place the reader in the midst of decorated pavilions, rented circus tents, and the massive concrete Coliseum situated on the Columbus fairgrounds. In order to accurately recapture the events that transpired during the 1919 exposition programs have been reproduced as they were recorded and include words of introduction, corporate prayers, hymns and public addresses. The material included in this book was delivered both spontaneously and with well-crafted articulation, revealing both the immediate notions of speakers alongside the more reserved and carefully prepared thoughts of the participants.

The unpublished transcripts of the exposition total over 1700 pages and include ecclesiastical representation from the African Methodist Episcopal Church, Colored (now Christian) Methodist Episcopal Church, Methodist Church of Canada (now United Church of Canada), Methodist Episcopal Church, Methodist Episcopal Church, South, and Methodist Protestant Church. The speakers range from social activists to missionaries to ordained ministers to those considered the products of mission. Methodists such as Lena Leonard Fisher, Robert Elijah Jones, James Cannon, Jr., and Charles Albert Tindley share the stage with governmental leaders, civil rights activists, and military veterans including William Jennings Bryan, Alice Paul, and Sergeant Alvin York.

From World's Fairs to Missionary Expositions

The popularity of international expositions held in Chicago (1893) and San Francisco (1915) helped provide the impetus for American Methodists to think about ways that similar fairs could be used by the church to promote world missions. At these World's Fairs the Methodist Episcopal Church rented exhibit space to promote the work of its constituents and to introduce denominational literature and sell Christian products to global visitors. World's fair scholar Robert Rydell indicates that international expositions promoted both the political and financial motives of the country hosting the event and that fairs held in the United States functioned as "world universities" to showcase both the technological progress and national sovereignty of the United States.[2] For Methodists one additional component was fundamental to accurately portray the progress of the United States and to proclaim America's cultural superiority to a global audience. These expositions needed to sell world missions to visitors and to demonstrate how Christianity, in this case Methodism, would be used to foster the development and implementation of McConnell's notion of a "Worldwide Church."

During the mid-nineteenth century, missionary exhibitions were also created with the intent to demonstrate the cultural superiority of European nations that hosted the expositions. In addition to marketing the progress and expansion of European nations the exhibitions included non-Western peoples placed on review in recreated "native" villages. The displays included some of the actual homes of those exhibited as well as material artifacts such as weaponry and religious icons taken from colonized societies.

These expositions also focused on the advance of religion into colonized countries and highlighted the ongoing attempts to convert various people groups to Protestant Christianity. In *Reinventing Africa* (1994) historian Annie E. Coombes confirms that the first known Protestant missionary fair - the "Church Mission to the Jews" - took place in 1867 at London, England.[3] Coombes notes that these types of exhibitions were sponsored by Protestant missionary societies and by the last decades of the 19th century functioned as arenas for British mission groups to raise monies for work overseas and to inform fairgoers on the progress and reach of Christian missionaries in Europe and throughout the world. The Church Missionary Society of London was one such organization holding its first missions fair in 1882. The purpose of the exposition was to help develop interest in Protestant missionary work and to commemorate the ministry of Christians sent to West Africa as early as 1803. The fair showcased an assortment of display cases and wall hangings that identified the relics of mission and sought to demonstrate the need for more missionaries to work overseas.

The 1882 missionary exposition functioned as a promotional tool to illustrate the peoples and cultures of the regions of the world placed on display. Eugene Stock, editor of *A History of the Church Missionary Society*, noted the fairs included "articles of foreign manufacture, samples of food and clothing, models of native dwellings, and other objects of interest illustrative of native life, habits, and religions" from lands where Society missionaries had been at work.[4] To make the pavilion and exhibits reflect the distant lands they were meant to portray, missionaries brought material objects, weaponry, and food products to England for display in the exhibits. Stock emphasized that the early missionary fairs "enlightened thousands of hearers concerning the condition of heathen nations and the work going on among them" and functioned as a reminder of the progress of British colonial and missional work overseas.[5]

The earliest known missionary exposition in the United States was held in 1911 at the Mechanics Building in Boston, Massachusetts.[6] "The World in Boston: The First Great Exposition in America of Home and Foreign Missions" was a collaborative endeavor between the Young People's Missionary Movement and several Protestant missionary organizations.[7] The exposition placed missions work on a stage for all to view and was intended to evidence the work of missionaries in the United States and around the world. Over fifty organizations, including the Board of Foreign Missions and the Board of Home Missions and Church Extension of the Methodist Episcopal Church, participated in the exposition. Methodist church leaders including S. Earl Taylor and Ralph E. Diffendorfer were present at Boston and used their experience at the fair to identify how missionary expositions might sell missions to Methodist constituents. The impression of the Boston fair on both Taylor and Diffendorfer would later surface at the end of the decade as American Methodists planned a much more expansive and expensive exposition.[8]

A series of other fairs sponsored by the Missionary Education Movement were held during the same decade in a variety of cities including Cincinnati (1912), Baltimore (1912), and Chicago (1913). Exposition guidebooks highlighted the extensive use of films, pageants, and lantern slides to describe the advance of Protestant missionaries in the United States and overseas. These events offered fairgoers a kaleidoscope of humanity from areas of the world few had been able to visit. Placed on stage, missionized peoples were evidenced in ways that popular magazines such as *National Geographic* and *Missionary Review of the World* could not replicate.

The Centenary Fund Drive

The 1919 Centenary Celebration of American Methodist Missions was held during a year in U.S. history saturated with racial violence in the forms of public lynchings and urban riots. American women demonstrated their influence in the social and political arenas as suffrage advocates by the hundreds of thousands held rallies and parades challenging the U.S. Congress and President Woodrow Wilson to provide legislation guaranteeing all women the right to vote. Many Americans, including those affiliated with both the Northern and Southern denominations of the Methodist Episcopal Church, fought an ongoing crusade against the production, distribution, and consumption of alcoholic beverages. Additionally, post-World War I patriotic interests were blended with a sense of concern over the place of the United States on the world stage. At the same time President Wilson was on a national tour marketing the concept of a League of Nations, Methodists at the fairgrounds watched warplanes stage mock battles in the skies above Columbus as anti-aircraft guns replicated the sounds of battle from the grandstands below.

In the decade prior to the 1919 exposition, Protestant missionaries and mission organizations had asked Americans to contemplate how they might involve themselves in the advance of Christianity and to consider ways they might contribute financially toward world service. As noted earlier, Protestant missionary expositions were seen as one technique to help sell world missions and to provide fairgoers with opportunities to view Christian converts from around the world on exhibit in recreated villages and homes. These venues would not only demonstrate to visitors the worldwide activities of missionaries but also encourage fairgoers to think toward the future; to convince Christians that missionaries and missions organizations were charting a course to physically and spiritually reconstruct the world.

The destruction wrought by World War I had altered some of the ideals put forth by mission advocates. Prior to the conflict leaders of Methodist mission agencies imagined that their missionaries would help establish a global "Christian civilization" throughout the world. This "civilization" would look, many hoped, remarkably Methodist and Western as missionaries interpreted the teachings of Christ from a Wesleyan perspective and attached societal and cultural expectations from their experiences as American citizens. Yet, even in the midst of the Great War some Methodist leaders believed the U.S. government and its military forces were making the world a safe arena for the establishment of democratic practice that would eventually result in peace and economic prosperity.

These notions were worked out in the mission bureaus at the same time Methodist military leaders and soldiers fought in the trenches and seas of Europe. S. Earl Taylor, graduate of Drew Theological Seminary and Secretary of the Board of Foreign Missions, contended that there were "things which governments cannot do" for which American Methodism had an answer. Taylor responded in *The Centenary Survey of the Board of Foreign Missions* that the Methodist Church and its agencies planned to reinforce "spiritual and moral forces" within the United States while simultaneously removing "ignorance and superstition" from distant countries. To eradicate "ignorance" and "superstition" overseas meant Methodist constituents needed to construct colleges, establish hospitals, and build churches. These facilities would cost the church millions of dollars and require numerous workers to labor in mission fields thousands of miles from the United States.

In the early twentieth century some American Methodists were concerned that missionary organizations needed more money to be fully effective in the quest to spread Christianity throughout the world. In *The Cost of Christian Conquest* (1908) William N. Brewster challenged readers to have "a radically different attitude" about contributing financially to world missions and argued that domestic and foreign missionary work, in order to succeed, required a "new point of view" to reach those in the pulpit and in the pew.[9] Brewster's words foreshadowed a series of Protestant fundraising campaigns between 1916 and 1919 that would eventually bring in millions of dollars for church-sponsored missionary organizations.

Between 1916 and 1919 Protestant traditions including the Northern Baptists, Northern Presbyterians, and the Disciples of Christ sought additional funding for their mission agencies in order to construct new schools and hospitals, to increase the number of missionary workers, and to distribute Christian literature across the world. Methodists were not to be outdone as leaders of the Methodist Episcopal Church and Methodist Episcopal Church, South, collaborated on a multi-million dollar fundraising crusade to raise awareness and money for world missions.

John Lankford's 1963 essay, "Methodism 'Over the Top'" introduces the efforts of American Methodists to raise funds for missions by means of the Centenary Fund Drive. Leaders of The Methodist Episcopal Church and Methodist Episcopal Church, South, challenged members to raise millions of dollars a year for five years to cover the expenses of Methodist missionary activity.[10] Hand-written pledges were made on cards that were given out at Methodist churches and schools across the United States. Some donations for the Centenary Fund arrived in the form of actual cash but a bulk of the contributions were sent in on promissory notes – to be paid-in-full in the months and years following the Centenary exposition. The initial funds pledged by the Methodist Episcopal Church alone were in excess of forty million dollars with Southern Methodists also planning a substantial contribution. On the eve of the fair the actual pledged totals from Methodists tallied far in excess of original estimates and topped at nearly one hundred fifty million dollars. Centenary organizers hoped that the exposition would help draw in pledges by demonstrating the monetary needs required for the conversion of the world to Christianity.

A Methodist 'World's Fair'

The Centenary Celebration was held at the Ohio State Fairgrounds from June 20 to July 13 to commemorate the one hundred year anniversary of the founding of The Missionary Society of the Methodist Episcopal Church. Fair organizers claimed they agreed upon Columbus as the venue for the exposition after the results of a church-sponsored survey revealed that one in every twelve residents from Ohio attended a Methodist Episcopal Church and that approximately one million Methodists lived within six hours of the city.[11] The city was also a central location for the U.S. railroad system and a series of well-traveled roadways connected Columbus with cities including Cleveland, Cincinnati, Pittsburgh and Chicago. Celebration organizers marketed the exposition by advertising "Methodist auto caravans" of churchgoers that planned to visit the fair. Organizers also connected the dates of the exposition to the summer vacation schedule of Methodists by distributing to churches over one hundred thousand road maps with directions to the fairgrounds. The periodical *Zion's Herald* noted this Methodist pilgrimage to Ohio announcing that, "all Methodist roads will lead to Columbus [where] hundreds of thousands of visitors of all religious faiths and from every part of this and foreign countries are expected to attend."[12]

The exposition was a multi-million dollar investment and the final product was considerably larger than earlier U.S. Protestant fairs that had rented one building in a downtown location. The Columbus fairgrounds hosted over sixteen thousand exhibits representing the people and products of thirty-seven countries including the United States.[13] Eight large exhibition halls, regularly used for the

annual Ohio State Fair to display agricultural commodities, functioned as international pavilions filled with the people and reconstructed landscapes of regions worked by Methodist missionaries. These buildings showcased the global progress of the church by informing visitors of the locations of Methodist missionary outposts that, by 1919, reached into Africa, Asia, Latin America, Europe and North America.

Planners of the Centenary Celebration of American Methodist Missions sought to capture the interest of the American public fascinated by earlier international fairs, colonial exhibitions and missionary expositions. Through a combination of international displays, the latest technologies, and dozens of public addresses American Methodists were able to create a "Methodist World's Fair"[14] that would bring money to the coffers of mission agencies and help entice volunteers to join the church on the march toward the expansion of Protestant missions around the world. The Centenary Celebration was seen as one such event that would give American Methodism a platform from which to broadcast its current work and future hopes concerning global missions. Staged by leadership from the Methodist Episcopal Church and Methodist Episcopal Church, South, the exposition provided visitors with opportunities to view "the world" at the Columbus fairgrounds.

In the months and years prior to the fair Methodist church leaders had asked missionaries to gather items indigenous to their countries of placement including pieces of actual homes and dozens of material artifacts. As a result Methodists packaged and transported dwellings and cultural artifacts from Africa, Asia, Europe, North America, and South America for placement in the exhibit halls at Columbus. Once organized and displayed in the various international pavilions visitors were able to view just how far American Methodist missionary work had expanded into international venues. Inside the pavilions visitors were made aware of attempts on the part of Methodist missionaries to bring Christianity to people groups who were now the products of mission.

The three-week fair featured dozens of interactive exhibits on the recipients of domestic and foreign missions. These missionized players were asked to act out their daily lives and performed "native" tasks while on display before interested American viewers. Visitors toured eight pavilions designated with international titles and themes including "The Africa Building" and "The China Building." Families from regions including Korea and North Africa were asked to simulate the work of indigenous industries, cook and eat dinner, and clean their "homes" while being carefully observed by American fairgoers.

The fair functioned as a venue of exchange between both viewer and those viewed. On one level the exposition educated visitors on the history and current progress of Methodist world missions. In this way organizers created exhibits, dispersed information through lectures, and handed out booklets and pamphlets describing the work of Methodist missionaries. The fair also functioned on another level, providing visitors opportunities to learn about themselves as Americans while at the same time watching "foreigners" practice "strange" religions and perform domestic responsibilities within the recreated "native homes" of the fairground pavilions.

8   Voices from the Fair

The exposition also reflected early twentieth century consumer interests in leisure and entertainment. Visitors interacted with Christian sports athletes, rode camels through a simulated "African desert," and examined Hindu fakirs lying on beds of spikes. Methodist Fred B. Smith, a part-time journalist for the YMCA magazine *Association Men*, noted that the intersection of popular entertainments and Christian missions at Columbus created an environment "for enjoying what was the best in a circus, a county fair, a picnic, grand opera, the drama and the Church – all at one time."[15]

The Celebration was also recorded on film as Hollywood mogul David Wark Griffith sent a camera crew to record the activities of the fair for future generations of Methodists. In the weeks prior to the fair, Griffith toured the various pavilions under construction and remarked, "What particularly impressed me was the wonderful opportunity the Methodist Centenary Celebration gives the people to visit the entire world. Extraordinarily impressive are the foreign villages represented where not 'supers' [actors portraying indigenous peoples] but real natives brought from foreign lands demonstrate the daily existence in those countries."[16] For both mid-Ohio Methodists and notables from Hollywood the exposition functioned as an arena for entertainment, Christian missionary education, and ethnological evaluation.

The fair attracted over ten thousand Methodist ministers and over one million curious visitors each paying fifty cents to enter the front gates of the exposition.[17] As Methodists were entertained they were also informed by the missionary-oriented nature of the exposition that, if heeded, provided serious intercultural implications. Visitors could attend films, illustrated lectures, and dramatic pageants and then proceed to dine at a Methodist church-sponsored restaurant along the Midway. At the same event they also heard speeches addressing the immediate need for large amounts of money and additional missionaries to serve around the world. In these halls the peoples of distant lands and the practices of religions other than Protestant Christianity called for their attention and their money. Placing "the world" on exhibit at Columbus informed visitors of the global activities of Methodist missionaries. Impassioned speeches called for volunteers and for the funds necessary to reach people in need of Christian salvation and Methodist benevolence.

Chapter Summaries

Chapter One includes a selection of addresses that evidence how American Methodist missionaries were working to not only convert the people of Africa to Christ but also how the Methodist Episcopal Church and Methodist Episcopal Church, South, were working to help bring attention to the plight of African Americans in the United States. On "African Day" well-known Methodists including Robert E. Jones, Joseph Hartzell, and Alexander Camphor spoke of the involvement of missionaries in Africa. Through their work the people of Africa were being converted to Christianity and influenced by the teachings and cultural expectations of American missionaries. On "Negro Day" Philadelphia minister Charles A. Tindley, Isaiah Scott, and Randall Carter identified the social injustices at work in the United States. For these church leaders a home missionary impulse was needed to create safe environments for Black Americans who deserved respect and recognition in a nation dedicated to injustice and segregation.

Chapter Two includes a variety of speeches from representatives of women's and men's groups actively patronized by American Methodists. On "Woman's Day" speakers from the Methodist Woman's Foreign Missionary Society, Woman's Christian Temperance Union, and the National Woman's Party evidenced the concerns over issues of gender and representation. Lena Leonard Fisher, Anna Gordon, and Alice Paul gave speeches that highlighted the work of Methodists in world missions, global Prohibition, and women's suffrage.

A well-known fraternal organization that included thousands of Methodist men was also represented at the Columbus fair. The Methodist Minute Men held their national convention on the fairgrounds and brought in well-known speakers including Josephus Daniels, James Cannon Jr., and Christian F. Reisner. These individuals presented an approach to world missions that highlighted how Christian laymen were working to convert the world to Christ. Representatives for the Methodist Minute Men had traveled the United States speaking in churches, auditoriums, and movie theaters promoting both the Centenary and the Methodist Church.

Chapter Three includes speeches that broadcasted some of the social concerns of early twentieth century American Methodists. On the eve of national Prohibition the Woman's Christian Temperance Union joined forces with groups of Methodist men to celebrate the removal of alcohol from American society. As a result of the Nineteenth Amendment enacted during the second week of the fair American distilleries could no longer legally produce or distribute alcoholic beverages. Well-known temperance advocates including Anna Gordon, William Jennings Bryan, and Clarence True Wilson promoted their concerns regarding the residual effects of alcohol and how Methodists had led the charge to remove the saloon from American cities.

Chapter Four includes speeches that link the work of Methodist domestic missions with the advance of Americanization. The chapter also includes addresses that helped link American Methodists with the work of the U.S. military and the rebuilding of nations destroyed by the ravages of the Great War. For example, Henry Roe Cloud appeared on stage to inform audiences of the Americanization and Christianization of Native Americans. To celebrate the victory of American forces Albert Read and Alvin York described for audiences how Methodists had been the first to volunteer to serve the country and how the United States now needed American Methodists to help with rebuilding efforts overseas. The chapter also highlights how many American Methodists supported the controversial League of Nations plan proposed by President Woodrow Wilson and a speech by William McAdoo informed audiences of the roles that Methodists played in this endeavor.

Notes

1. Francis John McConnell (1871-1953) received degrees from Ohio Wesleyan University and Boston University. He was an ordained minister with the New England Annual Conference of the Methodist Episcopal Church and the Methodist Church. McConnell served as President of the Federal Council of the Churches of Christ in America and was an active participant in the Methodist Federation for Social Action. His wife, Eva Thomas McConnell (1871-1968), worked for several years as the vice-president of the Woman's Foreign Missionary Society of the Methodist Episcopal Church. Nolan B. Harmon, *The Encyclopedia of World Methodism, Volume II* (Nashville, TN: The United Methodist Publishing House, 1974). 1480-1481. All biographical and geographical information for the remainder of the book are from *The Encyclopedia of World Methodism, Volumes I and II* unless otherwise noted.

2. Francis J. McConnell, *Democratic Christianity* (New York: The MacMillan Company, 1919), 58 and 72. For additional information on Bishop McConnell and family see his autobiography *By the Way: An Autobiography* (New York: Abingdon-Cokesbury Press, 1952).

3. Annie E. Coombes, *Reinventing Africa: Museums, Material Culture and Popular Imagination in Late Victorian and Edwardian England* (New Haven and London: Yale University Press, 1994), 173.

4. Eugene Stock, ed., *A History of the Church Missionary Society*, Vol. 3 (London: Church Missionary Society, 1899), 306.

5. Ibid., 666 and 696.

6. For a scholarly treatment of missionary fairs and particularly the 1911 World in Boston event see Erin L. Hasinoff, *Faith in Objects: American Missionary Expositions in the Early Twentieth Century* (New York: Palgrave Macmillan, 2011).

7. *Handbook and Guide of the World in Boston: The First Great Exposition in America of Home and Foreign Missions* (S.l.: s.n., 1911), 105.

8. S. Earl Taylor, Secretary of the Methodist Board of Foreign Missions and General Secretary of the Centenary Celebration, served as Consulting Secretary for the Boston event. Methodist minister Ralph E. Diffendorfer organized the "Children's Section" at "The World in Boston" and later became a General Secretary for the Methodist Episcopal Church and worked as a speaker for the Home Missions exhibits at the Columbus fair.

9. William N. Brewster, *The Cost of Christian Conquest* (Cincinnati: Jennings and Graham, 1908), 103.

10. John Lankford, "Methodism 'Over the Top': The Joint Centenary Movement, 1917-1925," *Methodist History* 2:1 (October 1963): 27.

11. "Methodist Centenary Celebration, State Fair Grounds, Columbus, Ohio, June 20-July 13, 1919, official reports and records" compiled by Alonzo E. Wilson, Director, Division of Special Days and Events, 12. See also, Nancye Van Brunt, "Pageantry at the Methodist Centenary," *Methodist History* 35:2 (January 1997): 106-118.

12. "From the Ends of the Earth," *Zion's Herald*, 21 May 1919, 655.

13. "Centenary Celebration Columbus," *Columbus Evening Dispatch*, 4 July 1919, 15.

14. "The Methodist 'World's Fair,'" *Central Christian Advocate*, 26 July 1919, 12.

15. Fred B. Smith, "In Stride with the Christian World: An Exposition de Luxe," *Association Men* (August 1919): 876.

16. "World to See Centenary Celebration," *Central Christian Advocate,* 2 July 1919, 8. There is no extant evidence that suggests Griffith was actually at the fair during its three-week run. The film made on the fair has not been located by the author.

17. Smith, "In Stride with the Christian World," 876.

Chapter Two

Methodist Missions and Racial Identities

Introduction

The addresses of Chapter Two take place over three days. The days were given the monikers "African Day", "Negro Day", and "Southern Day." Chapter Two includes a selection of addresses that evidence approaches American and Canadian Methodist missionaries used to convert the people of Africa to Christianity. The speeches also demonstrate how the Methodist Episcopal Church, Methodist Episcopal Church, South, Methodist Church of Canada, and the Colored (now Christian) Methodist Episcopal Church were working to help bring attention to the plight of African Americans in Canada and the United States. On "African Day" well-known Methodist bishops including Robert E. Jones, Joseph Hartzell, and Alexander Camphor spoke of the work of missionaries in Africa.

Daniel Mumpower, missionary to Africa for the Methodist Episcopal Church, South, spoke on how the denomination had recently planted a mission station in the Congo. He addressed the audience concerning medical missions and highlighted a new hospital in the country and claimed it had been relatively "easy" to convert Africans to Methodism. He hoped that the Methodist Episcopal Church and Methodist Episcopal Church, South, would work together to convert the peoples of Africa to Methodist Christianity. Reverend James Doyle followed Mumpower and spoke of how the Methodist Church of Canada planned to be involved with missions work in the diamond mines of Africa. Samuel Zwemer, editor of *The Moslem World,* spoke of the challenge the Muslim faith presented to the Methodist work in Northern Africa. According to Zwemer, Methodist missionaries had been significant contributors toward the Christian conversion of Africans. These same indigenous peoples had also been influenced by the teachings and cultural expectations of American missionaries.

On "Negro Day" Reverend Irving Garland Penn presided over the sessions held in the massive fairgrounds coliseum. Themes presented included: social equality, the Black soldiers of World War I, lynching, and the progress of the leadership of African American churches within the Methodist Episcopal Church and Methodist Episcopal Church, South. Speakers also indentified the contributions of African Americans to American society and to Methodist missionary history. Charles A. Tindley, a well-known orator and minister of East Calvary Methodist Episcopal Church in Philadelphia, gave a rousing address challenging the audience to think about how African American soldiers had served in the Great War and also argued for "social sameness" for Black Americans including a memorable section of the speech that may remind readers of the "I have a Dream" speech of Dr. Martin Luther King, Jr. almost half a century later.

William Asbury Christian, President of the Female College of the Methodist Episcopal Church, South, presented on the academic and intellectual progress of African Americans in the American South since Emancipation. He pressed the audience to consider various social injustices (e.g. lynch mobs) that African Americans encountered in society and the difficulties faced while trying to acquire jobs and homes. Robert E. Jones, Editor of the *Southwestern Christian Advocate* of New Orleans, spoke on the work of the Black Church and also predicted the unity of the Methodist Episcopal Church and Methodist Episcopal Church, South, with the later formation of the Central Jurisdiction in 1939. He made strong statements regarding the lynching of African Americans and how the American South needed to make radical adjustments to its treatment of Blacks in order for racial justice to gain traction.

Francis J. McConnell, Bishop for the Methodist Episcopal Church, spoke on how lynching activities had negatively affected the perception that international peoples had of the United States. McConnell also discussed the tensions over labor issues related to African Americans and the American Federation of Labor. Perhaps most significant for the audience that day was how McConnell argued for the advance of Black Methodists in self-governance related to church leadership. The final speaker on Negro Day was Reverend Randall Carter, Bishop of the Colored Methodist Episcopal Church in America. Carter referenced the timing of the Centenary Celebration, exactly three hundred years after the arrival of Black slaves from Africa and one hundred years after the founding of The Missionary Society of the Methodist Episcopal Church to support the work of John Stewart to the Wyandot peoples of Western Ohio. He also presented the audience with a list of important Black Americans who had made significant contributions to American society including Booker T. Washington, Paul L. Dunbar, and Frederick Douglass.

The third section of the chapter includes speeches on "Southern Day." The first address by Irving Garland Penn provided examples of the progress of Black Americans in the Negro Department of the 1895 Atlanta Exposition as well as the work of the Freedmen's Aid Society. Garland highlighted the ongoing struggles of mob violence and the work of some Methodist denominations to help elevate African Americans to church leadership. The final speech of the chapter is by Charles H. Tobias. Reverend Tobias spoke of the contributions of African Americans to the music culture of the American South and also highlighted the work of Black soldiers in the Great War.

African Day Program

Monday Afternoon, June 23, 1919

...The meeting convened at two o'clock, in the coliseum, Bishop J. C. Hartzell, chairman

...Invocation by Mr. Robert E. Jones...

ROBERT E. JONES:[1]

O Lord, our Father in Heaven, we worship Thee this day. We magnify Thy glorious name. We thank Thee for all the privileges that are ours; for the privilege of worship; for the privilege of love; for the privilege of hope; for the privilege of faith. O Thou God of all the nations, in Thy presence we come, pouring forth our heart in gratitude for all that has been done, for the uplift of mankind.

We thank Thee Lord for the signs that we see, for the ray of hope that is ours, that nations are being born anew, that the dark places of earth are being lightened, that men who were in their trespasses and sin are being emancipated by the power of the life of Jesus Christ. We thank Thee, O Lord, that the home field and the foreign field are becoming one under the sway of one Master, one Lord, one faith, one hope, one love; and may we realize today that Thy people are one; one in yonder parts of the world and one here; that it is one humanity, with one common God, the Father of us all, and one brotherhood in faith, in hope, in trust, in service.

We thank Thee O Lord for what has been done for the redemption of Africa. We thank Thee that Africa has been rolled on the heart of the world; that the world turns toward Africa, rich as it is in its natural resources, rich in its ivory, rich in its gold, rich in its coffee, rich in all of its materials, rich yet more in the men and the women who are to save through Jesus Christ, and we thank Thee, our Father, for the men from the day of Livingstone[2] on down to the present, and the day that those men gave their hearts and lives for the redemption of Africa.

We thank Thee for that host of men and women consecrated, self-sacrificing, giving up all, burying themselves in Africa's life, that Africa may rise and shine. O Lord God, we thank Thee for the missionaries who have gone to Africa, and while the continent is still dark, there are places of light all through that continent.

Hasten the day, O God, of all the nations when Ethiopia shall stretch forward her hand unto God; when they, too, shall join in with the rest of the world and help crown Him Lord of all. O Lord, our Father, may we this day realize our duty toward that dark continent; our duty to give ourselves as well as to give our means, and may we so tie ourselves to that dark and long neglected continent until she shall come into the full blaze of Thy glory and sing Thy song, and lift their voices unto Thee in prayer.

O Lord God help us to realize all that the Centenary means to us in teaching us the brotherhood of man, that we are one – one through Thee, one through Thy redeemed blood, one in our hope, one in our pilgrimage toward that one Heaven.

Help us to love Thee, and help us to serve Thee. Our Father in Heaven, we lift up to Thee a prayer of gratitude and thanksgiving for Bishop Hartzell; for all that he has done for people in this country and in Africa; for what he represents to us in his life, in his sacrifice, in his service. We thank Thee for his inspiring leadership; for what he has been able to do.

Touch men here and there, and as we pray Thy blessings for him today, so likewise do we pray Thy blessings upon Bishop Camphor, upon Bishop Johnson,[3] upon Bishop Scott,[4] upon all those who have administered in Africa, and hasten the day when not only those in Central Africa shall be saved to God; when the cross shall be triumphant, when Jesus Christ shall reign from one end of Africa to the other, and Thy name shall be glorified; but also in all those foreign fields may Thy name be supreme.

Now, Father, we give ourselves to Thee. Hear us in prayer. Accept us as we come unto Thee with the burden of our heart for the salvation of our redemption, and at last bring us unto Thyself, and the praise shall be Thine, world without end. Amen.

...Music by the Kaffir Boys' Choir...[5]

ROBERT E. JONES:
There is only one man in Methodism to introduce on Africa day as the presiding officer and genius of the meeting, and that is Bishop Hartzell.

JOSEPH CRANE HARTZELL:[6]
I want to say to you one word concerning these Kaffir singers. Mr. Palmer (sic) tells me that he has trained fifty boys of this type and not one of them has been a failure. They are now missionaries and citizens of the country. Africa has two great missionary fields – two great mission problems. The one has to do with the one hundred million native black Africans – one hundred millions – as many as in the United States, and they are doubling in numbers every fifty years. That means in fifty years there will be two hundred millions. In three hundred years there will be as many black people in Africa as there are people in China or India.

The other great problem is the Mohammedan problem. There are fifty millions of Mohammedans in Africa, and these Mohammedan forces are making Mohammedan converts among these millions of black people faster than all the Christian missionaries are making converts.

Today we will bring before you information of these two great mission fields of the world. We have speakers here from different cities of the continent who will speak briefly. We have missionaries here from different cities of the continent whose faces I want you to see – heroic men and women who are leading the forces in this work.

North Africa is the center of the Mohammedan work of the church. Portugese (sic) Africa, Rhodesia, Liberia on the west coast, and Gold Coast on the west coast, Madeira Island on the west coast, the Congo mission in the heart of Africa – these are the continental strategic centers where the Methodist Episcopal Church has planned her forces, and I want you to get that picture in your mind.

I am going to call upon Bishop Camphor first. Bishop Camphor was educated in this country. I knew him when a boy. He has lived in Africa for a number of years. In the last general conference he was elected a bishop for Africa, and Bishop Camphor, a scholar, a prince, a man whose life is consecrated to Liberia and West Africa, will speak to us a few moments. (Applause)

ALEXANDER PRIESTLY CAMPHOR:[7]

I can never confront the African situation without feeling very much like the little boy who was very fond of sugar, and when suddenly he found himself in the presence of a great pile of sugar he said, "Oh, for a thousand tongues and more time to do this thing justice!"

But ladies and gentlemen, under the limitations of time, I must only touch here and there upon my great question. Whatever may be the drawbacks to Liberia[8] – and there have been not a few – these drawbacks have never outweighed the points of strength, and the advantages that the republic of Liberia offers. As early as the founding of Liberia in 1822, when her problems were greater and more stubborn than they are today, the founders of Liberia and her friends in America never lost hope in the Liberian enterprise. They faced their problems manfully and heroically, though they were confronted by a deadly climate and by savages and untoward [untold] experiences that are unnameable, yet they persevered and continued until this day. I believe that the secret of the perseverance of the Liberian people lies in the fact of this strategic importance of that republic, and the many points of strength that it offers.

In this country we frequently hear of the failure of Liberia. We frequently hear that Liberia is without force, without vision. I stand before you this afternoon to say that there is not a place anywhere in all of Africa that offers the advantages that Liberia offers for the development of Christian missions.

In the first place, Liberia is an American organization. Liberia is American in spirit and in purpose and in aims. Liberia is American planted. It was fostered by American philanthropy, and the spirit of the people is American, and more than that, it is tremendously Methodist. The Methodist people own more land and have more people in Liberia than any other church, and then the government has no bias against missions. The government is friendly toward missions.

It offers freedom, exemption from duty. It offers protection of life and property, and every encouragement possible within its power to the missionaries. Not even North Africa nor South Africa nor East Africa nor Central Africa offers the points of advantage for missionary work as in Liberia. The country itself is very resourceful. It has mines; it has fine timbers. It has all kinds of products that are remarkable, and this is giving to Liberia a brighter outlook than in the past. Just recently the American government made a loan of $5,000,000 to this republic.

The editor of Munsey's Magazine made this remark. He said that when news reached him from Washington that this government had agreed to loan Liberia $5,000,000 he was surprised, and he didn't know why this loan was made, for he said, "Money sent to Liberia never returns, but," said when he heard from a Methodist bishop what Liberia did in the last war, "I am prepared to change my mind."

Liberia played a very prominent and heroic part in the last war. She sent soldiers to France, and when the German submarine went to Liberia to punish her because she had joined the allies and had declared war on Germany, Liberia had the courage to stand up manfully and defy Germany with her powerful submarine. (Applause) And although the commander of that submarine ordered the republic to destroy the allied property in Liberia, the government said, "No, we'll do no such thing!" And she didn't.

So that, my friends, I want to say to you today that that little negro republic possesses elements of strength and power that are worthy of our consideration. The Methodist Episcopal Church has been in Liberia since 1833. Our missions were planted all along the coast, and we are now penetrating the interior. This Centenary, I am hoping, will give us the men, will give us the means, whereby we may be able to penetrate even the most distant sections of Liberia, and thus carry out the prayer and the plan of the fathers of Liberia, that it would be an open door for the evangelization not only of Liberia but for the evangelization of the entire African continent.

We have our educational institutions, our colleges of West Africa, and our affiliated schools, and in these schools we are training our men and women for work in our theological school in Monrovia.[9] We are training our ministers and workers so that they shall be able to go out as torch bearers to their brothers and sisters in the farther regions beyond.

The Mohammedan problem is encroaching upon us as it is in other sections of Africa, but I am glad to say that so thoroughly is Liberia in principle Christian that Mohammedanism will not have much of a foothold in Liberia. I think perhaps the best thing that will express to you the spirit of Liberia is the national hymn of that republic, and I give this in conclusion. One writer has said, "If you would know a people, study their hymns and their songs."

Liberia has expressed herself nobly in her national hymn, it is:

"All hail Liberia. A-hail!

>   This glorious land of liberty
>   Shall be ours,
>   Though new her name,
>   Green be her fame,
>   And mighty be her powers.

>   With joy and gladness in our hearts

United we will meet the foe
With valor unpretending.

Long live Liberia, a happy land,
A home of glorious liberty by God's command.

All hail Liberia. A-hail!

In union strong success is sure,
We cannot fail.
With God above
Our rights to prove
We'll over all prevail.

With heart and hand our country's cause defending,
We'll meet the foe with valor unpretending.

Long live Liberia, happy land,
A home of glorious liberty by God's command."

This is the sentiment of Liberia, and with this sentiment Liberia will succeed. (Prolonged Applause)

JOSEPH CRANE HARTZELL:

Our mission in Liberia was organized only thirteen years after Stuart (sic) opened the mission among the Wyandotte Indians. This was the first foreign mission of the Methodist Episcopal Church. The Methodist Episcopal Church has recently opened a mission in the Congo state, and I am going to ask Dr. Mumpower, who represents the Methodist Episcopal Church in the Congo state, to give in a very few moments the story of the inception and the outlook of that work.

DANIEL L. MUMPOWER:[10]

Any one who expects to hear me had better take a front seat. The least a physician speaks really the better off he is in his profession. As I had the honor of being a physician, I have never made much of a presentation of being a public speaker, but I am glad this afternoon to speak to you a little bit about the opening of the Congo mission of the Southern Methodist Church.

This was established in February, 1914. It has, therefore, been in existence for the last five years. We of the Southern Methodist Church believe that the Congo mission illustrates in a peculiar way the proper undertaking of a new mission work. First of all there was made the survey in order that there might be properly selected a field, and then after the survey was made, it was presented to the church, in order that the church might consent, and in order that the resources of the church might be behind the undertaking.

Then after this, there was selected for the mission field three missionaries; one who should represent the pastor's work, one the industrial work, and one the medical work; representing in a way the three forms of service as carried on by our Lord and Savior during His earthly career.

Since 1914, at the time when the mission was organized, we have now about two hundred church members, and about six or seven hundred probationers. Most of you who have labored out in Africa understand that the problem before the missionary is not asking so many men to come in, and so many converts to come in, but rather the problem of being careful as to whom are taken in. We could have many more than two hundred in our churches if we were willing to take in all who would come to us, who have come to us in the past.

We have now established the good hospital, which is constantly full. The people have shown themselves very willing to submit to anything that we as missionaries have said, though at first they were very suspicious. Gradually their suspicion has been overcome, and now we say we have no trouble at all in bringing to them our message.

The people are not antagonistic. They are to some extent indifferent, but there is given to us a free chance and a good opportunity to present the gospel of Jesus Christ. We have now, fortunately and happily, I am glad to say, a good Centenary movement on among our people out in Central Africa. The native church has voted that hereafter any person who is admitted into the church shall be admitted upon one basis, and that basis is the basis of tithing, (Applause) along, of course, with the other – a belief in Jesus Christ.

Fortunately, too, we have about ten or perhaps fifteen native evangelists, and they are being supported by the native church. We do not call upon our home church here in America for any support of the native evangelist, because we wish our native church to get the benefits which come to them through this matter of self-support.

I wish to say in regard to the Congo, just as Bishop Camphor has said in regard to Liberia, that there is no place in Africa which offers a more fruitful field for the gospel of Jesus Christ. I think you will hear every missionary who speaks to you this afternoon tell you that his field offers the most brilliant, you might say, or the best opportunity for the cause of Jesus Christ.

This proves to you that any field out there where the cause of Jesus Christ is pressed is a field that is fruitful in the harvest. It gives me great pleasure also to say that we are trying to do our part in making pagan Africa a Christian continent. We realize, as well as our friends in North Africa, that it is exceedingly difficult to win a Mohammedan to Christianity, but in comparison it is not difficult to win a pagan to Christianity.

If you can give the proper time and can have the proper number of workers to present the cause of Christ to him you will not experience any great difficulties. That is one reason why we as churches – as Northern and Southern Methodists – should be very diligent in presenting the gospel of Christ to these people in Central Africa, because their hearts are open, and they are willing to receive our message, but once Mohammedanism has got its grip upon the hearts of the people it is exceedingly difficult ever to loosen that grip.

22 Voices from the Fair

We pray – we ask you – that as we go back into our fields in these few months, that the prayers of Methodism will follow us who are laboring in the Belgian Congo. You who belong to the Methodist Episcopal Church know of the work of your people in the southern part of the Belgian Congo, and we hope that it will be possible for us in time to come that the work of the two churches will be united – the Southern Church working up to the North, and the Northern Church working down to the South. (Applause)

JOSEPH CRANE HARTZELL:

Our Canadian brethren are entering Africa also, and we have a distinguished member of that church here, and he will speak to us five minutes and give us an idea of their plans of going into that country. With the church in the South, the church throughout the North, and with the Canadian church going hand in hand into that continent, we see what God must certainly bring to bear. We will now hear Mr. Doyle.

MR. DOYLE:[11]

I count it a great privilege to come down from the country of the north, the Dominion of Canada, and take part with you in this great Centenary Celebration. Our country is large. If you put it by comparison, we find that the Dominion of Canada is territory as large as the British Isles, France, Holland, Belgium, Spain, Portugal, Japan, and the United States, all added together, less Alaska.

That may seem like wild exaggeration, but if you go over your atlas and take the area of the countries that I have mentioned you will find that what I have stated is correct. We only have a population of about eight million, and about one million of those are Methodists. We are glad to convey greetings to you from about one million Methodists of Canada. (Applause) About a hundred and twenty-five of those are present in this Centenary Celebration.

I come myself from one of the western provinces, Saskatchewan. I have been required to spell that a number of times since coming on to the grounds here. It does not seem familiar to most of the American people.

May I quote from the late J.J. Hill, your great railway magnate? When he was giving an address at a banquet in the city of Winnipeg in the province of Manitoba he said, "Gentlemen, I want to tell you," and J.J. Hill knew the resources of countries as well as any man, perhaps, in the world, "there is no province in the Dominion, there is not a state in the Union, there is no country upon the face of the globe, that has got as much strong, valuable, arable land for its size as the province of Saskatchewan in your fair Dominion."

I am simply quoting Mr. Hill. Saskatchewan is about the size of Germany, and yet she has less that seven hundred thousand people. Only about one acre in ten of our land is occupied. Before the war we were receiving a stream of immigration into Canada at the rate of six per cent of our total population. We were receiving a stream from the United States into Canada of about one hundred and thirty thousand a year. We are just now laying the foundations of what we are going to be, and we want to lay them well, and lay them soundly in the great principles of the Christian religion. We want to stand with you, and Dr.

Stevenson has just whispered to me as I came out to speak, that we have thirty-five Canadians in Africa under the Methodist Episcopal Church, carrying on this great business of the Evangelization of the World. (Applause)

In our last general conference it was agitated that the day had come when the Methodist Church in Canada, as a church, should turn her face toward a new mission field and into the mines of Africa, and we believe it is a field we should enter. We want to stand with you of the M. E. Church, and the M. E. Church, South, and of the Methodists the world round, to lift up our banner.

I know you Americans take great delight in hoisting your stars and stripes. We in Canada have the same joy in putting up the union jack, and we are glad to see these two flags float side by side in every mission field on the face of the globe. (Applause) And, brethren, we will never rest until we join in the same great flag rope and we hoist the flag up and up and up and up, till the flag floats above the union jack and the stars and stripes – the blood-stained banner of the cross. (Applause)

JOSEPH CRANE HARTZELL:

Now, I am sure that anybody who leaves this audience before this meeting is completed will make a mistake. What wonderfully good things we have had! We have got more splendid things to come. We are to have one or two addresses on Mohammedanism, the last will be by Dr. Zwermer, the Editor of the "Moslem World," the best known and trusted leader of our time in the Protestant propaganda in the Mohammedan world.

I speak of this so that you may sit still, if possible, until this meeting is completed. We have now referred to the work of Methodism in barbaric, black Africa in part. I wish I could introduce to you here today that splendid company of men and women down yonder in Portugese (sic) East Africa, where we have one of our fine mission establishments. I wish I could bring to you here that splendid company of men and women in Rhodesia, under the union jack, where we have our great missions. I wish I could introduce others, but there are three or four here that I want you to see face to face.

We have Doctor and Mrs. Springer,[12] who a few years ago made the trip across the continent of Africa by appointment, and since that I have been enabled to organize a conference in the Belgian Congo. I am sorry to say that he has been called to another appointment. I want you to know them and their work, but I want to have them stand up for you in a minute.

The Reverend Doctor Richards (sic) and his wife. Dr. Richards began in Africa thirty-six years ago, and as organizer and translator (sic) of the Christian Scriptures in the two different languages he has worked everywhere. I want you to see him.

... Dr. Richards arose – received with applause....

Dr. Blackmore is from North Africa.

...Dr. Blackmore arose – received with applause...

Dr. Blackmore says he is an Englishman, but he says that he is more than half American since he came here. Dr. Frease, the Central Superintendent, will speak to us for a few moments.

DR. FREASE:[13]

North Africa presents to us one of the greatest – I had almost said the greatest – tragedy of Christian history. The gospel has spread even more rapidly along the African coast than it did in Europe.

The great Christian civilization which grew up along the North African coast sweeping west of Carthage gave thousands more to the discussion of fine doctrinal points than it did to seeking to save the people beyond; the results being that the great Mohammedan wave of invasion swept over that great region in the seventh century. The Christian church went down into a ruin more complete than anywhere else that I can think of.

Even in Egypt remained the pope; even in Asia remained the Armenian; even in other sections of Mohammedan lands remained the Christian Greek, but in North Africa, Morocco (sic), Algeria, Tunis and Tripoli the Christian church disappeared. It was a great church. We see that from the monumental ruins still existing.

Just west of Algers, a little seaport, fishermen's town, this day are ruins in which we can trace clearly the remains of five great Christian churches. The great Carthage cathedral can still be traced, and other churches there. All up and down that great land it is said that some forty thousand Christian churches were destroyed, and from that day till about ninety years ago – rather seventy years ago – North Africa Mohammedanism fought Europe, and always during those centuries had the upper hand.

Why, you know almost within the memory of people in this building today the barbaric pirates scourged the Mediterranean, came out into the Atlantic, and defied all the Christian powers. When I go downtown in Algers and look at the old port and see the buildings there, I remember that in 1830, as there had been for all the years of centuries beyond that, there had been on an average ten thousand white European Christian slaves. When I go to Tunis and stand in the old slave market there, I stand on a place where other thousands of white European Christians had been sold into a slavery worse than death, but in 1830 France took Algers, extended her sway over Algeria in 1881, to the protectorate over Tunis a little later. Just before our great war we know that France was acknowledged as the sovereign in Morocco, so that even today that great Mohammedan section, one of the most difficult in the whole world, has come under the sway of European civilization. Under France there are millions of Europeans who have crossed the Mediterranean to live in Algers and Tunis. They have constructed thousands of miles of railways; ten to fifteen thousand miles of some of the finest automobile roads in the world, and under the impact of that European civilization, and trade, and education, and literature, Mohammedanism first began to tremble and to stagger and to fall, and as this great war came on and France in the desperate need as she was of men began, timid at first, to draft the Berber and the Arab of North Africa into the trench armies – then as she grew bolder, drafted them all, so that the whole young manhood of North Africa has gone out into France, either to fight in the armies as over three hundred thousand of them did, or to work in the fields, to labor in the work shops.

These men were torn, as I saw them, from their desperate cases, from their mountain homes, from their villages, into valley and into plain, and they are coming back, as I saw them, changed for good, and all Mohammedanism is disintegrating in North Africa. (Applause)

Seated on this platform are some venerated leaders – Bishop Hartzell, who with the prophetic foresight of a great statesman and leader, saw in North Africa one of the great strategic centers of attack upon Mohammedanism. When in 1907 at a great Sunday School convention he was pleaded with by the delegates there to undertake for our church to go into North Africa, he did so. For mark you, up to that time no great Protestant church of America or of Europe had undertaken mission work in North Africa.

Amidst the greatest difficulties and obstacles Bishop Hartzell went forward and founded the mission, taking over with him some missionaries who at the risk of their lives had established work there in Tunis and Algers. He asked me to come from India to superintend that work, and I came. I have done my best under his leadership, and we took over other missionaries in Constantine.

Brother Blackmore is one of them – a type of those magnificent English missionaries, I should say British, for they are Scotch and English and Irish. Professor Beech of Yale University wrote to me and Bishop Hartzell and others, and said that he has never seen a finer type, nor a finer group of missionaries, better equipped, in the world.

So God has planted us there as a great church in Morocco, in Algeria, and Tunisia and Tripoli, just at the time when He was breaking up the great paganism, when Mohammedanism was to disintegrate, and He has given us these ten years to get ready for the great task that lies before us, for North Africa is different from the rest of Africa – separated by the Sahara Desert.

We have white people there. The Berbers are a white race – fifteen or sixteen millions of them – then there are about three or four millions of Arabs, and they who were the most intolerant of Moslems today are the most accessible.

Ten years ago I said to the missionaries, "We must establish homes to receive the children of the Kabyle and Arab to train them." They said, "It can't be done. We can't get the children." I said, "We must try it!" Bishop Hartzell backed me up, and we did try it, and today we have nearly a hundred and fifty Kabyle and Arab boys and girls in our six homes, going to Tunisia and to Algeria, and the missionary at Algers tells me that he just received seventeen new boys in that beautiful new property we bought for that home only two months ago, and that he dare not take more because he does not want to increase the proportion of new boys too rapidly.

The only obstacle to that work today is our ability to receive and take care of these boys and girls. Already four or five of the boys and four or five of the girls have been married and established Christian homes. Already they are representing the Methodist Episcopal Church – consecrated, earnest, capable workers.

The Methodist Evangelical Church of France[14] has just turned over to us their only station in North Africa, and under the blessing of this Centenary campaign, with the war and emergency funds, we are preparing a great forward movement, with an increase in missionaries, with an increase in all that we need, and with the French government ten years ago hostile, and today friendly and favorable and glad to have us there and supporting us in every way, we promise to go ahead and as their lines of railway cross the Sahara, we believe that with a growing Christian church in North Africa, by these rails we are going to be able to solve the great problem of black Africa. May God grant it! And I am sure that God is preparing for us in that great field one of the greatest triumphs the Christian church has ever had. (Applause)

JOSEPH CRANE HARTZELL:

I want now to introduce to you Dr. Samuel M. Zwermer (sic), Editor of "The Moslem World," the best posted man on Mohammedanism we have in the Protestant world. I take great pleasure in introducing Dr. Zwermer.

SAMUEL M. ZWERMER:[15]

(Opened his address by loud calls) Fourteen centuries ago that was the call that rang out over North Africa. Thirteen centuries ago with that battle cry Mohammedanism challenged the church of God and won out. Thirteen centuries ago they swept away the Christian church from North Africa in the short space of one hundred years, and we speak of that as the Mohammedanism challenge to the church of Jesus Christ, but today it is no longer the challenge of Mohammedanism. It is the challenge of Methodism to the Mohammedan world, for the Methodist Church, North and South, the Methodist Church of Wesley, who said, "The world is my parish," has today challenged the Mohammedan world in three of its most strategic centers.

In the first place, your church has challenged Islam in India. In the second place, your church is challenging Islam in Malaysia; and in the third place, your church has challenged Islam in Africa. In India, where Mohammedanism has a massive strength, in Malaysia where Mohammedanism is still plastic and yields to the impulse of the power of the gospel, and in Africa where the great rival of Christianity has been and is Mohammedanism – I say the Methodist Church has met that challenge, and they have met the challenge in the same spirit as David met the challenge of old Goliath.

Goliath stood with spear upraised, and all Israel ran away as though they were defeated. And then David, good man of God, arose with his pebbles from the brook and his heart of steel, and his faith in the God of Israel, and he said to Goliath what you and I are saying today to the Mohammedan world – "Thou comest to me with a sword, and with a shield, and with a javelin; but I come to thee in the name of the God of Israel, whom thou has defied."

And I say this afternoon that the leaders of the Methodist Church are following in the footsteps of that early missionary, who went single handed into North Africa, and as he was preaching the love of Christ way back in 1310 to the Mohammedans of North Africa he was stoned to death, and that lonely grave is today proving the truth of the old church father [Tertullian] who said, "The blood of the martyrs is the seed of the church."

I hold in my hand a pamphlet by one of our missionaries in Malaysia. It is entitled, "Islam's Challenge to Methodism." The book is so good and so full of meat, and so full of facts, that you ought to know that I regret to say that the title is incorrect. The title does not show the old Methodist faith that attempts the impossible, and glories in the power of God. The title ought to be "Methodists' Challenge to Islam." (Applause) And I want to say today in this presence that the most baffling problem and the biggest problem, and the final problem to bring the whole in the subjection to Jesus Christ is the Mohammedan problem. Every denomination knows it. The church of God knows it. The politicians know it, and around the peace table today in Paris they have left the hardest nut to be cracked last.

Not a word have you heard today or yesterday in regard to the fate of Persia and Turkey and North Africa and Egypt. They have shoved aside that problem as too big and too baffling until they have brought Germany to her knees in repentance and peace has been declared. And then the problem will be what a re-united Christendom will do with the one who has challenged our civilization, who has murdered eight hundred thousand of our fellow Christians, who has dragged in the mire the name of Jesus Christ, who has prostituted the most sacred churches to the worship and the honor of Mohammed.

Then the problem will be whether a united Christendom will again put the cross above the crescent, and the answer to that question is the Mohammedan problem. A few months ago I saw a very interesting cartoon. It represented a huge turkey sitting on a colossal egg. In the background stood Madam Europe armed with a butcher knife, and there came John Bull from the left of the picture. The egg was marked "British Mohammedan Subjects" and John Bull called out to Madam Europe, "Sh! Do not kill the bird. I have him setting."

Well, the whole question is whether it is worth while to have the turkey sit any longer upon that egg, which most of us believe has long passed the hatching period, which most of us believe is rotten, and worse than rotten – a civilization which has degraded womanhood, and childhood, and manhood; which has flouted the truth of God; which has displaced Jesus Christ in His majesty and honor; and we are not willing, as Americans, that that bird shall sit and hatch that egg. (Applause)

We believe there is a greater liberty, and a holier program, and a higher ethics for the Mohammedan world of India and Malaysia and Africa than any program which the young Turk or the old Turk has yet shown the world, and here today in the name of the body of the Christian missionaries, whatever may happen at the peace table, whether you are pro- or anti-Wilsonites, whether you believe in a league of nations, or do not believe in a league of nations – here and now I lay before you not the mandatory of the peace table, but the mandatory of God for the evangelization of the whole Mohammedan world. (Applause) And this mandatory of God is ours, not only by the record of God's word, not only by His eternal promise, and his gracious promises in the gospel that the kingdoms of the world, and therefore of Mohammed (sic), shall be the kingdom of Jesus

Christ, not only the character of Jesus, who loves little children, who loves degraded women, who loves the uplift of our common humanity – but that mandatory is the mandatory of America for three great reasons.

We forget our history so soon. Do you realize this afternoon that a hundred years before Bishop Hartzell threw down the challenge to the Mohammedans of North Africa the fathers of our republic who framed its constitution, from the days of George Washington and Jefferson, flung down the challenge to Mohammedan Africa, and when Great Britain and France and Spain and Portugal were paying a million dollars in gold every year to the pirates of the Mediterranean, to the Mohammedans who enslaved Christians, it was the American Government that sent our little fleet into the Mediterranean under Steven Decatur[16] and swept it clear of Mohammedan pirates and established the freedom of the seas. (Applause) That is our mandatory.

One of the most glorious chapters that you and I must remember is that chapter of the Barbary wars. We did not fight for territory. We fought against the Mohammedan pirates to establish the freedom of the commerce of the world, and our missionaries were eighty years late. If only Methodism had gone in then! If only the Presbyterians had then established their work! But the work that a century might have done may fall ere the hours of the setting sun; and the motto this afternoon for you and me is that old watchword that Admiral Togo[17] put at his masthead when the fleet of Russia had sailed all the way around the Red Sea and the Indian Ocean and came to grapple with the fleet of the Japanese Government. In that battle he said, "I want a watchword today that will put courage into the hearts of the Japanese sailors," and so he put up at the masthead of the admiral's ship of the Japanese navy these words: "The destiny of an empire," and under that watchword they smashed the Russian fleet and won the day, and today you can see the masthead of Methodism, as at the masthead of the Christian church, as you think of Africa, "The destiny of a Continent."

Shall it be Christ's or Mohammed's? Would you like your girls and your boys to be brought up to the measure of the stature of the fullness of the camel driver of Mecca, or of the Son of God, Jesus Christ, the Savior of the world? And that destiny depends on your response to the mission of the Methodist Church in Algeria and Tunisia and along the coast of North Africa; and not only in Africa have you challenged this great giant, but at Singapore and in Malaysia.

It was about a year ago that I was in the harbor of Singapore and visited your Methodist missions on shore and talked with them and planned with them on the strategic value of the position that God had given them. And I tell you here this afternoon that the Methodist Church under a glorious leadership of your missionaries in India and Malaysia has occupied the very Verdun of the Moslem world in Southern Asia.

If you draw a circle around Singapore of a few hundred miles, you have within that circle no less than forty million Mohammedans, and these forty million Mohammedans are Moslems of only one or two hundred years standing. They are still plastic. They are not Mohammedans as in North Africa with thirteen centuries behind them; but they are Mohammedans who yield to the message of God's love, who would crowd your schools and hospitals and buy literature, but the Methodist Church has never yet had an adequate program, a big program, a program of progress, among the Mohammedans of Malaysia, and I beg of you when Dr. Shelleber (sic)[18] goes back to lift high that royal banner, that you will stand by them, and I prophesy that the Methodist Church will see mass movements and revivals, and a great ingathering, not only in Africa, but in Malaysia for God. And there you have the mandatory for India, too.

Kipling says in one of his poems, "By the bones along the wayside you shall come to your own." There is not a cemetery in Bombay or Lucknow or Calcutta or Delhi where you cannot point to the graves of Methodist missionaries – men and women and children, who lay down their lives. No poppies grow there. The sun is too hot. The sky is like brass. The earth is like iron, but in that soil they lay down their lives, and may God forgive us if the Methodist Church does not advance over the graves of its pioneers to plant the banner of victory in Bombay and Lucknow and Calcutta until the whole of India is covered with the knowledge of the glory of God, as the waters cover the Bay of Bengal. (Applause)

That is your task, and the challenge comes to us not only from the dead, and not only from the living, but the challenge comes to you from the throne of God, and from those who have passed away in the service of the missionaries now on your fields. I wish you could see them today. We who are here are off of the job. We are on vacation. We stand here as those who are back on furlough, to regain our strength and go back to the trenches. But God knows that every one of us are thinking, most of all in the quiet moments of this Centenary, of the small, thin line of battle over there.

I wish you could hear them; hear them as they cry; hear them as they plead; hear them as they sigh for reinforcements; as they call to God in the prayer of that old hymn, one of the beautiful poems of our American poet when he said, "The cry of the dauntless." Every one of them a dauntless soldier.

They are not here, so let me give their cry to you. I can see them way up in Quenta, way down in Java, far to the east in Bengal and Burma, far to the west in Algeria, and along the whole line of Methodism what are they saying to you. Listen: "More than half beaten, but fearless, facing the storm in the night; reeling and breathless, but tearless. During the lull of the fight we who bow not but before Thee, God of the fighting clan, lifting our faces we glorify Thee."[19]

"Give me the heart of a man. What though I stand with the winners, or perish with those that fall; only the cowards are sinners, fighting the fight is all. Strong as my foe he advances. Snapped is my blade, O Lord see their proud banners and lances, but spare me this stub of a sword."

That is their spirit, and you have only given them a stub of a sword. You have cut their appropriation. You have delayed their reinforcements. You have not given them equipment. You have not added to them all they needed to sweep the enemy back. But with this Centenary movement; with this vision of God; with this new inspiration; with this new leadership; with this sword of triumph – if we will hear that trumpet which has never sounded retreat, we will march under that banner which has never known defeat, and we will say with Clemenceau,[20] the Tiger of France, that "Over against the Mohammedan World, no matter how strong or how mighty, the last fifteen minutes of the battle is to be ours, and in the name of Jesus Christ, Mohammedanism by faith has already fallen, and the division of Mohammed's empire is yours." (Applause)

Negro Day Program
Monday Morning, July 7, 1919

...The meeting convened in the coliseum at 11:30 A.M., Dr. I. Garland Penn presiding temporarily...

IRVING GARLAND PENN:[21]
The presiding officer for this morning's service will be Dr. W. H. Logan, pastor of the Tabernacle Episcopal Church, Galveston, Texas. We will have a selection from the United Quartettes, entitled "I want to be a Christian Soldier."
...Singing...
Dr. J. C. Sherrill, of Tennessee, will lead us in prayer.

JOSEPH C. SHERRILL:[22]
O Lord, our heavenly Father: we thank Thee for the great world movement that made this occasion possible, and we are here at this hour in Thy name. We ask that Thou wouldst be here with us, and we pray especial blessings upon us today, as we come here to add our part toward making this great occasion what it should be; and we pray especial blessings upon him who shall speak at this hour. We pray that Thou wouldst pour out upon him the holy spirit, and as he shall speak and as the words in which he shall utter his thoughts come forth from his own heart, may they find a happy reception in our hearts.

We pray now, heavenly Father, for Thy special blessings upon us during this entire day. May the entire program, as it shall be carried out today, be carried out in Thy name. O Lord, may it show forth the results of the work in which Thou hast been doing for us through men and women, for the onward march of Thy Kingdom through all the years that have passed, and, our Heavenly Master, may it also show forth and be the means of outlining a program that shall be far-reaching in the years yet before us.

Be Thou with us today. Hear all that we shall take recognition of, all that shall be said and done today, and may we leave this hall, bound to go to our various places, better prepared to render service for Thee in the years to come, than we have been before in all the days of our lives.

Hear us, I pray Thee, in Thy name, and baptize us with the Holy Spirit, and may we be Thine, and entirely Thine, to the honor and glory of Thy name, through Jesus Christ, our Lord. Amen.
...Singing by United Quartettes...

I. GARLAND PENN:
We all know the story very well, when Benjamin Franklin wandered into Philadelphia, poor indeed. He was almost stranded, and we know of his career. Later a boy of African descent entered the city of Philadelphia, wandering about, a stranger, knowing not where to go or what to do. Finally he wandered into a church and was happily saved, became its janitor, later entered the ministry, and in his own conference was sent as pastor of the church where he was once

janitor and where he was converted. Later in his career he was sent to that church as pastor. It was a good sized church, able to hold all the people who had hitherto attended, but when he began to preach, the church suddenly grew too small and he added a few wings, consoling himself, (and his officials cooperating with him) that they would have ample room as soon as the doors of the main auditorium were opened and the wings added. However, it was found to be too small, so they thought they would move the location to a church much more spacious, and they established East Calvary. They said there they would have plenty of room. However, at the first service they found that the church was overtaxed, and so it has been going on for years.

Now the Board of Church Extension proposes to build him a church that will seat 3,000, and I predict that after the first service shall have been held, the people in Philadelphia will ask, "When are they going to build a church that will hold the people who come to hear Charles A. Tindley?" (Applause)

There is no royal road to greatness, and, as some one has said, there are no barriers to a boy of ambition, filled with the Holy Ghost in the Methodist Episcopal Church. (Applause) And, whatever may be the experiences of us here today, here is one who is honored in his own country, pastoring his own church. It gives me great pleasure to present to you the speaker of the hour, Dr. Charles A. Tindley, pastor of East Calvary Church, Philadelphia. (Greeted with applause.)

CHARLES A. TINDLEY:[23]

I am not so very strong in voice and not so very strong in strength, especially when it comes to size up with a great building like this. Now, I will have to have the attention of the people, so, instead of saying to me "louder", you be quieter. (Applause)

I am happy this morning to be called upon and privileged to say a word in this presence, in connection with this great day, this day set apart for the peoples of my race. I am not over-much in love with the people of my race, nor am I under-much in love with the people of my race, but because I love people in general, the people in my race are included. I have no apology for my race, because I did not make them, and I hope I will have nothing to do with unmaking them. I have no excuses to make for their color, because that was the business of their Creator, and He must have liked it because He is making so many of them. (Applause)

When it comes to a matter of seniority or priority, my race comes in for a first consideration, because we represent the oldest color in the world. (Applause) The Bible said "The evening and the morning were the first day", and not the morning and the evening. (Applause)

However, we do not dispute the right of other people to a share of the blessings of the world just because we came here first.

...The band was asked at this time to give a selection while the crowd was quieting. The band played "Onward Christian Soldiers"...

(Dr. Tindley Continuing):

Let me say this, as a repetition: I am happy to be here, to take part in a program that is entitled "Negro Day." You know, we seldom get a big day like this, we seldom get a chance like this, and perhaps because this is the biggest thing the world ever saw, we get the biggest place in it that we ever got upon any other occasion, anywhere else, or at any other time. The world is moving and it is carrying with it everybody, and thank God we are in the crowd, and we are moving also. We don't object to having this day called "Negro Day," if you put a big N and one G, but if you put a little n and two g's in it, your (sic) are not talking about us any more than other people who deserve that same thing. (Applause)

We come today to join with you in helping to make this world better for the tomorrows that shall come and for the yesterdays. We have come to say to you that we are with you in every upward climb in every big business for God and for man, in every work of betterment for everything that God made in this world. We recognize that we must prepare the way for God, in order that God may do what He wills to do for mankind, for God never does anything, we recognize, for an individual, but that individual can do for thousands or millions. God has made this great world as a big plant of raw material, in which everybody who does his duty and her duty can develop into the highest possibilities that God made for them. It is a fine, old world! Once I wanted to leave it, but I don't now, it is a fine, old world. This world has a splendid echo, it speaks back to anybody; whatever anybody says, it answers him exactly. If you praise God, the world shouts back in praises to God. It is your echo. If you curse the world, it curses back; it is your echo. The world answers you every time. And if you want to get that good compliment from the world, give it one and it will give it back to you. If you want to get a blessing from this world, hand it one, and it will hand it back to you. If you want to get abused by the world, abuse it and it will abuse you back – it is your echo. No race knows that better than my race.

So, we have come to join with you in helping to give the world a blessing, that we may receive as an echo a blessing in return.

I came to speak to you this morning about the flag of my country, my country, oh, yes, my country! I was born here with you – yes, some of you; others of you were shipped here. (Applause) And you came by way of the golden Gate of California and some other gateways that led in the immigrants.[24] . I came by way of birth, and so I am a citizen of this country. (Applause) I don't begrudge you a good place here, but I ask of you the chance to occupy some little corner pretty comfortably for myself here, because I am one of the aborigines. (Applause)

We were brought here to be your guests, they tell me; you furnished ships free of charge; you brought us here and you gave us our lodging free and gave us our clothing free – if you can call that clothing – and gave us our food free and charged us nothing for 250 years; and now do you expect us to leave? Not on your life! (Applause) We are not charging you a great deal, but we feel somehow that when you talk about citizens, that we have a right to stand up and be counted, because of being born here and because of helping to clear up the forests and to make the fields and the institutions. If that constitutes an element that enters into citizenship, we count again. If helping to fight for the country is an element that enters into citizenship, we count once more. (Applause) We are citizens of this commonwealth.

Do you blame us because we are colored? If you do, we can't help ourselves. We were made by the same hand that made the dogs and the hogs and the chickens and the horses. There are other things that are black and white, red and yellow, mulatto and striped, grissly-gray and spotted – we are all in the same crowd of variegations that you are in and did not do it ourselves. Do you blame us? (Applause)

We are sorry that we don't bring to you on this blessed day a greater reputation for learning, a greater reputation for morals, a greater reputation for material wealth, a greater reputation for lots of other things; we are sorry we don't bring you a greater reputation along these lines, but you are friends here today and you will receive kindly, I am sure, and with appreciation as well as consideration, any little thing that we say in the matter of excuse for not bringing to you what ought to be brought and what you would like to see us bring today, namely, better education or more education, more material wealth, a larger reputation for good morals, and a whole lot of other things that belong to citizens before they become really good. We say, we are not able to bring you up to the full measure, one hundred percent of all these beautiful qualities; but if you will give us the same time that you had yourself for making these things, and leave us the ladder that you climbed on, and brace it at the top with the same strong bracing that you braced it with for yourselves, and put it on a foundation at the bottom as strong as you rested it on for yourselves, and then don't write us up until we have had as many years to climb as you have had – if you will do that, we believe that you will think that we are made out of better stuff to begin with than you are. (Applause) And I don't believe black folks are better than white folks – I don't believe it! (Laughter) I believe, therefore, that they need all that anybody else needs, and some more, in order to be what they ought to be; and until they get that, I don't think anybody ought to sit in judgment upon them. (Applause)

I want to talk about my flag for a minute. Sometimes when I am talking, I take my pattern from my father's old flint and steel gun. He packed his shot, and she scattered her shot and killed a lot of birds, but nobody knew where she was going to hit. Sometimes when I am speaking, I scatter my shot and nobody knows where I am going to hit.

This is a beautiful day we live in, a day of all the days, and an age of all the ages, that we live in. The world is waking up as never before to a sense of brotherhood and democracy, and all that makes for the Utopian accomplishment of the highest and greatest dream of all the dreamers of the world, until today there is an enlarged and removed horizon, because a new day has dawned. I heard the roosters crow for the new day just a while ago. The roosters that crowed for the new day were in the shape of all the whistles in Philadelphia, all the whistles in New York, all the whistles in Buffalo, all the whistles in Chicago, all the whistles in San Francisco, all the whistles in Columbus, and all the world over, all crowing for a new day. The Kaiser had taken off his helmet and undone his iron fist and bade the world a sad farewell and gone to dream, to rise no more until the new Kaiser came on the scene. (Applause)

The rooster crowed for a new day for our world, and so the dawn has come. Thank God when the horizon is removed and a new day has come to our world. Are negroes glad? Very glad because they have helped to bring the new day and hail all the blessings that the new day brings; because they belong to this new day, thank God. (Applause)

And the flag of our country in the new day has a new meaning, a meaning that it never had before. Thank God for our flag, the flag of our country! And what is the new meaning of the flag? First of all, the red of the flag stood for the blood of the victims and the enemies of the country. And, as the devotees of the flag, we fought and men died; we won and they lost; we rose and they fell; we triumphed and they went down, and the red in our flag stands for their blood, because we were the victors and they were the victims. Have our people any right to rejoice in a triumphant flag of our country, the greatest country the world ever saw? Have our people a right to rejoice in that marvelous victory; yea, verily, for where Old Glory has gone, my folks have gone. (Applause) And they went with a will and with patriotism, the old flag floating at Boston and over the Commons there, but her proudest wave was over the blood of Chris Maddox (sic),[25] . baptizing the new soil for the new day, and "My Country, 'Tis of Thee, Sweet Land of Liberty."

And then we followed the flag to Yorktown, behind the greatest man of them all, General Washington, and we went to Lake Henry with Mr. Perry – we were there. Then over in Mexico and then back again to Antietam, and to Gettysburg, and to Fort Wagner, and to Appomattox Courthouse – we were there. Then over on San Juan hill, where the greatest of them all rode his horse proudly up that marvelous hill, and behind him shouted a crowd of black men, saying, "There will be a hot time in the old town tonight!" (Applause)

And then, when the Kaiser put on his field glasses and saw the dreams of an extended world and had the dream of a world emperor and the world as an empire, and said to his men, "Go, get the spoils and take the hinges off the gates of the empires and take the emperors off their thrones; bring me them as a trophy and crown me lord of all" – when he said that, we looked into the face of our President, the greatest man perhaps in the world, and said, "Do you need us, sir?" Nobody answered us for a while, and the Kaiser boasted and strutted around, gathering more feathers and more plumes and more starch and more dignity. We asked again, "Do you want us, boss?" Nobody answered us, and by and by one day our good man passed into the White House, and peering through the windows, he saw faces of men whose nationality he could not detect. He pushed the button and said, "Send me a black battalion to keep guard on the greens around the White House." (Applause) Our boys got on a double-quick trot. They came, stood erect, facing the White House, and bowed, and in that bow said, "Mr. President, say your prayers and go to bed, for negroes are on guard." (Prolonged applause)

I say to America – East, West, North and South if you put negroes on guard; if you give them a chance to breathe, a place to stand; if you give them liberty enough to stand straight, they will guard the world! (Applause)

That stripe of red in the flag is going to change now – it has changed in the new day, and in the new light it doesn't stand now for the blood of our unfortunate victims, it doesn't stand now for the blood of those whom we have sent down to defeat, but, like Jesus Christ, we are coming out of this great war with our garments stained with our own blood, representing that we are willing to sacrifice that other people may live and have a chance to live. (Applause)

And the new day means a sacrifice forever. We are staining our war with our own blood.

Then comes the next stripe in our emblem, that stripe of white, representing peace, if you please. Ah, friends, it is fine to have peace when others who are enemies and who assail you are beaten down and powerless, and you stand monarch of all you survey, and in full possession of the territory. That is peace! That is military peace! That is the peace of the world! But our white stripe in the flag stands for a nobler peace than that. It stands for that peace that makes us happy because we exist, but goes out to seek others who are less happy and fortunate than we are and gives them a chance to exist also! (Applause) A peace that picks up the fallen, that saves the unfortunate and brings life to death! Thank God for a stripe like that in the flag!

What have negroes to do with that stripe? Very much. We lay claim to a peaceable nation, thank God, a peaceable race. In the days of the bloody war of the sixties, our men like watchdogs slept all night on the doorstep, with a hand on the knob, and with the other hand on the meat axe, guarding the mistress and her children, while the masters went to war. (Applause) We are the same stuff now, thank God! (Applause) We are made of the same stuff today. No bombshells have been thrown by our folks. (Applause)

The Bolsheviki sent us notice that if we would join them, they would help us to get free. We said, "Nothing doing!" (Applause) We don't want freedom along that line. We never killed that we may live, but we live that others may never die. (Applause)

I call upon the flag of my country. There she floats, bless her old stripes. (Applause) I say, "Flag of my country, have you any charge against your negro constituency in the country?" Flag of my country answers me, "There are three awful spots on you that are disgraceful, that no waters shall ever be able to wash out, that no reformation will make people forget – three spots on you which are disgraceful. One was put there when the immortal Lincoln died." I examine the spots, and they are not put there by a black hand, but by a white hand. (Applause) "You had another spot when the immortal Garfield died, but it is not put there by a black hand, but by a white hand." (Applause) "You had another spot when McKinley died, but no black hand put it there – it was a white hand." Old Glory, answer me, if we ever disgraced you in all the world? We have not, Old Glory. (Prolonged applause)

Old Glory, we had more trouble to follow you in these years just gone by than any other race in the world. We had to go over 13,000 heaps of ashes to the remains of our brothers and sisters, fathers and mothers burned at the stake; we had to go under 12,000 tree limbs, from which our bodies hung ready to be riddled; but we took hold of your four corners, shut our eyes, and jumped forward. (Prolonged applause)

Answer me, Old Glory, do you recognize me? I am a member of the same race that made you cover up the heaps of all the lynching and Jim Crowism and relegation and segregation, and went in to die for you. Do you recognize me? (Prolonged applause)

Old Glory, I lower my voice just a moment. I paid a sum that was equal and more than equal to all I had to pay. My boy, Old Glory, twenty-three years of age, educated out of my own pocket seven years long in the college, had entered the University of Pennsylvania to take his course as a physician. He went to your defense last August. On the third day of October word was sent to his father and mother, "I die in No Man's Land, that the country might be free." (Applause)

Old Glory, do you charge me any more for citizenship? If I paid my way through, can't I be a citizen now, when I have given my boy to die for your perpetuity? (Applause) If I buy a ticket, won't you let me have a decent car to ride in? If I pay my bills, won't you let me live on a clean street somewhere? If I can do the work, won't you let me earn an honest living anywhere? (Applause) If I am a true man, won't you let me vote for them to rule me? Old Glory, answer me; answer me or blot out your stars and come down! (Applause)

One other thing about Old Glory and I must stop. Old Glory, you have a good many stars, but your stars are blending together. It is said, Old Glory, that one great man once, oh, not long ago, for in this very war, had one star in his window turned to gold, and somebody said, "Why aren't there a couple of more stars in your window?" He replied, "Because I didn't have but one boy to send." "And why does your star now shine as gold?" "Because my boy died."

Old Glory, way up above the skies my Father in heaven had one son, when the war was on between sin and civilization, He had just one boy to go to war; that was His only begotten son, Jesus Christ. He fought well for three years and died, and there is one star now in the window of glory because God had one son to die. (Applause)

All the stars blend in that one star. Old Glory, I put your stars all in one today and say to you, "Is that the star of hope?" If it is, Old Glory, brush the clouds away and let the black boys see it, as well as the white boys. (Applause)

When my grandchild lifts his head from the cradle, Old Glory, and sees your star, will it mean for him a clear road to honor, a clear road to wealth, a clear road to manhood; will your star shine on him as it does on others, or will you put up a wall ahead of him and say, "Because you are black, hitherto shall you come and no further." Old Glory, tell me, does your star shine for me as well as anybody else? (Applause) If it doesn't, in the name of God, come down! (Applause)

In closing this little talk, I pay my respects to you by saying, don't be afraid to give us a chance in this world. You said that if you educate us, we will become bumptious and unruly and we will want social equality. Don't you be afraid. Of course, we have a few fools, but you wouldn't think we were advancing if we hadn't bred a few fools in all this time. (Applause) We have some people now who are actually contemplating suicide. That shows that our people are rising. (Applause) Our folks are actually losing their sense now, because they happen to have some. I think it is a big sign. You say that if you educate us, we will want social equality, but you mean social sameness. We don't want social sameness, we want social equality. Social sameness will mean, your table is the same table as mine. We don't mean that. It means your food is the same food; we don't mean that. It will mean that your bed is the same bed; it doesn't mean that. It will mean our house is the same as your house; it doesn't mean that. That is social sameness. But social equality means a house as good as yours, if we can buy it. (Applause) A table as clean as yours, if we can produce it. (Applause) Food as well cooked as yours, if we can cook it. A wife just as intelligent and sweet as yours, if we can find her. (Applause) Not social sameness, but social equality. If that is what you mean, make the most of it, for that is what we want in this broad world.

You mistake us when you say that if you educate us, we will want white women for wives. Listen to me a moment: we may have a few fools – if we didn't have, we would be different from any other race in the world. (Applause) Don't rate us by our fools, for if we rated you by your fools, we would do you an injustice. (Applause) Don't rate us by our criminals. Don't rate us by our rogues. Don't rate us by those who are bad, but rate us, if you can, by those who are trying to be good. (Applause) Don't measure the height of our tree by the lowest limb. Measure from the root to the top. We measure you from your Wilson down. (Applause)

When one steals, don't burn up our town, for we don't all steal. (Applause) When one lies, don't discredit the whole race, for we don't all lie. Of course, we have a few fools, but we are the most independent race, when it comes to women, you ever saw in your life.

God knew that we were color-loving folks. We like a variety of colors. God knew that. (Laughter) He knew that and He knew that just as we looked for colors – when we go to buy a suit of clothes we look for colors – in things of that kind, when we go to get a wife, we look for the same thing. God knew that, and He made us all kinds of colors, from chalk to charcoal. (Applause)

While you are getting difference in sizes and different shapes of head and a little different complexion and different hair, we can walk about in our garden and get any sort of color that suits our fancy. (Laughter)

We have a few fools, but not all fools. We think our women are getting to be the prettiest women the world ever saw. (Applause) If one of them finds that her husband is falling out with that kind of color, she goes to a paint shop and gets another brand. (Applause) I saw one the other day who was actually blue. (Applause) I think, however, where she was dealing they gave her the wrong stuff, but she put it on and became blue.

No, no, we don't mean an intrusion, we don't mean bumptiousness, but because we are human, we mean that we ought to have whatever a human person has in the world. We ought to have a fair chance in the race of life, high ceilings above a head and a ladder to climb; to dare to live without fear or dread, and a chance to be manly and a man. (Applause)

People of Columbus, with these words I give the keynote of Negro Day. Give us a chance in the world to take care of our families, a chance in the world to educate our children, a chance in the world to buy all our money can buy, and enjoy it after we buy it; a chance in the world to live where it is best for us to live, without cross bones being put over our doors and a notice to move in four hours. Give us a chance to do what other men do, and you have the finest, most trustworthy, everlastingly indefatigable eternalists around you the world ever saw. (Applause) These people will die by you, if you let them live by you. (Applause) A chance to live is what we want, only a chance to live.

Somebody gave me a dream the other day – and I am not a good dreamer – but they gave me a good dream. This dream was that a black boy went to school and graduated in his class of white and colored children, and on the graduation day he was surrounded by friends. When he was out in the world, he married a girl who graduated with him from the same school. All the other boys who were white got employment in the trade that he was trained in. He went to this factory and they turned him down just because of his black face. The other boys said, "George, we know you; we have eaten with you; we have shared our scanty fare with you in school, and we wish you could share our job, but sentiment is against it." George went to another place, only to get the same reply, the same words and the same treatment. That continued for some time, until George came home one day disgraced, disgusted, heartbroken, with a wild stare in his eye. He said to his wife, "I can't make it. I have got it in my head, I have got it in my muscles, but I can't get employment because my skin is black." He looked at his boy and said, "You are doomed in this world because you can't change your color." Then he looked at his wife and said, "You are doomed because you can't change your color." He drew a knife from his pocket and plunged it first of all into the bosom of his boy, and said, "I would rather see you die, than to have you walking around heartaching, like your father, for things that you can't get." He turned around to his wife and plunged this dagger into her bosom and said, "I would rather bury you than to see you sitting here, longing for comfort that I am unable to give to you because they won't give me a chance to get it." Then he prayed to God, and this is what he said in his prayer: "O God, why did you make me black? I didn't do you any harm; my parents didn't do you any harm. Why did you make me black? Why have you doomed me to segregation and disgrace? I am penniless and ragged, with brains and heart and muscles equal to the test to make a good living, but I can't because social barriers keep me now. God, if I come to you now will you forgive me?" – and he paused a while and then plunged his knife into his own bosom, crawled between his dead wife and dead child, prayed once more, and died.

People of this country: that is the picture that I want everybody to carry away. But you are too good to let my boy suffer that way, you are too good to let my girl suffer that way. I step forward and say to you, in the name of God, unlock the factory doors, unlock the business places, open the avenues, give me a chance to earn a living, bring back my wages, make my boy happy and my wife happy, or you will make me kill myself and kill my loved ones doomed to all eternity. God save my race! God save the world! God save democracy! God save the Nation! (Applause)

I. GARLAND PENN:

I want you to see a lineal descendant of John Stewart, the pioneer missionary to the Wyandotte Indians. Her name is Mrs. Alice Stewart Evans, and I present her at this time.

...Mrs. Evans was greeted with cheers...

...ADJOURNMENT...

Negro Day Program
Monday Afternoon, July 7, 1919

...The meeting convened in the Coliseum at 2:30 P. M., Dr. I. Garland Penn presiding as Chairman...
    ...Music by orchestra...
    ...Music by Second Regiment Band...
    ...Music by Colored Chorus...

HERBERT STANZELL (sic):
The Chairman of the afternoon is Dr. Penn of Cincinnati and I am happy to present him to you now.

IRVING GARLAND PENN:
We will be led in prayer by Bishop Scott of Nashville.

ISAIAH BENJAMIN SCOTT:
"O Lord, Our Lord, how excellent is thy name in all the earth." We approach Thee today as the giver of all good, the Father of Our Lord Jesus Christ and our Father in Heaven, and we pray that as we approach Thee we may so do acceptably and that we may humble ourselves before Thee. We pray that Thou wilt look in mercy upon us, forgive all our sins, strengthen us for our day and generation and fit us for each and every responsibility of life. We pray today that these exercises may be conducted to the best possible purpose, that they may tend to encourage and strengthen the people in whose interests they are held and that such information may be given out as shall be beneficial to all concerned.

And now, Lord, as we come, we would not come in our strength, we come pleading our unworthiness and looking to Thee as our Father and our God.

We pray for our Church and for all the churches, but especially do we pray for Methodism today, that while she rejoices in what has been accomplished in the past, and while she rejoices in the splendid showing made in the Centenary, she may also look to Thee and may accept what has come to her a given of God, and instead of seeking to glorify herself, glorify the Lord Jesus Christ.

And we pray, O Lord, for our country, for him who is at its head, the President of the United States. May he be more and more fitted to the responsible tasks that come to his hands. We pray that he may have strength and wisdom and vision, that he may have the desire to do the right thing in every case.

We pray for our people, the people here whose interests are discussed today. O Lord, God, may they be in that frame of mind that shall cause them to desire to be what Thou wouldst have them. May they be in that frame of mind that shall enable them to see their own shortcomings, the necessity for their own development and improvement. Direct and strengthen and help them and while we suffer disadvantages and in some cases persecution, we would not pray that the fires be quenched, but we do pray that we may come out refined because of the trials and better fitted for the responsibilities of life.

O blessed Christ we thank Thee for what Thou hast done for us in the past and we pray that more and more we may look to Thee as the giver of all good. Bless us now and strengthen us. Bless those who shall speak to us. Grant that they may have wisdom and guidance. Grant that we may be enabled to get some uplift, some vision, some strength, some purpose of heart to go forward in the great task of life. Lead us now and guide us in all things and save us, through Christ we ask it. Amen.

IRVING GARLAND PENN:

We are to lose no time in the introduction of speakers. This is Negro Day. It has been eminently successful so far and we have a very fine program for the afternoon. The first speaker of the Afternoon is a representative of the Methodist Episcopal Church South, a Virginian. I happen to know him; we were boys together. I know he has a great message for you, and we were greatly delighted when the committee nominated Dr. W. Asbury Christian of Blackstone, Virginia, President of the Female College of the M. E. Church South in that town, and we present him to you as the first speaker, Dr. W. Asbury Christian. (Applause)

WILLIAM ASBURY CHRISTIAN:[26]

Mr. Chairman, Ladies and Gentlemen: Let me please make a request that those who are moving about there, take a seat or go out so that those who remain can hear what is to be said. (Applause)

It gives me great pleasure to be able to speak to you on this occasion. I love to speak to the colored people and I love to speak in their interests. (Applause) There is so much fervor among them and I don't wonder that there are so many good colored preachers. A man who can't preach to the colored people can't preach at all. (Applause) And they are so appreciative. I don't think I have ever made a talk to the colored people that they haven't shown their gratitude for any word that I have said, sometimes expressed in their own way but nevertheless from their heart.

I remember once preaching to a colored congregation and as I came out an old woman took hold of my hand and said, "God bless you honey; you've got a white face but you sho' have got a black heart." (Laughter and applause) And I appreciate very much the intent and meaning of what that good woman put in that familiar and homely way.

I feel that I should begin my talk for this afternoon by congratulating the negro race. I do not know of any people who have made the wonderful progress in three hundred years that the negro race in America has made. (Applause) When I look back over their history I am persuaded that God overruled the avarice of the men who inaugurated the slave trade for the betterment of the race of the colored people. It was an awful hard school and yet God has taught a mighty lesson in that school.

But this progress which the colored race has made is not a point at which they can rest. It is rather a stepping stone from which they can reach to higher things. There is a great future before the colored race and if we stand by him and lend him our aid he will make good. We do not need to nurse and cuddle the colored race. They are not asking for extraordinary privileges; they are not making unusual demands; they are asking for the cooperation of men, for the sympathy of Christian brotherhood, (Applause) for the protection of the law, (Applause) and if you give him these he will work out his own salvation. (Applause) So God will work in him both to will and to do of his good pleasure. (Applause)

Now to accomplish this, let us remember that we must understand one another; we must be patient with one another; we must sympathize with one another. The negro of America, ten million strong, is a mighty power that can be trained and used for the advancement of the Kingdom of God. (Applause) And let me say that if you do not train him, if we white people don't help to train him, the devil will take hold of him and curse us both. (Applause) Let the best element of the white people and the best element of the colored people cooperate in this great work of advancing the race.

And why should this be thought strange or unusual? The worst element of the white race and the worst element of the colored race have no trouble getting together to wreck and ruin both races. (Applause) We have problems to solve and we can't solve them overnight. Friends of the colored people must stand firm and must be earnest in their work. I know the colored man has had many a false friend and among them is the politician who wants to use the negro to get into office and then cares no more about him. (Applause)

I can illustrate that by a little story that was told of a leading politician in Virginia. It was said that he went up to the gate of Heaven and knocked. St. Peter opened the door and said, "Colonel, are you mounted?" He said, "No I am afoot." "Well," he said, "You can't come in here unless you mount." So he came on back and he met colored Sam. He said, "Sam, would you like to go on in to Heaven?" "Yes," he said, "Colonel, I certainly would." "Well, St. Peter told me I couldn't get in unless I was mounted; you let me ride you up to the gate and we will both go in." He said, "Yes sah, hop on." When they got up to the gate he knocked and St. Peter said, "Are you mounted?" He said, "Yes." "Well," said St. Peter, "Tie your mount on the outside and come on in." (Laughter) And he turned and said, "Good bye, Sam, that is all I want with you, you can go where you please."

We want men who have the interest of the colored man at heart. (Applause) Like a good friend of mine, a physician of one of the best families in old Virginia, one dark and stormy night he got a message to come and see old Uncle Bob, as they called him. His wife said, "Doctor, are you going out in this storm?" "Well," he said, "It is mighty bad but I have got to go; the old man is suffering and he needs me," and out he went. When he came to the creek, the creek was swollen, but he tried to ride over. He didn't get over. The water dashed him off his horse and drowned him and drowned his horse, but I have often thought that when my good friend the doctor went up before my Lord, he said to him, "Come, ye blessed of my father, inherit the Kingdom prepared for you, for I was sick and ye came unto me." (Applause)

We must see in the humblest man and the humblest woman an immortal soul for which Jesus Christ died. (Applause)

Now I want to make a few suggestions as I pass along. I was sitting at a dinner table in Baltimore some months ago where there were a great many wealthy men and leaders of the race. We were talking about helping the negro and ameliorating his condition. I said, "Gentlemen, if I were a moneyed man and wanted to do a great service to the race and to God I perhaps would not use my money as you would use it." One said, "Well, how would you use it?" I said, "I would use it to make possible for the negro a clean, healthful, comfortable home." (Applause) For the foundation of our nation is the home. I thank God whenever I see a colored man owning his own home. I know that he has prepared against a rainy day, and not only that I have observed in my travels that the fewest number of colored people who own their homes are ever in the criminal courts. (Applause) Now think of that. When they are crowded in cellars and packed in garrets and stuffed in little cabins, oftentimes without even a pane of glass, in the name of all that is true and right, how can you expect people under such conditions to develop the beauty and strength of a home life that God has blessed many of us with? (Applause)

And I say today, let the colored man have a clean and comfortable home; let him own it; (There is no place like home; be it ever so humble, there is no place like home) We have got to do it with the work of education. We are doing some of it but we are just on the fringes. We have got to do a greater work in educating the colored man, and let me say that preparatory to educating him, you have got to pay the father and the mother a living wage so that they can send their children to the schools (Applause) and not to the fields and factories to eke out a poor existence, and then to raise them up in ignorance. (Applause)

We have got to have leaders. I congratulate my friend, the Chairman, upon the great work his bureau is doing in producing leaders. I am not casting any reflections upon any other denomination or any other class of leader, but I must stand here and say, as I go up and down through the Southland, the best, most upright leaders among the colored folks that I meet with, are our Methodist leaders. (Applause) I thank God for the great church that is able to bring forth these men of God who are bent upon uplifting their race and ushering in the Kingdom of God. They are teachers of religion, not a religion of fervor only, but they are men who strive to instill into the hearts of their peoples the great principles of the gospel of Jesus Christ that show themselves in the beautiful fruits of life, the fruits of the spirit that make magnificent characters and beautiful lives.

Now let me say in closing one word that I want to emphasize. I do not think it is any more just to charge the negro race with the crimes of some of its members, than it is to charge the white race with the crimes of some of its members. (Applause) But let me stand here and say that you can't suppress crime by crime. (Applause) If the people who have had advantages, trample under foot the law, in the name of reason how can you expect the unlettered and the ignorant to respect the law that they trample under foot? And I stand today as a southern man to say that the time has come when this mob violence which eventuates in lynching, must stop.[27] (Applause) The strength of the law is its power to protect the weak. The weakness of law is its failure to overcome the strength of the lawless. Let our Methodist people go out from this place with a renewed determination that in our pulpits and in our homes and in the street we shall cry out against mob violence (Applause) and insure the humblest man in the community of a fair, speedy and just trial, and we will do more to conquer the criminal than by mob violence.

Methodism has never failed before any great proposition. The liquor traffic vaunted itself and Methodism was the David that led the armies of the living God until it was brought low. (Applause) We have led the way in the great work of missions. Now let us lead the way on the great onward movement of the protection and advancement of the colored race and show to men by our own lives the mighty teachings of Jesus Christ that "Whatsoever Ye would that me should do to you, do Ye even so to them." (Applause)

I. GARLAND PENN:
This meeting starts well. We are now to have an address from one of the ablest editors, without respect to race, in our country, Dr. R. E. Jones, (Applause) Editor of the Southwestern Christian Advocate of the Methodist Episcopal Church, located at New Orleans.

ROBERT E. JONES:
Mr. Chairman, Ladies and Gentlemen: The negro constitutes one-tenth of the population of the United States of America. He will not go to Africa. He himself is against amalgamation; his presence in American life is a stubborn fact.[28] If he is a vexation and an annoyance, don't blame him. He did not just grow, as Topsy did, he is God-made, and God was as wise, as good, as just, as loving when he made the negro as when he made the other nations of the world, and the time will come when God will vindicate the why and the wherefore of the making of the negro peoples of this world to the satisfaction of all concerned. (Applause)

Has the Christian Church a message for this problem that is educational? Rural, city, economic, industrial, political and social. If we do not find in the church a message, then to what source shall we turn? Is there a leader who will stand forth as a champion of the cause of this black man? Some fifty odd years ago Abraham Lincoln banked his all on the negro. He had supreme faith that the negro was worth while and the negro redeemed the faith of Abraham Lincoln.[29] (Applause) Lincoln called him to fight; he responded 200,000 strong. Lincoln gave him his citizenship; he reports today in response to his citizenship a billion and a half dollars of property, a reduction of his illiteracy to 33%; he reports today as a loyal, tried American citizen. (Applause)

Every man who has touched the negro race with an unselfish motive has been lifted up from obscurity unto world fame. There is a message. Who gives the message? Who assumes the leadership? The negro turns to the church; his religious temperament and tendency suggests to us our method of approach and attack upon the problem. A gospel that is to be representative of the life of Jesus Christ and his spirit must be a gospel that will include all men of all races. If we accept the fatherhood of God then we must accept the brotherhood of man. (Applause) The negro turns to the church in his darkest hour with an open heart, hoping to find in the church a friend, a counselor, a helper. We are today in the midst of a discussion of the union of the two great Methodist bodies in this country. In some sense, the negro was the cause of the separation. The negro records himself today as opposed to being longer standing in the way of the union of these two churches. If the wiping out of sectionalism will come by the union of these two churches, then the negro offers his heart and hand, but in the coming of this reunion of the two great Methodist bodies of America the negro must have in that reunited church, a self-respecting relation, a relation that is thoroughly democratic and a relation that is true to the principles of the New Testament.[30] (Applause)

Somehow I cannot quite conceive how a church can open its doors to a part of the races of the world and shut its doors in the face of certain peoples in American life. If we welcome the Chinaman and the Japanese and the Hindu and the Bulgarian, then in the name of Christ, the doors of the church must swing on easy hinges and the negro must have the same place in the church as the other races of the world. (Applause) It is one thing to preach brotherhood; it is another thing to live brotherhood. (Applause)

Before Booker Washington died, and if you please he was the pastmaster in good will and inter-racial relationship, he said, "The world is watching America today to see what America's attitude is to be toward the negro." My friends, the world is watching Methodism today. What will be united Methodism's attitude toward the negro? Will Methodism accept him as a brother? (Applause) Abraham Lincoln said that if he met two men on a plank, a white man and a black man, he would push the negro off or he would push the white man off, "but," said he, "The plank is broad enough for both, neither need to get off." I am here to declare that on the platform of Jesus Christ the plank is broad enough and strong enough to hold the North and the South, the East and the West, the black and the white, in one great fellowship. (Applause)

With the black man of loyalty – and I think, modestly, we may say the negro has been loyal all the way along – he has fought in every war of the Republic from the time that Chris Maddox (sic) fell on Boston Common on down to the war of 1812, down through to San Juan, and then there comes to us the brilliant story of the achievement on the Western Front. The soldier who lies nearest to the German line today – the American soldier who lies nearest to the German line today – is a negro American soldier. (Applause)

With this as a background, we stand and plead today for life, for life! How I thank this good man from Virginia that he has spoken so forcefully, so eloquently against mob violence. The negro tells the sad story that since 1889 nearly four thousand have been lynched. Fourteen hundred men and women have been lynched since 1900 and it is commonly understood that this lynching is for the crime of rape.[31] Let me speak frankly, friends, but truthfully. The negro race does not cover the criminal element of our race with even a strand of thread; we do not shelter, we condemn without reservation every criminal whatever the nature of his crime. (Applause) I am happy to tell you that I have not known, of all those men that have been lynched, a single person; as a matter of fact there is almost a gulf between us and the criminal class of our people. Bishop Charles B. Galloway said, after careful investigation, "No negro who came out of our schools was ever accused of a crime of rape."[32] (Applause) But here is a master fact – it is very unpleasant and I regret that there is a single case of that – but there were five times as many cases of rape in one county of New York City as were alleged against the whole negro race for the last five years. (Applause)

However, we are not so much concerned today about the lynching of a hundred men or two hundred men, but may I speak with you frankly? What strikes terror to the heart of my people is this: that any negro may be lynched and there will be no redress for it. (Applause) And we plead today to the American people that we may have life; that we may live secure. This calls for a strong utterance of the press of our nation. With a background for our loyalty, may I speak frankly with you? We responded to the call of the nation; we did not shirk; we did not run; we marched up like a man and offered ourselves to the nation for the defence (sic) of the nation and for the defence of the doctrine of democracy. Let me say the negro is passed up somewhat. He has lived to see the day when it is a good deal more popular to be a negro than it is to be a German. (Applause) Somebody said that there was German propaganda among us, and somebody said, on the other hand, that the negro could be bought, but no German money ever bought a single negro anywhere in America. (Applause) We walked squarely up; we fought; we died. Hear me when I say if you American people (and we have got something of your spirit) launched the American Republic on the proposition that taxation without representation is tyrany (sic) then we submit to you today, ladies and gentlemen, that fighting without representation, is tyranny. (Applause) And the negro wants today, everywhere in this country, the right to vote, the right of self-determination. (Applause) And there need not be the revision of a single constitutional amendment anywhere in the country north or south. We accept any standard whatever that standard may be and we will walk up to it, or report to God the reason why. (Applause) What more than that? Realizing that there are privileges in democracy the negro assumes his responsibility. Do you ask me what we purpose? We purpose to show to the American people that in our hearts there is love for everybody. Thank God I stand today as a representative of a race which does not hate any race; loves and forgives and we promise you that we shall love North and South, East and West, friend and foe, (Applause) in God's name. That is our policy.

Further, there are dangerous sputterings in American life. It is not all over yet. Here and there you hear wild talk. The Bolshevistic movement is on, but may I say to you, friends, if the day comes in any labor movement or any sort of an organization where America is threatened, you can look back with security upon 12,000,000 negroes, and we will stand ready.[33] (Applause) At the bottom of all of our race trouble practically is what we call racial integrity. Now you can't talk on much about racial integrity because I don't know what race I belong to myself. (Applause) But I am here to say to you my friends, if there is a man here, North or South, who believes in racial integrity, the negro will meet you more than half way and join hands on racial integrity. (Applause) We will sign a contract today, written in our own blood, to build the wall so high that no white man can go over it and so thick that no negro can go through it. (Applause) We want our homes sanctified. If a man who robs the virtue of a woman deserves death, then that applies to all womanhood and they must be secured. Bless the women. (Applause)

Hear me, not for a single moment do I approve in any way whatsoever of mob violence, but when a man stands up and defends his womanhood he is my man; I honor him, but if that man protects the womanhood of his race, if he is consistent, he must protect the womanhood of my race. (Applause)

The next great forward step in this great race questions (sic) is to come from the South. With all due regard to what the North has done, with thanks and gratitude for their men, for their money, for their counsel, for their love, for their prayers, for their tears, for their blood, the next great forward movement in the uplift of the negro must come from the southern men of the South. Somehow I think the southern white man is well nigh omnipotent. When he gets ready he could walk up today and give justice today and no one would dare say against it. Woodrow Wilson is my President. I honor him; I love him: I pray for him; I teach my boy to pray for him. There is a triumvirate in American life. Two have been named, Washington and Lincoln. If Woodrow Wilson will apply his doctrine of democracy to all men, without regard to race, Woodrow Wilson will fill the third place in the great American triumvirate.[34] (Applause)

Finally, down in South Carolina a boy went to the front. He was from one of the aristocratic families of South Carolina. His mother sent him away with her tears. She kissed him, good bye, she gave him his sweater, his socks, and when he had gone she put on the front door a service flag. By and by the black boy, George, was to go. He said, "Miss Mary when I go are you going to send me off as you did your son, Frank?" She said, "Yes, George," and she gave him his sweater, his socks and sent him away with her, "God bless you". He said, "Miss Mary, are you going to put a service flag on the door for me?" She said, "Yes, George, I will," and when George had gone she put on the kitchen door a service flag for George. By and by that boy came back on a furlough with his shoulders thrown back, with his heart beating true to all the principles of American democracy.[35] He saw the service flag on the front door for himself. He walked to the rear door and saw the service flag for George. He said, "Mother, for whom is this service flag on the kitchen door?" That aristocratic southern white woman said, "My son, that is for George." Then as true an American as he was, and as true a son as he was, he lifted himself and said, "Mother, any man who is good enough to give his life for the Republic it is not enough to have a flag for him on the kitchen door, that service flag must be on the front door with me." (Applause) And so that southern man walked to the kitchen door and took that service flag down, walked to the front of that house a put it on the front door.

Whatever you say about discrimination, underneath it all there are in the south a great number of southern people who want to give us a fair chance and a square deal (Applause) and we say to the American people today, "Take the service flag off the kitchen door and put it on the front door; give us proof of our American citizenship." (Applause)

I. GARLAND PENN:

My friends, the negro has no better friends anywhere in the world than the Bishops of the Methodist Episcopal Church. (Applause)

We are delighted to have one of those Bishops present to speak to us at this time, as it is a special privilege to have Bishop Francis J. McConnell, of Denver, Colorado, to speak to us at this time.

FRANCIS J. McCONNELL:

I wish to speak to you for a little while this afternoon about the significance of the negro question for the new international day into which we have come. I am not talking to anybody here just as a black man, I am not talking to anybody here as a citizen of the North; but I am talking to you all alike, as citizens of the United States, about to enter into new relationships with the other nations of the world.

The other day the final terms of peace were signed, so far as the United States was concerned, which provided for a League of Nations among the nations of the world. We have been saying very many things in the past few years about making the world safe for democracy, and as we come into this new League of Nations, let us remember that there are certain things we must do and certain things we must not do, if we are to come around the council tables of the nations with clean hands and speak out of sincere spirits. The thing that distresses me about this lynching question, to which reference has been made, is just this – not that it reflects upon the South, not that it reflects upon the North, merely that wrong is done to the black man; it does all that, but it does this also: it brings us into the council chambers of the nations very liable to be misunderstood, very liable to be questioned, and everything we say concerning democracy. (Applause) I am not here to cast reproaches upon the white people of the South; I believe it is perfectly true, as their leaders have said, that ninety-five percent of the white people of the South are in favor of doing away with lynching, altogether. I think it is true, of course, that ninety-five percent of the people of the North are in favor of doing away with lynching altogether. I know that my own section of the country – reared, as I was, in Ohio and educated in New England, and living pretty much over the country – I know that my own Northern part of the United States has not been guiltless so far as lynching is concerned; that the fair annals of the state of Ohio too many times have been blackened in this way, and one of the latest great outrages was the outrage in East St. Louis.[36]

Now what happens? When we stand in the council chambers of the nations, Germany says, as she said in attempting to justify her outrages, "Let us not hear anything about this matter from a nation that permits lynching." It was not just to say that, but there was not any very easy way to answer it.

I was down in Mexico – I go to Mexico once every year; I have been going there for the last seven years. One time I was in Mexico in very troublesome times, when it looked as if there might be an outbreak of war between the two nations because of the way the United States was charging Mexico with maltreating citizens and doing crimes against the spirit of humanity. I remember how completely my lips were sealed and how little there was for me to say when a Mexican paper came out with three columns full, having kept a record for a year of accounts of lynchings in the United States. It reflects upon us internationally.

Now I have a suggestion to make. If ninety-five percent of the people of the South want lynching stopped and yet are unable to stop it; if ninety-five per cent of the people of the North want lynching stopped and yet as individual communities are unable to stop it, what then is the sensible thing to do? The sensible thing then to do is to call in the power that can stop it. (Applause)

I have seen enough of labor disturbances to know that one reason why the State Militia cannot handle the labor question when rioting breaks out is because they are related and inter-related one way and another; they have their local interests. There is one authority in the United States that is not supposed to have local interests, and that is the authority of the Federal Government. (Applause)

And I think that the next step to take on this whole abominable business, North as well as South, is to put upon the statute books of the United States a federal law that will deal with this matter. (Applause) And I say that not because I am interested in any one particular section. I refer to the entire United States – not Alabama, not Georgia, not Tennessee, not Ohio, but the United States! The Federal Government should see that he gets some protection against this awful crime! (Applause) And we cannot go into the council chambers of the nations unless, as a nation, our faces are set as a flint against this thing.

Now, in the next place, let me say this. Reference has been made here to the fact that twelve million negroes in the United States, laborers most of them, are full of the right kind of Americanism and will stand against Bolshevism, will stand against labor radicalism. I want to say this, and I am not saying this as a threat to anybody but simply as the statement of a fact. The fact is just this: With seven million five hundred thousand men of working age killed; to say nothing of those dead from disease, with seven million workmen killed in this last war, there is really a dearth in the labor market. Unionism is bound to spread, in spite of the attitude of the American Federation of Labor toward negroes.[37] Unionism is bound to spread, until Unionism has touched practically every man who cares to come near it. The only man who will stay out is the man who cares to stay out. I am not saying it is right; I am not saying it is wrong; I simply say it is inevitable. We talk about the I.W.W., for example; what is the trouble with it? The I.W.W. man is a man who has no home, he is a man who has no permanent job, he is a man who has no wife. You make it impossible for the negro to have a home! You make it impossible for the sanctity of his home to be respected! You make him feel that he is not a part of the ordinary laboring force of the community, and what do you do? You make it possible, then, for the radical agitator to play upon his feelings about the matter. The negro always has been an American. He does not stand for that type of internationalism which does away with national boundaries. And I say simply this: that in this international day, this new day to which we have come, the best thing we can do is not to talk about philanthropy for the negro, not to hand him out gifts, not to talk about benevolence, but to see that he gets a fair day's pay for a fair day's work! (Applause)

If he raises $3,000 worth of cotton, when he takes $3,000 worth of cotton to the gin, he shall get $3,000 for it! (Applause) And if you can deal fundamentally justly with him, just along the lines of simple economic honesty, you are going to put up a bulwark against a thing that is over-radical and against a thing that is unsound, and you are going to inject into an international labor movement, that is bound to come, a great stream of sound Americanism.

Now in the next place let me say this: That Woodrow Wilson has been talking, and we are all talking about the relations between the so-called more favored nations and the so-called less favored nations, the contact; we are talking about trusteeships for backward nations, and all that kind of thing. Here is one place where the question is being asked more and more, "How is the negro giving an account of himself?" And I want to say this, from the point of view of one looking out upon this matter from the international standpoint, that one of the most hopeful signs today is just the way the negro is proving himself in all the church relationships; in all the relationships, that I have seen him capable of self-government. (Applause)

I held three Methodist conferences this last spring and winter, the Mississippi and the Louisiana conferences. In one of those conferences there were seven district superintendent reports read one after the other. They were the best set of district superintendent reports I ever heard read. (Applause) And after I heard those reports, I knew better what to do, I knew more what was expected, what was the nature of the situation, than from any similar set of reports I had ever heard. I went into conference, at the cabinet meetings, with three different sets of district superintendents. I never heard one man in a cabinet meeting say an unworthy word against his brother; I never heard one man present a brother's case, except in terms of the utmost fairness. Now, dealing with the men in that way, seeing them face to face, I want to tell you now the astonishment to me is not that they have made so many mistakes, but that they have made so few. When you consider the fact that they have had in these relationships only a half century of self-government, the progress made by the negro preachers, by the negro Methodist preachers, in self-government is great beyond anything that I can say. And, seeing them at that range, I say that it is one of the most hopeful experiments in international relationship.

Now, may I say this: I am not going to criticize one of your race, but I do not have much sympathy with one of Booker T. Washington's doctrines.[38] It was this: that the negroes should train themselves primarily to be an industrial people. That is all right, I suppose, but what you need is better trained preachers, and what you need is better trained leaders along intellectual lines;

not that you should lead any one man, but to lead yourselves and do the best for yourselves. (Applause)

You see, this question is reaching out everywhere. Maybe you will not see it. I do not expect to see it. Maybe your children will not see it, but your grandchildren will see the time when the question will be raised, "How soon can the peoples of the earth that are looked upon as backward peoples, the peoples of Africa and the people of some of the other nations, how soon can they be entrusted to any measure of self-government?" – and the only place that has been tried out has been here in the United States. While you have been denied political rights, we all understand that nevertheless where you have been given a chance – and this is the shame and the condemnation of it all – where you have been given a chance, you have governed yourselves wisely and well. (Applause)

Why, take this matter of discipline. Honestly, brethren, it is your own affair; it is none of my business, but take this matter of discipline. If I were going to find any fault with the discipline that Methodist preachers in the colored conferences put upon one another, it would be just this: that they are a little too severe. (Applause) A little too severe! And in some of those conferences I felt, time and again, (white man, though I was) disposed to interfere, in dealing with the matter as you dealt with one another. I think the problem, at least in an ecclesiastical relationship, has shown this, that there are great possibilities for development there, and you are doing exceedingly well with the problem.

Now there is something else; just this: Democracy means in these days what? Does it mean that everything is to be melted down into everything else? It does not! It does Not! I am simply taking the words out of the lips of the speaker who just preceded me, when he said that you do not stand for race amalgamation. Personally, I think when that matter is raised, it is all a bugaboo. (Applause) It is all a bugaboo! You do not wish to be set aside by yourselves. You wish, on the other hand, to develop yourselves, and yet you wish to come into friendly contact, into contact of cooperation with other peoples that you looked upon as brothers in the Kingdom of God. And the present movement in the whole world of democracy is just this: When you find anything in a race anywhere that is worth developing, develop it to the full; and then that every race meet every race on a plane of brotherhood and of mutual respect. (Applause)

We are coming to that more and more.

Now, about this matter of church union, I am not here to talk about that, and it would be in bad taste while the matter is in debate today, but I want to tell you what I think is the sentiment of the great mass of the Methodists everywhere: That since the relation between the negro people and the Methodist church is what it is, since they have come in good faith and we have taken them in good faith, whatever adjustment is made, must be an adjustment to which the negro freely, and under no compulsion whatever, consents. (Applause)

It all comes down to this: Did God make the races different for any particular purpose, or did He not? Now I don't know why he made me white; I haven't any idea why He did. I don't know why He made you black, and I don't know why there are yellow races and I don't know why there are red races, but I am perfectly sure that when the time comes, we will see that there is some abundant good reason for it. And now we are all already beginning to get a glimpse of that very sort of thing, namely, that every race had its distinctive contribution to make to that sum total called civilization. (Applause)

I am not here to disparage the white race; I am in doubt sometimes just what our part is – I don't know. (Laughter) I think I can see the part of some of the races to the great sum total, but in the final system of things and the final day, we are going to have a govern society, built up not of people all alike, but of people, different people maintaining their differences, people maintaining their ways of looking at things and their ways of speaking, and their ways of doing things, and yet through their representative at least meeting on the plan of mutual Christian brotherhood and respect.

The good Lord knows that I don't want to go to heaven if there are too many people there like me. (Applause) And if they were all like me, that would be the condemnation of heaven for the rest. (Laughter) I don't want a heaven all black, and I don't want a heaven all red, and I don't want a heaven all white, but I want each race to bring its contribution, so that we can get to the place where we don't discuss these questions in these ordinary terms at all, don't raise some question, but let each race work out its thought, have it stand by itself and be proud of itself, and have some kind of respect for itself. (Applause) After all, we cannot respect things except as they are inherently respectable, and the thing for the white man and the thing for the black man, first is to make himself worthy of respect. (Applause) When we do that, if we make ourselves worthy of respect and respect ourselves, why then we can get along measurably comfortably, whether the other fellow respects us or not, if we have that kind of thing firmly fixed. But my idea is that in the end each one of us is to make his own distinctive contribution to this great total. That is the movement.

In England today there is a very significant political movement. It is the movement they call Federalism. That does not mean what the Federalism of our fathers did. It means that people of a distinct point of view, people of a distinctive occupation shall be enabled to group themselves together and impress their own distinct point of view on society, and their representative shall meet the representatives of people of other points of view. And that is my ideal of a democracy: Each race, each nation standing for its own point of view, respecting every other nation; meeting upon a plane where these things can be discussed, where they can be handled in the light of Christian brotherhood.

My word, then on the whole, is one of congratulation and of hopefulness. I see dark days ahead of us, unless we Christianize more thoroughly all our relationships; unless we Christianize industrial relationships, unless we stand for more fair play and common honesty and common decency in our relations back and forth. I am not disposed to raise some of these other questions until we deal with this first.

My first concern, my first regret, my first problem in dealing with the negro is just this: (seeing how many times the people of the North, I will say, have dealt with him; not casting any reflection upon the people of the South) That he shall get common, fair play and a man's chance. That is what I am after! (Applause) That is the essential thing: life, liberty and the pursuit of happiness; and this world ought to be big enough so that the white people and the black people can each in their own way pursue life and pursue liberty and pursue happiness under Christian standards, and not be everlastingly getting in one another's way – it ought to be big enough for that. (Applause)

I was on the Western Front for a while this last year. I used to see the negro soldiers "over there." They asked me to speak to them and I went, and I have heard them singing in their tents and singing in their barracks, and singing in their meetings this – I don't know but that I have heard it sung there – "I'se goin' down to the edge of the Jordan one of these days; I'se goin' down to the edge of the Jordan one of these days!" That is the spirit in which those men went to the front, and after I heard them sing that song, some went down to the edge of Jordan, and some went out into the stream, and some went across. They went across for what? They went across for that flag, that means so much to you, as it means so much to me. They went across, that all the world could come out into a new promised land, free from militarism, free from the appeal to force, free from the appeal to autocracy; and I rejoice today that I cannot understand some things done in Europe, I am disappointed in some things about the peace treaty and all the rest of it, but I believe, friends, just this, that there is a promised land at least of measurable greatness just ahead of us.[39] I want to say this also for myself – and I am sure I represent the great mass of my church – I was not asked here to speak as an individual; I am speaking in a sense as a representative of the Board of Bishops of the Methodist Church, though they do not know what I am going to say and I am not holding them responsible for what I am going to say – I do think this: that the black man has had his share in bringing us into that promised land; he has done his part, and as my feet push over that Jordan into that new promised land, as we come to a land that means a new internationalism and means a new day and means a new League of Nations, for myself I desire this: that I shall not have a liberty or a joy purchased by another man, without holding myself responsible to the best I can do to pay my debt to him. (Applause) And if he has played his part – and he has – in bringing us into that new promised land, then I say that he and his children are entitled to their part of the liberty and the life and the pursuit of happiness that belongs to them, and they cannot be left out. (Applause)

There is no way of getting rid of you, and we do not care to do it. (Applause) You are born faster than we could transport you to Africa – everybody knows that – and nobody has any desire to transport you to Africa. You are here and you are here to stay! (Applause) You are here and you are here to stay! And, inasmuch as we worship one God, inasmuch as we hale (sic) one Master of us all, inasmuch as we bow down to one common altar, then let us forget things just as far as we can, let us forget our prejudices and let us meet around our tables, and wherever we discuss these matters, try each to understand the point of view of the other, try each to find where God has called him to work in this world, and to hail every man as a friend and hail every man as a brother, and wish everybody "God-speed," and look toward the new day that is to come. (Applause)

I. GARLAND PENN:
Now, my friends, after the last speaker, we are to have a solo, from a celebrated soloist, which will last five minutes. But now the last speaker we are to hear from is Bishop R. A. Carter, of the Colored Methodist Episcopal Church in America. Bishop Carter.

RANDALL ALBERT CARTER:[40]
I had a great speech prepared for this occasion, but as usual, they have made me the "mop up" man, and now my speech is in the identical fix as the man who bought a new pair of pants one evening to go to a picnic next day, and after all the stores were closed, he tried the pants on and found that they were six inches too long. He told his wife that, as well as his mother-in-law, and they decided that there could be no remedy for those pants, and the picnic was spoiled for him next day. After going to bed, the good wife, as all good wives usually do, having her husband's predicament in mind, arose about two hours after they had gone to bed, got a pair of scissors and needle and thread, cut the pants off six inches, sewed them up again, and hung them up and went back to bed. About an hour after she had gone back to bed, the mother-in-law, having in mind the predicament of the next day, stole up, got a pair of scissors and a needle and thread, cut off six inches of those ill-fated pants, sewed them up, and went back to bed. And next morning, when he arose to put on his picnic pants, instead of the pants being six inches too long, they were a foot too short. (Laughter) That is the condition of my speech now. The other speakers have cut it all to pieces and said practically all that I meant to say.

It is, however, no accidental coincidence that the Centenary of the arrival of the American negro in this country comes so near to the Centenary of the beginning of American Methodist missions, which were begun through the consecrated courage and faith of a negro man, John Stewart.[41] (Applause) It is rather God's sovereign gesture to this nation to set itself to settle this race problem justly and to give the negro, the descendants of the negroes who came to this country three hundred years ago and the descendants of John Stewart, whose spirit has gone marching overseas and lands for a hundred years and now returns to receive the homage of the earth in this wonderful celebration in the city of Columbus, a just reward. (Applause) John Stewart, the negro pioneer missionary, was an illustration and example of the potent possibilities of his great race; and I say "great" deliberately and advisedly. (Applause) For, as Dr. Lyman Abbott has truly said, "Never in the history of mankind has a race made the progress, educationally and materially, which the negro race in this country has made in the last fifty years." (Applause)

That the negro race has a great history in the past and that her civilization was suddenly arrested, is the impartial testimony of explorers and travelers in Africa. Dan Crawford, the great English missionary and the explorer, who spent twenty-three years in the heart of Africa, in his book "Thinking Back (sic)", the

Bantu tribes boast the same kilt, mortar, pestle and cooking ware of the Moslem period; but why should we wonder at this, for is not Egypt the back door to Africa?[42] That the negro race is at present backward and of arrested development is admitted and apparent, but that it is inherently inferior to any other race, there is no evidence whatever.

In considering the negro in this country, it must be borne in mind that he was brought to this land three hundred years ago, and for two hundred and fifty years he was kept in the most brutal and degrading slavery recorded in history. Small wonder that he should seem so stupid, base and immoral.

Then Crawford adds: "All who work among the slaves know that bondage of body conduces to bondage of brain. That is to say, as the slave has been valued in coin, in commerce, he accepts the valuation and really becomes as dead and metallic to all human susceptibilities as literal coin. Why, then, be surprised? It is ridiculous for a man to go and treat a negro as a demon and then express surprise that he is not an angel. If you breed slavery into the bone for centuries, how can you annul it all by the cash payment of an hour? Thus, because the negro while enslaved was like all other people in a similar state, it was confidently asserted that he was innately stupid, brutish, shiftless, improvident, immoral, and incapable of mental and moral development. But when the cruel bonds of slavery were broken and cast away from the negro, he awoke from his centuries of lethargy, as from some horrid nightmare, and his history since his emancipation reads more like a romance than like reality."

At the taking of the census of 1910, it was shown that in less than forty years the negro had reduced his illiteracy three per cent. Reliable statistics show that the negro had contributed for his own education in that time one hundred and four million dollars; that he had established and was maintaining a large number of colleges, seminaries and academies, and that in less than half a century he had produced such characters as Douglas (sic), the orator, Henry O. Tanner, the painter, Paul L. Dunbar, the poet, Booker T. Washington, the constructive statesman, Dr. Daniel H. Williams, the first Sergeant, and Granville T. Woods, the inventor, whose genius placed him on the pay rolls of the New York Elevated Railroad and the Bell Telephone Company. (Applause)

A wise philosopher said, "If one of the race demonstrates genius in the finer things of civilization, civilization has come through him to that race."[43] The negro left his master's plantation with no material possession; he had never been taught to save and accumulate anything; he had rather been encouraged to have nothing. He was supposed to be incapable of knowing the value of things, and was taught to be too shiftless and indolent, without an overseer, to even make a living. It was freely predicted that he would soon starve and die out.

Yet, the United States census of 1910 reveals that this supposed half brute and half human had taken so kindly to freedom and the opportunity to own something, that he had become the owner of 430,499 homes in the cities of the South alone; (Applause) that he owned and operated 890,370 farms in the South, valued at $1,140,792,526; that he had invested at the same time millions of dollars in various business enterprises; that he owned more than $5,000,000 worth of school property, more than $40,000,000 worth of church property, and that he had on deposit millions of dollars in the various banks throughout the country. (Applause) To the charge he was naturally immoral, if not unmoral, the census of 1910 shows that in the negro population of fifteen years over 64 percent of the males and 73 percent of the females had married and the proportion of divorces at that time was seven tenths percent for the males and one and one tenth percent for the females. (Applause) I submit that that is not a bad record for a people who had been encouraged to be immoral and live promiscuous lives for centuries of slavery, for the gain the children of that sort of living brought their masters. It has been said, and truly said, that the weight of character and strength of intellect tell in impact (sic) and I contend that the negro has shown both in his contact with the civilization which has been none too free for his progress and advancement. One of the pastimes of the critics of the race has been that the negro was, by statistics, degenerate physically, that he was deteriorating as a man, that he was a menace to his white neighbors because of his disease-breeding and disease-bearing characteristics; if a negro wasn't in this country, than a fountain of youth would spring up in every cross-road and sprinkle the health-giving waters over the population there of. (Applause) And one of the stock jokes of the press and the rostrum was the negro's flat-feet and his love for whiskey. There seems to be no way to successfully contradict these allegations since the doctors said so, and everybody knows that doctors are never mistaken.

Then came the great war and the United States was drawn into it, and the nation-wide draft was on, and the young men of all races and colors were commanded to register and were called to the training camps to be examined and tested by the most expert physicians in the land, for only the fittest could stand the strain of this world's most savage war, and we, inexperienced, began to compare the results of any examination and finally gave their findings to the public in official bulletins, a profound silence settled upon all the editorial sanctums and rostrums which had hitherto so gladly published and repeated what the learned doctors said in days past and gone. Concerning the negro's physical degeneracy, first came Dr. Isaac W. Brewer, of the United States Medical Reserve Corps, who published the figures on the physical and mental condition of the drafted men for the National Army, which figures showed the rate per thousand of rejections, and for what disease, white and colored being given separately. Dr. Brewer tabulated 28 diseases, and in only 9 of the 28 diseases do colored men show a higher percentage. Here they are:

Tuberculosis – per 1,000 rejected men – 19.2 for colored; 34.1 for white. Alcoholism – rejected per 1,000 – white 34.1; colored 7.8. Diseases of the genitor-urinary system – white rejected per 1,000 – 25.2 per cent; colored 7.2 per cent. Flat-feet – white rejected per 1,000 – 55.7, and colored 44.8 per cent. (Laughter) This is a showing that the negro comes to the august tribunal of American public opinion today and asks for a verdict on; and they say in passing, that we have been loyal, and I may say in passing that we heard during the perilous days of the war acknowledgments made that we hadn't been treated right and there had been mistakes made for which justice hadn't been done us, and we heard promises that if we could "carry on" and help win the war, that when the war was over we would get the things that had been denied us in the days past.

How nobly we "carried on." Our witness is in heaven and our record on high. And now we come to claim our reward, we come to have every promise fulfilled that was made to us. (Applause) We do not appeal to the white politicians, but we appeal to the Christian churches here represented and to the Christian churches throughout this land, open your mouths and from every pulpit and rostrum, in every editorial sanctum thunder that negro baiting must stop in this country. (Applause) That the burning of, and lynching of negro men and women must cease, and that the trial of negro criminals must be transferred from the pine thickets and oak groves back to the court house and the orderly processes of the law. (Applause) And we come not alone, but we come accompanied by our sons, who lost a leg or an arm, across the seas; we come leading black boys from the trenches, groping in the darkness at noonday, upon whose blinded eyes the light of the sun will shine no more. We come, supporting weeping widows and mothers, whose sons and husbands fell upon Flanders Fields, where the poppies grow, and upon the blood-stained slopes of France, where now the lilies bloom, and we come, believing that we are well deserved of our country. Lo, over us hovers a great cloud of heroic deed, bathed in glory and shining in light, and we hold out our hands to the American public today and plead that we gave our lives that the black men might have these things. See that we did not die in vain! (Applause)

I. GARLAND PENN:

My friends, let me say that we have a very accomplished singer of our race here, who was to give us a solo. It is Mrs. Hardy, who was graduated some years ago from the Yale Conservatory of Music, but unfortunately Professor Kraft has gone away with the key to the organ. However, I want to introduce Mrs. Hardy to this audience. (Applause)

We are much obliged to you for remaining with us this afternoon. You are all dismissed now.

Southern Day Program
Wednesday Morning, July 2, 1919

I. GARLAND PENN:

Mr. Chairman, brothers and sisters, on an occasion like this it seems that it is a wise thing that I should take the advice of a member of my race who gave to another member of my race some advice when they were discussing the late war.

One Negro said to the other, "What is the use of my going over to fight the Germans? I haven't anything against the Germans. They have never done anything to me," and the other Negro said to him, "Well, now, there is no use of your talking like that. They are getting your name, and they are going to bring you before the Draft Board, and they are going to examine you. They are going to send you to camp and they are going to drill you and then they are going to put you on a ship and send you overseas and then they are going to send you up to the front line trenches and there you use your own judgment." (Applause)

I think it is very important that I should use my judgment on an occasion like this. And then, as a preface to what I am going to say, may I say what another has said that "there is so much good in the worst of us and there is so much bad in the best of us, it ill behooves any of us to talk about the rest of us." (Applause)

I want to say, Mr. Chairman, some things today concerning the South which I steadfastly believe.

First, I believe that there never was a time in all the history of the country when the South was more willing to help the Negro to be somebody than this very day. (Applause) I speak out of an intimate knowledge for I am glad to be called a Southerner and particularly a Virginian, and I would rather be from Lynchburg, Virginia, than any other city in Virginia, and so I have some intimate knowledge of these white people in Virginia and Georgia, for I happened to be the Commissioner in charge of the Negro Department of the Atlanta Exposition in 1895 and I came intimately in contact with those gentlemen in Georgia, and I say with that experience of twenty or thirty years up to this day that today the Negro can claim more of the best South – that it is more willing to help him financially in his school work and to encourage him generally than at any time in the history of our existence in this country.[44] (Applause)

We received a letter the other day in the office of the Freedman's (sic) Aid Society that told us this significant fact, that in the State of South Carolina there has been appropriated, I think it is $100,000, in addition to the regular appropriation for the State School, to erect a monument on the State School Grounds for the colored people in Orangeburg to the memory of these black men who fell overseas, fighting to make the world safe for democracy.[45] (Applause)

The State of Tennessee has made an appropriation similar to this and certainly a large appropriation for the education of the colored people in that state.

And the other day I heard this significant fact which every one ought to know, that in the State of Texas, in spite of the fact that some people believe that the South does not believe in the higher education of the Negro, the Board of Regents of the State Normal School for colored people at Prairie View wiped out the line and established Prairie View School as a college for the education of the Negroes in the State of Texas. (Applause)

Now then, I steadfastly believe another thing. There never was a time in all the history of our country when the South appreciated the loyalty of the Negro to the flag. And let me say, my friends, that well this is, for the Negro contributed his part in this late war, and it was a great thing, and I am sure our Southern people, as well as the Northern people, appreciated that fact.

It was a great thing that you had when we declared war against Germany as loyal a people as the 10,000,000 black people in this country. (Applause) For, Mr. Chairman, you could pick out of that 10,000,000 black people, black soldiers and place them around the White House and be absolutely certain that there weren't any Germans in the crowd. (Applause)

The fact of the matter is, it is said that when the black troops overseas went over the top after the Germans they went so fast, and made the Germans go so fast, that the Germans lost their field glasses, and the Negroes picked them up, and some of the white fellows were a little jealous of the Negroes having so many souvenirs as the fine German field glasses to bring back home and one white soldier asked a Negro soldier how they got so many field glasses. This Negro soldier said, "Why, these Germans when they saw us coming they don't need any field glasses." (Applause)

And, Mr. Chairman, the very color of the Negro, the distinctiveness of Negro loyalty and so forth made him, perhaps, worth more, and thank God, that I lived to see the day when one black man was worth more than two hundred Germans. (Applause) I think the South as well as the North appreciates this as never before.

Now I believe, Mr. Chairman, that there never was a time in all our history when we wanted to square ourselves in this country, North and South, with the preachments of our President overseas, and when we were so ashamed as we are today of anything that occurs in our country, North or South, that does not square with making a country decent to live in, or making America safe for any citizen of America safe to live in.

There never was a time when we were so ashamed by mob violence. There never was a time, as now, when we propose to do whatever we can and as fast as we can to square ourselves with our preachments concerning democracy the world over, and I expect to live to see the day when America will be rid of every single thing that now taints her, and the South will take as big a lead in this business as any other section in our country. (Applause)

Now then, let me say again, my friends, that in the South the Baptists and the Methodists have a great chance with the Negro. You know all Negroes are

Baptists or Methodists anyhow, and if they are anything else, a white man's tampering with their religion. (Applause) Now, no church is doing more for the Negro in this country than the Methodist Episcopal Church, and then in the South no church is doing more than the Methodist Episcopal Church, South. (Applause) And I believe you are going to do more and more as the days come and go. (Applause)

My friends, we are glad to have here among these young people on this platform a quartet from Payne (sic) College at Augusta, Georgia with these quartets from our Freedman's (sic) Aid School, and I turn to these young people who have been singing songs that we are every day becoming prouder of, songs we will not – please God – give up, songs which we will continue to sing.[46]

What shall I say to these young people in these few minutes I have? I say to them, "Young people of my race, with your life before you look out upon this audience today and see that the purpose and the plan of the South, as of the North, in having two Negroes on this program today means for you as for them a new day, (Applause) and of this new day I say in the lines of Addison: "The dawning – tongue and pen to aid it. Hopes of honest men aid it. Paper aids it. Type aids it, for the hour is ripe, and our earnestness must not slacken in its play. Men and women of the South, black and white, clear the way." (Applause)

CHARLES HENRY TOBIAS:[47]

Mr. Chairman, ladies and gentlemen, the first word I want to say is that this last piece that was sung is the composition work of a negro. (Referring to "The Old Flag Never Touched the Ground")[48] (Applause)

If Dr. Penn can qualify as a Southerner, I even more can qualify. I was born in the state of Georgia and received my intellectual nurturing in a college maintained by the Methodist Episcopal Church, South. (Applause) Because of that fact I feel today that I am better prepared than a good many colored men here to approach with calmness, with dispassionate vision, and yet with utter frankness, some of the questions in which all of us have mutual interests.

Dr. Penn referred to the fact of having two colored men on the program today. I want to say that you could not have had a Southern Day without negro representation. (Applause) When I say that I have in mind the fact that the negro is intricably (sic) interwoven in all the history and traditions of the South, all that is distinctive in Southern literature, and in Southern song is colored by the negro, seen through his eyes, and spoken through his lips. Take out the negro characters in the Southern novels, blot out the stories of Chandler Hardy's "Plantation Lyrics of Many Poets" and what is left that is characteristically Southern in literature was produced South of the Mason and Dixon Line.

Blot out from a Southern song book "My Old Kentucky Home," "Swanee River," "Old Black Joe," "Massy's (sic) in de Cold, Cold Ground," "Carry me Back to old Virginny," and "Dixie," the South's national anthem, which is itself written in negro dialect, and what have you left that is distinctive of Southern song? (Applause)

So I say that we belong here today by virtue of the fact that our contribution to all the history and traditions of the South is as considerable as the contribution of any other group in the South. (Applause)

Now, my friends, I want to say this: I have heard mentioned this morning that beautiful tradition, dear to the heart of Southerners, of the black mammy, but I want to say in the spirit uttered by one remark in the speech of General Carr that while we revere the memory of the black mammy in the South, the time has come when we, as Southerners, must face the proposition of dealing with the sons and grandsons of black mammies.[49]

It was not black mammy that went a half million strong in response to the call to the colors across the sea. It was the grandsons of black mammies that went. (Applause) Since it seems in order to recite the records of soldiers here today, let me recite the record of a single black regiment – the Three Hundred Sixty-Ninth. (Applause) A hundred and nine days under continuous fire, they never had a man taken prisoner, they never lost a foot of ground – the first of the allied troops to lay foot on German soil; (Applause) the nearest to the front when the armistice was signed; (Applause) two hundred individual declarations of the Croix de Guerre, and the whole regiment cited for bravery.[50] (Applause)

I want to say, my friends, that I believe that our Southern people here today are prepared to hear the next statement that I make – that in the light of such achievement as that it is positively unthinkable that the men who have made that contribution to the cause of world democracy could ever think of the application of the principle of world democracy to all the peoples of the earth, and then regard themselves as the only exception to the rule. (Applause)

This one other thought in the moments I have left. There is, of course, in the mind of us all here now – and I speak as one bred to the soil – the interests of the preservation of democracy – nay more, the interest of the preservation of life itself, and there need not be charge and counter charge for us to face this truth. We can face it dispassionately, we can face it with the utmost frankness, and let others suggest what they will or may for the immediate solution of the problem of lawlessness, but the ultimate solution, and the one that will give lasting benefit is a recognition of the sacredness of human personality, whether it find itself expressed in black or yellow, or whatever color it may be. (Applause)

I know that I look into the faces of men and women who not only would not do wrong to another individual consciously, but who from the bottom of their souls hate wrong and hate the ways of vileness that rise up and spread over our whole country. I know we hate it, but what we want to impress upon you in connection with that thought is this – that in order to have these things put down, it is necessary for us to go out in the spirit of the crusader, in the spirit in which Dr. Stuart said, that we went out to kill the liquor traffic with the same determination to see human and social justice done to all men, and the work will be done!

Just this one other thought. Whenever a group of people in any section of the country have their personality cheapened by disfranchisement, by discrimination, by anything, it makes it easy for the lawless element of the community to victimize that man for no man who is rendered cheap in the life of a community will be safe in the hands of the lawless element of the community. It is only as we regard every man as a man that the lawless element will respect his personality and regard him as it regards that element of citizenship that is always respected in the community.

Just a year ago in our country the personality of the German suddenly found itself going down, and it became a possible thing with the lawless element, because of the fact that German stock had gone down, to pounce upon Germans within the community and to do away with them, thinking that nothing would happen. It is the logical outcome of the attitude toward personality; hence our President's proclamation against violence.[51]

I say, my friends, today in all calmness of spirit that if we ever are to remedy the thing in this broad land that we call lawlessness, it will come by putting in an increasingly larger emphasis upon the Godlikeness of man's personality, whether it expresses itself in black, yellow, in brown, in red, or in any of the hues which God has colored the races of mankind. (Applause)

Notes

1. Robert Elijah Jones (1872-1960). Jones was a bishop and ordained elder with the Methodist Episcopal Church. He was educated at Bennett College and Gammon Theological Seminary. He served in several churches as a member of the North Carolina Annual Conference and later became assistant manager for the *Southwestern Christian Advocate*. In 1920, Jones was elected bishop with the Methodist Episcopal Church. Jones and Matthew Clair (elected the same year) were the first African Americans to be elected to the episcopacy of the Methodist Episcopal Church.

2. David Livingstone (1813-1873). Livingstone was a Protestant medical missionary from Scotland assigned to southern Africa. He studied theology and medicine at the University of Glasgow and became widely known for his work in Africa as a result of his book *Missionary Travels and Researches in South Africa* (London: John Murray, Albemarle Street, 1857). For additional information on the life and work of Livingstone see A.N. Porter, *Religion versus Empire?: British Protestant Missionaries and Overseas Expansion, 1700-1914* (Manchester, England: Manchester University Press, 2004).

3. Eben Samuel Johnson (1866-1939). Johnson was a bishop and ordained minister with the Methodist Episcopal Church. Born in England, Johnson moved to the United States and was educated at Morningside College in Sioux City, Iowa. He served in various churches as a member of the Northwest Iowa Annual Conference. In 1916, he was elected a missionary bishop and served in Africa until his retirement in 1936.

4. Isaiah Benjamin Scott (1854-1931). Scott was a bishop and ordained minister with the Methodist Episcopal Church. He was educated at Central Tennessee College in Nashville and later received a Doctor of Divinity degree from New Orleans University. He served in various churches as a member of the Texas Annual Conference and later became president of Wiley College and editor of the *Southwestern Christian Advocate*. In 1904, he was elected missionary bishop to Africa until his retirement in 1916.

5. Balmer's Kaffir Boys Choir was a traveling musical group directed by J.H. Balmer. They performed throughout Europe and North America during the late 19th and early 20th centuries. They first appeared in the United States at the 1893 Chicago World's Fair. The singers represented the Basuto, Khoikhoi, "Red" Kaffir, and Zulu Tribes of

Africa. Their performances included songs and narratives of life in Africa. For Centenary exposition audiences the choir represented the potential result of Methodist intercultural and missionary work to Africa – to produce talented African young men who had been both civilized and Christianized by missionaries. See "Balmer's Kaffir Boys' Choir," *University of Wisconsin Bulletin* 826 (1917): 5.

6. Joseph Crane Hartzell (1842-1928). Hartzell was a bishop and ordained minister with the Methodist Episcopal Church. He was educated at Illinois Wesleyan College and Garrett Theological Seminary (now Garrett-Evangelical Theological Seminary). He served in various churches as a member of the Central Illinois Annual Conference and the Louisiana Annual Conference. Hartzell worked as corresponding secretary for the Freedmen's Aid Society and was founding editor of the *Southwestern Christian Advocate*. In 1896, Hartzell was elected missionary bishop to Africa until his retirement in 1916.

7. Alexander Priestley Camphor (1865-1919). Camphor was a bishop and ordained minister with the Methodist Episcopal Church. He was educated at Leland University, New Orleans University, and Gammon Theological Seminary. He served Pennsylvania and New Jersey churches as a member of the Delaware Annual Conference. In 1897, he was appointed president of the College of West Africa in Monrovia and later served as president of Central Alabama Institute in Birmingham, Alabama. In 1916, he was appointed missionary bishop to Africa (Liberia) and died the following December, only six months after his speech at the Centenary Celebration.

8. The initial work of the Methodist Episcopal Church in Africa began in 1822 when Reverend Elijah Johnson met with a group of indigenous peoples for religious services in Liberia. In 1833, Melville B. Cox arrived as a missionary and by 1836 the region had become an officially recognized Annual Conference.

9. Monrovia Seminary, established in 1839, was first Methodist school for theological education in Liberia. In 1898, the name of the school was changed to the College of West Africa.

10. Daniel Leeper Mumpower (1882-1969). Mumpower was a medical missionary assigned to the Congo region of Africa by the Methodist Episcopal Church, South. He was educated at Central College (Missouri), Yale University, and Vanderbilt University. A trained pharmacist, Mumpower worked in the Congo from 1913 to 1923. He returned to the United States and accepted a denominational appointment for the MECS. In 1932, he returned to work as a practicing physician until his retirement in 1965.

11. John Doyle was Superintendent of Missions for the Methodist Church in Canada. His responsibilities included the oversight of the regions of Northern Saskatchewan and Northern Manitoba. See *Annual Report of the Missionary Society of the Methodist Church in Canada, Newfoundland, Bermuda, West China and Japan* (Toronto: Methodist Mission Rooms, 1919), xxii-xxiii.

12. John McKendree Springer (1873-1963) and Helen Emily Springer (1868-1949). John Springer was a missionary bishop for the Methodist Episcopal Church. He was educated at Northwestern University and Garrett Biblical Institute. He was assigned to the Rhodesia (now Zimbabwe) and Congo missions and retired in 1944. Helen Emily Springer was a missionary for the Methodist Episcopal Church. She was educated at the Women's Medical College of Philadelphia. She was assigned to the Rhodesia (now Zimbabwe) and Congo missions and authored several hymns while translating the Bible and other Christian literature into various indigenous African languages. In 1907, both John and Emily made a well-publicized trek across the center of Africa from the Indian Ocean to the Atlantic Ocean.

13. Edwin Field Frease (1864-1938). Frease was a missionary and ordained minister with the Methodist Episcopal Church. He studied law and received a Doctor of Divinity degree from Taylor University. He was a member of the East Ohio Annual Conference and served in missionary appointments in India and North Africa. He was appointed Superintendent of the North Africa Mission of the MEC and retired in 1932. "Rev. Edwin F. Frease," *New York Times*, April 23, 1938, 15.

14. Evangelical Methodist Church of France

15. Samuel Marinus Zwemer (1867-1952). Zwemer was a Protestant missionary sponsored by the Reformed Church in America. He was educated at Hope Academy and College (Michigan) and New Brunswick Theological Seminary. Zwemer spent over 30 years working with Muslims of North Africa and editing his journal *The Moslem World*. In 1929 he was appointed as a professor of Christian missions at Princeton Theological Seminary. He later taught at the Biblical Seminary of New York and Nyack Missionary Training Institute. Alan Neely, "Zwemer, Samuel Marinus," in *Biographical Dictionary of Christian Missions*, Gerald H. Anderson, ed., (Grand Rapids, MI: William B. Eerdmans Publishing Company, 1999), 763.

16. Steven Decatur, Jr. (1779-1820). Decatur was an officer with the U.S. Navy during the Barbary Wars and the War of 1812. See Robert J. Allison, *Steven Decatur: American Naval Hero, 1779-1820* (Amherst: University of Massachusetts Press, 2007).

17. Togo Heihachiro (1848-1934). Hiehachiro served as an Admiral with the Navy of Japan. The "Silent Admiral" was a highly respected naval officer who fought in the Russo-Japanese War of 1904-5. See Jonathan Clements, *Admiral Togo: The Nelson of the East* (London: Haus Publishing, 2010).

18. William Girdlestone Shellabear (1862-1947). Shellabear was missionary to the Malay Peninsula region for the Methodist Episcopal Church. He was also professor of missions at Drew Theological Seminary. He taught the Malay language at Drew and at Hartford Theological Seminary in Connecticut. See Robert A. Hunt, *William Shellabear: A Biography* (Kuala Lumpur, Malaysia: University of Malaya Press, 1996).

19. An altered version of the John Neihardt poem "Battle-Cry." John Neihardt, *The Quest* (New York: The MacMillan Company, 1916), 148-149.

20. Georges Benjamin Clemenceau (1841-1929). Clemenceau was Prime Minister of France when this speech was given at the Centenary exposition.

21. Irving Garland Penn, Jr. (1867-1930). Penn was an educator, journalist, author, and minister with the Methodist Episcopal Church. He was educated at Rust College and Wiley College. He worked as a news correspondent for several papers including the *Richmond Planet* and *New York Age*. He was a member of the Lexington Annual Conference and worked for many years as Assistant General Secretary for the Colored Conferences of the Epworth League and as corresponding secretary for the Freedmen's Aid Society of the Methodist Episcopal Church.

22. Joseph C. Sherrill was a missionary and minister for the Methodist Episcopal Church. He was educated at Philander Smith College and Gammon Theological Seminary. He served several churches in Arkansas. In 1899, Sherrill was appointed as a missionary to Liberia (Monrovia) and later served as president of the College of West Africa and George R. Smith College (Missouri). See Kenneth C. Barnes, "On the Shore Beyond the Sea: Black Missionaries from Arkansas in Africa during the 1890s," *The Arkansas Historical Quarterly* 61:4 (Winter 2002): 329-356.

23. Charles Albert Tindley (1851-1933). Tindley was an ordained minister with the Methodist Episcopal Church. He was educated at Boston University School of Theology

and later received honorary doctorates at Bennett College. Tindley was a member of the Delaware Annual Conference and served several churches in Delaware, Maryland, New Jersey and Pennsylvania. In 1902 he was appointed to the Bainbridge Street church which later changed its name to Tindley Temple. During his ministry at Tindley Temple the church reached nearly 12,000 members designating it as the largest Methodist church in the world.

24. The Methodist Episcopal Church appointed immigration workers at both Angel Island in the San Francisco Bay area and Ellis Island in the New York City area.

25. Tindley refers to Crispus Attucks, an African American killed at the "Boston Massacre" on March 5, 1770.

26. William Asbury Christian (1866-1936). Christian was an ordained minister with the Methodist Episcopal Church, South. He was educated at Randolph-Macon College and Vanderbilt University. He was a member of the Virginia Annual Conference and served several churches throughout the state. Christian was president of Blackstone College for Girls and President of the Anti-Saloon League of Virginia. He retired in 1932.

27. Christian's 1919 address was given during a recent resurgence of the Ku Klux Klan throughout the United States. The Klan had emerged in the post-Civil War American South but had been largely repressed by the United States Government. Following the establishment of Jim Crow laws in the late nineteenth century, a revived Klan emerged during the second decade of the twentieth century. The D.W. Griffith film *Birth of a Nation* and an appearance by the Klan in Atlanta in 1915 sparked another surge in Klan membership. By the 1919 Centenary Celebration lynchings and race riots had received national attention. Christian's address would have been received with mixed emotions at the fair as some Northern and Southern Methodists were still trying to suppress the rights of African Americans. See Shawn Lay, "Ku Klux Klan in the Twentieth Century," *The New Georgia Encyclopedia*, July 07, 2005, http://www.georgiaencyclopedia.org/nge/Article.jsp?id=h-2730; see also Nancy MacLean, *Behind the Mask of Chivalry: The Making of the Second Ku Klux Klan* (New York: Oxford University Press, 1994).

28. Jones seems to reference the Society for the Colonization of Free People of Color in America project initiated in 1816. The motivation of the Society was to move African Americans to Africa in such locations as Liberia and Sierra Leone. See Eric Burin, *Slavery and the Peculiar Solution: A History of the American Colonization Society* (Gainesville: University Press of Florida, 2005).

29. Jones references the Emancipation Proclamation of 1863. For additional work on Lincoln and the Proclamation see Eric Foner, *The Fiery Trial: Abraham Lincoln and American Slavery* (New York: W.W. Norton, 2010); and Allen C. Guelzo, *Lincoln's Emancipation Proclamation: The End of Slavery in America* (New York: Simon & Schuster, 2004).

30. The settled outcome of discussions related to African American Methodists and the merger of the Methodist Episcopal Church and Methodist Episcopal Church, South, resulted in the formation of the Central Jurisdiction of The Methodist Church in 1939. For further study on the discussions related to racial discourse and the merger see Morris L. Davis, *The Methodist Unification: Christianity and the Politics of Race in the Jim Crow Era* (New York: New York University Press, 2008).

31. For additional information on the history of lynching in the United States see Crystal Nicole Feimster, *Southern Horrors: Women and the Politics of Rape and Lynching* (Cambridge, MA: Harvard University Press, 2009); and Philip Dray, *At the*

Hands of Persons Unknown: The Lynching of Black America (New York: Random House, 2002).

32. Charles Betts Galloway (1849-1909). Galloway was a bishop and ordained minister with the Methodist Episcopal Church, South. He was educated at the University of Mississippi. He received honorary doctorates from the University of Mississippi, Northwestern University, and Tulane University. As a member of the Mississippi Annual Conference he served churches in Port Gibson, Jackson, and Vicksburg. He was editor of the *New Orleans Christian Advocate* and was well-known for his preaching eloquence.

33. Jones references the recent activities of the Russian Revolution of 1917. For additional information on the Revolution, reactions in the United States, and issues of labor uprisings see Norman E. Saul, *War and Revolution: The United States and Russia, 1914-1921* (Lawrence, KS: University Press of Kansas, 2001); and Daniel H. Kaiser, *The Worker's Revolution in Russia, 1917: The View from Below* (New York: Cambridge University Press, 1987).

34. President Woodrow Wilson and the League of Nations are discussed in a later chapter. For additional information on Wilson and his involvement with marketing the League of Nations see John Milton Cooper, *Breaking the Heart of the World: Woodrow Wilson and the Fight for the League of Nations* (New York: Cambridge University Press, 2001).

35. For additional information on African American soldiers during the Great War see Gail Lumet Buckley, *American Patriots: The Story of Blacks in the Military from the Revolution to Desert Storm* (New York: Random House, 2001).

36. For a detailed account of the 1917 race riots of East St. Louis see Harper Barnes, *Never Been a Time: The 1917 Race Riot that Sparked the Civil Rights Movement* (New York: MacMillan, 2008).

37. For more on the African American labor issues and American Federation of Labor see Julie Greene, *Pure and Simple Politics: The American Federation of Labor and Political Activism, 1881-1917* (New York: Cambridge University Press, 1998); and Julius Jacobson, *The Negro and the American Labor Movement* (Garden City, NY: Anchor Books, 1968).

38. Booker T. Washington (1856-1915). Washington was an author, political figure, and popular voice for African Americans during the late nineteenth and early twentieth century. He was educated at Hampton University and Virginia Union University. Washington was instrumental in the founding and success of the Tuskegee Institute of Alabama. McConnell's critique of Washington in his speech echoed others including author W.E.B. DuBois who criticized him for his accommodationist approach when confronting racial discrimination and violence. For biographical attention on Washington's life and his role in race relations see Robert J. Norrell, *Up From History: The Life of Booker T. Washington* (Cambridge, MA: Belknap Press of Harvard University Press, 2009); and Michael Rudolph West, *The Education of Booker T. Washington: American Democracy and the Idea of Race Relations* (New York: Columbia University Press, 2006).

39. McConnell references the conversations taking place at the Paris Peace Conference related to President Woodrow Wilson, his Fourteen Points, the League of Nations. See Margaret MacMillan, *Paris 1919: Six Months that Changed the World* (New York: Random House, 2002).

40. Randall Albert Carter (1867-1954). Carter was a bishop and ordained minister with the Colored (now Christian) Methodist Episcopal Church. He was educated at Paine

College and received honorary degrees from Allen University and Lane College. Carter was a member of the South Carolina and Georgia Annual Conferences serving churches throughout Georgia. He was secretary to the Epworth League of the CMEC and was an active member of the Federal Council of the Churches of Christ in America. Carter's speech at the Centenary exposition was published in his book *Feeding among the Lillies* (Cincinnati, OH: The Caxton Press, 1923), 256-272.

41. John Stewart (1785-1823). Stewart was a licensed minister and missionary for the Methodist Episcopal Church. He is recognized as the first U.S.-based missionary supported by The Missionary Society of the MEC. Stewart served at the Wyandot Nation reservation near Upper Sandusky, Ohio. In 1823 Stewart died after complications with consumption. His gravesite at the Wyandot Indian Mission is recognized as a Methodist Heritage site for The United Methodist Church. See Christopher J. Anderson, "John Stewart," *African American National Biography*, Vol. 7, Henry Louis Gates, Jr. and Evelyn Brooks Higginbotham eds., (New York: Oxford University Press, 2008), 403-404.

42. See Daniel Crawford, *Thinking Black: 22 Years without a Break in the Long Grass of Central Africa* (New York: George H. Doran Co., 1912).

43. Carter, *Feeding among the Lillies*, 259.

44. Penn was placed in charge of the exhibit which championed the progress and work of African Americans in the U.S. South. For additional information on the fair and the exhibit see *The Official Catalogue of the Cotton States and International Exposition, Atlanta, Georgia, U.S.A., September 18 to December 31, 1895, Illustrated* (Atlanta: Claflin & Mellichamp Publishers, 1895).

45. The original Society was organized by the American Missionary Association in 1861. In 1866, the Freedmen's Aid Society of the Methodist Episcopal Church was formed. The purpose of the organization was to support the educational training of African Americans by providing schools with teachers, housing and supplies. See Dwight Oliver Wendell Holmes, "The Freedmen's Aid Society of the Methodist Episcopal Church," in *The Evolution of the Negro College* (New York: Teacher's College, Columbia University, 1934), 102-119; see also James S. Thomas, "Methodism's Splendid Mission: The Black Colleges," *Methodist History* 22:3 (April 1984): 139-157.

46. Paine College was established in Augusta, Georgia in 1882/1883 through the joint efforts of leaders affiliated with the Colored Methodist Episcopal Church and Methodist Episcopal Church, South. The school is named for Bishop Robert Paine who was instrumental in missionary work to African Americans and in memory of his assistance with the formation of the CMEC.

47. The author has been unable to locate biographical information on Charles Henry Tobias.

48. See James Rosamond Johnson, Bob Cole, and James Weldon Johnson, *The Old Flag Never Touched the Ground* (New York: Jos. W. Stem & Co., 1901).

49. For historical and contextual analyses of the phrase "Black Mammy" see M.M. Manning, *Slave in a Box: The Strange Career of Aunt Jemima* (Charlottesville, VA: University Press of Virginia, 1998); and Micki McElya (*Clinging to Mammy: The Faithful Slave in Twentieth-Century America* (Cambridge, MA: Harvard University Press, 2007).

50. For additional information on this regiment see Stephen L. Harris, *Harlem's Hell Fighters: The African American 369th Infantry in World War I* (Washington, DC: Brassey's Inc., 2003).

51. For an examination of the tensions and animosities German-American Methodists faced during World War I see Donald Carl Malone, "German Methodism and the Great War," *Methodist History* 9:4 (July 1971): 3-21.

Chapter Three

Women's Missionary Societies and the Methodist Minute Men

Introduction

The addresses of Chapter Three were proclaimed on "Woman's Day" and "Minute Men Day." Representatives of several Methodist women's missionary organizations, the Woman's Christian Temperance Union, and National Woman's Party evidenced concerns about world missions, social justice, and universal suffrage. Speakers included well-known early twentieth century women including Lena Leonard Fisher, Daisy McLain Bulkley, Martha E. Abt, and Alice Paul. Thousands of women gathered together on Woman's Day to showcase themselves as mothers, concerned wives, *and* mission-minded activists. They were deliberate to demonstrate how they had contributed to Methodist missionary work and the quest to take Christianity and American values to North America and overseas. Their presence at the fair modeled for fairgoers what it meant to be socially, religiously, and politically active as American Methodist women.

Lena Leonard Fisher presented her case for a "new patriotism" that involved the need for more American women missionaries to take Christianity around the world. Fisher pushed audiences to consider membership in the Woman's Foreign Missionary Society and encouraged attendees to serve in locations devastated by the Great War. Daisy McLain Bulkley, Field Secretary for the Colored Conference of the Woman's Home Missionary Society, located the work of women in the United States specifically to African American women and children. Bulkley was particularly interested in character-building and how Methodist women needed to be more involved in the Christian education of the home and the church. Martha B. Abt gave a lengthy address on the importance of urban social services, the care of persons with disabilities, and encouraged

Methodists in attendance to help create a Federal Department of Public Welfare for the care of American children. Perhaps the most notable presenter on Woman's Day was suffragist Alice Paul, head of the National Woman's Party. Paul strongly encouraged the audience to become more active in political maneuvering in order to give women the right to vote.

Methodist men held several conferences and meetings throughout the duration of the Centenary exposition. On "Minute Men Day" representatives from the Methodist Episcopal Church and Methodist Episcopal Church, South, spoke on the involvement of men in the history of American Methodism. Several laymen marketed the Minute Man campaign and sought to draw more men into the local church, raise awareness for world missions, and acquire funds to support missionaries and missions organizations. Ministers and military leaders including Christian F. Reisner, Elmer T. Clark, Bishop James Cannon, Jr., and Secretary of the U.S. Navy Josephus Daniels addressed audiences in a standing room only coliseum.

During the three-week fair Methodist men were highly visible in exhibits, pageants, and parades. The Centenary Celebration, for these men, illustrated the significant contributions of men of faith and functioned as a location to add additional members into denominational fraternal organizations including the Methodist Brotherhood and Minute Men. The men and youth of these organizations were regarded as the future combatants of American Methodism's religious and ideological war on claiming the world for Christ.

Reverend Christian F. Reisner presided over the events of Minute Men Day and spoke of the need for more laymen to get involved with the local church. He chastised laity in attendance for their active involvement in civic organizations such as the Rotary Club while ignoring the important roles they played in the local church. Reisner claimed he needed more laymen help build congregations and share evangelization responsibilities. He also championed the need for recreational centers and motion picture theaters in local churches claiming "every church must serve its community, or it will go out of business, and unless we get busy the saloon crowd will get busy and beat us to it."

The Methodist Minute Men held their national convention on the fairgrounds and brought in a well-known military presence and Methodist Minute Man. Josephus Daniels, Secretary of the U.S. Navy, charted a brief history of the Methodist movement and called laymen to move quickly toward the evangelization of the world. He also called men to help the United States eradicate the production and consumption of alcohol and to help stamp out sexually transmitted diseases among the branches of the U.S. military. Daniels also used the stage as a platform to promote League of Nations documentation proposed by President Woodrow Wilson. At the conclusion of the rally over five thousand Methodist men pledged to support the controversial legislation.

Woman's Day Program
Tuesday Afternoon, June 24, 1919

The meeting convened at 2:30pm in the Coliseum, Miss Belle H. Bennett, President Woman's Missionary Council, Methodist Church South, presiding...

BELLE H. BENNETT:[1]

In today's program, we have not attempted to bring the whole scope of woman's work to you. If we had done that, there would probably be standing before you at this hour that great woman, Dr. Anna Howard Shaw[2] who for nearly twenty-five years has been a preacher of the gospel in the Protestant Methodist Church.[3]

We could have brought before you the great women of this land representing that world movement which for more than a century has been bringing women to that long sought political, industrial and religious freedom which is coming, coming now so quickly. The great amendment of prohibition would have found here women who represented the W.C.T.U. before the Anti-Saloon League was known. You would have heard women who have had their part and their struggle in all of this great movement.

We can say today, "God is marching on and we, the women of this great land and of all the lands of the earth where the great messages of Jesus Christ have been taught, are following Him."

We come to you with just one great episode of the women's missionary work. One hundred years ago when that little group of Methodist men gathered around the table in New York, it was only a little while later that there gathered in a parlor of one of those uptown homes a group of Methodist women, and women's missionary work began.

It was not until after the middle of the century that all over the land just women such as you see here today gathered themselves together and general conferences of Methodism authorized the organization of that great women's missionary work which is now bringing millions of money annually into the treasury of the church and sending out around the whole earth women to preach and teach and live the glorious gospel of Jesus Christ.[4]

The first speaker of the afternoon will give you the message from the word of God on which all that we do, all that we are is founded. Mrs. James Spilman.

MRS. JAMES SPILMAN:[5]

In the twenty-fourth verse of Paul's letter to the Colossians: "I fill up my part of the sufferings of Jesus Christ which are behind." That is the one thought that I wanted to leave with you at this hour, that now in the saddest and greatest century that the world has ever seen, you and I as individual fellows of the Lord Jesus Christ must, so to speak, stand with Him under this great load of the world's suffering and of the world's sorrow.

It is surprising beyond expression when we look into the utterances of Jesus what he said about the questions that we allow to worry us. Christ said little about the immortality of the soul and the great future and that sort of thing, but the greater part of the message that he brought while he was on earth had direct bearing on his followers rendering a Christian service to men and women in need.

I say it reverently, devoutfully and thankfully that Jesus Himself could not know how to work with a man until He became a man. For that reason, He came through the channels of the virgin birth. He was the son of the carpenter and later He was the man god who went about doing good.

Sometimes you have people come to you and say, "I sympathized with you in that great sorrow that came to you." There is a mother bent over the couch, the life of her child going out. Some one who learns of this goes to the mother and says, "I have come to offer sympathy." The person who gave that sympathy might have been honest. She was the friend of the woman who was suffering. Yet, we all recognize this thought: no person can sympathize with another person until they have a similar experience. People can feel sorry for you, but to really sympathize with you, that person must have passed through a similar experience.

So Jesus, when He undertook the program of working with man, had to come to earth and become a man. After He became a man, He became sorry for him and could sympathize with him. We are told time and again that Jesus saw the multitude and they looked to Him like sheep that had no shepherd and He had compassion on them.

We find, then, that the primary principle of the life of Jesus Christ was not philosophy, though He was the greatest philosopher that ever lived. It was not science, though He was the greatest of all scientists. But, it was a feeling of divine compassion for suffering humanity.

So, I lay upon your heart the fact that if we help Jesus Christ, that in our hearts there must be a great compassion for this suffering world.

The next thought: if there is a compassion in our hearts akin to the compassion in the heart of Jesus, we will do that thing that Jesus so often did. He left the multitudes and withdrew Himself and went into the mountains and poured out His soul to God.

Just now we stand on the summit. The great crisis faces us that unless the gift of the millions is backed up with real prayer and definite service, the Centenary will not be the blessing that we want it to be. Really, the church must pray as we have never prayed because we face a task such as we have never faced before.

Jesus had compassion for people. That compassion led Him to pray and that compassion followed by prayer, led Him to dedicate his life to a life of service. Therefore, it is said of the Lord that He went about doing good. So, we, in our lives, as Paul expresses it, for my part, we, individually, won't have a feeling of compassion for this world. We want to learn how to pray for the world, and then, wherever we live and whatever may be the circumstances of our lives, to our very best ability we want to dedicate ourselves to a loving service to humanity and thereby help to fill up the sufferings which are behind in the life of Jesus.

We must stand with the Christ under the load of the world's sin and the world's sorrow, thereby making our church and this movement the greatest blessing that the world has ever seen. "For my part, I fill up that which is behind the suffering of Jesus." Shall we pray.

Our gracious heavenly Father, we come into Thy presence at this time to thank Thee for this movement, for all that it means to the great churches of Jesus Christ. We thank Thee, our Father, for the love in the hearts of men and women who have planned it, for those who have put their strength and time and talent upon the altar of God for this service.

We thank Thee, our Father, that it is possible for us to be here together and to see these great things that thrill our hearts, and to hear the messages that make us happy when we feel that we can have at least a little part in helping Jesus Christ to bring the world unto Himself.

Bless, we pray Thee, these Thy handmaidens. We ask it in Jesus' name. Amen.

BELLE H. BENNETT:
The men and women who have been working in the mission fields of the world, have learned long ago that no land can be evangelized by foreigners. It must be the trained children of that land who shall give to the people the knowledge of Jesus Christ and His love. Now, for a moment, we will listen to the singing of the little Japanese children from San Francisco who are the product of one of the schools of the Women's (sic) Home Mission Society of Methodism.

CHILDREN OF SAN FRANCISCO:
...Singing of Japanese national hymn, American national anthem, American song "K-K-K-Katy." Japanese children's "yell"...

BELLE H. BENNETT:
There are some men and women that all men and women know can be said of them, "Ye did not choose me but I chose you and appointed you that you should go forth." The two women who bring greetings to you this afternoon, Mrs. W.F. McDowell and Mrs. W.P. Thirkield, wives of those two splendid Bishops of the Methodist Church – Mrs. McDowell, President of the Women's (sic) Home Mission Board comes to us today from Washington City; Mrs. Thirkield comes to us today from far off New Orleans. Mrs. McDowell speaks first.

CLOTILDA LYON MCDOWELL:[6]
Mrs. Thirkield and myself are just a trifle sorry for Miss Bennett today, and I suppose she wonders why. Well, it is because she never lived in Ohio. And, I am a little bit sorry for Mrs. Thirkield because she wasn't born in Ohio. To be sure, some of us didn't remain in Ohio, but maybe we could not help it.

Fifty years after the missionary work of the Methodist Episcopal Church was started, the Women's (sic) Foreign Missionary Society was organized, and today

I bring you greetings and a welcome from more than four hundred thousand women and young women and children who are members of the Women's (sic) Foreign Missionary Society. Next fall we shall be finishing a five years' Jubilee Campaign. We hold our Golden Jubilee Meeting in the city of Boston where the society was organized fifty years ago.[7] During these five years, we have [been] working and working hard. We set for ourselves goals and have kept before us certain figures that we want to reach at this Jubilee Meeting.

But, do you know that the thing that concerns us most today is not, after all, lest we might fail to bring in the two million dollars which we hope to bring as our annual offering this year, but it is a real deep concern lest some of us, somewhere, may fail to comprehend the full significance of this pregnant hour, and failing to see it, may not seize it in its swift flight. You will hear that said or something like it every day during this Centenary Celebration. That is our chief concern today. The world today waits for the message of salvation in a new way. Again and again you will hear that in the coming days.

But, a message means messengers and messengers mean money, and money means more women at work and more intelligent work. So, do you see, we have been talking right around in a circle, and we are back again, thinking of goals and figures. They, after all, are only the means to the end which we want to attain, and we have been trying through all these five years to keep before us the one great aim and never lose sight of it, that they might know the only true god is Jesus Christ whom Thou has sent. That is our aim. That is why we have goals. That is why we have set for ourselves goals and figures and while we are working to reach this goal and attain these figures, "Expect great things from God; attempt great things for God" an old saint has said. "Bring you all the tithes and prove me if I will not pour you a blessing." Do you see, one depends on the other. The blessing and expectation come to those who do and give their all. To this fellowship of expectation, to this fellowship of service, of activity, we invite every Methodist woman in the land today. (Applause)

BELLE H. BENNETT:

Now, Mrs. Thirkield, the President of the great Home Mission Board, will speak to us some words of the need of our own great land.

MARY HAVEN THIRKIELD:[8]

That beautiful tribute of Victor Hugo to his wife comes to mind today as most applicable to women in missionary service at the Centenary Celebration. He said, as he looked into her eyes, "Thou shalt be my heart while I will be thine arm."

Back of Methodism was the warm pulsating heart of womanhood and out from that English rectory went our founder of Methodism because a Christian mother Susannah (sic) dwelt within. In New York City the warm heart of response came from a Methodist woman as Barbara Heck threw open her doors to the pioneers of Methodism.

But, today as we come with the same heart of love and the same heart of sympathy, we come banded with both hands of service. We have gone beyond

Victor Hugo and we have taken husband and wife, man and woman, and as co-partners in this work, thrown our hearts' love into the activity of our hands.

One hundred years ago, as we look backward today at the beginnings of missionary work, Harriet Stubbs stood by the side of our earliest missionary in the Wyandotte Mission and years afterward Harriet Skidmore stood in the halls of Methodism in New York City and helped bring into organization our great Foreign Missionary Society.

Down in New Orleans Jennie Culver Hartzell caught the germ of service and threw out her heart into the arm of power and Mary Helms of the Southland stood by her side.

So, together we come today; together we have served; together we look out into the new century and accept the challenge of the future.

I bring you the greeting of an organization of our church and nation, the Women's Home Missionary Society that has been so busy with our arm and hand and heart that God has marvelously blessed us with power.[9] At our first annual meeting twenty-five hundred dollars was reported from the general fund and seventy-nine hundred as the total income. Last year one million one hundred and fifty-five thousand ninety-nine dollars and seventeen cents was reported in the treasury of this society of Methodist women, and I speak today for two hundred seventy thousand members, including all ages and all departments.

We come to you with a look backward of gratitude and joy but we come to you with the look forward of danger and a call for service. Today our flag and our nation stand in the limelight as never before and no matter how many vital issues are settled in the halls of Congress, back of all must be the Christian home, building as the foundation for the future. So, as we listen to the edicts that are coming out from Washington of women's suffrage, let us not think merely of freedom of ballot but let us think of getting busy to train women to so use the ballot that it shall count for righteousness.

As we listen, we hear the bells a ringing the victory of the seed sowing of Christian women as prohibition looms in the air. Prohibition may drive out the evil den of the saloon but it calls in the Christian home and attractive center of womanhood. Let us accept the challenge and with arms and heart united with our brothers share not only the Centenary but share in the task that the Centenary lays upon us. (Applause)

BELLE H. BENNETT:
Five Mexican girls, the product of the mission school on the Rio Grande will sing to us now...singing by Mexican girls...

It is not often given to any one family in any church or any country to give one hundred sixty years of service to God's cause. The two women who speak to you now and their brother, Bishop Leonard, have given that number of years.

Mrs. Lena Leonard Fisher who speaks to you now is the Jubilee Commissioner of the Women's Foreign Missionary Society.

LENA LEONARD FISHER:[10]

A new age has gone forth in the whole world and its most marked characteristic is a new type of patriotism, a world patriotism. To the women of Methodism, to the daughters of this great denomination fifty years ago and through fifty years until now, to these women the new patriotism is not new, the patriotism for which we have been standing for half a century. They have given its cardinal principles a most practical demonstration in their efforts to reach out to the Christ-less women of the whole world.

It is not my province this afternoon to outline for you comprehensively the principles of this great world patriotism but my task for the next few moments shall be to simply note a few of these for which the women of Methodism in their welfare work have stood for half a century.

The first which I would note is that new patriotism must reckon with human suffering. They tell me that a wounded man belongs not to one division of the army but that he belongs to the whole army, and so I would say that it is perfectly logical reasoning when we affirm that the sick folks of the world do not belong to any one country or any one race but to the compassion of the whole world.

What a record was made on the western front of France in the matter of relief for human suffering! In the four years and a half during which the great war raged, three thousand five hundred war hospitals sprung up along France's flaming front and the Red Cross of America alone sent out a great army of ten thousand doctors and nurses. Why, the equipment in these war hospitals and the efficient service rendered was the last word in scientific efficiency.

But, the new patriotism goes beyond France and its war hospitals. The new patriotism listens with ears wide open to the cries of anguish of half of the human family, whose cries sound to heaven unheeded, unrelieved. It is said that nine million men fell on the European battlefield. Every year for a number of years, thirty-three million people have died from diseases, all of which were relievable, many preventable, but they died without medical attention.

In passing this point, I would leave in your heart of hearts this statement which is no fiction but which is an accurate statement of fact: that today fifteen hundred millions of women and girls are living under a system of faith whose very laws visit upon them torture – mental, physical, spiritual – as dreadful and unspeakable as that which was visited upon the womanhood of any of the invaded countries of Europe. And for these five hundred million, there gleams no Red Cross. So, we must reckon with human suffering and in this day when fast trains and fast boats and the wings of the aeroplane are bringing that unnamable, vague thing which for years we have called the orient, and we have it at our doors, to them must be given the ministry of healing.

The women of Methodism by our hospitals are doing their utmost for the relief of the suffering of these, who, unless women minister unto them, in the majority of cases must be unrelieved.

As the second factor in the new patriotism which is of fundamental importance, I would mention the doing of the difficult task. I think that that picture which we have of Abraham Lincoln as he was leaving his Springfield home when the gray mists of the morning were hanging over the town and he stood on the rear platform of the train a very wonderful one. I think his utterance was most pathetic when he said to his friends and neighbors, "I go to assume a task more difficult than that which has ever devolved upon any man since Washington."

The new patriotism calls for the doing of the difficult task and we as Methodist women have no reason to hang our heads in this our golden year, for fifty years ago a little group of eight women with the blessing of God gripped a difficult task which has made for the eternal salvation of thousands of women in Christian lands. Today the difficult task that stares at the women of Methodism.

The first part of the difficult task, I should say, was a call to the youth of our great church for overseas service for Jesus Christ. The Women's (sic) Foreign Missionary Society counts upon her honor roll the names of nine hundred eighty-three women, six hundred of whom are in active service today. At the end of this year, our high year, our glad year, we shall be sending out after the Boston meeting, possibly one hundred of the fairest daughters of Methodism who will go into the twelve different countries to preach the unsearchable riches of Jesus Christ. So, I would say to the youth of our church, the difficult task is yours.

When the news came to us from across the sea that Douglas Haig and his soldiers were fighting with their backs to the wall, what if reinforcements had not gone forth to that thin line over across the Atlantic? But, think of that other thin line where the fight is strong, where overworked men and women stand today and they are calling to you. Who should be the recruits for this thin line in lands where Jesus Christ is not known?

The second part of the difficult task is directed to us who are here at the home base and who must direct the great campaign in this great world warfare. It is to the women of Methodism today and it is this: the difficult task of keeping up our war standards in two particulars. First, in the matter of our giving. O, friends, do you know that we relegated to a place of honor but some obscurity that magical slogan which the women of fifty years ago had about two cents a week and prayer. We are not on the two cents a week basis in this day. That has been an excuse. We are not talking about two cents. We are not talking about pennies at all. I believe that the reason the philanthropic interest through so many years has been measured by one cent is because we used to teach the children, "Hear the pennies dropping." Never have the children sing that song again because it has produced men and women who were willing to keep on dropping pennies.

We must keep up to our war standards in the matter of our giving. It is not how little can I give but how much can I give, not that we are begging for this great work but that we are asking our constituency to help us finance the greatest enterprise in all the world, the cause which eventually must be triumphant in the world.

The second part is that we must keep up our standards in the matter of service. O, how skillful the fingers of American women have become! How we have learned to roll surgical dressings and bandages in the war days! O, friends, when the last war hospital shall be evacuated, shall our fingers forget the cunning they have learned? We must keep our standard of service.

The new patriotism has but one measure. It is not measured by blood. It is a fine thing to be a daughter of the American Revolution, somebody whose father fought back there for the freedom of this nation. But, friends, the point today is not who was your grandfather, the point today is what are you as the granddaughter of that early American patriot doing in the age in which we live! (Applause) You are aristocracy.

The aristocracy of the new patriotism is not measured by blood, it is measured by the service. It is said that a Canadian general went into a hospital in London. He almost stumbled over the Duchess of Conneaut as she was scrubbing the floor. He looked down at her and said, "It seems to [me] there should be some one else to do that." She looked up at him and replied, "This floor has to be scrubbed and there is no one else to do it. Why should I not scrub a floor?"

We women of Methodism have been scrubbing the floor of the world for fifty years and the time is still here when we must wield our mops and brooms. There is the debris of war to be swept away. There is the debris of wrecked childhood and oppressed womanhood to be cleared away and our service must be kept up at the concert pitch at which it was on the day the armistice was signed.

Finally, I would say that the new patriotism reckons with the fact that there is a very wonderful human material outside the white race. This has been a cardinal principle in the work of the Women's (sic) Foreign Missionary Society for fifty years. As a nation we have been most provincial.

I remember once that my mother met an old lady in New York, one of the women from our neighborhood. The lady remarked that she was starting on a western trip the next day.

"You are going on a western trip! Why, where are you going?" my mother said, supposing, of course, that she was going at least part way across the continent.

"I am going to Buffalo."

As a nation we have gotten about as far as to Buffalo before this war came in recognizing the value of human material outside the white race. Do not forget that when the armistice was signed, it was the forty-three thousand American negro soldiers who were nearest the Rhine! (Applause)

Do not forget that these splendid black fighters, whose liberty and freedom was gained for them by the strong right arm of Abraham Lincoln and the unconquerable armies of the North, were the men who sprang to the defense of liberty. Not only these men, but there were a million and a half men who marched from India to France's front. Thirty thousand of them died on the Fields of Flanders and France. Ten thousand among this million and a half were Methodist boys who heard their first ideals of liberty and freedom from the mouths of Christian missionaries and preachers. And, they went to fight alongside your boy.

There were two hundred thousand Chinese boys who went over and did work behind the lines of France, without which, victory would have been absolutely impossible. There are women in Africa today, down in the timber land, down in the jungles who strain their eyes across vast distances to see the return of men who will never come back. There are women on the sands of Arabia who saw their men ride forth one day and who will never see them come back. Little Burma sent five hundred fighters to the western front.

Friends, here is the point: it is the mothers of these men for whose salvation we labor. These heroes who helped defend the altars of freedom for a world, these men were raised by women. Their mothers and their sisters are entitled to their share of the heritage which was won by these men. (Applause) It is for them we labor. It is for their cause, we believe, that Jesus Christ Himself placed his hand upon that little group of eight women in Boston fifty years ago, his hand which has been upon our mothers all the way through, his hand which is now upon the great host of four hundred and twenty-five thousand women in the Women's (sic) Foreign Missionary Society, for last fall we passed our jubilee goal by twenty-five thousand women and today this great army knows that it is for these in whose cause we march that they might know Him, Jesus Christ, whom to know aright is life everlasting.

Oh, that all of us women, all who are here today, would allow your lives to become points of contact between Jesus Christ and these women who sit in darkness! It is our great privilege to usher these oriental mothers and sisters into the great new age, the dawn of which is upon us. Will you help us now as we enter into the second half of the last fifty years of our first century of service, to lead these also into the light of Jesus Christ?

A new age dawns. The trees are alive with song for Joseph dreams his dreams again and Joan leads her armies into life, and somewhere near the Master from His hurt hands and heals world again. (Applause)

BELLE H. BENNETT:
Mrs. Woodruff, another member of the same family will speak to us now.

MAY LEONARD WOODRUFF:[11]
Forty years ago there stood a man in one of the great cities of our nation before just a little group of women and he uttered this sentence: two fields will present themselves for your special consideration. First, the frontier South and West, and, second, the great cities will claim your activities.

For forty years the Women's (sic) Home Missionary Society has been working out that program and we come today to tell you of the advance which has been made under this banner. We were called upon to uphold Christ before the women of our own country. It was because under the Stars and Stripes there were women who had never heard the story of our Lord and Savior Jesus Christ.

In those days the work of this organization was in the continental United States. We had no thought when we made the pledge that wherever the flag should wave, there in the name of our God would we set up our banners, that we would cross the seas to the island possessions of our country, and that there we would be called upon to minister in the name of Jesus Christ.

Our pledge made in those early days has been redeemed, for wherever Old Glory has waved, there we have gone. And, we come before you today to say that wheresoever Old Glory shall wave, there the Women's (sic) Home Missionary Society will go with a story of the Lord Jesus Christ.

We realize that today we are facing a new period. We realize that today home missions means more than it has in the history of our land. We know that today we cannot labor for the home missions under the Stars and Stripes, but that we labor for the uttermost parts of the earth, for a saved America means a world's salvation and redemption.

The Women's (sic) Home Missionary Society of our great organization was first called together to the Southland to labor among the millions of negroes, to gather the girls into our industrial homes and schools. And, on this platform today you will hear from two women who have been trained by the Women's (sic) Home Missionary Society, one of whom has gone to the dark continent and done a wonderful service under the Women's (sic) Foreign Missionary Society.

Today we are not confining our efforts for the negroes to the Southland. We have only to suggest to this audience that a migration has occurred; from seven hundred fifty thousand to one million of these people have come from the Southland to the Northland.

A few weeks ago it was my privilege to be in the black belt of the South and I want to say to you today, I did not miss one who had migrated to the North. It seems as though they were all there. But, they have come, as we know, to the Northland and we must meet this situation. We must see a new opportunity and to these people, who gave, as you have heard in the great war of their best, we must give the chance of men and women under our flag. So it is that we go with our industrial homes and schools, that we minister to the womanhood in order that the womanhood may uplift that race.

Again, the Women's (sic) Home Missionary Society in the Southland goes into the homes of the mountain highlanders. There, in sight of our Southern states, are six million of these people and they must have their opportunity. You know how they have not been reached with education and Christianity. We must go to them.

And then, the Latin Americans, numbering today more than three millions under our flag have come up over the border from Mexico. They have come from that Roman Catholic country. They have come here not as Roman Catholics. They have come as people who have absolutely lost their God and we must go to them with a message of salvation.

Sweep on up the Western coast, if you will, and glance for a moment at the orientals, eighty thousand Chinese. I heard Jennie Hughes a few weeks ago make one of those wonderful appeals that it seems to me only she knows how to make. She pled with the women to think of the two thousand Chinese students at our universities and colleges.[12] I plead with you for eighty thousand Chinese and I beg of you that no Chinese under this flag may ever return to China without having the touch of Jesus Christ.

Miss Hughes said, "I came into one of the colleges. I found a young woman whom I had known in China.

"'Of course, you have given yourself to the Lord Jesus Christ.' And, looking Miss Hughes fully in the face she said, 'I have been here for four years and no one has spoken to me until you came of my Savior."

Don't let that ever happen again. There are one hundred thousand Japanese. You listen to the singing of our Japanese children today. How many of us as American citizens ever take time to go where these people are under the Stars and Stripes to know that they are bringing their oriental religions, their oriental customs here and that unless we stay them, they must influence to a large degree this country.

Then we come to speak briefly of the work in our insular possessions. Think of Alaska and the Aleutian Islands with more than one half million people! You know the story of the epidemic that has swept away the adult population until hundreds of hundreds of children have been left. Our government has said to the Women's (sic) Home Missionary Society, "You must be responsible for these children."

Go to the islands of the Pacific. Look at the Hawaiian Islands. You will find nearly two hundred fifty thousand of the most cosmopolitan population you have ever known. If you could go there as we have done, you might be taken as we were by Mr. Yasumori, who is here on the grounds in the Hawaiian exhibits, and he would show you the Buddha school where two thousand children are brought in for special training. As you entered the compound, if you asked, "What is this house?" the reply would be, "Here are where the young men and women are being trained for Buddhist propaganda." We asked, "Where are they to go?" He replied, "Back to the orient or to the United States of America."

Go to that wonderful land of Lehua and as you drive out you reach the town of Lahaina. There you will find a Mormon temple erected for the ministry for the people of the mid-Pacific Island. They told us that their church membership in the Church of Latter Day Saints was more than four thousand, but they had more than seventeen thousand adherents.

A party of nine Methodists went through that temple. We saw those rooms where these strange rights (sic) and ceremonies are performed. We saw the mural decorations on the wall that we cannot describe to the audience this afternoon. But, friends, we are here to say that the gospel of the Lord Jesus Christ must be given to these people if we shall fulfill the pledge we have made to our flag and to our God.

Then, this year is the child's federal year of our nation, the opportunity of childhood under the flag. If you go to any foreign country, you will find the childhood of that country. If you go to China, you will find the Chinese children. If you go to Japan, you will find the Japanese children, but here you find under our flag the children of the world, and one of the greatest opportunities of this nation today is its childhood. We must make the children true Americans and we have come to realize that simply speaking the English language, that simply the knowledge of our laws, does not make Americans in spirit. We must train the childhood of this nation that they may be in the future what we would have them to be as American citizens.

You have heard the story of the East Side teacher in New York who said, "Last fall we opened the doors to twenty-eight nationalities. This June when the schools closed, we opened the doors to one nationality – American children." In order to make childhood what it ought to be, as American citizens we should be intelligent on this subject. We should not only prosecute our work in missions but as Christians, as Protestants under the flag, we should have something to say with reference to our public schools. (Applause)

You have heard the story of the little Italian boy who for some misdemeanor was being chastised by his father. He went down into the alley and the gang met him. They said, "Did he nearly kill you? Did he hurt you?" He drew himself up and said, "No. I didn't care for the beating, but it made me mad that that old Dago dared to whip an American boy."

You smile. But, friends, go back of the smile and what does it mean? Do you realize that between the child in the public school and the foreign parent in the home is being created a tremendous chasm, a chasm that we believe must be bridged as we must go into the homes of the foreigners and give to them not only the English language but the American spirit backed up by the gospel of the Lord Jesus Christ.

Then we come to speak just a word of this year of Americanization. We are talking of Americanization everywhere. This term today means more than the old problem, as we called it, of immigration. It includes immigration but it includes so much more – that Americanization must reach every man, woman and child under our flag, and it must be a Christian Americanization. We must give to these people not only education, we must give them the gospel of the Lord Jesus Christ.[13]

Do you know that today there are five million five hundred thousand illiterates in the United States? Some one at once will say, "Yes, but they are almost all foreigners." Listen. One million six hundred thousand only are foreign born. In our army there were seven hundred thousand boys of draft age who could not read or write.

Did you hear the story of the boy, who on Mother's Day at camp went into the Y.M.C.A. hut and there were the posters all around – "Write to Mother on Mother's Day, Have you written to Mother" and other such sayings. This boy sat down and took paper and pen, and wrote and wrote and wrote. The Secretary came around the first time and said, "Are you ready to give me your letter?" The boy said, "No." Again he wrote and again the Secretary came and received the reply the second time. The next time the Secretary asked him the question the boy looked up and said, "I am just a fool. I haven't any mother and if I had, I couldn't write to my mother today."

Oh, friends, this is one of the most important things for us to consider in this matter of Christian Americanization. When you come into the realm of the religion in our country, what do we find? One hundred five million in population! Forty-three million only are members of any church – Jewish,

Roman Catholic or Protestant, leaving sixty-two millions unchurched and without God in the world.

Some one here will say, "What are sixty-two millions?" I will tell you. You must add one factor to the sixty-two millions, composed of two little words and that will make the responsibility of the sixty-two millions yours for time and for eternity, and those two little words are "our own." If you add those, you have a problem, you have your problem for time and eternity.

What about the false faiths that have risen among us? I will not speak of the isms and cults that are so prevalent but let me say to you as we have suggested, that Buddhism is making long strides under our flag and those Hawaiian lands are one of their strongholds.

When you come to speak of Mormonism, what does it mean? It means defiance of the laws of God and of our land. I want to say to you today that we are asleep on this question. Senator Smoot just a few weeks ago said in Brooklyn at the dedication of one of the churches, "Today we have four hundred fifty thousand members in this country, and please God, they shall multiply over and over again."[14]

I sat in a Mormon tabernacle a little over a year ago. I heard Brigham H. Roberts who was sent back from the halls of Congress to his harem. He had been appointed a chaplain in the army of Utah. At the close of that address a little woman took both my hands in hers and said, "Oh, think of it! He is chaplain of the Utah troops."

Friends, these are things we must know. They are issues to which we must be awake in this day and in our generation. We must save not only the United States of America for America but we must save the United States of America that the world may be saved for our Lord and for His Kingdom. (Applause)

BELLE H. BENNETT:

Before we go on with our program, I want to ask you ladies and gentlemen if you saw in one of the recent papers that there has been a proposition to rescind the gentlemen's contract with Japan. Now, as far as I know, and I think I know something from personal observation, the gentlemen's contract was kept better by the Japanese than it was ever kept in America. I came over on shipboard with a large body of cultured Japanese men and women. Those men did not get through the custom houses and I did and yet these men and women were to be allowed just as we were allowed, to come to Japan. Will you kindly study the gentlemen's contract with Japan and see if you approve of rescinding it?

Most of you know that Japan is the one nation, the one Christian nation, where Christianity had its first converts among the educated and cultured people of the land. In all other lands we have had to go down into the market places, the highways and the byways.

We will now listen to Miss Suiga San sing.

…Singing of Suiga San…

Mrs. Daisy McLain Bulkley will speak to you. She is the Secretary of the conferences of the negro people of the Methodist Episcopal Church and will tell you of the work.

Friends, before she comes to the platform, as a Southern woman, may I say to you that we have nearly ten millions of these colored people in the South, the most religious people in the world. They are an imitative people. The great body of them are in the adolescent stage and these people don't always get your front door religion. They do exactly what they think the better class of people around them do. If they come North in a great body, as they are, see to it that you set them an example that will make them the people that you want them to be. We are trying to do it in the South but we have not known them in their homes or in their workshops to any great extent and that is the danger with us in the South and with you in the North. But, God has given them to us and they are a mighty heritage which we must see to it is given back to Him as a Christian people.

DAISY MCLAIN BULKLEY:[15]

When I came to the Centenary grounds a few days ago, as I looked around here and there and greeted my brothers and sisters from the ends of the world, I said, "Verily, has the world come together in the city of Columbus." When I went into our various exhibits and looked here and there at the marvelous display that the church has brought to us, I declared, "Today I would rather come here as a representative of John Stewart than as a representative of a Michelangelo or any other race under the sun."

Michelangelo saw the form of an angel in the rough rocks of Florence, Italy. John Stewart saw the image of Almighty God in his brothers and sisters of the Indian race in the state of Ohio.

This Centenary Celebration will for all time establish recognition for the negro race as a contribution of the religious uplift of the world. The negro no longer occupies his traditional role of recipient. During the great world war the negro himself became a freer of men.

Then I declare unto you as I look over this great church and realize today that this Methodist Episcopal Church took the initiative in giving this great school to the world, not to Methodism but the Methodist Episcopal Church through the Centenary has given the opportunity for all Protestantism to become educated, to receive information and inspiration, to receive an enlargement of vision, that the world might go back to a larger service for our King.

I would rather stand here today as the representative of the great Methodist Church than any other, not because I lay any stress on Methodism or denomination but, friends, because this great Church has taken the initiative. Friends, when I realize how opportune this Celebration is after having heard just a few days ago of a church in New York moving up her hour of worship, not that her membership might have more time for devotion but that her membership might have more time for sports and pleasure – the American people are rearing a generation of pagans because of their utter disregard of the Sabbath, because of the Sunday moving picture, because of the Sunday baseball – I thank God that the Methodist Episcopal Church has taken the initiative in bringing the world to her knees.

As I look over America and think of the great ministry to the American people and realize that there is no phase of American life that is not being touched and influenced by this society; when I look back and realize that the needs of the negro girl gave impetus to this great organization, I thank God for the great sisterhood of the world, and I want you should know once for all that the fundamental work of the Women's (sic) Home Missionary Society is character building.

The character of a nation determines the destiny of that nation. Our homes are not trade buildings to send our young women out to be domestic servants. The real objective of the work is the fitting of every woman for her God-given sphere of home builder, brain, hand and heart trained to be fully alive to the highest usefulness, her whole being atingle with a hunger for the best in life. No better investment, no greater contribution could be made to the national life than this nobler aspiration to the coming womanhood.

The Woman's Home Missionary Society wants you to understand that money invested here is transmuted into character. Gold is refined into life processes for the kingdom. The society has always tried to make you understand that the true foundation and the only education that will make this old world better is religious education for all the people. (Applause) If this old world is to be made a safe place for all the people, then all the people must have religious education.

My dear friends, we would have you understand today that democracy will not come through the signing of the decision of the Peace Conference, nor will it come through the League of Nations, as important as it may be. Democracy is not a material thing. Democracy is a spirit. Democracy is the attitude of soul and mind. Democracy can only come when great majorities of the people have attained a spiritual, moral and mental attitude that will lift democracy to a higher level. There must be a process of leveling up and not down. If every individual, every man and woman, is to become a factor in the national life, in the life of the world, then every effort must be made to improve the quality of the individuals.

Do you ask how far has the Women's (sic) Home Missionary Society succeeded in doing this? I declare unto you today that from one school for negro girls there have come five wives for Methodist ministers, twelve wives for college presidents and seven missionaries.

> There is but one great fellowship of love,
> Throughout the whole wide earth.
> In Him shall true hearts everywhere,
> Their high communion find.
>
> His service is the golden cord,
> Close binding all mankind.
> Then join hands, sisters of the faith,
> Whate'er your race may be.
> Who loves my Father, as a child,
> Is surely kin to me." (Applause)[16]

BELLE H. BENNETT:
Miss Martha E. Drummer will speak to us of the dark land of Africa.

MARTHA E. DRUMMER:[17]
While I was sitting here, I was thinking what is bigger than this Centenary. And, I thought, the opportunity in Africa. (Applause)

The Centenary is all right, if you will seize your opportunity in Africa. While I am talking about that great neck of the woods, you will be thinking and praying for all the dark places of the earth's heathen races. I know you will. Your hearts have been big enough. You have had enlargement of the heart since I was here six years ago. At that time you were singing, "Brighten up the corner where you are." Now when I come back you are singing, "Brighten up the corners everywhere." (Applause)

Thirteen years ago I signed up for overseas service, thanks to the women of Methodism. I am so glad you sent me. I wish I could wake up there tomorrow morning. When I walked through the Africa building, I didn't see a badge for my little garden spot, it is just a little kitchen garden. I come from Angola, Portuguese West Africa, about two thousand miles below Liberia. Don't ask me about the neighbors in Liberia. In Angola I was three hundred fifty miles from the coast, just a plain bush woman, and I couldn't tell you much about anything but the bush.

I am so glad there have been no dreadnaughts or destroyers our way, but I am glad you sent builders our way. I thank God for the builders over the world. We are building temples the world cannot see. We are building for eternity, building characters in that world over there. Lift up your eyes and behold the vision of our Christ. He loved underdeveloped humanity. He loved the sick and loathsome of society. Let us get His program to make the world safe to live in. His program is love one another as I have loved you.

Now, when you are thinking of all the dark places, you won't miss Africa. It isn't large. It is only one fourth of the earth's surface. In that little kitchen garden where I work, there are only about eight and a half million natives. I want you to think about those people way back there in the bush. I want you to see them. Oh, yes, that wonderful, that beautiful sunny Africa which was good enough for Livingstone is good enough for Christ. Africa needs Christ as a refuge today just as much as Jesus needed Africa in Herod's day. Oh, send Him back to us. Send us the light. Africa has only been touched. In the place where I have been working, thanks to you, I have been going back from village to village trying to do good. For eight years I taught in your schools there and I learned the manners of the people of the bush. If they said, "Ku ku ku ku," I said, "Ku ku ku ku." I have gotten as near the people as I could to let them see that you are really letting the light burn. Continue to let them see it burn. We need you. We need your money.

When they have the missionary with them, people say, "Let us sing 'Icy Mountains'" but, oh, please, don't sing "Icy Mountains."[18] The church of God is too cold toward missions now. Then, "Waft ye winds the story." But, the winds won't do it unless this Centenary puts some gold and silver and men and women into the winds, otherwise the story will never get there.

Let us have your best. Your best is none too good for Africa. We need the very best you have and the most of it. I am not going to tell you all about it. But, you remember the song, "Where are the nine?" We have only nine out there trying to do the work but as I go about there from place to place trying to tell the story of the gospel, the people have received it gladly and they are just as hungry as they can be for something that is new. They are begging for teachers in every village, and somehow they got medicines associated with the Methodist missionaries. They are coming to us for physicians. "Is there any balm in Gilead?"

Come over and help us. If I were to give you one cry today, it would be, "Come over in Africa and help us." The opportunity is great if you want to do something big and hard for Jesus Christ.

Come to Africa. I welcome you to that great space and those hungry hearted people who are waiting for that Christ who said, "And if I be lifted up, I will draw all men unto me." (Applause)

BELLE H. BENNETT:
I want the women whose names I shall call to stand before us just a moment: Mrs. Lois Parker, last remaining founder of the Foreign Missionary Society of the Methodist Episcopal Church; Mrs. Clementine (sic) Butler, the daughter of one of the founders; Mrs. Alma Matthews (sic), the missionary with the longest service at Ellis Island; Miss Atkinson from China who has been on the field there nearly thirty years and the first member of the Chinese Women's (sic) Missionary Society to visit this country. Mrs. Parker last year completed sixty round years of service.[19]

Friends, I have the pleasure of introducing to you one of our dear friends, Mrs. Anna Gordon of the W.C.T.U.

ANNA GORDON:[20]
Dear friends, it is a wonderful privilege to be here today. We are very sorry that the meeting of the Women's (sic) Christian Temperance Union was placed at the same hour with this great meeting of the missionary forces of our Methodist Church.

You see I am armed for the battle of the Lord through the Methodist missionary organizations but we had our W.C.T.U. gathering, and although we hoped we could adjourn in time to have the closing moments with you, I am privileged to do so and to bring you the greeting of the world's Women's (sic) Christian Temperance Union and the gratitude of every heart beating beneath the little bow of white for what you have done to help establish the temperance work of women around the world.

But for these blessed women and the missionaries in every land, but for the bishops of the Methodist Church in every land where we have tried to do our temperance work, we could not have had a Women's (sic) Christian Temperance Union. It is like shaking hands with one's self to thank you all but we do so from the depths of our hearts, and in this glad new era, with gladness and glorious singing, we go forth under the banner of the King of kings and the Lord of lords to take the world for Christ His own kingdom. The Women's (sic) Christian Temperance Union cannot do it but all of us together with God's blessed help will plant the banner of total abstinence and purity and prohibition in every land under the sun. (Applause)

BELLE H. BENNETT:
Now Mrs. O. N. Townsend, together with Miss Barge, has something to say to you.

MRS. O. N. TOWNSEND:[21]
I want to say something to the people in front of me for the people who are behind me. I never was so proud I am a woman as I am today.

A little girl once said to her doll, "Lucy, I heard a story this morning in Sunday School. God made a man. God put him to sleep, and took out his brains and made woman."

This morning Miss Barge and I felt as if we had invited a lot of people to our house and everybody was cross from the hired girl down, and the potatoes had to be substituted for the asparagus. We couldn't have any bands, and, lo, the bands were on my own arms. In other words, women of Methodism, if we can't have what we want, let's want what we can get.

Miss Barge and I have worked hard for this day. I am proud of it. I am proud of you all, every one of you and I am rather proud of Miss Barge.

But, I tell you I am not willing any longer to say that the Red Cross is the greatest mother on earth. "The Greatest Mother of Earth" – just look at that poster. Won't you adopt it? That woman has in her arms the world. In her right arm she has the cross of Christ. On her arms she has the bands of the Women's (sic) Home and Foreign Missionary Society and she says, "With both hands earnestly." Shall we not have that for our poster, for our guide? Like Joseph of old, shall we not ask our Master to strengthen the arms of our hands? O, might God of Jacob, come to the women of Methodism today. Come to the armed women. Come to those who have put both hands to this work, and may we for once and all say now:

> Here, Lord, we give ourselves to Thee
>   It is all that we can do to serve
>   The present age, my calling to fulfill.
>   O, may it all my powers engage
>   To do my Master's will."[22]

Now, Carrie, what have you to say?

CARRIE BARGE:[23]
I think we have been getting a world vision today and that is the only kind of a vision that will meet the present situation.

I am proud of Mrs. Townsend and I am proud of you. I thank God I am a Methodist woman.

I would be ashamed of myself this afternoon if I could not look the world in the face and say, "I am interested in every creature, in every land in God's world."

I wonder how many women who are here this afternoon can stand on both feet and say, "I belong to both missionary societies?"

How many of you wear both armbands? All of you who belong to both missionary societies, please stand.

…Majority of audience rises…

Now, I am going to ask another question. All of you who belong to the Women's (sic) Foreign Missionary Society, please stand.

…Majority of audience rises…

Now then, another question: I want every woman in the house who joined the missionary societies today or who is going to join, who pledges herself now that she will join the Women's (sic) Home and Foreign Missionary Societies, to please stand.

…A number of women in the audience rise…

Then listen while you are standing. We are going to give you a privilege that never was granted Methodist women in all the history of Methodism. We are going to give you the privilege of coming to the platform and shaking hands with the three Presidents of the societies, in just a moment.

I have had leadership in the missionary society of Southern Methodism for twenty-five years. For the last fifteen years there has been a good deal of talk about union between these great Churches. Let me say that in all these years, I have never heard a single woman object to union. What is the matter?

When Sir Douglas Haig sent back that message to this country that the men behind him were a thin line, it was just a little later when he sent back the message, "So close are we upon our munitions, day after day, that if the women stop for one hour in France and England in the making of munitions, we go down under it. Germany will be victorious." One hour! Now, friends, the women of England, of France, of all those lands are looking to you for help. Today the doors are wide open into far-off Russia and Poland and all of those lands, and yet today we have but one tenth of the womanhood of our Methodism in these missionary societies. May I ask what is the matter? What is the matter with the motherhood that can give her boys to the front trenches when she is unwilling to stand for Jesus Christ in these far-off lands?

You are not the women to talk to because you are all missionary women, but won't you go out and talk to the others? Won't you go back to your closets and pray day by day that He may lay His hands on the finest young womanhood, saying, "Go yet into all the world." I leave this message with you.

While the orchestra plays, we want every woman who has joined these societies to come to the platform and have the privilege of shaking hands with these three magnificent women.

MRS. O. N. TOWNSEND:
   Let everybody come to the platform!
   ...Audience marches to the platform where they are received by the speakers of the afternoon...

   ...ADJOURNMENT...

Woman's Day Program
Tuesday Afternoon, June 24, 1919

...Meeting convened in the Big Tent, Mr. E. K. Hester presiding as Chairman...

E. K. HESTER:[24]

I have great pleasure in introducing to you the speaker of the hour, a woman who during the War Council Work in Chicago delivered a thousand addresses and received a medal for doing that. She reached 85,000 people, and she is a woman who is more conversant with social conditions in the great city of Chicago than any other woman of the day. She brings to you for only a few moments this afternoon a message on "City Welfare." I take great pleasure in introducing to you Mrs. Martha E. Abt who will now address you.

MARTHA E. ABT:[25]

I am indeed glad that it is my opportunity to speak at the Centenary on Woman's Day, because women in the last two years have really come into their own. And coming here today, which is Woman's Day is a privilege indeed.

The late war has taught us many things, and among the problems to be solved is that of reconstruction and social service. Reconstruction may mean many, many things, but we must work with one end in view and that is the reconstruction of our social service either in village, town or city.

It doesn't make much difference after all where we work because the problems are all the same. Each town has its individual problem and each problem is individual to that town. Chicago had many, many problems and then they were overlapping one another just as the agencies overlapped one another, so we tried in our way to solve some of those problems by our Department of Public Welfare.

There isn't any reason whatsoever that every town and village in the whole United States could not use a Department of Public Welfare, and they could have them. It is only a group of men and women working together. The ultimate end is all the same – the care of our children – and that is the greatest problem in America today.

Twenty-five percent of the boys who composed our late national army could neither read nor write the English language, and ten percent could not read nor write any language whatsoever, to the shame of America.

No matter what we do, no matter what work is done abroad, there are great things to be done at home, great things to be accomplished, which must be accomplished and which can be best done in our own communities.

Everywhere you go you hear the talk of community centers. That is more needed than anything else today – community centers, where boys and girls may be cared for, may be amused, where their amusements may be supervised. I was in a small town in Ohio last Sunday, the town in which I was born and raised and married. On Saturday evening while down there I observed there wasn't a place to go, not even a moving picture house. On Sunday morning I spoke in church, and my greatest plea was for supervised amusements. One can scarcely understand the heart of the child. When we grow up we grow older and we seek quite old amusement. We feel we know enough to want to see the things that we like, but not so with the child, and I pleaded with those people to build a community house, to build it by taxation and keep it up by taxation, so that every man, woman and child in this little town might participate – not build it by any sect or creed and keep one child out because he might belong to some sect or creed, and another child because they might be in a lower social strata than the people who built this community house, but build it by taxation and keep it up by taxation so it might belong to the community, and be called a community house in name and fact and in deed. Have someone come in then who understands supervised amusement, and you would be surprised what little trouble you will have with your young folks.

We get them in the city after you are through with them in the country, and if I had the time this afternoon I would like to take you with me through the Courts of the City of Chicago and the County of Cook, and I would show you the ultimate end of some in our penal institutions.

It isn't a pleasant subject, but it is a subject upon which we Americans must be awakened.

While down South last year I heard a noise under my window and looking out I saw a little colored boy down there about twelve years of age, and he was peeling potatoes. It was five o'clock in the morning. The little chap was early at work and he kept talking to himself, and this was his monologue, "Just can't go anywhere – worked all year – wanted to go to picnic today, and all I get is 'you lazy nigger, you must stay at home' – I ain't been lazy. I just wants to go to the picnic" and he would take the potato and throw it down to the side of the pan, and he would say to the potato, "Come back here, old potato, and let me finish peeling you – but it (sic) does want to go to that picnic – never asked for any day in the whole year and now I can't go, just have to stay here and work, work, work – that's all I know." The heart of that child was bound up in the little picnic, the only thing the little fellow had to look forward to perhaps the whole year long, and then he was denied the privilege of going. The heart of that little colored boy isn't any different from the heart of every other little child in the whole United States. A child is a child no matter what the color of the skin, or their station in life. They are just children longing to go somewhere and to have something to do.

And so I am pleading for liberty for them, for supervised amusement for our children. You can't know what it means.

I am going to plead with you people who do not live in the city to have your children instructed in the mysteries of life and what it means, and instruct them properly because the saddest things we get in the Courts are due to a lack of understanding. We have little girls that are mothers from the age of ten years on in our County hospital, and the only cry that we hear is that "I didn't know."

Years ago, the first of July, in every city in the United States, in every church in every city, Herbert Hoover's famous letter was read where he asked for the conservation of food, and the women to work in the great war, and this is the text of that letter. I heard it read in the Old First Church in Salem, Massachusetts, the oldest church in New England, and he said: "Upon the women of America devolves the losing or the winning of this war." We raised the boys that went to this war. I gave my boy. He was a tank commander, and I was awfully glad and thankful to God when he came back to me the eleventh of April, sound in body and in mind; and upon the women of America depends the reconstruction of the life of America.

They talk about Americans assisting foreigners or people born on alien soil to become Americanized. The greatest thing in America today is the Americanization of Americans. You have got to make them understand what America means, what the ideals of America are, and how to live up to them.

In the Court of Domestic Relations of the City of Chicago are heard all the troubles that men and women have that they want adjudicated in Court without resorting to the divorce courts. Seventy-five percent of those are people who are born on foreign soil, about twenty-five percent are Americans.

Not long ago a Polish man was brought in there for beating his wife. He had beaten her terribly. The wife stood there bearing the signs of her punishment. He didn't deny beating her, but he gloried in it. The judge said, "Do you deny beating your wife?" "No," he said, "I beat her." The judge said, "Why did you beat her?" He said, "She my wife, I have a right to beat her." "Why," the judge said, "no, you haven't any right to beat her." "Well," he said, "in Poland we beat our wives; they belong to us. She belong to me, so I beat her." "Well," said the judge, "remember, you are now living in America and Americans do not believe in beating their wives. It isn't Americanism. Neither is it American for you to beat your wife, and so you must not do it." But the only thing the judge could do was to put the man on one year's probation, and tell him if he again beat his wife what would happen to him. Well, American men, as a rule, do not beat your wives, or if they do the wives do not bring them into Court as much as the foreigners.

But we must raise our boys and our girls with the idea that the home is a most sacred thing, the most sacred thing on the face of the earth, because the nation is just as strong as the home, and when the home ties disintegrate and do not progress, then the nation cannot progress, because the nation is made up of peoples, and the peoples make the home.[26]

I was talking to a woman whose boy died in service. She was complaining bitterly about the Government. Naturally, she resented the giving of her boy because she didn't understand the necessity for it, and I asked her, "What is the Government, who is the Government, what does it mean?" Well, she thought a moment. She said, "I guess it is just us," and I said, "You are just right, the Government is just us and no one else." It isn't some great, intangible thing – something that is far removed from everybody and everything, but it is just us, and the better citizens we are, the better men and women we are, the better children we raise, the better government we are going to have, because after all the old United States is just us.

Going around among the cities and the states as I did during two years of war work, I learned a great number of things. I heard a great many ideas and exchanged thoughts and ideas with a great many people, and an astonishing thing I have found was the absolute lack of education. People said, "Don't go to this crowd to talk to them, they ought to understand. They are an intelligent body. They can read." Perhaps they do, but people do not always read intelligently nor understandingly. And when I would go out to my Red Cross meetings, and I spoke one thousand hours from May 1, 1918, to December 23, 1918, starting in early in the morning, sometimes giving as high as eight addresses in a day, I have found the people were more than willing to work, but they wanted to know why. They wanted to know why the supplies were needed. Why they were asked to do so much, they wished to know.

I came back from New York last fall with a nurse who had been through that hell of Chateau Thierry and she told me how our boys came back seven hundred an hour, broken in body, torn almost to shreds. Some of them didn't live to get to the first dressing room after they were brought back. Those were American boys. They weren't foreign boys, because they belonged to our First Division and the Sixth Brigade of Marines who went in 8000 strong, and 2000 came back.[27]

After I could take those messages to our women, then they understood why it was so necessary to go on with the work, and it is just as necessary now in communities to build up your communities, and go on with your community work, because you must live with those people, and be with one another all the time.

It is alright to send your money away some place else, but you need a great deal of it right here at home, because the taxpayers after all are the ones that must pay the bills, the court bills where crimes are committed and men and women are taken into Court and sent to penal institutions. Your taxes must pay the bills. You pay in the long run, and so it is absolutely up to every community to keep your community clean, to build up your home life and your community life to such a degree that you will have no criminals.

Our greatest crimes are committed by those who are feeble-minded. In the State of Illinois alone we have over 500,000 feeble-minded children, men and women. Every community has someone in that condition, and I am going to tell you and ask you to watch that person – see that that person does not marry and bring forth of its own kind.[28]

We hope in the next decade or two, since there are no alcoholic liquors to be sold after July first, that those who are feeble-minded caused by alcoholic beverages, will, of course, bear no more feeble-minded children – that that phase of the question will be taken care of, but there are other phases that must be taken care of.

About four years ago Chicago was startled to read in the papers of the murder of Mrs. Coppersmith and her little baby boy, John, two years old. Chief Schuttler sent two men over to my office and asked me if I would go out on the case, and I told them I would. With Captain O'Brien, the Chief of Detectives, and two men from the Chief's Office, two as we call, undercover men, I went out on the South Side. We investigated, asked questions and looked everywhere, and it all resolved itself into one boy, a feeble-minded youth, who was known in the neighborhood as a "goof." He had never harmed anybody. No one ever knew an unkind act that this boy had ever committed. He was just a harmless boy. He never had a chance. He was born of alcoholic and syphilitic parents. At the age of two he had to have a mastoid operation, and at the age of nineteen, when he was in the Court on trial for his life, he had a hole in back of his head almost as big as a dollar. The only thing that this boy could do was to work in a butcher shop, and what do you suppose they had him doing? They had him killing chickens. Well, when he went to deliver Mrs. Coppersmith's materials for her dinner that morning he attacked her. She resisted him, and he went to a drawer and he took out a butcher knife, and he found a hammer. He first hit her in the head with the hammer, and she hollered, and the next thing, of course, he took the knife and he slit her throat from ear to ear. That's the way he did with the chickens when they hollered – cut their throats. That's all he knew. Little John toddled in, two years of age, and seeing his mother lying on the floor, covered with blood, he started to cry. Well, the chickens cried, and he cut their throats, so he cut little John's throat.

The boy was arrested. They could not get a confession out of him. He would not confess. He didn't know anything. His mind was a blank. He didn't realize that he had done anything, and his sister came in and asked if I couldn't help her.

I sent Doctor Davis, a brother of Colonel A. B. Davis, who came back with the Thirty-Third Division from France the other day, and he, together with Clarence Dare [Clarence Darrow?] and myself, went over to the County building. He examined this boy, and at two o'clock that afternoon went back and had a full confession from Russell Petty of how he killed this woman and her child, and why. That boy was not to blame for that murder because the state was cognizant of that child's condition from the time he attended public schools at the age of six. During the trial every teacher that he had ever had came in and told the trouble that they had with him, how he could not learn anything, and how they put him in the backward classes, and he couldn't accomplish anything. Nothing was done with him at all, or about him. He just simply roamed the streets until this psychological moment when his brain went all together and Mr. Coppersmith gave his wife and baby because the State did not take care of that boy.

And what were the results of the trial? We pleaded "Guilty." There was nothing else we could do, and threw ourselves on the mercy of the judge. The boy was sent to Joliet for the remainder of his life, and the State Legislature immediately went into session, passed a bill to care for the feeble-minded of the State of Illinois, both children and grown-up people, and it took the murder of Mrs. Coppersmith and her son to make Illinois wake up to the care of her feeble-minded.[29]

That is your problem, because there isn't a city or a village or a hamlet in any county of Illinois, or any county in Ohio that hasn't its feeble-minded, and they propagate and propagate. Go out to your institutions and find out how many of you have and take stock, and when you have a right to vote on a proposition to care for them, vote "Yes" every time. That is one of our problems, and that is the problem that is staring America in the face today.

Let me speak to you further along those lines. Out at Fort Sheridan we have United States General Hospital No. 28. I go out there quite frequently. I am one of the few that are privileged to go in the psychopathic department. There we have any number of boys who have been shell-shocked, who couldn't answer a question that you would ask them to save their very lives. I saw one great, strapping, handsome fellow sitting by a window who hadn't spoken a word for ten months. They would take him out of bed and put him on the chair, and there he would sit looking down at the floor, never even raising his eyes unless an attendant would come to him and bring him something to eat, and take him out and bring him back and sit him down again. That is in Hospital No. 28, where we have hundreds of boys like that. Those boys would have been psychopathic sooner or later. It took the shock of the war to set them off, as we say now. It would have come later on in life.[30]

When our people in the United States learn to recognize mental illness, and treat it in the same as you do every other illness, when you demand that your insane be cared for, not as criminals, but as you would a dear one that you would send to the hospital and have the very best of medical care taken of him, then indeed are we going to live up to the American ideal of things.

Too often has a person been dragged into the Courts who is mentally ill and made a show of, asked questions, everybody comes in and testifies. What good is it? They don't know what they are talking about, and it certainly is humiliating to the family, and no good is accomplished.

Cook County has progressed more in the line of the care of her insane than any other county in the United States. We have a Lunacy Commission that listens to the stories of people who have to tell about the insane and they are not a part of it. No one except those immediately concerned are ever allowed in that court room, and after their story is heard and that of the nurse and the doctor under whom they have been in observation for ten days or two weeks, then, and then only, is the patient brought in. He is talked to by an alienist, the best that America [can] afford, and after the alienists have rendered their opinion and decision, and if it means an institution for that patient then that patient is put in a private car, constructed especially for them and sent to either Chicago Hospital, Elgin or Kankakee, the three hospitals for use in the northern part of the state. They are given the best care the medical men know how to give them. You cannot get through there, as a visitor. Our people are mentally sick and are not on parade, thank God, in Illinois. You can't go through as you would to a circus, and look them over and see what you think of them. We are shielding them from that, and it is the last few years only that we have had sense enough to do that. You wouldn't parade a sick person anywhere, so why parade your insane, mentally ill? But take care of them and guard them, and look after them, and restore them, if possible, to their status as citizens of this United States.

You know the war is over. We must remember that the boys who are coming back, the boys that were gassed, in the next few years are going to have a severe test. We are going to have more insane than the United States ever dreamed of, especially the boys that are gassed, because while the gas will eat up the lining of the lungs, or corrode it, it also permeates to the brain, and in a few years we are going to have a great many of our soldier boys mentally ill. Those boys must be cared for, and up to now there is not one place in the whole United States where Uncle Sam has a government hospital for the insane. They were talking about apportioning them among the States, among the small hospitals in the states, that is, insane hospitals. And let's not allow it. Let us have Uncle Sam build, if necessary, in every state, or he may zone the states, and have a hospital for those boys, because it is coming just as sure as you are sitting in this tent today, and so be prepared for it.

My time is up. I can no longer take your time to talk about social services and reconstruction, but do go back to your communities with the thought of supervised amusement for your children, have swimming pools if you can by any manner, hook or crook, have moving pictures for your children, because the moving picture is perhaps the greatest educational thing in the world – keep out the other kind – they are too harmful, because what the eye sees and the ear hears, a child never forgets. Hold-up after hold-up have we had when we used to allow the moving pictures to be uncensored. We do not allow it in Chicago nor in the State of Illinois any more, and I hope you do not allow it in the state of Ohio. Have a place where your children may go and have their little parties, have a room for your Woman's Clubs and have all the women in town in it. Have it working in unity just like you did when you worked for the Red Cross, and instead of making bandages for the boys over on the other side, build citizens in your own community work with your own children. Have ideals and live up to them.

Teach your children what it means to be an American. Four years, since 1914, the thin line of Belgians, the British, the French and the Italians stood between the German hordes and America. Their battleships made it possible for us to send our own boys across the water, but God Almighty won this war, and the United States was the instrument he used. And so now let we citizens of America build to greater ideals and build better American citizens to keep on progressing because to progress means America.

...ADJOURNMENT...

Meeting of National Woman's Party[31]
Wednesday Afternoon, June 25, 1919

...The meeting opened at 2:30, Mr. Herbert Stanzell (sic) presiding...

HERBERT STANZELL:
We are favored with two speakers this afternoon – Miss Paul of the National Woman's Party, and Mrs. Virginia May Murray following her as Secretary of the National Travelers' Aid Society. I am very happy to introduce the chairman of the afternoon, Mrs. James Rector, member of the National Advisory Committee of the National Woman's Party.

MRS. JAMES RECTOR:[32]
Ladies and gentlemen, in this great Methodist Centenary you are bringing religious thought up to date. We feel that we should like to bring suffrage up to date, and in bringing it up to date we have to bring the thing so far as the very threshold of the liberation of the women from a political slavery. Susan B. Anthony commenced her campaign many years ago. We have added state by state until we come to this time – six years ago – when Oregon, Kansas, and Arizona came in together. That factor changed the political history of women. Up to that time it was felt that we did not have enough votes for women to cast to influence the political situation at Washington. When those three states were added four million women voters came in to cast their vote. At that time Alice Paul, whom I am about to introduce, saw this political change and immediately started to work to get the thing nationalized. She wanted a federal amendment. Of course, you know that as long as women were citizens of and voters of a state that was as far as it went. We might keep on being citizens and voters of a state, but still we would be no better off, for there is an amendment in our constitution denying women the right to vote. We should not be – you might say – United States citizens until that was abolished.

Miss Paul saw that with these four million women voters we had a reserve force which we could use for the entering wedge. That meant that the suffrage states controlled a fifth of the Senate, a seventh of the House and a sixth of the Electoral College. She immediately took advantage of that fact and started her campaign. Feeling that she could not educate the women of the country or all those four million women to an understanding of their political power, feeling that she could not educate the entire population of the United States to an understanding of what was going on in Congress, she felt this was one little group of five hundred thirty-one then that she could concentrate on – she and her organization – and she did this: She said, "There are two political parties. One party is dominant, the party in control. Therefore the dominant party is absolutely responsible for the measures that are passed under the administration. They are also responsible for the measures that they failed to pass under that administration."

The next thing was to gather these four million women voters so that they would have one plank in their platform, and that plank was suffrage. They would hold that vote as a holy vote, casting it only for suffrage. Any man or any group of men who opposed suffrage would not receive their vote. At that time – six years ago – there were some very wonderful and remarkable things going on in Congress of which we were, most of us, ignorant. We didn't know – those of us from the suffrage states – that the very men that we had put in power, that we had sent to Congress and to the Senate – we didn't know that they were going there and casting their vote against suffrage.

That was something that Miss Paul went out into the West for and among the suffrage states, and her organization showed them up. She showed that those women are putting in men who went back and caucused against them, and their vote had to count against suffrage. That was a part of the campaigning that was necessary to be done to win what we have today.

Of course, at the head of this body of responsible men, which has happened to be the Democratic Party ever since we have been working this way, was the President. The task has been to educate the President from absolutely not only a negative, but an anti side, to the place of urging this legislation which you know he has done. At first we went to him with deputations. Women of the country said, "Why bother the poor man? He is so busy and so overrun with everything, we can wait," and they didn't realize that that meant four million women waiting and waiting for their political liberty. They didn't realize that four million women didn't count as sufficiently important, or their numbers sufficiently important, to impress five hundred and thirty-one little men of Congress.

So we continued our deputations, and an unheard of thing happened. The President said, "I have seen these three deputations. I don't believe I can see any more." At least, we think he said that, and when the big deputation from New York of important women came down they called on the president to gain an admittance to get an appointment, and they waited and they waited, and an appointment came.

Finally, Miss Paul telephoned, "We have waited and waited for the appointment from President Wilson. Will you kindly inform him we are on our way to the White House." That was unheard of at that time. That got us publicity all over the country, and then we were bothering the President again. Some of us even felt that we mustn't bother the Congressmen, and I don't wonder, because Congress was so busy passing Porkhouse Bills that it couldn't take time to free four millions of waiting women.

Then began our timidity, and our women's nature evidently showed forth, and we waited and we waited. Alice Paul tried to convince some of the suffrage leaders six years ago that this national campaign must be launched immediately. At that time they were so used to the old state dog trot that when an airplane came across the sky they couldn't believe it to be so, and they said to her, "You can go ahead with your committee work, but we can't allow any funds. You will have to raise them all yourself."

Alice Paul did. She raised $30,000 immediately and with that she flamed forth in the biggest suffrage demonstration that has ever been known in history. That was the famous parade and pageant that was staged in Washington on the eve of President Wilson's inauguration. At the head of that parade road a new banner – an absolutely new banner it was – "We Demand the Enfranchisement of Women of the United States."[33]

You know that was very new. For three years later women were saying to me, "I don't like that word 'demand.' I think you ought to ask for things, but I don't like that word 'demand.'"

You see, back of that idea was this – that most women believe that the right way to get anything was to coax and wheedle, and when we couldn't do it, and when we couldn't be polite, we had to go back home and wait. You see, that also was the idea that men were gods, and had to be propitiated.

Alice Paul came into the field and she said that women were goddesses, and they might demand of their gods what is their right to ask. I think that released women from a certain type of mental bondage which came along with suffrage. In that demand we saw at once, I think, that we had the power. You know you can't demand anything if you haven't got a reserve force back to say, "I want that thing. I demand it. It is my right. I have such and such a thing to back me up."

It was Alice Paul's work to get out among those four million voters, those women voters, and tell them what power they had – that they had the power to back up a demand, and it was her business to educate these five hundred thirty-one men to realize that the women could use that power.

After many, many deputations to President Wilson the war came on, and still suffrage was far from us. President Wilson said, "Well, ladies, the tariff and the currency have to be decided first, and I cannot give your cause any consideration this session of Congress. You must wait." Well, pretty soon the tariff was out of the way and the currency was out of the way, but we were still waiting. We had to think up something new to influence President Wilson to again change his mind. Then came a campaign in the western states against those men who went back to Congress from the suffrage states and voted against us. I think there were some forty-nine campaigns against it, and only nineteen were returned.

Men began to wake up and to find that women were on to them a little bit, and that they would have to be very wary of what they did about the suffrage issue after this, and that it was not longer expedient for them to deny suffrage altogether. Then came the war, and at that time something almost happened to suffrage that happened to suffrage in the Civil War.

Women were about to step aside and go over into war work and wait until the war was won before urging their cause. They did that in the Civil War. They worked like veterans, and when it was over their promises were unfulfilled. Suffrage almost lost in that war. It had to be kept alive. All of you, I know, are going to recall that suffrage during the war period had been kept on the front pages of the papers. You have seen pickets, you have seen banners, you have seen speeches burned, but we have kept right on the front pages of the papers, and we haven't gone off for one instant, and suffrage is now with us.

The pavements in Washington were very cold and we warmed them up with hot bricks. The air was very cold and we warmed it up with some very hot banners. And after a while there was left a very cold corpse in Washington, left behind while some went abroad, and that corpse was the corpse of unredeemed promises. We burned that to ashes – not for the sake of the ashes, but because it gave quite a good bit of heat.

I always say this – that there are several methods of heating. There is the direct and the direct indirect, and there is the indirect, and you know that the direct method is cheapest to maintain. It gives the most heat, and the cost to install is the least. The direct indirect and the indirect are both expensive to install and to maintain.

Alice Paul moved her little boiler plant right up to the White House, and she turned on direct heat and the bricks were warmed and the air was warmed, and the pages of the newspapers were hot, and now we have suffrage at our doors. There is still work to be done. I know this audience comes from many states. If you belong to a state that is not ratified, you must go back to that state, start a fuss, and see to it that the men who are responsible get into action.

If you have got a legislature that tells you they are not going to meet until next year, tell them to get busy. We are all fighting for you. Get busy. We want you in an extra session right now to ratify. Now is the time. We don't want it next year. We want to get into this 1920 election, and we must have it within three months, and if you have any money pour it into the coffers of your suffrage organization so that they can have a freer hand to get together and put pressure on these men to get publicity to work, and get this thing ratified. We must have it within three months.

It is not only cruel and utterly useless to wait longer than that, but it is unnecessary. Our legislatures are for the people, and women are people, and they are certainly enough in four millions to get that done – don't you think? I thank you. Miss Paul will now speak to you of the work that has been done in Washington direct.

ALICE PAUL:[34]

We are glad to have the opportunity of appealing to you men and women who come from so many different states to help us in carrying this suffrage campaign thru to its final conclusion. The movement for suffrage, for women, for the opportunity for women to direct their own lives is just what our great foreign war was fought about – for the right of people to direct their own lives. This movement has been going on in America before the Civil War – long before the negroes were enfranchised. All these years, and years and years women and men have worked that women might be politically free. And now today we have almost reached the conclusion of this fight.

We began our work in Washington just six years ago. After six years of lobbying of Congressmen, six years of going to prison, six years of every kind of effort, the suffrage amendment has at last been passed by both Houses of Congress and has come to the various states to be ratified. Our measure must now receive a majority vote in legislatures of thirty-six different states. Now, you men and women who come from those states, you can help in seeing that this long struggle of over seventy years is brought to a conclusion before this summer comes to an end. We at Washington have done everything that we knew how to do. We have finally succeeded in our work. There is nothing more that we can do at the national capitol. What you can do is to see that whatever state you come from is the next state to endorse this action taken by Congress. You can see that your state legislature supports this position of President Wilson, supports the position of the National Democratic Party, supports the position of the National Republican Party, and without any further waste of time sets the seal of the approval of your particular state upon this measure. Ohio has done this. Pennsylvania did this yesterday. Seven states have taken this action, and twenty-nine states more must take it.

Now, the part that remains is very easy compared with what has gone before. It is this little part of finishing up this task and seeing that all American women are politically free just as English women are and German women are, as women in Australia, in Canada, New Zealand, in Norway, in every part of the globe excepting in America, are free. Now, it is that task that we turn over to the women of every state, and we turn over to you as representatives who come from these different states to do the very utmost that you can to help in this campaign. (Applause)

MRS. JAMES RECTOR:

Mrs. Winters, the state chairman of the National Woman's Party, has a little announcement to make to you.

MRS. WINTER:

I would like to know if any people in the audience would like to become members of the National Woman's Party. I would be so glad to take your names and your addresses. We do want new members.

...ADJOURNMENT...

Minute Men Day Program
Saturday Morning, July 5, 1919

The meeting convened at 12 o'clock Dr. Christian F. Reisner presiding.

> ...Several musical selections were rendered by the Great Lakes Band...
> ...Singing of "Joy to the World"...
> ...Singing of "Onward Christian Soldiers"...
> ...Singing of "Over There"...

CHRISTIAN F. REISNER:[35]
I want to introduce a splendid man who is the head of the Methodist Minute Men of the South Church who also wears the same badge we do, please God, and we hope before many weeks there will be no South Church or no North Church but just one Methodist Church. (Applause) I want to clasp hands with Mr. Clark, the head of the Methodist Minute Men of the South Church. (Applause)

ELMER T. CLARK:[36]
I am glad of this opportunity to greet the Methodist Minute Men of the nation. I am not sure that I can make myself heard in this great building, but I am glad of this opportunity to greet, in the name of the Minute Men of the Southern Methodist Church, the Methodist Men of the nation. (Applause)

In the Southern part of the United States the Methodist Minute Men aroused the church as no man ever dreamed that it could be aroused before, and we believe that to them is due a large part of the credit for the tremendous enthusiasm with which the Centenary Movement went over the top. We hope to make our organization permanent for the glory of God and the progress of his Kingdom in the world. (Applause)

CHRISTIAN F. REISNER:
Now, if you please, let every regularly accredited Minute Man in the house stand up.
> ...Audience complied with his request...
> ...Now I want all the Minute Men to go through all the yells...
> ...At this point the Minute Men in the audience gave their series of yells, consisting of:

> A-M-E-N
> PRAISE THE LORD
> OLD JOHN WESLEY
> MINUTE MEN, MINUTE MEN, MINUTE MEN.

I am sure we want a message from the Chairman of the Centenary Commission of the South Church, Doctor Pinson. (Applause)

DOCTOR PINSON:[37]

I am not a Minute Man. Those who hear me, say I am about a Forty Minute Man. I don't want to be "skinned alive." If I did I don't think that there could be a better day than this to take the hide off. (Laughter) I am glad to say that the Minute Men of our section not only did great things when they go into it, but they got it on the ground floor and got it about a hundred percent strong and stayed right in to the end of the whole campaign. (Applause) Thank God not only for what these Minute Men North, South, East and West have already done but for the discovery of that mighty power that they are capable of wielding in the future. (Applause)

...Singing of "Jesus Lover of My Soul" to the tune of "Silver Threads Among the Gold"...

CHRISTIAN F. REISNER:

I think it is only fair for you to know a few of the men who really put the Minute Men Movement over the top. Some of these laymen gave practically all their time. I am going to introduce my area chairman and then ask Mr. Clark to introduce three of his district chairmen. We will not try our district chairmen for we have too many of them. First I will introduce Arthur Stock of Detroit. (Applause) The next is Fred Long who moves people out of St. Louis. He is a storage man but I tell you he made folks go when it came to Minute Men business. (Applause)

FRED LONG:

Gee, but I would like to make a speech, but Reisner won't let me. (Applause)

CHRISTIAN F. REISNER:

The next is Nordeman. He comes from a suburb of Columbus [Ohio], Chicago.

MR. NORDEMAN:

Of which New York is a suburb. Greetings from Chicago. (Applause)

CHRISTIAN F. REISNER:

The next fellow has been working for a dollar a year. It is all he can earn. He is the Secretary of the Government Praying Commission. He lives in a suburb of Chicago and is the Area Chairman, Watson Moore of New York.

WATSON MOORE:

We Minute Men believe in the power of prayer. (Applause) Nothing else can save New York, and not even Chicago. (Applause)

CHRISTIAN F. REISNER:

The next is a fellow who died many years ago but he came to life when the Minute [Men] aroused him and he showed the kind of stuff there is in him, and I am going to ask the Boston bunch of Minute Men over there, the only crowd that came in a special car, to stand. (Applause) Mr. Dorchester, the Area Chairman of Boston.

MR. DORCHESTER:
Methodist Minute Men I bring you greetings from Bunker Hill. I want our boys to stand up and give you our yell.
...The Boston delegation of Minute Men gave their yell...

CHRISTIAN F. REISNER:
We have a lot more Area Chairmen but I want to present, before I present Mr. Clark, another fellow who didn't do anything but sleep on Pullman cars, what time he wasn't talking, the National Secretary, Mr. Parker. (Applause)

MR. PARKER:
I think we want to say to you gentlemen that our friends over the seas who have just returned have told me that those places there in the mountains and the valleys that were cursed with the poison shells are now blooming with the flowers of blue and of scarlet and of gold. God, through nature, has healed those cuts by the beautiful flowers and it is part of our work as Minute Men through the gospel of the Bloody Christ to scatter over this world the flower of the gospel of God and make the desert blossom as the rose. Thank God we can do it. (Applause)

CHRISTIAN F. REISNER:
There is a little town near Washington that I came pretty near forgetting. It is so beautiful; they are so friendly; it is so close to the south. It is proper to introduce the gentleman from this town before I introduce Clark. His name is Price. He is a lawyer. You wouldn't believe it to look at him, and he is the Area Chairman of Baltimore.

MR. PRICE:
Mr. Chairman, Ladies and Gentlemen (Laughter) – report had come to me that some ladies were sitting over there on the other side of the house. (Applause) I am from the Washington Area. I believe in the Minute Men, so much so that I bought an official Minute Man car this spring – the Lexington – the same as Dr. Reisner drives. (Applause)

CHRISTIAN F. REISNER:
I don't know whether they gave him his car or not. He advertised it; I didn't, but it is owned by Methodist Minute Men, and one of the owners said that he gave 35 times as much to the Centenary as he did to missions because he got to talking and when he opened his mouth he put his foot in it. (Applause)
Now Mr. Clark will introduce three of his district Chairman.

ELMER T. CLARK:

I want to present to you first one of our Minute Men Chairmen who made a record of 100% in Minute Men organization and in the Centenary Drive, Mr. J. H. Dickey of Kentucky.

J. H. DICKEY:

The great Baptist laymen of Louisville, Kentucky asked the Presiding Elder, Dr. Thompson of that district, what was the greatest factor in putting the Centenary across? Dr. Thompson said it was the Minute Men of the Southern and the Northern Methodist Churches. Men I congratulate you for doing the greatest thing that has been done by the laymen in the United States of America. (Applause)

ELMER T. CLARK:

We have another 100% Chairman in this audience. I am glad to introduce to you now Mr. C. M. Ledbetter of Georgia.

C. M. LEDBETTER:

The Minute Men helped to put into the church some real, first-class business methods. Now there is another drive on Minute Men and laymen must join by prayer and consecration and put religion into business until we can convince the world that business and the social life and even politics can be run according to the Ten Commandments and the Sermon on the Mount. (Applause)

ELMER T. CLARK:

Mr. H. Griffin, one of our Chairmen from the State of Arkansas.

H. GRIFFIN:

I greet you from Arkansas, the coming state of the Union, (Applause) where Minute Men really work and on the first day of the drive several districts went over the top. Two Conferences of Arkansas went over the top by a large majority, raising over two and a half millions. (Applause)

ELMER T. CLARK:

We have a man here from the State of Tennessee. He said that he did not want to be presented and would not make any speech, but on account of the record which the Minute Men made in the State of Tennessee I want you to look into his face. The Minute Men of Tennessee made a record of 97% in organization and this man that I want to present to you is Mr. Ben Hickens, one of our Chairmen in Tennessee.

BEN HICKENS:

I am glad to represent the volunteer state, and we had volunteers for Minute Men and our Minute Men are now volunteering to continue this glad work and we believe we have a bigger drive on than the one we had in the Centenary and that is for our revival. (Applause)

CHRISTIAN F. REISNER:
What is the matter with the Southern Church?

AUDIENCE:
They're all right!

CHRISTIAN F. REISNER:
If you will give close attention I want to present to you a man who in my judgment – I am speaking my personal convictions – is one of the men who is doing things for the Kingdom of God in a perfectly matchless way, one of the General Secretaries of our Board who has been an advisor on our Council. I am sure you will be glad to hear him and you can hear when he stands here, Dr. Edgar Blake.

EDGAR BLAKE:[38]
Mr. Chairman and Gentlemen of the Minute Men Movement: I very greatly appreciate this very generous introduction of my friend Dr. Reisner. My regret, however, is that it is not entirely in accord with all the facts in the case. It reminds me of a good maiden sister who was congratulated on her approaching marriage by a friend and the maiden sister said, "I regret exceedingly that it is not true, but thank God for the rumor." (Applause)

Mr. Chairman, as I was looking out of my window this morning upon your wonderful parade downtown there came rolling up to my ears from the street below something like this, "One, two, three, four, five, if he talks any longer, hit him, kill him, skin him alive." Mr. Chairman, I do not know whether I quite got all the words but the sentiment, I think, I absorbed. I do not intend to be skinned at this time and therefore I shall confine myself to the Minute Men limitations. Indeed I think it was Dr. Mott who said that if a man can not strike oil in five minutes he ought to stop boring. (Applause) And I commend that, Mr. Chairman, as an unusually fitting sentiment for the Minute Men Movement. I would like at this time to make this statement as an official of the Centenary Movement and say that in the judgment of many of us the most significant find of this Centenary Movement was the Minute Men and that no single factor in this great movement has contributed quite so much to the success of it as has that movement which is represented here this morning.

I would like also to make this further statement, if I may, and I do it very gladly. As an official of this movement I would like, Mr. Chairman and Gentlemen, to express the admiration, the appreciation and the gratitude of the Centenary Organization to the man whose vision and whose genius has made possible the discovery and utilization and the achievements of this great Minute Men Movement, namely Dr. Christian Reisner. (Applause)

...Three cheers were given for Dr. Reisner...

CHRISTIAN F. REISNER:

The biggest privilege that ever came to any man was to have the joy of working with the finest bunch of fellows on this earth, the Minute Men. (Applause) I want to say further that it has been a great joy to know the leaders of Methodism as they have come into contact with this movement during the drive for the Centenary. There is one man who has stood out in patience and calmness and actually said to me once in awhile, "Go ahead." That means something you know, to turn some folks loose. I am sure we want to stand and give the Minute Men's salute. Then after we have given the Salute we will remain standing as I introduce to you the man who has cooperated with everybody and whom Dr. Blake so splendidly helped from the first of January on, the man in whose heart was born this movement and who has carried it like a child because he walked with God, S. Earl Taylor.

...Audience stood and gave Minute Man Salute...

S. EARL TAYLOR:[39]

I find myself using a word that I have not been accustomed to use, and I am using it a good deal these days. That word is 'Amazing." I use the word in connection with the Pageant. It is an amazing thing. I use the word in connection with the parade last night. It was indeed an amazing thing. (Applause) And I have no other word to use to describe my feelings as I consider this Minute Men Movement than the word "Amazing." (Applause) That in so short a time with so little chance for preparations a hundred thousand men should equip themselves and stand on the platform in the pulpits of our churches and acquit themselves like men, and across the nation sound the call to advance, has been to me amazing.

Now in the days of the Laymen's Missionary Movement some wag said that the only idea he saw about these uprisings of laymen was that they sat down so quickly. But I am hoping Mr. Chairman, that this great Minute Men's Movement will not sit down now that the drive is over. (Applause) Having discovered our strength as laymen I hope we will gird our loins and perpetuate the organization in some great powerful way and that we will now go forward into this new century, strongly emphasizing the notes we have been pressing of prayer and stewardship and a forward move by the church and with it all and above it all in this coming year sound the note of evangelism that we may bring men and women to Jesus Christ. (Applause)

The great outcome of the Centenary Movement and of the Minute Men Movement ought to be the greatest world-wide revival the church has ever seen. (Applause) And I am praying that these men here may go back with the fires burning in their hearts and upon their lips. I congratulate all who have had part in this movement, but I can only say, in behalf of the Centenary Movement, God bless you. (Applause)

CHRISTIAN F. REISNER:

We are sending the Boston Minute Men out after Secretary Daniels. They will bring him in in a few minutes. (Applause)

I want every man in this house who began tithing within twelve months, either new or renewed his tithing to stand.

...Great numbers of men stood and received liberal applause...

Dr. Blake, who is to carry a big burden in the Centenary for the next few months, Dr. Taylor who also will carry a burden, I want them to hear our pledge that every one of us here who will promise, by God's help to go out and win one or more souls to Jesus Christ – I want you to get on your feet.

...Practically all the audience stood up...

I am going to ask Dr. Taylor and Dr. Blake to lead us in a word of prayer.

DR. BLAKE:

Almighty God, Thou hast used thy servants in a marvelous way in the years that have gone by, Thou who hast been using thy laymen in the most wonderful fashion in these recent days, lead us now, we pray Thee, that after the movement on in these recent times there may come that which shall powerfully extend the kingdom of our Christ and Thy son throughout the earth. We ask it in the name of Jesus Christ our Lord. Amen.

CHRISTIAN F. REISNER:

Our loving heavenly Father, we do thank Thee for the achievement of the Centenary period. We thank Thee for the way in which men and women have given themselves to Thee unstintedly. We thank Thee, O God, for the great financial outpouring that has caused our hearts to rejoice. We thank Thee for the increasing volume of prayer. We thank Thee for the men and women who have learned the higher, deeper lessons of stewardship. We thank Thee especially for that consecration of life whereby our sons and our daughters, our young men and young women have given themselves to Thee and now, O God, help us to see, as David Livingstone saw years ago, that the end of the exploration is but the beginning of the enterprise, and help us now this day to reconsecrate ourselves to Thee and O God wilt Thou send thy fire down upon the church and upon this great company of laymen and the men they represent and wilt Thou use us mightily in the coming days to thy glory, and then O Lord when Thou dost give success wilt Thou give humility? May we not think we have done anything because Thou hast used us but may we see that we are instruments in thy hands, and in the last great day, O God, may we gather around the Throne, rejoicing, bearing our sheaves with us, because we have decided without reservation to live for Thee and to die for Thee, and let us in the end and in this day also give Thee all the praise through Jesus Christ our Lord. Amen.

CHRISTIAN F. REISNER:

We have had all kinds of big guns. Today we want to give you just a vision of a few of the great men in both churches. I want to present to you a tremendous fighter for the glory of God who is always a big gun, Bishop James Cannon, Jr. of the Methodist Episcopal Church South.

JAMES CANNON, JR.:[40]

I am always glad to serve in any capacity for the church, and I suppose that it is an entirely proper thing to serve as a stop gap and a filler-in at times, and I am glad to make that contribution at this present moment. I want to call your attention to one thing that is going on on the ground. We are holding an Evangelistic Service at the big tent every night. Bob Jones is doing the preaching and if you want some spiritual quickening and refreshment and emphatic declarations of the old truths and of how Minute Men can call sinners to repentance, come around and worship with us at the big tent every night at eight o'clock. It is my lot as an officer of the church to appoint men. Well, I started to say serve, yes, to lead to serve. One of the great problems that confronts the appointing power of our church is not simply what men we have to appoint but when we send a man to an appointment who will be there to hold up his hand, and "We will at your right and at your left, fully behind you, carry on the Master's work?"

I am sure every Bishop of both churches rejoices to believe that the Centenary Movement has developed in the laymen this spirit of serving and that we will all feel greatly encouraged when we send our ministers to the charges, to realize that there is a stronger cooperating force in those charges than there has ever been before. (Applause)

CHRISTIAN F. REISNER:

I want to introduce all our Area Chairmen and one of the men who gave nine-tenths of his time and out of his not great riches, but out of his real treasure, he gave a large gift to the Centenary. Our Buffalo Area went over the top first. I am sure you want just to see and hear a word from Francis Baldwin, the Area Chairman of Buffalo.

FRANCIS BALDWIN:[41]

The Centenary Movement got to my heart when it was launched at Niagara Falls. I was there. It has grown with the days as they have come and gone. I have been greatly interested in all its work. We have gone through one stage. We have put up the money. The Minute Men whom I had the privilege of leading in the Buffalo Area, as part of this great Army, have done magnificent work, but there is more to do. There is the consecration for life service; there is the putting of our church in the position to do the work that God wants it to do and the biggest helping power in the earth, and we Minute Men can do it if we keep our feet on the ground and our hearts right and our heads in the air and use the thinking capacity that we have.

I know that the Methodist Church, as one branch of the great Christian Army of the world, is a mighty power to save the United States and then to save the world. The Minute Men must do their work. (Applause)

...At this point the hymn, "Faith of Our Fathers" was sung...

...Secretary Daniels entered the Coliseum, escorted by the Boston Minute Men...

CHRISTIAN F. REISNER:
Now let us give the Secretary the Minute Men Salute.
...The Minute Men stood and gave their yell...

>Amen! Praise the Lord! Old John Wesley!
>Minute Men, Minute Men,
>One, two, three, four, five,
>If he talks longer – longer than that
>Shoot him – kill him – skin him alive!

Mr. Secretary, we have tried to give you today that which has not been given to any man on the ground; namely, a group of men – only these at least two-thirds are Minute Men. In our church they spoke to forty-three million people. The Minute Men of the two churches certainly made it possible to have subscribed at this minute nearly $170,000,000. (Applause)

We Methodists do not know any South Church or North Church. (Applause) We remember the old colored man who said he was a member of the Methodist Episcopal Church of God, and his wife was a member of the Methodist Episcopal Church South of God. (Applause) We know Secretary Daniels to be one great big magnificent Christian statesman, and a Methodist. (Applause) On this moment we remember that he was one of the first national officers to kick booze out of the front and back bar. (Applause) And thus, in my judgment, Secretary Josephus Daniels was called to the Kingdom for such a time as this, and did more to help bring in national prohibition than any other man I now know. (Applause)

He is an American – fine, strong, clean, capable – because he is a disciple of Jesus Christ and a member of the organized body of Christ on earth. No man could better address this country on the program the Minute Men have dedicated themselves to – that of winning a million souls to Christ – than our good Secretary Josephus Daniels. (Applause)

JOSEPHUS DANIELS:[42]
Minute Men of this epoch-making day, ladies and gentlemen, it is most fitting that this Centenary of Methodism should be held in the capitol of this great state of the central West, which in days of stress gave to this republic two presidents belonging to the Methodist Church, both of whom illustrated by their lives and their expressions the spirit of the great faith to which we belong.

After the great Civil War when there were men North and South who retained something of bitterness in their hearts, the first voice in America that carried from the Gulf to the Lakes was the immortal expression of General Grant: "Let us have peace." (Applause) And when our other great martyred president, with the love in his heart which always dominated him for every part of this republic, advocated that brave men who had died fighting courageously should be alike honored all over the republic, he preached the gospel of love which did more to unite this republic than anything except the experiences of this great war. And so we gather in a commonwealth in which the early settlers heard the Methodist hymns which were one of the greatest foundation stones upon which this commonwealth is erected. Their faith and their zeal have made largely the robust character of a commonwealth whose pure Americanism is a hundred per cent.

Whatever may be said about our church, one thing is true of it, and must always be true if it fulfills its holy mission, and that is that Methodism is Christianity in earnest. (Applause) You have welcomed to this historic and inspiring gathering men of other creeds, but you have no welcome, and there is no welcome among Methodists anywhere for any man who lacks faith and zeal and enthusiasm. (Applause)

The Methodist Church was born in a college, and hastened to a factory. (Applause) That education and culture and knowledge in a church that does not attempt to lift up the life of the humblest toiler is not the education that Christ approved. (Applause) We belong to a church that has a robust faith. We know in whom we have believed, and we are persuaded that He had the power to keep what we have trusted to Him.

There is no ethics, no morality, no uplift for the world that does not find its life and power in the Lord Jesus Christ. (Applause) We belong to a church which in America, in point of numbers, leads all the Protestant Churches, and that is a matter of profound gratification, provided the church is at work. We believe in a church in which every man and every woman must be as consecrated and active as the minister in the pulpit. (Applause) We have seen in this Centenary movement that the spirit of laymen – at work for a defined object – has born large fruit, and we recall in the early days of our church when the ministers had no pulpit and preached on the streets and in the lanes.

Not only did the ministers preach, but the laymen of the church held their classes, and felt called to preach in lay fashion the eternal gospel, and the success and glory of our church is that in its early days it recognized dependence upon men in the pew as well as men in the pulpit. Unfortunately for us, in other days the laymen of the church did not fully understand what the word "laymen" meant. They thought a layman was a man who ought to lay down; (Applause and Laughter) and let the preacher pull the wagon of salvation. And many of us illustrated that in our lives, and the ministers toiled and struggled while we threw a few nickels in the basket and said: "Parson, go to it!" (Laughter)

If this Centenary movement had not raised a dollar, if it had not brought the inspiration and outlook and hope to the church, the fact that it has caused laymen asleep in the amen corner to wake up was worth all the effort. (Applause)

In the early days, I say, it was the laymen who were a mighty power, and today in this presence of Minute Men, who wisely chose a name that is stimulative of patriotism and religion – for, brethren, we have learned that patriotism and religion are one and inseparable now and forever – when I speak of laymen and our work in the church, I do not refer only to men, because, confidentially, brethren, there are very few of us who ever did anything worth while that the laywomen didn't inspire and lead us in it. (Applause)

I think that the character in fiction which is the most beautiful ever portrayed is George Elliott's (sic) picture which he has drawn of Dinah Morris, the Methodist preacher, whose beautiful character made her a living evangelist, and when Methodists get ready to canonize saints I shall propose that we canonize Susan A. Wesley first of all; (Applause) because she was the inspiration of sermons and songs of her sons.[43]

Only three days ago the whole nation – more than the whole nation, the progressive men and women of all the world – bowed their heads when the news flashed over the wires that Dr. Anna Shaw was dead – a great woman, who like a warrior died as she saw victory coming to her life purpose. (Applause) She was bred and educated and given the impulse of her life in the Methodist Church, and before she entered upon the great reform to which she gave her life was a minister in the Protestant Methodist Church (sic). (Applause)

If I were asked to say what were the greatest and most lasting achievements of Methodism, I would not say our organized church, powerful as it is, mighty and militant – I would say rather that Methodism had not only given the world a great and powerful revival agency, but it had touched every church in Christendom with its blessing. (Applause)

All the men and women whose lives were touched and whose souls were awakened by the preaching of Wesley and Whitefield, and those who came after – if they were in our church the number would be ten-fold those we now have in our membership, (Applause) and I, for one, rejoice that this great church to which we belong has not only carried the light that never was on sea or land to those within its communion, but it has carried it to men in other communions and brought in men who had no creed.

One of the most illuminating books I ever read was Edward Eggleston's – "The Circuit Rider." If any young Methodist here has never read it, I advise him to buy it.[44] It is the best picture of pioneer Methodism in this community, and Illinois and the central West ever written. You recall – those of you who read it – what the Irish schoolmaster said about the Methodist. He said, "These Methodists are narrow people." But I have observed that a narrow stream runs strong.

Taking to ourselves virtues that are common to all the churches, we never had narrowness in the sense of illiberality and lack of brotherhood with all good men has never touched our church. It never can, but we remember that straight and narrow is the road that leads to everlasting life. (Applause) One of the dangers of our age is the latitudinarianism and a so-called breadth that lacks the strength and power of faith and effort and success. What we need – what the world needs – is that clear-cut and plain preaching of a gospel that makes men who profess faith in Christ love all the world, but to walk forward in the paths laid down in the Scriptures. (Applause)

This great church of ours – and you will observe that I say church and not churches (Applause) – should go forward ever in the light of that faith.

A few weeks ago I had the pleasure of being in Paris and talking to some of the great men who were writing the Covenant of Peace – the greatest document since Christ's Sermon on the Mount. (Applause) Mr. Lloyd George said that one of the things that troubled him most was that he had to devote his days and nights to studying the conditions and needs of countries that he didn't know existed, learning geography.

We have destroyed sectionalism in America. The great organization, political and social, doesn't know any Mason and Dixon's Line. Thank God, it has gone. (Applause) And yet there are lineations (sic) in this great Christian church of ours – an organization divided on sectional lines. I agree with you, doctor, I do not want to belong to any Methodist Church North of God or South of God, or East of God, or West of God. (Applause) There is no geography in the Kingdom of Heaven. (Applause)

I met this morning a distinguished bishop, a strong colored man, minister from Liberia, who preached the same doctrine we believe, and Methodism everywhere must unite and hold up their hands of their faith in every land, every clime. (Applause)

For nearly four years – at least for more than three years – the allied armies in Europe fought with courage but without success. The British Army was commanded by a great British general – hard headed and hard fisted Scotchman – that great man, Marshal Haig. (Applause) The French army with splendid dash and spirit fought against odds and held to it and said: "They shall not pass!" under the direction of the great French general, that masterful and quiet man, General Foch. (Applause) The American army was growing larger all the time, fought under our splendid and brave general – General Pershing, (Applause) and yet there was lost motion; there was division of council; there was lack of unity.

Not many days after America entered this war the great man, now on the sea, who is our President, (Prolonged Applause) and that great man in Britain, the little Welsh lawyer, Lloyd George, (Applause) proposed and insisted and urged that there could be no proper handling of the allied forces until they had unified command. (Applause) When that command came the allied forces, with that masterful Frenchman in command, marched on to victory. (Applause)

What is the lesson to us? We have a Methodist Church North, and a Methodist Church South, and a Protestant Methodist Church, and a Wesleyan Methodist Church, and I don't know how many more – all of them believing the same doctrine, preaching the same gospel, advocating the same things, and one is marching under General Haig, and one under General Pershing, and one under General Foch, and they lack unified, strong leadership. Out of this Centenary we shall not come with pride and glory and living up to our opportunity if we content ourselves with raising one hundred and fifty or one hundred and sixty million dollars.

Why, you can waste that much money in division. What we want, what we must have, what must be the goal is that Methodism in America shall be united and inseparable. (Applause) It has been the claim, it has been the record of the Methodist Churches – I used the word "Churches" in the past tense, I refuse to use it in the present tense, I know nobody can use it in the future tense – we have had the record and claim enunciated by our bishops and other leaders that the Methodist Church is a prohibition church. (Applause)

The millions of men in our country and over the seas who have battled against the evil of intemperance have always known that among the Methodists there was a militant fight that could never end until the saloon evil was put out of business. (Applause) Working hand in hand with men of other faiths and with men who did not belong to any church, but wished to end the evil, this Centenary movement is held at a time when forty-five out of forty-eight states have ratified the amendment to the Constitution that gives us prohibition. (Applause)

Those who believe in it have given the Methodist Church credit for advancing along the lines and going over the top, and those who have opposed it have declared that the agency which they feared most was the militant Methodists of America and with its inclusion in the Constitution, which makes it as much a permanent part of the national government as any clause in the Constitution, we are resolved that that amendment and the laws behind it shall be enforced to the limit. (Applause)

I was born in the South during the Civil War, but neither I nor any of my ancestors ever believed in the doctrine of nullification.[45] (Applause) That evil has been banned, but Minute Men of the Methodist Church, Christian men of all churches, men and women of America, we must hear the call and mobilize to fight another evil – an evil that has been helped and strengthened by the drink evil. We must here and now mobilize the Christian, the moral forces of America for a war to the knife against immorality in America. (Applause)

Until this war began men in our church were ignorant, and many of them indifferent, to the fact that five per cent of all the men in America were infected with a moral disease, and when the summons came to war the shock, the humiliation came to all of us that of the men of military age, two and a half million of them were in the throes of a disease which destroyed their morals and made them unfit to fight.

It was a revelation to me. It was a saddening thought that in a Christian land – so-called – we had permitted and winked at and gone to sleep while red light districts destroyed the manhood of America. (Applause) The trumpet call to men of faith and men of courage is to swear on the holy altar that we will not cease our warfare against the social evil until no red light district can live in any town or hamlet in America. (Applause)

The army and the navy have been fighting this blot, and this menace, and this weakening of our manhood. Five years ago in the army one hundred eighty-five men out of every thousand were infected by this self-composed disease. The Secretary of War has fought it earnestly and sincerely until it now has been reduced to less than eighty-three in a thousand. (Applause) In the navy we have made quite as large a reduction, and yet in the very menace of the submarines, when every man was needed, enough days were lost by men in the navy who had been disqualified by their sin to man a great dread-naught. Upon the urgent recommendation of the Secretary of War and the Secretary of the Navy, army officers and navy officers and social workers have organized a social hygiene board and given the money to fight this evil, and I call upon you because I have the honor to be the chairman of that board – I call upon you and all good citizens, to unite in your communities on a doctrine of education. Gentlemen, we have been silent too long.[46] (Applause)

Men in the pulpit have sometimes hesitated to bring this question before their people. The President has hesitated to discuss it, and the cancer has grown. What we have been doing has been putting a little salve on it instead of the surgeon's knife. What we need are surgeons in America to cut out this cancer that is destroying our youth. (Applause)

I observe that I am violating the rules of the union. (Referring to the fact that he is talking overtime)

...Yells of "Go on!" from the audience...

And I fear that I have been speaking more than four minutes. One thing more – when he had no pulpit, when he had no church, when he had only a handful of followers, when mobs tried to break up his meetings, John Wesley proclaimed a slogan – "The world is my parish."[47] (Applause)

The church that is satisfied to have a good Sunday School, and take care of its own preacher and board and stop there has never seen the light; has never heard the voice: "Come over into Macedonia and help us." (Applause)

This Centenary movement is to bless our own people; bless them how not to help them to help themselves, but to bless them with a vision of the world's needs and of our duties to the world. (Applause) To the practical man, John Wesley showed no wisdom and no judgment when he left his handful of people in Great Britain and crossed the seas to preach the gospel to the Indians. (Applause)

It wasn't practical. It was not according to the old rule, but the soul of an Indian in Georgia was as great to John Wesley as the soul of the king of Great Britain. (Applause) "The world is my parish" must carry the gospel to the ends of the world. I was proud today to see on this ground that we had in India and China and the isles of the sea missionary efforts put to the fore-front. It must be carried forward until working with other Christian churches we must in our generation – not fifty years hence – we must see that the gospel is preached to every soul in all the world. (Applause)

"The world is my parish" – that is a Methodist doctrine, as enunciated by Wesley. It is the creed of all Christian churches in their large movements, because we are united so closely with other Christian churches that we march side by side, and step by step with them.

But the principle – "The world is my parish" – has leaped across seas and mountains. It no longer has application only to religion – religion the forerunner; religion to blaze the road; religion to open the way – but we have lived to see the day when statesmen of twenty-three nations have declared the doctrine – "A man liveth not unto himself, and no nation liveth unto itself."

We have come in an hour when our right and our duty to mankind demands that as we made sacrifice to win this war we shall make sacrifice to make peace permanent to all the world. (Applause) I read in the papers, as Mr. Dooley would say, that a certain distinguished United States Senator had said that if Jesus Christ would have come onto the earth and asked him to vote for the League of Nations he would not do it.

My reply to him is that nearly two thousand years ago Jesus Christ came into the world for the sole purpose of peace on earth, good-will toward men; (Applause) and his coming to save men must save nations, and now that the hour has come, the hour has struck, when twenty-three nations – all the allied forces in the world – are resolved to enter into a covenant, a solemn covenant, written by the wisest men of our generation, representing a billion eight hundred million people, who have drawn up this covenant to make war a sin and a crime and at last let this generation witness the fulfillment of the prophecy sung in Bethlehem, I am one of those who believe that the American people are going to end war and not permit the lads who gave their lives for world peace to die in vain. (Applause)

MR. MOORE:
This resolution is proposed:
"Resolved, that we, as a group of Christian men and women assembled at the Methodist Centenary Celebration, do most heartily and earnestly endorse the effort to secure the League of Nations, which shall serve to preserve the peace of the world."
...The resolution was seconded immediately...

CHRISTIAN F. REISNER:
It is moved and seconded that we adopt the resolution. All in favor say "Aye." It is unanimous. (Applause)

JAMES BALDWIN:
Mr. Chairman, I have a resolution written by an official and a member of the Methodist Episcopal Church, South, which I take pleasure in reading:
"Five thousand Methodist Minute Men send greetings to the magnificent convention, and express their conviction that unification is a vital necessity to the future of Methodism. We pray that the Divine wisdom may guide you in preparing an acceptable plan for elimination of all differences. Only as a unit can Methodism accomplish its mission in this mighty day for the world and its need."

CHRISTIAN F. REISNER:
This goes to the Unification Committee at Cleveland, which meets Monday and the resolution is that we urge them to arrange for absolute unification so we will have one Methodist Church.
...The resolution was seconded...
All in favor of it say "Aye"; those opposed say "No."
...The resolution was adopted...
Secretary Daniels tells me one of the oldest sailors in service is here, and he wants to say one word.

W.H. HARDY:

Mr. Chairman and Mr. Secretary of the Navy, this is the greatest privilege of my long and eventful life. I enlisted in the United States navy on the thirteenth day of July, 1852. I enlisted on the United States Frigate Mississippi, in command of Commodore Matthew C. Perry, who was the first to introduce prohibition in the United States navy. He did not believe in booze, and it was the worst offense that a man could commit to become intoxicated on board Commodore Perry's flagship, and I wish to say today that Secretary Daniels has carried out the work that Commodore Perry began, and God has blessed him in his efforts. (Applause)

...The audience sang the doxology...

CHRISTIAN F. REISNER:

O Lord our God, we thank Thee for this wonderful session, and we pledge Thee to live as becometh the sons of such a Father – God – to carry His gospel to all the world until Christ shall be King everywhere, and brotherhood shall bring peace on earth. Bless Secretary Daniels in his great work. Bless our President, and give him rare wisdom. Bless our Senate and our House that they may do God's business. Bless these laymen, O God, that they may put Thy words in flesh and help build the Kingdom everywhere for His sake who taught us to pray:

"Our Father who art in Heaven, hallowed be Thy name. Thy Kingdom come, Thy will be done, on earth as it is in Heaven. Give us this day our daily bread, and forgive us our trespasses as we forgive those who trespass against us, and lead us not into temptation, but deliver us from evil. For Thine is the kingdom and the power and the glory forever, Amen."

...ADJOURNMENT...

Minute Men Convention
Saturday Afternoon, July 5, 1919

...The meeting convened in the Big Tent at 2:30pm, Mr. H.W. Lewis acting as chairman..

...Singing by Colored Quintet...

H.W. LEWIS:

I would like to have half a dozen men lead us in short, heart-felt prayers – just a few words. Let us stand and bow our heads.

...Short prayers by several men...

...Selection by the Hadley Concert Company...

...Music by the Bennett College Quintet...

...Dr. Christian F. Reisner now presiding as permanent chairman...

CHRISTIAN F. REISNER:

I think we had better go ahead with our convention discussion, and if it is your good pleasure we will do that.

I have been traveling all over the United States. I have tried to find out from every section of the country whether they wanted the Minute Men movement continued. There was only one fellow that I have found that didn't want it continued. He had an article in the New York Advocate. He showed he was the first man that ever thought about the Minute Men idea.

Is there anybody here who doesn't believe that the Minute Men movement ought not to be continued? All those who believe it ought to be continued hold up your hands.

...It was unanimous...

Now then, why do you think it ought to be continued? Now no man can talk longer than half a minute. Give us a reason why you think it ought to be continued.

VOICE:

Because it utilizes the dormant forces in the Church.

VOICE:

I believe it is a spiritual blessing to the men.

VOICE:

I believe it should be continued because you have got an organization in the Church to take in and fill up when there is nothing else to do. (Laughter)

CHRISTIAN F. REISNER:

These Minute Men didn't all come from Ohio. They came here from Coast to Coast, and they mean business as sure as you are a foot high. We had a little meeting the other morning with only fifty men present and there were twenty-six states represented. Now when any man gets up after this, he must tell us his State and town.

BOSTON, MA:
We need the Minute Men to stir up the dry bones of the Church to get them alive. We don't dare to leave them now for fear they will go to sleep again.

GEORGIA:
We need the Minute Men because it will bring the spirit of union together with all the great forces of the two great churches, and the other churches that are connected with it.
...Several "Amens"...

DAYTON, OH:
Ever since the birth of the Church the cry has been that the women do it all. Now we are awake. Give us something to do, so they will keep still. (Applause)

RICHMOND, VT:
Because the Minute Men will keep the home fires burning.

INDIANA:
My father was a preacher. I have a son preaching to the Mormons in Utah, and we need the Minute Men to help him.

MASSACHUSETTS:
We are told that prayer is the energy of this great movement. We need the Minute Men because they are men that believe in prayer, and this is the demonstration of its answer, that the prayer of the mother, the prayer of the sister, and the prayer of the wife, thank God, has been answered.

TEXAS:
The Church has been fifty percent. We need the Minute Men to make the other fifty percent.

MASSACHUSETTS:
Because through the Minute Men the Church has learned the world is our parish.

SAN JOSE, ILLINOIS:
We believe the Minute Men ought to be continued because they have just gotten a start. Why stop them now? Let them go on.

SAN JOSE, CALIFORNIA:
We need the Minute Men to go into small places where there is no preaching. I believe there is a great work to be done in this way.

WATERLOO, IOWA:
I just talked to one of our Bishops in the India tea room. He said the Minute Men are to become the vital religious force of our Church. I believe that if we men go back and tackle the job that the work of the Minute Men will produce a large part of the 53,000 young men that are needed to go out and help bring the world to Christ. (Applause)

NEWCASTLE, INDIANA:
I think the Minute Men movement is needed to give the laymen a definite job, and to organize them on the job so it can be completed.

NAPLES, NEW YORK:
I have the honor of being from the same town that Mr. Parker is from. I believe the Minute Men should be continued because they have brought it to pass that when the Consecration Hymn is sung now we are not obliged to say, "Take my wife and let her be consecrated to the Lord." (Applause)

KNOXVILLE, TENNESSEE:
This movement has demonstrated clearly that the men of the Church have a message that the world needs, and that the world wants, and the world is anxious for. We can not afford to let this movement die. We have got in the next five years to do more for Christ than has been done in the last fifty years. It can not be done unless the laymen do it.

KEYSTONE STATE:
The Minute Men of Pennsylvania have kept the Church of Pennsylvania up on high gear, and now like Elijah we are going up on high. (Applause)

COLUMBUS, OHIO:
We need the Minute Men because it is an organization, and as I understand the Methodist Church is an organization now, and what are we going to do without men? It is the man power of the Centenary to do things with. Therefore, we must keep it.

HOOPSTON (sic), ILLINOIS:
I am from the original dry town of the United States. (Applause) It never had a saloon. It is called the Holy City. We need Minute Men that will get up and tell the congregation things that the ministers don't tell them. (Applause)

TENNESSEE:
I am glad to say that the Minute Men have awakened some of us lazy church people up, and I think they ought to be continued to keep us awake.

INDIANA:

We should continue these Minute Men simply because of their wonderful moral and spiritual backing to the minister of the Gospel, which will enable him to preach the Gospel of Jesus Christ to the salvation of the world.

CHRISTIAN F. REISNER:

I am going to have some preachers talk now.

BROCKTON, MASSACHUSETTS:

I want to tell you why we have such poor preachers. I know why it is, because we can't get anybody else to do the job any better. (Applause) As soon as anybody is able to do it any better than the preachers that are doing it now, we are ready to step aside and say, "God bless you. Go at it." Now then Jesus Christ has a man's job – that of winning a half million souls to Jesus Christ in the next year. The Minute Men are the gang that can do the job. We don't dare let them step aside. May God bless them as they undertake the task.

NEBRASKA:

The Minute Men's organization is important because it will foster and develop the initiative on the part of the laymen of the Church.

PENNSYLVANIA:

I believe that the Minute Men movement is vitally important because it is God's organization, because it isn't afraid to preach the law of God. It has made more tithers in the last year than the Methodist Church has in the last fifteen.

MICHIGAN:

We must have Minute Men because they do the work we can't get around to do, also because they have taught us how to pray, and that we must pray in faith believing, and you Minute Men have prayed that way. I can't get along without Minute Men. Neither can any minister here.

FREMONT, IOWA:

I believe in the Minute Men because it put new life and new energy and new zeal into the preacher.

CAMP HILL:

Because of the added effectiveness of the missionary message when it comes from a man other than the pastor.

FILLMORE, CALIFORNIA:

I believe in the Minute Men and want the Minute Men because we can not get along without them, considering the great work that we have to do. I want our motto to be 15,000,000 conversions in Methodist Churches in the next five years, and that is only one as your share a year in this great campaign, and I want the Minute Men with us on that greater undertaking than any we have yet undertaken.

MIAMI, FLORIDA:
I for one want the Minute Men continued because they are doing what I and every other honest pastor had been trying to get them to do in the whole history of the church – to take hold of the duties of the business of the Church, and run it.

CHRISTIAN F. REISNER:
Now may I say something, as a preacher of twenty-six years' standing? I have never been anything but a pastor. I never held any kind of job of any other kind. I was never out of my pulpit in that time more than half a dozen times. I believe in sticking to the job.

We preachers have tried to do too much of the work ourselves. Secondly, we have had to do it, because a whole lot of laymen would take a job and straightway forget it, until it is a nuisance to have to appoint some fellows on the committees because they never do anything. Third, we would have twenty times better preachers if you men would get into the game and run the Church like you run your business. (Applause) Some of you know that that is my particular hobby.

I will not preach to empty seats if there is anyway to fill them, and a miserable crowd of laymen will be the first bunch to stand around and talk about a preacher being a sensationalist if he uses a new method. And I say you business men have no more right to say that the Church is sensational because it uses a new method than your grocery store or your dry goods store is because it uses a new method. (Applause)

If the Minute Men will go into their local church and say, "By God's Grace this Church is going to be a success" every pastor will back you up, and lead you and be a bigger man. The trouble is, first, you pay your preacher so little that he can never raise his head in decency. (Applause) Why think of it – the street sweepers of New York City get nearly twice the salary that the average Methodist preacher gets. Now I say, business men, the Minute Men ought to do this, first, the Church of Jesus Christ shall be the most honorable institution in the community. We will pay our preacher so he can live like other folks. Next, we will put our Church on the map. You hold your Rotary Clubs, and your Exchange Clubs and your other meetings and yell yourselves to death, and if you will jump into the Church of Jesus Christ with the same enthusiasm and snap and go, you can put it in the forefront in your town.

There is no power on earth like you fellows have got. Why, men, we couldn't have raised one-tenth of the money we raised if you laymen hadn't done the talking and the boosting. We preachers were scared to death. When I started into the game the first of October, the first thing I did was to visit the preachers meeting in this country. I spoke at the Chicago Preachers' Meeting. I got a terrible frost when I went in there, and yet I had the best treatment in Chicago of any city in this country when I got through. Those fellows treated me like a prince. I went into the New York Preachers' Meeting, and I had a hard time. They put me on to the tail of another man's speech. They wouldn't give me time. And the preachers were afraid of this thing. I don't blame them for they have been carrying the load all the time, but the laymen were not afraid, and because they were not afraid of it, they put it over.

Now, laymen, why don't you do the same for your local Church? I want you to be as fair about the Church of Jesus Christ as anything else, and don't be moss-backish. I went to a town the other day where three hundred families tithe – pay all their money into the Church Treasury. They don't distribute it around. They bring their one-tenth and drop it in without putting their names on it, and the Church Treasury distributes it. They had seventy-two automobiles come that night, and they went ten miles singing the Gospel for two hours before Church service. When I went in I had a house full to preach to – not a lot of empty chairs. And then at the close that night I went down stairs. I found that Church that was a thrill with spiritual life had put in a recreation room, and they had a bowling alley. Isn't that terrible?

I am not going to put a pool table in my Church. Don't misunderstand me, but I went into that Church. They had a bowling alley. They had a table in there – it wasn't a pool table, but it took more skill to play it than it does to play pool. They had iron wickets, and they used a long cue and a big ivory ball, and you had to billiard the ball against the side to get it through the arch. Now was that Church doing the Lord's business or not? Let me tell you there were three hundred young fellows there, and the pastor told me that they didn't find a boy in the town who when they came in they had to teach how to handle the thing. The saloons were closed and the three hundred boys in that little town filled their game room every Saturday night. Men, what I am saying is not to put pool tables in. Don't misunderstand me, but I say this, we have no right to throw rocks at anything because the Devil has used it. Am I right in that?

...Loud "Yes"...

I don't care what you shall put into the Church but in the name of sense let us get busy and get people for God. That is the big thing.

Now I am saying that you men have got to get into the Church, and when somebody talks down a thing don't you accept it until he gives a reason for it.

How many of you folks are opposed to motion pictures?

...Just a few hands up...

We have ten thousand feet of reels from this Exposition, including the parade last night. Would you like to have your people see that parade? Do you know that every foot of it has been taken by motion pictures and is ready to be shown? I want to tell you men that when I showed motion pictures in my church I was abused like a yellow dog. When I got the men to come here and take these pictures more than one preacher has berated me for doing it. I went out to see [David Wark] Griffith on the Coast, and I talked religion to him, and he told me that his mother was a Methodist. When I described this to him, he said, "I will send men to take motion pictures of that," and it will cost them $25,000. Then he said, "I will turn the original over and make the Methodist Church a present of it in memory of my mother." (Applause) Let us quit being moss-backs unless we can give a good reason for it.[48]

John Wesley wouldn't allow musical instruments in the Church because the Devil was using them. Now I don't know what you are going to put in your church, but I say the Devil hasn't got a thing on this earth, if in itself it is harmless, that I wouldn't take and use for the glory of my Christ.

...Several Amens...

And if I can stand by the side of a fellow in motion pictures or in a bowling alley or in some other kind of a happy recreation, and win him to Jesus Christ you have no right to berate me.

When I was a pastor of a Church in Kansas City there was a little dance hall opened on the corner, and I advertised against it. I said you have no time to go down to that dance hall, and the result was that the dance hall grew and grew. Then I said that I had got to beat them some other way, and I organized a social club and in less than three weeks we run the dance hall out of business, because we had something better.

Now, men, I am standing for this. Every Church in this country must be a recreational center. (Applause) Every Church must serve its community, or it will go out of business, and unless we get busy the saloon crowd will get busy and beat us to it.

Now I am not saying what you shall put in, but if I had my way I would at least put in motion pictures. I would put in something else, if it was nothing but boxball. And there are some other games I would put in, but you don't need to.

God is going to hold you Minute Men responsible. These preachers would do ten times what they do, if they weren't afraid of your criticism. They would do a lot of things they don't do now but for the three or four fellows on the Board who are always afraid they will do something sensational. They would rather have you be a dead one than sensational.

Laymen, go back home and say, "Our Church is going to be the biggest thing in this town, and we are going to do the thing that will get the people, and we are going to get the people so we can give them the Gospel of the saving Christ, who is the Divine Son of our Heavenly Father, who alone can save men from their sins." Use everything you can.

The Interchurch Movement is going to agree if there are three small churches in a town, two of them will close up, and one of them will be made strong. That is the agreement and if the Churches don't get into that agreement woe be unto those who don't. When I am pastor of a Church, that Church has got to be the biggest thing – not the Elks, not the Chamber of Commerce, not the library, not the Woman's Club, not the Bridge Whist Club, but the Church of Jesus Christ shall be the biggest thing in that town.

Now then if there are too many churches there that is none of my business. If I have done all I could do to get them to combine, then I am going to get busy and make mine big.

QUESTION FROM AUDIENCE:
What about making it a community center, rather than a local church affair?

CHRISTIAN F. REISNER:

Now that is a local problem you men can work out. I have helped a good deal in that sort of thing. I tell you this, if there were three churches in a town and we could agree to put in a community house, I would put that community house in, but I wouldn't turn it over to the worldly business men of the town. I would make the Committee to be dominated by the three churches, and I would keep the Minute Men and the Christian men in charge of that community house every week night. I wouldn't put a lot of don'ts there, but a lot of does, and a lot of religion.

I am ready for union work, if the other fellows are. If not, I am going to put my job over. If I was running a grocery store, I wouldn't sit around, waiting until the other fellow agreed with me. I would get the business.

I think it is a shame that there are six or seven churches in a town, but if the others won't, then let us do business. Then if you can't do that, get a new Church.

QUESTION FROM AUDIENCE:

Suppose you are by yourself in a big church, which would decry anything of this kind to be put in, or any new method to be put in, what would you do?

CHRISTIAN F. REISNER:

This is what I would do. I would first find out the fellow that I could most likely persuade. I would live with him until I got him. Then I would try to get two. I would have these two fellows be Minute Men, and have them go out and get two more, and then some night I would put on something that would surprise them. I would say to the Minute Men "You go and put on some stunts some Sunday Night." If I were you I would get two or three or four fellows to agree with me to buy a thousand roses some night and give them away. There you have made a break. When I put motion pictures into my church I went ahead and brought the machine in, and after it was done I asked the official board if I could. (Applause) I raised all the money myself. Now that is what I mean – go ahead and do some things for the glory of God, and take the responsibility. I never saw a Board that wouldn't back you up when you deliver the goods.

I wouldn't give a picayune for the fellow who won't make his local church go over the top. You Minute Men have got a taste of what you can do. Now you can raise the Church of Jesus Christ where it is going to be the biggest thing in the community.

When I went to New York City nine years ago they had regularly an audience of twenty-five to thirty Sunday nights in an auditorium that seated fifteen hundred people. I won't tell you all the details. The President of our Board of Trustees will be here next week, and you can ask him some questions. The loose collections for the year, before I went there, was $1400. For the month of March last year, the collection was $1400. We raised $70,000 in ten days and paid the debt and have a $20,000 endowment. We have 175,000 people there every year. We never have a Sunday without the invitation, and never a

Sunday without somebody raising their hand for prayer. I do some of the most unusual things to get an audience. When I get them woe be unto them. We get their money and some other things.

At this point I am going to tell you what Mr. McAdoo said to me. Mr. McAdoo said, "I think if you would like to have us do it the United Artists (Mr. McAdoo is the counsel for the United Artists) can take these reels and make a half million dollars for Methodism." (Applause) Now when you think that we are going to have millions of people see them, do you think they can see them without being impressed? Take that parade last night. It was most impressive.

Mr. Hamburg is here – the man who took "The Birth of a Nation" and took "Intolerance" and "Hearts of the World." By the way, we are going to show you "Hearts of the World" next week. We are going to have a motion picture convention. I want all of you preachers to be here. We are going to bring W.A. Brady out here, the President of the National Producers' Association. We are going to bring on the President of the Paramount Company, also the President of the Mutual and the President of the Vitagraph. They are coming out here next week to attend our convention.[49]

The General Manager of the Paramount people is a member of the Methodist Church. The Paramount people said to Doctor Marshall, "Everything you cut out, stays out for what isn't good enough for the Church isn't good enough for us." Marshall is censoring all the pictures. Now you know we were so afraid to get in on these things, and the Lord wants us to get in, and if we start see how we do get in. Have you seen the Pageant? One of the biggest men in the United States said the other day that was the most smashing thing that was ever produced in the world. (Applause) Let us not criticize but construct. When I was a young fellow a man gave me a motto I have never forgotten, "Never criticize anything unless you can suggest something better."

Now the last thought. You know, Irving Berlin wrote "I hate to get up in the Morning." He was very prominent in New York at the time, and I always tried to get the prominent to visit our Church. So I got hold of Irving Berlin and he came and sang.[50] He sang, "Everybody was in Step but Jim" and "I Hate to get up in the Morning" and then he sang, "When I Lost You." I asked him to do that. He wrote that when his sweetheart died, and two million copies were sold. They applauded again and again. That was a pretty serious thing to do on Sunday night, wasn't it? I confess it shocked me, but I want to say that those people were happy, and they thought of the boys in the Army singing, "I Hate to Get Up in the Morning" and it brought tearful memories to them of the lads over there, and when Irving Berlin left they applauded again and again, and he said, "All I can say is my father and my grandfather were Jewish Rabbis. God bless you." That night, my friends, I preached and gave the invitation and thirty-eight people stood on their feet for prayer. You see what I am getting at. I am going to use the bait that catches the fish even though I have to spit on the bait. (Applause)

It has been a great privilege to me to associate with Mr. Clark in this work, and I tell you we only have to know these Southern brethren to love them. I never knew they were so lovely until I have been seeing them lately. I don't wonder that they are so chummy down South. I think I will go down and take a Southern pulpit if I get a chance. My cousin, a Southern Methodist, came up to New York the other day. He said, "If you will come down and be my pastor" – I won't tell you how much money he told me he would give me, but he is in the oil business and he doesn't know the value of money. If I go to the South Church it will have to be soon or there won't be any Church, South, or Church, North. (Applause)

I am glad to introduce Mr. Clark, the head of the Minute Men of the South Church, and I know he will tell you about some of the plans for the future of the Minute men. Then I will follow very briefly giving an outline of ours. Then I am going to ask each of the area chairmen to say a word.

ELMER T. CLARK:

My friends, I am glad of this opportunity to speak a word to you about the permanent organization as we propose it down South of the Mason and Dixon line.

We used to think that we were a pretty hard and closefisted set down there, more or less orthodox and set in our ways, but when I heard Doctor Reisner tell about the trouble that you brethren up here have about putting an innocent moving picture show or a bowling alley in your Church, I think that we down there are pretty liberal after all. And I can assure Doctor Reisner that if he accepts the invitation and comes down South of the Mason and Dixon line to preach that nobody will berate him, if he puts in his moving picture machine. (Applause)

We have multiplied hundreds of our churches where they operate moving picture machines in connection with their Sunday evening services, and those churches are among our most progressive and efficient churches.

Now in regard to our Minute Men, it would be simply a repetition to say anything about the excellent work that they accomplished in the Centenary Drive.

Down in our Church the Minute Men in our organization reached an efficiency of 88% for the entire Church. That is, there was a Minute Man organization in 88% of all of our churches, including our little country churches and the congregations that worship out in the school houses in the woods.

And after the great drive was over, and we investigated the record we found that there wasn't a single church in all of our denomination which operated the Minute Men according to our schedule that failed to go over the top. (Applause)

Our goal, as you know, in the Centenary drive was $35,000,000, including our credits, and we raised that amount and reached that goal on the first Sunday afternoon of the drive, and during eight days we oversubscribed it fifty percent. And the Minute Men of our Church are recognized by all people as being important factors in putting over our drive.

Now there isn't any doubt in the mind of any Methodist down there as to whether the Minute Men should be permanent or not. We have already settled that question by sounding out everybody, and we haven't discovered any man who even dreamed that our Minute Men organization ought to be discarded.

We have not yet determined on the form that our permanent organization of Minute Men is going to take fully. You know, down in our Church the Minute Men are a part of the Publicity Department, and we do not make very many plans for the Publicity Department until the Centenary Commission has outlined their policy. And we function to that, and so in these coming months and years whatever policy the Centenary Commission and the Church shall officially outline the organization of the Minute Men is going to function to.

But there are three or four lines of activity that we are going to follow. And one of them is that we are going to see to it that all the members of our Church are lined up and enrolled in active work in this League of Intercession. (Applause)

That has been a tremendous success in our part of the country, and we are going to set a month after a while in which the Minute Men will devote their exclusive attention to the matter of prayer, and at the end of that month we are going to have a drive, and when that drive is over we expect to have most of the membership of our Church enrolled in this League of Intercession, giving themselves constantly to God in prayer for the extension of His Kingdom upon the earth.

And the second thing that the Minute Men are going to do is to see to it that all the preachers and all of the official members and nearly all of the common, ordinary members of our Church are tithers. (Applause)

Do you know that only forty-six percent of our preachers are tithers? I don't know what the percentage is up here, but in the Southern Methodist Church, so far as we can tell from the records, that is, judging by those who have signed up the tithing card only forty-six percent of our preachers are enrolled. Now the Minute Men are going to see to it that the preachers do better than that.

And when they get the preachers lined up, they are going after the Official Boards. When they get them lined up, they are going after everybody else. And so we are going to set a period of time in which our Minute Men will stress the matter of Stewardship, and that only.

And at the end of that period there will be another drive, and after that drive, we are all going to be tithers.

And then we are going to do another thing. Our Minute Men have got to see to it, in cooperation with other branches of the Centenary work, that we have a great many hundred of the best young men and women of our Church as missionary volunteers. (Applause) We need several hundred of the best, the best blood and brain of America to be preachers and foreign missionaries, and deaconesses and home missionaries, and all that. I am speaking of those who are to give all of their time to the work of the Kingdom.

And we are going to have a certain section of our program that will be devoted to Life Service, and in this section the Minute Men will not do anything else except hunt for young people, the best and the strongest and the most intelligent, who will go out and carry the Gospel for us into all parts of this world.

And then overtopping everything else in interest, at least, and in importance, is the great evangelistic movement for which we are planning next spring.

During this fall and winter we are spending our time – I mean my organization is – not the Minute Men especially – but the Publicity Department is spending our energies in investigating conditions from an evangelistic standpoint everywhere in our Church. We are trying to find out exactly how many people around our Churches ought to be reached, and we are finding out some strange things.

We have found this, and you can find it out in your Church if you will make a careful investigation, and if your Church is an average Church. You will find out that there are three times as many people unreached, surrounding your Church who will never be reached for Christ unless the influence of your Church does reach them, as you have on your roll. I was a little bit startled when I first heard that, but we have put on evangelistic surveys all over our country, and it will average that percentage everywhere. There are three times as many people around every Methodist Church, with an instinctive leaning towards the Methodist Church, with some point of interest at which they touch the Methodist Church, but who are not Christians, as there are members of that local Church. (Applause)

We are finding out who these people are, and what they think, and how they are living, and just what their attitude towards the Church is. And when we have completed this survey, and have laid our plans, we are going to have an intensive evangelistic campaign in which we hope to reach and to save multitudes for the Kingdom of God.

And the Minute Men are going to do that thing. Why, down in our country the Minute Men almost had a revival before the campaign came off. I know Minute Men who have absolutely been born again through their speaking campaigns, and you know them. I know Minute Men who became so interested in this matter that they went out to solicit their friends for subscriptions to the Centenary campaign, talked religion to them, and I know Minute Men who actually went in to business offices and had prayers with people, and brought them to the altar and saw them saved in the good, old, orthodox way. I know that a Minute Man who can stand in the pulpit and speak for three minutes on missions can preach an evangelistic sermon out in the country somewhere. And I know that a man who can go out and tackle his neighbor to give several thousand dollars for missionary purposes can also go out and tackle some other neighbor to surrender his heart and his life to Christ. And so our Minute Men are going out into this evangelistic business.

And another thing they are going to do is to pay a whole lot of attention to the Churches out in the country. Methodism is a rural church. We have in our denomination about 15,000 churches in which there is held a service only once a month. Think of that! Fifteen thousand Methodist churches in our denomination that are closed three-fourths of the time!

Hitherto they have tried to be closed because there was no person to open them. If a preacher has four points on his circuit he can't be in all four of the churches each Sunday, and so three Sundays out of the month 15,000 of them are closed.

Our Minute Men opened them. We sent out to these country churches little teams of Minute Men to hold services in all of the churches which would not have any services otherwise. And so before the campaign closed our churches, nearly all of them, were having regular services every Sunday. We are going to keep it up. And these Minute Men are going to continue their visits into the country churches until it can no longer be said of Methodism that any considerable percentage of her churches are closed on the Lord's Day, when they ought to be open preaching the Gospel to the people.

Those are the general things that our Minute Men are going to do. We have not perfected our permanent organization, and we do not intend to perfect it here or very soon, for that matter. But we have in our Church an organization known as the Laymen's Missionary Movement.

It hasn't been doing very much these last years and the Minute Men of our Church have made up their minds that they are going to take over and absorb the Laymen's Missionary Movement, and so before our organization is completed we expect to merge our Minute Men's organization with the Laymen's Missionary Movement so that the Minute Men will be the whole thing so far as the work of the laymen is concerned.

In other words, we do not want to perfect in our churches two laymen's organizations running side by side and covering the same territory to a certain degree. We expect to have one organization, a combination of the Laymen's Missionary Movement and the Methodist Minute Men which will function according to the lines which I have suggested.

This is a great day for Methodism. It is a great day for the laymen of the Church, and it became a great day for the Church because the laymen determined to make it so.

Now the thing that happened up here happened down there with us, that is, every man that I ever heard speak who had cold feet on this proposition was a preacher. It is the truth. Our preachers were not very much frightened – some of them were at first, but the laymen were never frightened. I never heard of a layman who said that it couldn't be done, and the only time I ever heard a layman challenge our objective was to challenge it upward. And the only objections that we ever heard were not from the Minute Men, but from the preachers themselves, but, thank God, this success has eliminated all of that timidity from our preachers, and we are going forward to still greater things in the Kingdom of God.

And our Minute Men will always be at the fore in the carrying out of the movement which the Church must project and make succeed in this, the mightiest day of human history. (Prolonged Applause)

...ADJOURNMENT...

Notes

1. Belle Harris Bennett (1852-1922). Bennett was a missionary and active laywoman with the Methodist Episcopal Church, South. She was elected to several denominational positions including president of the Woman's Parsonage and Home Missionary Society and president of the Woman's Missionary Council. At the 1910 General Conference of the Methodist Episcopal Church, South, she spoke to the assembly on the rights of local women laity. The speech was the first time a woman had addressed the MECS assembly since its 1844/5 founding. Bennett was active in raising funds for the establishment of the Scarritt College for Christian Workers in Kansas City, Missouri, as well as Bennett College in Rio de Janeiro, Brazil. When she convened the meeting at the exposition Bennett was the lone woman representative for the Joint Commission on the Centenary of American Methodist Missions.

2. Anna Howard Shaw (1847-1919). Shaw was medical practitioner, author, and ordained minister with the Methodist Protestant Church. She was born in Newcastle-on-Tyne, England, and moved with her family to Michigan in the United States for her childhood years. She was educated at Albion College, Boston University School of Theology, and Boston University. She worked at churches in Massachusetts before becoming the first ordained woman minister of the MP Church in 1880. Shaw was active in suffrage and eventually became president of the National American Woman Suffrage Association. She authored *The Story of a Pioneer* (New York and London: Harper & Brothers Publishers, 1915) and passed away on July 2, 1919, only one week after Woman's Day at the Centenary Celebration.

3. The Methodist Protestant Church was formally organized in 1830 at Baltimore, Maryland. The new Methodist denomination was the result of dissatisfaction with the episcopacy and lay representation at General Conferences of the Methodist Episcopal Church. The first General Conference of the Methodist Protestant Church was held in 1834 at Georgetown, Maryland. Early leaders included Asa Shinn, Nicholas Snethen, and Anna Howard Shaw. By 1936 the MPC had a membership of nearly 200,000. In 1939, the Methodist Protestant Church merged with the Methodist Episcopal Church, South and Methodist Episcopal Church to form the Methodist Church.

4. Several missionary agencies for women were active during the Centenary Celebration. The Methodist Episcopal Church sponsored the Woman's Foreign Missionary Society (founded in 1869) and Woman's Home Missionary Society (1882). The Methodist Episcopal Church, South, sponsored the Woman's Missionary Council (1910), and the Methodist Protestant Church included the Woman's Foreign Missionary Society (1880) and the Woman's Home Missionary Society (1916).

5. Lucy Lee Mahan Spilman was a layperson in the Kentucky Annual Conference of the Methodist Episcopal Church, South. She was educated at Sue Bennett Memorial School and was later elected as president of the Woman's Missionary Council of the Kentucky conference. She was an active fundraiser bringing in nearly $20,000 for domestic and foreign missions work. She was also a leader in the Armenian Relief program. In 1922, Spilman served as an alternate lay delegate to the General Conference of the Methodist Episcopal Church, South. See William Elsey Connelley and Ellis Merton Coulter, *History of Kentucky* (Chicago: The American Historical Society, 1922), 144-145.

6. Clotilda Lyon McDowell (1858-1930). McDowell was a teacher and denominational executive. She was educated at Ohio Wesleyan University and worked two years as a high school teacher following graduation. After the death of her young

daughter, McDowell accepted the presidency of the Woman's Foreign Missionary Society of the Methodist Episcopal Church. She served in that capacity from 1908-1921. Upon her death in 1930, President Herbert Hoover remarked, "Such lives as hers are the true servants of humanity, their influence far exceeding the confines of any race or creed, and are inspiring examples of service for all." *Minutes of the One Hundred and Forty-seventh Session of the Baltimore Annual Conference of the Methodist Episcopal Church, First Methodist Episcopal Church, Baltimore, Md., June 2-8, 1931* (Baltimore, MD: Press of the Horn-Shafer Company, 1931), 408-410. For further study of McDowell's life and work see Herbert Welch, *Men of the Outposts: The Romance of the Modern Christian Movement* (New York: The Abingdon Press, 1937), 229-244.

7. The Woman's Foreign Missionary Society of the Methodist Episcopal Church was founded in 1869 as a means to "extend the Gospel to women by women." The WFMS was the central organization for women's missions with several local branches existing in Baltimore, New York, and in Minneapolis among others. The WFMS sent its first missionary, Dr. Clara Swain, to India in 1870. By 1939, WFMS missionaries were serving in Africa, China, and Latin America. Following the 1939 merger of the Methodist Episcopal Church, Methodist Episcopal Church, South, and Methodist Protestant Church the WFMS became an agency within the Foreign Department of the Woman's Division of Christian Service. Over 1,500 missionaries were sent between 1869 and 1939. For further study of the WFMS see Hilah F. Thomas, Rosemary Skinner Keller, and Louise L. Queen, eds. *Women in New Worlds: Historical Perspectives on the Wesleyan Tradition,* Two Volumes (Nashville: Abingdon Press, 1981 and 1982).

8. Mary Haven Thirkield (1860-1935) was an author and denominational executive. She served as fifth president of the Woman's Home Missionary Society of the Methodist Episcopal Church. Thirkield authored a biography titled *Elizabeth Lownes Rust* (Cincinnati: Jennings & Pye, 1903).

9. The Woman's Home Missionary Society of the Methodist Episcopal Church was officially organized in 1882 at Cincinnati, Ohio. The agency emerged out of concern for women and children in American cities as well as for the conditions of the residents of settlement houses throughout the United States. The first president was former First Lady Lucy Hayes. WHMS missionaries worked with Chinese immigrants in California, Native American peoples in the American Southwest, and African American women in North Carolina. After the 1939 merger, the WHMS became a division within the Woman's Division of Christian Service. By 1939, membership had reached over 250,000. For further study of the WHMS see Hilah F. Thomas, Rosemary Skinner Keller, and Louise L. Queen, eds., *Women in New Worlds: Historical Perspectives on the Wesleyan Tradition,* Two Volumes (Nashville: Abingdon Press, 1981 and 1982).

10. Lena Leonard Fisher (d. 1930) was an author, professor of missions at the University of Southern California, and missionary for the Methodist Episcopal Church. She was educated at the Emerson College of Oratory (MA) and received a Doctor of Letters degree from Baldwin-Wallace College. She wrote three books *Lantern Stories* (New York: Eaton & Mains, 1913); *Under the Crescent, and Among the Kraals; a Study of Methodism in Africa* (Boston: Woman's Foreign Missionary Society, 1917); and *The River Dragon's Bride* (New York: Abingdon Press, 1922). During the Centenary exposition she served as the Jubilee Commissioner of the Woman's Foreign Missionary Society which celebrated its fiftieth anniversary in 1919. Fisher also wrote World War I-themed songs *As Her Soldier Boy Marched By* (1917) and *France-Land Lullaby* (1918).

11. May Leonard Woodruff (1862-1948). Woodruff was a missionary with the Newark Annual Conference of the Methodist Episcopal Church. She served as an executive secretary for Puerto Rico for the Woman's Home Missionary Society. In 1902, Woodruff started a school and home for orphan girls (now the Robinson School).

12. Jennie V. Hughes was a missionary to China for the Woman's Foreign Missionary Society of the Methodist Episcopal Church. She was instrumental in the founding of Bethel Hospital and Mission in Shanghai, China. Charles Luther Boynton and Charles Dozier Boynton, eds., *1936 Handbook of the Christian Movement in China under Protestant Auspices* (Shanghai, China: Kwang Hsueh Pub. House, 1936), 101.

13. "Christian Americanization" was the response of early 20th century Protestant Christians anxious about the influx of immigrants from outside the United States. Americanization was the process of emphasizing and inculcating the language and customs of U.S. citizens for those immigrating into the United States. Those who wanted to enforce "Christian Americanization" sought to convert non-Protestants to Christianity. For an early 20th century context Charles Alvin Brooks wrote, "Americanization means the extension of our ideals, of the American spirit, and of our language to every quarter and every community, until there shall remain no foreign colonies untouched by the full currents of our American life or out of harmony with the rest of America." Charles Alvin Brooks, *Christian Americanization: A Task for the Churches* (S.l.: Council of Women for Home Missions and Missionary Education Movement of the United States and Canada, 1919), 8-9.

14. Reed Smoot (1862-1941). Smoot was a U.S. Congressional leader representing the state of Utah from 1903-1933. He was educated at Brigham Young University and prior to his death in 1941 served as one of the Twelve Apostles of the Church of Jesus Christ of Latter-day Saints. For further information on Smoot see Kathleen Flake, *The Politics of American Religious Identity: The Seating of Senator Reed Smoot, Mormon Apostle* (Chapel Hill, NC: University of North Carolina Press, 2004).

15. Daisy McClain Bulkley was denominational leader for the Woman's Home Missionary Society of the Methodist Episcopal Church. She was educated at the Browning Industrial Home in Camden, South Carolina. She worked as Field Secretary for the Colored Conferences and served as a reserve delegate for the South Carolina Annual Conference at the 1924 General Conference of the Methodist Episcopal Church.

16. Bulkley quoted the poem "The Brotherhood" by John Oxenham (1852-1941).

17. Martha E. Drummer (1871-1937). Drummer was an African American missionary appointed to West Africa for the Woman's Foreign Missionary Society of the Methodist Episcopal Church. She was educated at Clark University in Atlanta, Georgia, and the Training School for Deaconesses in Boston, Massachusetts. She was assigned to work in Angola and spent twenty years (1906-1926) on the continent returning only twice for furloughs to the United States. Brenda Wilkenson, "Martha Drummer: A Woman of Courage," General Board of Global Ministries, The United Methodist Church, Accessed February 15, 2011, http://gbgm-umc.org/mission/news2000/gbgm021000bwbm.html. See also Lily Hardy Hammond, *In the Vanguard of a Race* (New York: Council of Women for Home Missions and Missionary Education Movement of the United States and Canada, 1922), 131-147.

18. Reginald Heber and Lowell Mason, *From Greenland's Icy Mountains: A Missionary Hymn* (Boston: James L. Hewitt & Co., 1827).

19. Lois Lee Parker was a missionary to India and co-founder of the Woman's Foreign Missionary Society of the Methodist Episcopal Church. Clementina Butler (1862-1949) was an author and missionary for the Methodist Episcopal Church. She

served as executive secretary of the Woman's Foreign Missionary Society from 1889 to 1933. Alma Mathews (d. 1933) was a missionary for the Woman's Home Missionary Society of the Methodist Episcopal Church. She was assigned to Ellis Island to work with immigrants arriving to the United States. The Alma Mathews House, an early orphanage for woman immigrants and now United Methodist retreat center, is named after Mathews. Guide to the Alma Mathews House Board Minutes, General Commission on Archives and History, The United Methodist Church, Accessed February 15, 2011, http://archives.gcah.org/eadweb/gcah2437.htm. Virginia M. Atkinson (1861-1941) was a missionary to China for the Woman's Missionary Council of the Methodist Episcopal Church, South. She was educated at LaGrange Female College and served in the Soochow and Shanghai regions of China. She founded the Atkinson Academy for Boys and the Davidson Girls' School. Guide to the Virginia M. (Ginny) Atkinson Papers, General Commission on Archives and History, The United Methodist Church. Accessed February 15, 2011, http://archives.gcah.org/eadweb/gcah739.htm.

20. Anna Adams Gordon (1853-1931). Gordon was an author, songwriter and president of the Woman's Christian Temperance Union. She was educated at Lasal Seminary and Mount Holyoke College. Gordon worked extensively with Frances Willard and traveled the world advocating temperance. She served in various capacities with the World League against Alcoholism and the National Council of Women. She wrote hymns for publications including *The White Ribbon Hymnal, or, Echoes of the Crusade* (Evanston, IL: National Woman's Christian Temperance Union, 1911); and *Marching Songs for Young Crusaders: Temperance Songs for the Cold Water Army* (Evanston, IL: Nation Woman's Christian Temperance Union, 1890). For additional information on Gordon see T. Jason Soderstrum, "Gordon, Anna Adams," in *Alcohol and Temperance in Modern History: An International Encyclopedia*, Jack S. Blocker, David M. Fahey, and Ian R. Tyrrell, eds. (Santa Barbara, CA: ABC-CLIO, Inc., 2003), 273; and Julia Freeman Dean, *Anna Adams Gordon: A Story of Her Life* (Evanston, IL: Woman's Christian Temperance Union, 1928).

21. Townsend was an Executive Officer for the Homeopathic Department of the Zanesville (Ohio) City Hospital.

22. Lyrics from "A Charge to Keep I Have." Charles Wesley, *Short Hymns on Select Passages of Holy Scripture* (Bristol, England: Printed by E. Farley, 1762).

23. Barge was a Field Secretary of Young Peoples' Work for the Methodist Episcopal Church.

24. Everett Knight Hester (1863-1941). Hester was an ordained minister with the Rock River Conference of the Methodist Episcopal Church and later The Methodist Church. He served in several Illinois churches including Antioch, Harvard, Mt. Carroll, and Winnebago. Hester retired in 1935 and died of pneumonia on May 9, 1941. *Journal and Year Book, One Hundred and Second Session of the Rock River Annual Conference of The Methodist Church, Wilmette Parish Methodist Church, Wilmette, Illinois, October 5-12, 1941* (Chicago, IL: Printed by the Conference, 1941).

25. Martha E. Abt was the Chairman of Contagious Diseases for the Chicago Political Equality League.

26. For recent scholarship on women, missionary work, and notions of "home" see Barbara Reeves-Ellington and Kathryn Kish Sklar, *Competing Kingdoms: Women, Mission, Nation, and the American Protestant Empire, 1812-1960* (Durham, NC: Duke University Press, 2010).

27. For additional details concerning the battle and its historical context within World War I see David Bonk and Peter Dennis, *Chateau Thierry and Belleau Wood, 1918: America's Baptism by Fire on the Marne* (New York: Osprey Pub., 2007).

28. Helen MacMurchy, *The Almosts: A Study of the Feeble-minded* (Boston: Mifflin, 1920). See this volume for an early 20th century interpretation of mental disabilities. For recent scholarship see Steven Noll and James W. Trent, *Mental Retardation in America: A Historical Reader* (New York: New York University Press, 2004).

29. William J. Butler, *Laws of Illinois concerning Insane, Feeble-minded, and Epileptics, also Index and Analytical Brief of Laws and Prescribed Blank Forms to be followed in the Commitment, Care, Detention, Parole, Discharge, etc., of Insane, Feeble-minded, and Epileptics* (Springfield, IL: s.n., 1930).

30. Reference to a condition known today as PTSD, or, post-traumatic stress disorder. For further study related to PTSD and war see Nancy Sherman, *The Untold War: Inside the Hearts, Minds, and Souls of Our Soldiers* (New York: W.W. Norton, 2010).

31. The National Woman's Party was founded by Alice Paul as an organizational voice for women's suffrage. Members made national headlines in 1913 by holding a parade at Washington, DC on the eve of Woodrow Wilson's presidential inauguration. For additional historical treatment of the organization see Christine A. Lunardini, *From Equal Suffrage to Equal Rights: Alice Paul and the National Woman's Party, 1910-1928* (New York: New York University Press, 1986).

32. Janice Rector was a local Columbus resident and active member of the National Advisory Council for the National Woman's Party.

33. *Suffrage Parade: Report of the Committee of the District of Columbia, United States Senate: Persuant to S. Res. 499, of March 4, 1913, directing said Company to Investigate the Conduct of the District Police and Police Department of the District of Columbia in connection with the Woman's Suffrage Parade on March 3, 1913: With Hearings and Lists of Witnesses* (Washington, DC: s.n., 1913).

34. Alice Paul (1885-1977). Paul was a suffragist and feminist affiliated with the Quaker tradition. She was raised in the New Jersey area and educated at Swarthmore College. Paul spent several years in England working with suffragists Emmeline and Christabel Pankhurst. In 1910, Paul joined the National American Woman Suffrage Association and became active in Congressional legislation toward an Amendment for suffrage. She gained national attention following a suffrage march in Washington, DC that turned violent. By 1916 Paul left the NAWSA to form the National Woman's Party and in 1920 Congress passed the 19th Amendment giving women the right to vote. For additional information on the life and work of Paul visit the following website: http://www.alicepaul.org/

35. Christian Fichthorn Reisner (1872-1940). Reisner was an author, editor, and church executive. He was educated at Midland College, Boston University, and Baker University. He was an ordained minister with the Kansas, Colorado, and New York annual conferences of the Methodist Episcopal Church. He served as a member of the Epworth League and Methodist Minute Men and was noted for his aggressive promotional activities and interest in motion pictures. Carl F. Price, ed., *Who's Who in American Methodism* (New York: E.B. Treat & Co., 1916).

36. Elmer Talmage Clark (1886-1966). Clark was an author, editor, war correspondent and secretary of missions. He was educated at Hendrix College, Birmingham-Southern College, George Peabody College for Teachers, and Temple University. He was an ordained minister with the St. Louis Annual Conference of the Methodist Episcopal Church, South, and served in various Missouri churches including

New Madrid, Cape Girardeau, and St. Louis. In 1918, he was appointed publicity and promotional director of the Centenary of American Methodist Missions and played a major role in advertising the Centenary Celebration throughout the MECS. He edited both *World Outlook* magazine and *World Parish*.

37. William Washington Pinson (1854-1930). Pinson was an author, ordained minister, and missionary executive. He was educated at Webb's School in Culleoka, Tennessee, and received a Doctor of Divinity degree from the University of Georgia. He was an ordained minister with the Tennessee, Texas, Georgia, and Louisville Annual Conferences of the Methodist Episcopal Church, South. His served many churches including locations such as Franklin, Tennessee, San Antonio, Texas, and Louisville, Kentucky. Pinson was general secretary for the Board of Missions and helped launch the Centenary of American Methodist Missions.

38. Edgar Blake (1869-1943). Blake was a bishop and ordained minister with the Methodist Episcopal Church. He was educated at Boston University School of Theology and received honorary doctorates from Wesleyan University and Depauw University. He was a member of the New Hampshire Annual Conference of the Methodist Episcopal Church and served churches in Lebanon and Manchester. During the Centenary of American Methodist Missions Blake worked as corresponding secretary for the Board of Sunday Schools for the MEC. He was elected bishop in 1920 and assigned for work in Europe.

39. S. Earl Taylor (b. 1873). Taylor was an author and denominational executive with the Methodist Episcopal Church. He was educated at Upper Iowa University and Drew Theological Seminary. Taylor served as secretary of the Board of Foreign Missions for the MEC and was the central figure behind the Centenary of American Methodist Missions. Following the Columbus exposition Taylor worked for the short-lived Interchurch World Movement.

40. James Cannon, Jr. (1864-1944). Cannon was a bishop, ordained minister, editor, and college president for the Methodist Episcopal Church, South. He was educated at Randolph-Macon College, Princeton University, and Princeton Theological Seminary. He was a member of the Virginia Annual Conference of the MECS and served as president of the Blackstone Female Institute. He worked as editor of the *Baltimore and Richmond Christian Advocate* and was elected bishop in 1918. Cannon was an outspoken critic of alcoholism and was active in both the Anti-Saloon League and the World League Against Alcoholism. He received national attention for participating in "The Anti-Smith Democrats" that fought against the candidacy of Alfred E. Smith during the US presidential election of 1928.

41. Francis Everett Baldwin (b. 1856). Baldwin was an active member of the Methodist Minute Men and a lawyer in Western New York. He served as chairman of the Prohibition Committee of New York State and ran for governor of New York during the 1894 election on the Prohibition Party ticket.

42. Josephus Daniels (1862-1948). Daniels was an editor, author, Secretary of the U.S. Navy, and U.S. Ambassador to Mexico. He was educated at the University of North Carolina Law School and received several honorary doctorates. Daniels was editor of the *Raleigh News and Observer* and was active in the Prohibition movement as a Democrat. He was appointed Secretary of the Navy upon the election of his close friend Woodrow Wilson to the U.S. presidency. As Secretary he abolished the consumption of alcohol by officers and soldiers. In 1933 he was appointed Ambassador to Mexico by Franklin D. Roosevelt.

43. Daniels references Dinah Morris, a Methodist local preacher in George Eliot's *Adam Bede* (New York: Harper & Brothers, 1859). Susanna A. Wesley was the mother and early educator of John and Charles Wesley.

44. Edward Eggleston and John Karst, *The Circuit Rider: A Tale of the Heroic Age* (New York: J.B. Ford & Co., 1874).

45. The doctrine of Nullification was based on the theory that a U.S. state has the right to nullify federal laws that the people of the state deem unconstitutional. Walter Kirk Wood, *Nullification: A Constitutional History, 1776-1833* (Lanham, MD: University Press of America, 2008).

46. Daniels references the American Social Health Association, founded in 1914, to educate soldiers on sexually transmitted diseases. Additional information can be found at: http://www.ashastd.org/

47. Wesley's actual wording was "I look upon all the world as my parish."

48. David Wark Griffith was a California filmmaker who had produced the controversial film *The Birth of a Nation* (1915) and the follow-up epic *Intolerance* (1916). The audience listening to Reisner give this talk would have been familiar with Griffith and his work. Griffith visited the Ohio State Fairgrounds several weeks before the start of the Centenary Celebration to decide what to film. He sent several staff including cinematographer Johann Gottlob Wilhelm "Billy" Bitzer who helped film the July 4th parade and the pageant spectacle *The Wayfarer*. The final product was titled *The World at Columbus* (1919) and the motion picture was advertised in several Methodist-related newspapers. The author has not located a copy of the original film.

49. "Motion Picture Day" was held at the Centenary Celebration on July 8. Members of the National Association of Motion Picture Producers including William A. Brady, William McAdoo, and John C. Flynn of Famous Players-Lasky met with Methodist media advocates including S. Earl Taylor, S. R. Vinton, and Christian F. Reisner. Both the NAMPP and the Methodist Episcopal Church had sponsored the building of a 10-story motion picture and lantern slide projection screen erected inside the horse racetrack at the Columbus fairgrounds. For further information on this event and the connections between the American film industry and Methodists see Christopher J. Anderson, "Silent Cinema: Projecting America and Methodist Missions" in *The World is Our Parish: Displaying Home and Foreign Missions at the 1919 Methodist World's Fair* (Ph.D. dissertation, Drew University, 2006), 80-118.

50. Irving Berlin (1888-1989). Berlin was a world-renowned songwriter of Broadway musicals and show tunes. New Yorkers in the Centenary exposition audience that day may have been familiar with Berlin's *Ziegfeld Follies* showing at the New Amsterdam Theater in New York City during the summer of 1919.

Chapter Four

Methodists, Prohibition and Universal Suffrage

Introduction

Chapter Four includes addresses that broadcast several social concerns of early twentieth century American Methodists. For nearly a century Methodists had been on the front end of several crusades to promote Temperance and later Prohibition in American society. On the eve of national Prohibition the Woman's Christian Temperance Union joined forces with groups of Methodist men to celebrate the removal of alcohol from American society. As a result of the Nineteenth Amendment enacted during the second week of the fair American distilleries could no longer produce or distribute alcoholic beverages. Well-known temperance advocates including Anna Gordon, William Jennings Bryan, and Clarence True Wilson promoted their concerns regarding the residual effects of alcohol and how Methodists had led the charge to remove the saloon from American cities.

    The first section highlights addresses given at the "Woman's Christian Temperance Union Program" on Woman's Day at the Centenary exposition. Several women leaders of the W.C.T.U. and the World Woman's Christian Temperance Union spoke of the historic crusade to eliminate the manufacturing, distribution, and consumption of alcohol. Anna Gordon, National President of the W.C.T.U., Frances Willard Wong, China representative of the W.C.T.U., and Hardynia K. Norville, representative for the World W.C.T.U. connected the work of Methodist women with the movement and also demonstrated how international Prohibition would radically change the home and the world.

    Anna Gordon chaired the session on Woman's Day and spoke on the educational and social work of the W.C.T.U. in the United States and around the world. As National W.C.T.U. President it was important for Gordon to chair the session and highlight her involvement with the movement. Her global connections to other Prohibition advocates were evidenced from the stage and her short addresses and introductions throughout the meeting provided a framework to demonstrate the interconnectedness between the North American W.C.T.U. and the larger World W.C.T.U. Frances Willard Wong reminded the audience that the China exhibits at the exposition provided a sketch of the life and work of Chinese medical practitioners, educational institutions, and missionaries. But, the displays at Columbus did not adequately portray the elimination of footbinding, the extent of opium use in China, or the ongoing battle with alcoholism. Wong called for more missionaries to go to China and pressed fairgoers to consider helping her "fight for the spotless purity of women." Hardynia K. Norville, a representative for the World W.C.T.U. from South America, brought several women to speak on behalf of world-wide Prohibition. Representatives from Argentina, Mexico, and Uruguay evidenced how the W.C.T.U. and women from North America had been key influences in the work in their countries. More importantly, the representatives confirmed that indigenous peoples from their own countries were active in the dissemination of literature and social justice work in prisons and communities.

The second section of the chapter highlights addresses given on "Prohibition Day" at the Columbus fairgrounds. The sessions were held at the "Big Tent" and at the coliseum. Speakers for the meeting included Clarence True Wilson, secretary of the Board of Temperance, Prohibition and Public Morals of the Methodist Episcopal Church, Purley Baker, representative for the Anti-Saloon League, former U.S. presidential candidate William Jennings Bryan, and Illinois Congressman Henry T. Rainey.

Wilson, perhaps the most influential voice on Prohibition in American Methodism, charted the history of the Methodist movement and its notorious relationship with alcohol. Wilson spotlighted several temperance advocates and in particular noted the emergence of the Temperance Society of the Methodist Episcopal Church in 1904. He called for each Methodist annual conference to appoint "anti-saloon men" to promote the work of the agency, recruit more workers, and raise additional funding. Wilson linked beer drinking to the German military and claimed that the U.S. Expeditionary Force in Europe practiced total abstinence. Purley Baker, a leader with the Anti-Saloon League, spoke on the history of the organization and the mobilization of the movement in Protestant churches throughout the United States. Baker cherished his work with the League and used the exposition stage as a recruiting stump to gather more Methodists into the organization by claiming "the Methodist Episcopal Church, North and South, has sent more men into the field and put more money into the treasury of the Anti-Saloon League than it has been the privilege of any other denomination in this country to do so."

In 1919, William Jennings Bryan was one of the most recognized and respected orators in the United States. At the exposition he was careful to note the significance of the day (July 1) claiming "where could we better celebrate the first dry day in a saloonless nation" than Ohio and more specifically at a large gathering of American Methodists. Bryan had made a run for U.S. president under the Prohibition Party ticket several years earlier and championed how the U.S. government had been influential in helping rid the United States of alcohol. As a politician, Bryan felt it important to also comment on his support of the controversial League of Nations covenant proposed by Woodrow Wilson. He supported the legislation and claimed "love and brotherhood" would remove war from the future of the United States.

U.S. Congressman Henry T. Rainey took the stage after Bryan. Rainey was the Chairman of the Special Committee appointed by the U.S. Treasury Department to write the Harrison Drug Law and to help remove narcotics from American society. Rainey used the stage to remind the audience that, while Prohibition had legally removed alcohol from the United States, another vice, narcotic drugs were rampant throughout America. Rainey noted the existence of over one million drug addicts in the U.S. that resulted in approximately $40 million in drug trafficking monies. Heroin and opium were rampant and Rainey reminded the audience to act on narcotic drug trafficking as much as they had pushed for Prohibition.

Woman's Christian Temperance Union Program
Tuesday afternoon, June 24, 1919

...Miss Anna A. Gordon, National President, Woman's Christian Temperance Union, presiding as chairman...[1]

...The meeting opened with the singing of the first and last verses of 'America'...

ANNA A. GORDON:
Let us together repeat our Crusade Psalm. We are in the dear, old Crusade State and we have the president of the Ohio State W.C.T.U. on the platform. Let us repeat those blessed words that have been verified in these wonderful days – the 146th Psalm.

...The audience repeated, "Praise ye the Lord, praise ye the Lord, Oh, my soul, while I live will I praise the Lord. I will sing praises unto my Lord while I have a being. Put not your trust in princes nor in the son of man in whom there is no help. His breath goeth forth; he returneth to earth; on that very day his thoughts perish. Happy is he that hath the God of Jacob for his help, whose hope is in the Lord, his God, which made Heaven and earth, the sea and all that therein is, which keepeth truth forever, which executeth judgment for the oppressed, which giveth food to the hungry. The Lord looseth the prisoners; the Lord openeth the eyes of the blind; the Lord raiseth them that are bowed down; the Lord loveth the righteous; the Lord preserveth the strangers, he relieveth the fatherless and widow, but the way of the wicked he turneth upside down."

...Invocation by Mrs. Romans: Oh God, our Father, we do so thank thee that we can thus assemble in the interests of this great cause, thy cause. We recognize that from the beginning our organization which is represented here today has looked to thee for guidance and direction. It has looked to thee for wisdom and for understanding, and we believe that the women who have answered the call have come at thy command.

Oh, Heavenly Father, we thank thee for thy guidance throughout the years. We thank thee that thou didst put it into the heart of womankind to champion a great cause like this. We thank thee for the victories which are being celebrated today, and we ask that thou wilt give us larger vision, that thou wilt enable us to understand thy will at this crucial moment, in these wonderful days of opportunity to spread this gospel of temperance, the Gospel of thy kingdom to all the nations of the world.

We thank thee for this opportunity. We thank thee for this great assemblage here, which is bringing together the peoples from the ends of the earth in one, common cause. We ask that thou wilt be very near the officers of the National Woman's Christian Temperance Union, that thou wilt direct and guide and stay and strengthen them for the larger work that is laid upon them at this present time.

Heavenly Father, be with our own state organization, with our state president, with all that support that work in this Crusade State of ours.

We ask that thou wilt bless the temperance cause throughout the world today. Be with us now throughout this meeting, help those who are to speak, to do and to say the things that are pleasing in thy sight. Help us to be humble before thee that we may understand thy will in all things. Go with us now throughout the day, throughout the days that are before us in this great assemblage here, and throughout our life, and finally save us, we ask, in thy everlasting kingdom of peace. Amen...

ANNA A. GORDON:

Dear friends, the Woman's Christian Temperance Union is organized in forty countries and we have for thirty-five years been helping lift the world to the light in our many departments of work, the work for the children, the work for the little people who are walking life's dusty road and must choose when two paths meet, the narrow or the broad. The children have always tremendously enlisted the mother heart of the Woman's Christian Temperance Union. The Society has been called organized Mother Love, and its child welfare work, its moral educational work, its work to protect children along the lines of industry and in every possible way has always been emphasized, but more and more today, we are seeking to protect the child in the midst. And we thought this afternoon, although everywhere on this wonderful ground, where we are having this most marvelous exposition of the missionary work of the Methodist Church – you see the costumes of other countries, you see the bewitching little people from every land, yet we wanted to bring to our meeting our own Loyal Temperance Legion children from Europe, Asia, Africa, North and South America, and so we have invited twenty-five little people, who represent as many countries where we have the Loyal Temperance Legion children at work, to come to our platform.[2] One of our Columbus white-ribboners has kindly taken this grouping of the children in charge and I think she is ready to bring them to the platform.

In Australia, they have a motto for the little people. 'We march with the morning," and as we look into the eyes of the young people, we realize that the dawn is in their eyes, and those of us who have spent many years in service for God, and for home and every land, are delighted that there are those with the dawn in their eyes who are going to carry our flag on to further victories.

...At this point the children marched to the platform...

Friends, these costumes which the children are wearing were sent to me as Superintendent of the Loyal Temperance Legion, branch of our organization, from the various countries, and many of them are choice National costumes. We are going to ask them to take their seats upon the platform and stay with us throughout our meeting. (Applause)

Now we are to have words of welcome from the President of the Crusade State Woman's Christian Temperance Union, Mrs. Florence D. Richard of Columbus.

FLORENCE D. RICHARD:[3]

I don't know whether I can speak this afternoon or not for I have been making speeches out of doors. You know, we have been burying old John Barleycorn. We have to bury him out of doors. It is not worthwhile to hold his funeral in the house. So I am a little hoarse.

But I come in the name of the Woman's Christian Temperance Union of the Crusade State to bid you welcome, to welcome our national president, Miss Gordon, and to welcome all these little folks from these various lands. Isn't it wonderful as you see them in their own costumes, and I am glad that the W.C.T.U. early started out thinking about the children. And Ohio is proud today – the Crusade State – to have this privilege of coming before you and greeting the people not only of Ohio, but of the nation and some from the world. We are delighted.

We are delighted to have you come to Ohio for Ohio is the best state in the Union, of course. There is no other quite so good. (Applause)

We are the fourth state after the original thirteen, so we are the seventeenth state of the Union. Ohio means beautiful. That's the meaning of the name, Ohio. It is an old Indian name. They name the river Ohio because it was so beautiful and we took our name from that. And when you stop to think about Ohio, it surely is a wonderful, wonderful state.

Why, we have the best warriors from Ohio. We have the best orators in Ohio. We have the best writers in Ohio. We have so many of the good things that we can scarcely stop to tell you. We have some poets, and among them some women, and among the writers there is none better in all the world than Harriet Beecher Stowe who did more to rid this nation of slavery than anybody else in all the land. Then we won't like to stop right there. We would like to tell you that we are the first state in the Union so far as some inventions are concerned, that it is Ohio men, Mr. Brush and Mr. Edison, who really and truly light the world today. You see they have turned night into day. Not long ago in a trip across the sea I went over to the Alps and I saw such a wonderful lighting by electricity and behold, when I got over there, it was Edison's latest arc light or lamp that they were using in Italy in the Alps.

So Ohio greets you, one of the greatest states in the Union, and it is great not only so far as its brilliant writers, all its brilliant men and women are concerned. It is the Crusade State, it is the state that first heard God's call. The lady who voiced the prayer this afternoon said God had called the women, and we really and truly believe that he did. We know that these women could not have gone out themselves, and so being the first state in the Union where the women heard God's voice calling them to an organization that meant the overthrow of old John Barleycorn, surely and truly we Ohioans ought to be happy this afternoon to greet our national workers, to say to them, we started the ball rolling; we are glad you caught the vision and joined in, but Ohio first of all, and we are rejoiced in that. It was God Himself who called the women of Ohio who responded.

I was coming from Washington the other day where I had attended the world great meeting, and our own national president spoke, and coming home on the sleeper there was a woman whom I thought I knew but we were in the same coach, and finally I spoke to her. I said, "You look sort of familiar. I ought to know you," and she says, "Well, I know you; you are the state president of the W.C.T.U., and I am Mrs. J.B. Foraker,"[4] and I said, "Well, I am glad indeed to meet Governor Foraker's wife," and then she talked to me about the Crusade and she told me something that I suspect the rest of you knew, but I had forgotten it. She told me about Mother Foraker, Governor Foraker's mother. She was one of our original crusaders, and you know how they used to go out in front of saloons and how they would kneel down and how they would pray, and the drug stores were sometimes as bad as saloons and they went one night to pray before this drug store in particular and the druggist didn't like it. He said they hurt his trade, and after he had warned the women away and the women wouldn't stay, he concluded he would have them arrested. So he arrested the women, Mrs. Foraker among the number. This druggist had gotten the wisest lawyer he could to plead his case and to take up the case against the women. There was a long table in this courthouse and this lawyer had books galore on it with little marks in them, and the women thought if that lawyer was going to read all that law to them why they surely were doomed – if he had that much law on his side.

Then Mother Foraker and Mother Thompson and Mother Stewart and a few others said they thought before they commenced the trial they had better go over in a little room and have a season of prayer, and they went over, and Mother Foraker was the one that prayed the longest and the loudest. She said, "Oh, God, it is your case, not ours; we are doing thy work, not our own, and you just plead our cause for us this afternoon." And then she said, "Oh, Lord, confuse and confound that lawyer; confuse and confound him." (Laughter) They went back and took their places and the suit proceeded. It wasn't quite time for the lawyer so he took off his glasses and put them in a little red case and laid them down on the table, and the case came over the table a little. There was a little dog running around the room and he saw that red case and he jumped up there, grabbed the case in his mouth and ran around the court room and out into the street and they tried to get the glasses, but they couldn't and that lawyer couldn't read one word that he had. (Laughter) They tried to get other glasses for him but not a single pair would suit, and God answered the prayer of Mother Foraker, and he was confused and confounded so that he couldn't say a word.

So I am glad that the women trusted in the Lord and went forward, and it is that kind of women, and it is the state of Ohio that started the ball rolling and amid just such scenes as that, for national, constitutional prohibition that greets you this afternoon. I am not to make my speech very long, but one thing that brought the victory, Miss Gordon, is the work among the children.

One of our writers says that if you save the children you save the nation tomorrow, and the nation is SAVED, please God, for we have reached the tomorrow. Isn't that splendid?[5] We have state-wide prohibition and nation-wide prohibition. We are delighted that this is true, and so today we gather to sing a new song unto the Lord for he hath triumphed marvelously. It is his work, and we bless Him today.

When the Commissioners selected the city of Columbus as the Capitol of the State, there were nine other cities under consideration, but they finally voted on Columbus. There wasn't a single house here in this vast area – not one, but a log cabin, and all the rest was a dense forest. See how much we have grown and see what we have done, and we welcome you to the greatest state and to the greatest city. Now we don't think it is great because of all our manufacturing establishments and all those things but it is great because of the men and women that possess it. You know at the Columbian Exposition when they wanted something that would represent Ohio, they took that story of Cornelia and put it in stone, and as you go down town you will see it. After the Columbian Exposition they brought it back here and I don't want any of you to go away without looking at it. I think it is sort of suggestive and historic and prophetic and everything else that a woman stands on the top of that great pedestal down there. She has seven men about her but she stands at the top, and I am glad that women not only have helped put out the saloon throughout the state and the nation, but that the good people of the state have given us Woman Suffrage and placed us on an equality with the men of the State of Ohio. (Applause)

So we greet you today in the name of all these splendid reforms, and we want to thank God for all these victories. A state dry, a nation dry! We thank God today for our Congress that gave us the Eighteenth Amendment, National Constitutional Prohibition, and we thank God today for our Congress that it is standing pat on war prohibition too, (Applause) and that they are not listening to the advice of President Wilson and Gompers – the two go together. We are glad of it. Down in Washington one man said that if there ever was a man that threw his money wrench into the political tool chest it was President Wilson, and I think so myself. But we thank God for Congress, for a Congress that will do its duty, and we want you to pray that Congress will continue to do so. Then we thank God for legislators in forty-five states that ratified this splendid amendment.

Now let me close with this thought. It is all mete and proper and right when we have gained great victories to thank God for it. I don't think this Centenary would be complete – I don't think it would be right to have this Centenary calling upon God and honoring and glorifying his name without a Woman's Day and giving us a little chance and a little part in it. You know, when great victories were gained in the days of Abraham Lincoln he didn't forget to thank God for all these things. Bishop Simpson, one of our good Methodist Bishops lived in Washington and he was Abraham Lincoln's spiritual counselor. I have heard Bishop Simpson tell this story himself. He used to go to the White House often and go into a private room with Abraham Lincoln and they would pour out their souls to the God of Battles. One morning the Bishop was going by the White House and Abraham Lincoln came out without his coat or hat. He wasn't very much for costume nor custom, and so he hailed the Bishop. He said, "Come over, Bishop, and let's praise God for these great victories, for don't you know, Bishop, Hooker has fought a battle above the clouds and the enemy has fled before him, our brave boys have stormed Missionary Ridge and taken it, General Bragg has surrendered and the enemy's flag no long floats from that ridge, but the Stars and Stripes have controlled – come over, Bishop, and let's praise God for these victories."

And so today our hearts are filled with praises to God for the victories, and we realize that his guiding hand has brought them about, and so we welcome you in the name of our Crusade State, Ohio, in the name of our nation and in the name of our Lord God of Hosts, who led us so triumphantly to victory. (Prolonged Applause)

ANNA A. GORDON:

It is my pleasure to present Mrs. Robert Karch who has brought this family of nations, a youthful league of nations, the children in costume, and I wish that she would let them stand, one after another, and tell the country from which they come.

...The children, representing various countries, were introduced in the following order: Burma, Australia, Norway, Chili (sic), Scotland, Egypt, Ireland, England, France, Iceland, India, Sweden, Japan, United States, Madeira, Newfoundland, Denmark, Canada, Syria, and Finland... (Applause)

...Singing of "The Morning Light is Breaking"...

ANNA A. GORDON:

May I have the great pleasure of presenting the corresponding secretary of our W.C.T.U. in Porto Rico. We are delighted to welcome Mrs. Andujar and these two good friends. Her husband and herself helped us greatly in having prohibition secured for that island.

MRS. ANDUJAR:[6]

I am very glad to be here this afternoon to present greetings from Porto Rico, and I particularly want to show you a sign that we have in the Porto Rican community. On July 16, 1917 the cocoanut smashed the bottle in Porto Rico – one hundred thousand ballots for the cocoanut and sixty-three thousand for the bottle, giving a majority of thirty-seven thousand for prohibition.

What do you think of that in a country that in four years was drinking alcohol, and the Jones Bill gave the Porto Ricans the option to vote for or against liquor.[7] (Applause) And of their own free will, with the missionary back of them, and a few other people – physicians and lawyers and some people of great power and influence – helped us to win this magnificent victory.

I was in the country on the mountains with my children, when my husband wired me that Cocoanut won by thirty-seven thousand majority, and what a wonderful thing that was: the liquor interests said if they hadn't selected just the bottle it wouldn't have been so bad, but the cocoanut was such a delightful drink and such a beautiful fruit, and when the bottle was put up for the liquor interests they immediately lost everything. I am very glad to have been with you this afternoon.

ANNA A. GORDON:

The lawyer to whom Mrs. Richard referred, who in answer to prayer was confused and confounded, is not the only lawyer who has met that fate in these last years. There are some very distinguished lawyers who are today confused and confounded in the opinions they have rendered, and we are keeping close touch with Washington, D.C. these days.

The repeal bills are before Congress – both Houses – and the Committee on the Judiciary of the House and of the Senate have those bills referred to them. It was my pleasure and privilege to be with that committee a few weeks ago in Washington, and the bill that has been introduced by Mr. Volstead of Minnesota, chairman of the House Committee, has been under consideration, and by a vote of ten to three, the House Judiciary killed all repeal bills. (Applause) And voted by a similar vote that they would send out to the House the opinion of the Judiciary Committee, that one-half of one percent alcohol forms an intoxicating liquor. (Applause) And the Senate is just as dry as the House, and nothing is going to influence the Senate Committee on the Judiciary to report any repeal bill to the United States Congress.

We are all hoping those bills will come up for discussion on the floor of the House and the Senate prior to July 1st, and what a celebration we will have everywhere if we can secure the decision of Congress against repeal. And we are sure to do so, for this Congress has a larger percentage of dry voters than the Sixty-fifth Congress.

Now, we have some of our own members of this office of the National W.C.T.U. I have been watching for our national corresponding secretary, Mrs. Francis P. Parks, who has assembled our beautiful booth with Mrs. George assisting our publicity director at the National W.C.T.U. headquarters, and if Mrs. Parks has not yet arrived I am going to steal a march on Mrs. Anna Pritchard George, and ask her to say a word for us, and I want you to know her. I want you to go to the booth in the Asbury Building and see the story of the Woman's Christian Temperance Union. Mrs. Anna P. George, director of our publicity bureau.

ANNA PRITCHARD GEORGE:[8]

I cannot tell you how glad I am to be here with you, but I want to invite you all to our booth. I want to tell you a little of what is there, and then I want to appoint you associate publicity directors, and I would like you to go all over this camp meeting ground and tell everybody about your booth, because you have the ownership of that, it belongs to you W.C.T.U. folks, and we are running it for you.

We have there the wonderful polyglot petition which has gone to all the countries of the world to be signed by over seven million five hundred thousand people, and we have the signatures there in mighty rolls, which reach from the floor pretty nearly to the ceiling and make a great, big round pillar. Then we have the proclamations that were sent out for world prohibition – the one which is included in the polyglot petition by Francis E. Willard, the one by Mrs.

Steven, and the one by our own President, Miss Gordon, which was sent out on the day that the armistice was signed.

We also have there a spot map of the world, which shows in what countries the W.C.T.U. is organized, and gives the dates of the organization in those countries and shows that our organization has been established throughout this world for thirty-five years.

We also have wonderful panels which show the war work in the reconstruction of the W.C.T.U., and we have other panels which show the work in the different countries throughout this world. You simply cannot miss coming to our booth. It is a vivid picture of the work of the organization, of the history of the organization, and of the march of prohibition within the last forty-five years since the W.C.T.U. was organized.

And so I want you all to start right in now. First, come yourselves and see with your own eyes what it all contains, and then go out on a mission tour and bring everybody to our booth that comes to this meeting. Thank you. (Applause)

ANNA A. GORDON:

We learn that Mrs. Parks, our national corresponding secretary, will be here later. We want her to tell you of our great Americanization school at Chautauqua, where we are to have a six weeks' training course in connection with the Chautauqua institution, which cooperates with us in our training school for Americanization workers, and how we are going to finance this great plan of our organization.[9]

So many human stories come to us at a place like this, touching incidents, too. Our hearts were all greatly saddened yesterday as we learned of the dear little Japanese boy, the little life that so suddenly flickered out and left a home and hearts desolate. But for his going, one of the distinguished men of Japan would have been upon our platform – a man who has helped the Woman's Christian Temperance Union in that far-away sunrise kingdom, Doctor Uki.

I saw him yesterday and invited him. He said, "Oh, I would love to come. I am fond of the work of the Woman's Christian Temperance Union. I always want to help the movement, but we have at that very hour the funeral service of the precious child, killed suddenly by an accident." I said to Doctor Uki, "We'll remember you at our service. We will remember all the Japanese friends who are here and who are so tenderly in sympathy with the family of the Osakis of Oakland, who have been so sorely bereaved."

I know, dear friends, you will lift your hearts in prayer to God at this hour for these good friends who came so far away from Oakland to help in this great Methodist Centenary Celebration, and who so soon will take home the lifeless little body of their precious child.

Oh, the whole world is one! Our hearts are all alike. We are sorry Doctor Uki isn't here. We wanted him to speak of the men's work in Japan, but we are honored to have with us a worker of the Woman's Christian Temperance Union from Japan, Madam Etsu Sugimoto, who has been at the head of our work among the young people. She is now in this country with her gifted daughters –

educating them, and Madam Sugimoto is to bring us a word of greeting from Japan.

ETSU SUGIMOTO:[10]

I feel I have to make some apology before I commence, and of course, my voice is very little, but I will try my best to talk as loud as I can. I always wear my own dress – that is, the Japanese dress – and so very many people ask me if I have just arrived from Japan, and many times I am asked, "Can you talk English?" And I always say, "Yes, a little bit." And because I wear Japanese dress some people take it for granted I have just arrived from Japan, but I must say this is my third trip to this country, and I came here just twenty years ago, and I claim Cincinnati as my American home, so I am very proud to be here, especially after I heard the address from the president of this Ohio state.

Moreover, I am very glad to know that Ohio means beautiful. In the Japanese language Ohio means good morning, and so nothing could be so beautiful to me as the cherry blossom in the morning ray of the sunrise. So if the Indian word Ohio means beautiful, and in the Japanese language it means the greeting Good Morning, Ohio must have some origin somewhere. Therefore, I have a double gratitude to be here, with the feeling of a right to be here as an Ohioan – as an Ohio and Japanese woman.

In Japan I look so different from other people so very many people have the idea I am a stranger to that land. Japanese women very often are considered as very different from American women, but really I must tell you that Japanese women of today have the same fight as you ladies have, only we fight not in the same way as you ladies fight.

W.C.T.U. workers in Japan have to fight just as hard as the women in this country. The way we fight is different, but we have the same problem to solve. Now, the labor question is coming on and the women's position is different. Women of Japan, until recent years, have had to remain in their homes, but now they bravely realize they must shoulder the work with her other sex, and so we have the same problem, and I must say with pride that the White Ribboners of Japan are doing the leadership part in almost every good work in Japan.

Madam Yajima is our faithful and efficient leader in every respect, and I must send her this word, that I have been here, and I know she will be very glad to hear that I could be here and meet you, and I am very glad that I am allowed to speak of her work in Japan. In another word, I shall tell her that in this Centenary work we are demonstrating the brotherhood of the world, and are looking forward to the time when Francis Willard will tie the whole world together with the emblem of a small ribbon.

ANNA A. GORDON:

We all want to send a message of greeting to our revered president of the Japanese Woman's Christian Temperance Union, Madam Kaji Yajima.[11] She came all the way from Japan to Boston for a convention. She could not speak a word of English, but she lead us in prayer at our precious noontime hour, using her own language, and every heart was lifted to the throne of Grace as that sainted woman prayed for us. And she is thinking of these friends far away. She knows of the great meeting here. Let us stand as we send the message to Madam Kaji Yajima. (Everybody arose)

I wish we could bow as sweetly and artistically as our friends from Japan. (Applause)

The beloved founder of the world Woman's Christian Temperance Union, Frances Willard, we believe, today knows the marvelous way in which the work of our organization has grown in many lands. We believe that she knows what has come to our own beloved country. We believe she knows what is sweeping over the whole world in the progress of this great temperance reform. She knows how the missionaries have helped our work, how those who are in the pastorate of all these lands in the Methodist church have helped us in our great work.

She knows that we have a namesake of hers, Frances Willard Wong of China, preparing in this country to go back to her beloved republic to spread the scientific knowledge in regard to alcohol among the young people of her republic. She knows that Frances Wong is on fire for the salvation of China, from this threatened curse of invasion of our breweries and distilleries.

Oh, we are so glad Frances is here on the grounds, and that she can be with us this afternoon – a young girl with the dawn in her eyes and the great hope that under Christ, the King, she may be the Frances Willard of China.

FRANCES WILLARD WONG:[12]

Miss Gordon and my dear friends, I feel this is my greatest privilege, that I speak to you this afternoon on such a happy occasion. I understand that Columbus is named in honor of the one who discovered America. Again I was told that Oberlin College in Ohio state was the first one opened to women, and in which the mother of our beloved Mrs. Willard was a student for quite a few years.[13]

I certainly consider myself as one of the most fortunate persons to be here for this wonderful Centenary Celebration. Now, friends, you have seen the physical side of China. You have entered the gate of China – a building – and you have seen the medical department where you were told of the need for medical work in China. You were told of those hard benches on which the patients have to wait, and you have seen the operating table which is not a regular one. You were told that our medical missionary over there – that their aim is not only to give physical help to their patients, but also spiritual help.

They have Bible women to preach to them. Again you have seen the industrial schools. You have seen some pictures of a few colleges in China. You have seen the chop suey houses, where you enjoy so much chop suey. You have seen the temple – how the people worship, and you have seen, and you have loved those beautiful embroideries done by hand, by your own girls at home. You have seen the bride's room, and many other things. In short, you have a general knowledge of the way of our people's living in China.

But now, my friends, it is my intention to tell you a few things that you cannot see with your eyes, but with your mind's eyes. I know you have been wondering to yourself what is China as a nation, anyhow? Some of them say,

"Well, China is old China – five thousand years old." Others say that China is a new China.

Now, friends, this is just what I have in mind to tell you – whether she is old or young. Truly there are two ways of thinking of China as a nation. One – she is an old man with gray hair and gray beard, physically he could not walk, mentally he could not think.

On the other hand, she is a child, but six years old. A child almost like those children over there. She is a child of six years old. What she sees is only beauty, youth, love, sympathy, confidence and truth. In the old China there is a fragment of tyranny, a fragment of autocracy, but in the new China there is the flag of liberty and a flag of democracy. (The speaker displayed the flag) (Applause)

Friends, as you see this flag you do not know how much it means to us, but only you can appreciate when you think of your stars and stripes. This means more than anything else to us young people especially. For this flag, by means of which, and for which our young people died in battles for democracy in 1911, is a great symbol to us. It is by means of this flag that our young people are here studying and preparing themselves to serve China as best as they can.

And it is also this flag, friends, that I am here speaking to you about, in order to create a better understanding of China – China as the young China, not the old. In spite of her age, China has done a great many striking things within these few years. She has freed her women from foot binding.[14] She has given an equal privilege to both boys and girls for education. She has opened the door wider for [the] gospel, and above all, she has prohibited the selling of opium.

You remember, friends, how you used to think and read and were told that because of opium there are thousands and millions of families which broke down. You were also told that children – thousands of them, millions of them – became beggars because their fathers did not take the responsibility. Again, you were told that little women of China were allowed three inches of feet, and that they were suffering because the men they married did not love them, because they loved opium better.

But friends, since we have the republic – the eight year old child – she has driven away the opium from her border. I know your heart rejoices just like mine. It is a long story for me to tell you just how it is done, but I am not going to, and I want to tell you, friends, that while China is striving for a new national life, she is facing another battle – a new battle – a battle against alcoholism.

I must congratulate you with my whole heart for the wonderful victory which you have over liquor in this country, but friends, my heart aches when I think of the liquor men going to China – that in 1911 the liquor exported to China was at a cost of half a million dollars, that in 1918 it was doubled, and in 1919 it was again increased. It wastes our wealth. It perishes our race, and above all, it lowers our moral standard of living.

Do you think it is safe to think your task is over? Not yet, your task is not over. There is a great battle for you to fight – a fight for the spotless purity of women. You know, friends, it is our supreme duty that we should go to those places and work for those who are suffering. China, as young China, cannot stand to have another menace come into her country. This does not mean, friends, that while I am asking your help that we do not realize that it is the Chinese people themselves that ought to work out their own salvation.

We do realize, surely we do realize it in our country. Two thousand students in this country have made an organization for the time being to start campaigns against liquor men. Again, our girls alone in the East, last October, upon learning that liquor men were going to China, raised hundreds of dollars and sent it to our beloved Miss Gordon to help the temperance work in China. They are going to have a conference in Boston to help work out a campaign against liquor in China. At this particular time, because China is young, we want your help.

As you go out, I am going to put some literature over there which we are sending to China by our girls here, and I want you to read it. Yes, our lives are busy in these days. There are so many things going on as the civilization becomes more progressive and our family lives become more complex, and also our social life and our industrial life. But friends, aside from this work, there is a time that we ought to say to ourselves, "Up, thou sluggard, and away to the bugle call. The day of battle dawns." I tell you, friends, that time is today. I thank you. (Applause)

ANNA A. GORDON:

We are greatly honored in having on our platform Mrs. Bishop Oldham of South America. Mrs. Oldham has helped our work, has helped Miss Norville, our world W.C.T.U. representative in South America, and I consider it a great privilege to present, for a word of greeting, Mrs. Oldham.

MRS. BISHOP OLDHAM:[15]

I am very glad, indeed, to be with you. You see I am very much badged, and belong to all the good things in which our church is engaged, and in which North America is engaged in all countries. Great honor has been put upon my husband and myself in sending us to teach the gospel in the great lands, and now at last you know we are in South America.

It has been my great privilege to stand alongside – you see I have here the little white ribbon bow – to stand alongside of Miss Norville and be one of the women to hold out our hands to help in that great land. You know we talk about it being a country where they drink light wine and where they do not have very much intemperance, but we who live there know that history repeats itself, and the light wines are the only thin entering in of the wedge, and the others come along in great numbers, and we are seeking to unite all the forces for righteousness in South America in fighting this great evil of intemperance, and we have been very much blessed and helped.

Miss Norville, your representative who is here, has done a splendid work in bringing together the people in higher living, and bringing them into touch with what the women of those lands consider is going to be the greatest evil – that is the evil of intemperance, and those women have lent themselves so happily to this work, and we have the inspectors of education and the others giving Miss

Norville free course in that land, so that she has introduced the scientific temperance teaching into all our schools in Argentina.[16]

As I live in Argentina, in Buenos Ayres, I want to say to you that I feel that we are all holding hands in a blessed work when we are seeking to girdle the earth with the gospel of the Lord Jesus Christ, and with the white ribbon of the Woman's Christian Temperance Union. (Applause)

ANNA A. GORDON:

Now, our Mrs. Parks has come in from the busy booth in the Frances (sic) Asbury Building, and I know Mrs. Parks, our national corresponding secretary, has a word for us.

MRS. PARKS:[17]

Madam President, friends and comrades, I am very glad, indeed, to have the opportunity of looking into your faces for a few moments. I have probably seen most of you today over in our exhibit booth. If you have not been there, I hope you will go. I had one of the most encouraging things occur while you were having your lovely meeting here, when a missionary from China, home on vacation, came in to get some information, and said that the Frances (sic) Asbury hall[18] contained more of inspiration for the worker from foreign lands than he could find in all the rest of the grounds – that there was there so much of the inspirational, so much of the things that the worker in other countries wanted to carry back, and that much of it was in such condensed shape that it was of very, very great value to him, and his head was almost bursting from the knowledge that he was trying to pack into the day. So I felt well repaid for having stayed away from this meeting for a little while, and having missed some of the good things, by having that word of encouragement.

Our president of the crusade, Mrs. Richard, encourages us at national W.C.T.U. headquarters, and always writes optimistic letters and says to us, "You dear women over there are always thinking of things for us to do." She was fully pleased with this program – our victory year program – giving concrete plans for our twenty thousand local unions, covering the real big things to be done in this victory year, telling of reconstruction work which is fitted to the old time plan, telling us how to do the work for the children, under the child welfare program, in our women's industry program, in our Americanization program, for the reconstruction period as well as for our great program for world prohibition.

I will take time only to tell you of one feature of this reconstruction work. The Woman's Christian Temperance Union has stepped forward with faith and with courage in the work of Americanization, for which there is such a demand in every community where there are foreign born people. The war has brought home to America the need for Americanizing all of the people of America, and because there were so few schools in the country where teachers could be prepared, the Woman's Christian Temperance Union, cooperating with the Chautauqua of New York, the birthplace of the Women's (sic) Christian

Temperance Union, is putting on a six weeks' Americanization school, beginning July 7th.

There are to be gathered there some of the greatest speakers and experts from the colleges and universities of America to talk on Americanization. The school will be under the direction of Mrs. Mary Clarke Barnes, superintendent of our Department of Americanization, and she will be assisted by these experts from colleges and universities, and by the practical workers of our own organization.[19]

The school will be a part of the regular summer school's program. In addition to the class work, there will be on five days of every week, for six weeks, Americanization conferences in the Hall of Philosophy. I am sure many of you are planning to go to Chautauqua, New York, this summer. We want you to drop into the Hall of Philosophy for the Americanization conference – to go yourselves, or to persuade your young people, your college graduates, to attend these classes, and get the benefit of this teaching in this new and much desired line of reconstruction work. (Applause)

…The assembly sang, "All around the World the Ribbon White is twined"…

ANNA A. GORDON:
We were just singing a wonderful hymn, written by Catherine Lent Stevenson[20], who has made the world a journey for the world Christian Temperance Union – a large hearted, big brained woman who has given the best years of her life to our work, and she has been called home. We love to think of all her radiant services. She put a motto up in Boston over the great organization in our world W.C.T.U. convention years ago that had a great significance.

We had been over in bonnie Scotland, and as they have a large organization of British women and Scotch women and women from Ireland in their British Women's Temperance Association, they divided the great hall in Edinborough (sic), where we met, into two divisions – one for the British women and the other for women from all the other countries who were coming over as delegates, and when our American women arrived at this beautiful hall in Edinborough (sic) – remember that one of them was from the old state of Maine. She had a mind of her own, and she thought she could find her seat.

The young lady usher said, "You will see that the doors are labeled, you can't miss it. You will find your seat from the label on the outside door. You go down this way and you will find it," and away went our friend from Maine. I don't know but what she expected to find the name of her own city in Maine, certainly she may have thought she would find Maine, and of course, she thought she would find the United States of America, the country from which she came, and when she couldn't find anything like that she came back to the young usher.

She said, "I am afraid you will have to help me. I thought I could find the door that I would go in properly labeled." Well, the young lady hurried her along down the aisle and came to a door, and said, "That is your door."

Our friend from Maine looked up at it and there was just one word on the door, and it spelled "f-o-r-e-i-g-n-e-r-s." Never had she been a foreigner, and she couldn't understand it, but that was a natural thing. Those who lived in England and Scotland were at home. Those who came from other shores were to them foreigners, and when Mrs. Stevenson heard the incident and we held a convention in Boston, she put in great letters over the organization, these words, "Ye are no more strangers or foreigners."

Oh, that is a beautiful motto for the W.C.T.U. and in our Americanization work, in our world's W.C.T.U. work. We are making the world a larger home, as Frances Willard so beautifully expressed it, and we are no more strangers nor foreigners. It is the spirit of this great assembly at the Centenary Celebration – every bit of service is rendered to make the world homelike, and we have a great twin continent to the south of us – Latin America, South America.

Oh, how we think about it! How we clasp hands with our comrades down there! They are represented today by our world W.C.T.U. worker, Mardinia (sic) K. Norville, who after missionary life for years in old Mexico, has been five years representing the Woman's Christian Temperance Union in the republic of South America.

I have the pleasure of introducing Miss Norville, who will present a distinguished company with her on the platform, and will translate for one of the distinguished educators of Uruguay.

MARDINIA K. NORVILLE:[21]

It is for me a very great pleasure to be privileged to present these two dear ladies from the two countries in which I have had the privilege of spending twenty-five of the happiest years of my life in Mexico. For twenty years I had the privilege to be side by side with this dear lady and her husband and family. Her girls were pupils in my school. Her husband was my counselor and warm friend in all of the different tasks to be performed as the principle [sic] of our American institute, and this dear lady was a mother to all the missionaries who needed love while we were in her beloved country of Mexico.

Doctor Valderrama[22] is at the head of the greatest Methodist school for boys that Mexico has ever known. He is the man who is producing character, great men, Christian leaders for Mexico, and this dear lady is the mother, I think, of ten beautiful children, and is here with three of them helping to put on this Mexican part of the Centenary, and so it is a great pleasure for me to be able to tell you about her.

They were always prominent in W.C.T.U. work. I remember so well the beautiful union meetings which we had there, all Christian denominations united, and it was her husband who brought about this beautiful union once every month – a great W.C.T.U. order, a great temperance meeting, because the men and women are united, I am happy to say, in Mexico and in South America in our fight against king alcohol. (Applause)

And now it is my very great pleasure to introduce Senorita Aurelia Viera[23], who is one of the most distinguished teachers of the republic of Uruguay, the smallest republic of South America, but one of the most progressive. The president of her republic was up here some six months ago visiting President Wilson at the invitation of our government, and he was so delighted with what he saw in Christian America, he especially was delighted with the speaker of women's activities at the front of all reform movements – that a man who doesn't progress, believing in God, but a man who loves the fruits of Christianity, went back home saying, "We want our women to have that kind of education. We want our women to take up this great reform movement and do for our country what I saw the women of North America doing."

And so when this president of the republic, Dr. Baltazar Brum, knew that Miss Gordon had called me to come to be here in the home land at the time of this Centenary and represent our South American work, he asked me to bring with him a delegation of Uruguayan women, that they might study the methods, that they might go home prepared to help, be more efficient leaders in a social reform for this very progressive little republic.

This Senorita who stands at my side is said to have been the teacher who has influenced for good more of the great men who are actually in the government today than any one teacher. (Applause) She began as a young girl to teach boys. She has given most of her life to the education of boys, and she continually says, "I didn't teach religion. You know they don't allow the name of God in the public schools of Uruguay, but I did teach my boys religiously. They must not lie, they must not steal, they must not touch a drop of any kind of alcoholic liquor."

She has brought up men and so she goes around in the government offices, the very highest positions, highest offices today, and she says, "This is my boy, that is my boy." And so they love her and when they came to choose a delegation to send up here they said, "We want to honor Senorita Viera by sending her as official representative of this delegation. We should like much for Senorita Balgonselca and Bomanteau to come also, and let us present them at this time."

I think Senorita Viera will say a word to you if you will allow me to interpret.

...At this point Senorita Viera gave an address in Spanish, Miss Norville translating into English...

MARDINIA K. NORVILLE:

She says that in their country they have a reform. They have women who are now reaching out after a higher and more liberal education, women who are beginning to want to be doctors and lawyers, who are wanting to know the highest and most useful way to spend their lives, but she says they haven't the custom of speaking in public as have the North Americans, and so she, for one, feels at a loss when it comes to speaking in public.

She says she comes from South America, a country very far and yet very near, because they have studied and know a great deal of this great country of North America. She comes from a little country, but a country that is rich in high ideals and they aspire to become a great country though they are small. She says they are rich in physical resources but they desire to have help from the great nation, such as this, that they may become richer in higher ideals. They need more of the example of this country which has already made such wonderful conquests.

She feels that they need North America because North America has made not only wonderful conquests in the commercial, in the industrial world, but also in the higher, the moral and spiritual world, that they need closer relationship with this country than they have had before.

She and Senorita Isabel have come from a country that loves North America, and desires to know you better. (Applause)

May I have the pleasure of presenting to you this dear young lady, Senorita Isabel Gonzales Vasquez, who is the representative, the native representative, of our World's Woman's Christian Temperance Union in Uruguay? She has given and is giving her beautiful young life and her heart's devotion to our temperance because she believes that the gospel of temperance means a new day for Uruguay.

She believes that in her country, so blighted by the drink curse, that we can reach the higher government circles through our gospel temperance, when perhaps those same rulers of the nation will not come to our evangelical churches, and reaching them through temperance we may help to unite the great forces of God with the government forces, and bring them to know us and understand us better.

...At this point Senorita Viera read from a paper...

MARDINIA K. NORVILLE:

I will not try to explain it at all. She wishes to say that the government of her country is upholding the women, and the most distinguished women of her country have united with the women of North America in their endeavor to try to overthrow King Alcohol. She tells you the names of these very distinguished ladies, their national president, the great champion of their cause, the wife of the patriot, we might say, of prohibition in South America, and she also wishes you to know that she brings the most loving greetings from all of these distinguished madams of her nation, and they wish to let us know that they wish to join hands with you in this forward movement for a world-wide conquest against King Alcohol. (Applause)

This young lady, Senorita Maria Regina Baumwell, comes from Argentina. She is here representing the school of Buenos Ayres, and is showing in the Latin American Building from day to day tables, object lesson tables invented by the vice-director of this school where she is a teacher. She looks very small to be a teacher, and yet she is a normal graduate, and we think a very bright, dear girl.

She is going to remain in North America and study in one of our finest colleges, and we hope she will return to her country as a great worker.

There isn't time for them to speak, but I would like for Senorita Isabel, if she will, just a minute to say something of the work that the young people are doing that she is leading so beautifully in the republic of Uruguay.

...The Senorita spoke in Spanish, Miss Norville translating...

MARDINIA K. NORVILLE:
She says that the national temperance league of Uruguay has for its basis the morality and the social redemption of its people. They not only work among the humble classes, but they have also found it a most wonderful work among the high classes of their nation, because of the great need for this work among that class. In all of these schools they have the privilege of giving scientific temperance instruction.

She says these public school children who receive temperance instruction not only receive these lessons, but their hearts have been touched, and they go with us to the places where the outcasts, where the outlaws, the poor criminals were. She says, "We asked the children to go with us to the penitentiaries and the jails, and so these dear children have grown with the young people of the evangelical church, and they have carried the gospel into the jails and penitentiaries and have touched the hearts of many of the hardest of men. While we were teaching them God, they have gone in and done what missionaries had not the privilege of doing – carrying the gospel of temperance in these prisons."

She says that at first it was absolutely impossible to think of having banquets among the high class, the social circle of the young people without champagne and wine, but now this custom is being changed, and now it is becoming the style for the young people to have their social gatherings without the use of any alcoholic beverages. They have even their tennis courts. They go into the universities and give their lectures there to the university students and the young ladies have resolved that their beaux and their escorts shall be total abstainers.

She says that her government is seconding the beautiful work of the women of their land in upholding them in this desire to obtain total abstinence among the high class, knowing that they set the example for the lower, and they think that the national temperance league has for its objects, its prime object, the forming of noble character among the youth of their land.

I think enough of our children are here to present the magnificent flag which belongs to the women of the W.C.T.U. of Uruguay.

Well, we are very sorry that our dear children misunderstood the hour. They are not in the habit of coming quite this early in the afternoon, and did not know that we desired them this early. But we will let them be and you will excuse the errors which new girls will make, who are taking the places of those who are not with us. We thought you would be glad to see this very handsome flag which was presented to the women of the National Temperance League, and so we are trying to present this afternoon the first tableau which was given in the first great temperance fete in Montevideo when the National Temperance League was organized at that time.

The minister of foreign relations, who is now the president of the republic and our warm friend, spoke, and as he looked into the eyes of that group of boys and girls gathered on the rostrum that night he said, "The hope of our land is in these boys and girls, and I want to pledge my hand and assure these boys and girls that they can count on me to stand by them and do all that I can to help them in this warfare against the vice in our land," and he is doing it.

...At this point Miss Norville presented the tableau of Uruguay, showing the character of the progress of temperance work in Uruguay...

...The assembly sang the Doxology...

...ADJOURNMENT...

Temperance Rally
Tuesday morning, July 1, 1919

...Temperance Rally at 10:00 A.M. at the Big Tent – Dr. Charles A. Gage, platform manager...
...Singing of the "Battle Hymn of the Republic"...

CHARLES A. GAGE: Bishop James Cannon, Jr. has charge of this meeting this morning.

JAMES CANNON, JR.:
I am chairman for the committee of the day, but Bishop W.F. McDowell, the Chairman of the Board of Temperance and Public Morals of the Methodist Episcopal Church, will preside at this morning's session.

WILLIAM FRASER MCDOWELL:[24]
I am sure that the first thing that you would like to do after thus being formally organized would be to stand up and sing "Praise God from Whom all Blessings Flow."
...Singing...

JAMES CANNON JR.:
I will ask you to remain standing and unite in prayer, which will be led by the Reverend Dr. Howard H. Russell.

HOWARD H. RUSSELL:[25]
Lord, thou hast been our dwelling place in all generations before the mountains were brought forth or before thou hadst formed the earth and the world, even from everlasting to everlasting, thou art God.
We bless Thee that thou art at the helm of the world, that thou art the God of nations and this morning, in a special way, we thank thee for the way thou hast led our nation in connection with the special reform and advancement of humanity, which is brought before our attention by this meeting this morning.
We thank thee Father that thou didst inspire a hundred years ago the stirrings of desire for better things in the hearts of thy children and that the leaders of the various churches began to be awake and to desire better things.
We thank thee thou didst inspire, in the course of the years of the past century, the leadership of those into whose hearts thou didst plant the desire for freedom from alcoholic beverages.
We thank thee for the prayers of the "Women of 1873" when they went from saloon to saloon and, inside or outside, knelt to pray.
We thank thee Father that thou hast fulfilled, in answering those prayers, the declarations of thy holy world, that prayer does not return void. We thank thee that the women themselves rose up from their knees to organize for action and

wonderfully have carried forward the education and organization upon this question.

We thank thee that later the churches themselves, the men of the churches leading off, organized together to bring to pass a political change in the laws of the states and of the nation under thine own inspiration.

We thank thee for what thou didst lay upon the altar of Methodism in duty and obligation and responsibility upon this question.

We thank thee that from John Wesley forward there was instruction that the liquor was the devil's kindling-wood and that it ought to be not used as a beverage, and that its sale ought to be suppressed.

We thank thee for what, in the past quarter century, Methodism has been permitted to do through its great organization in the cooperation which has brought to pass the victory for which we, this morning, sing "Praise God from Whom all Blessings Flow."

We thank thee that that faith which they led out to inspire and carried upon their banners in the very vein of the fighting hosts of the last quarter of a century has inspired other church organizations to fall in line, some reluctantly, but at last practically all of them, until today we sing unitedly, regardless of sect or creed, regardless of political relations – "Praise God from Whom all Blessings Flow." As a result of this cooperation and its success we hope that in the future other great wrongs may be righted, other great sorrows may be alleviated and other great reforms brought to pass through the cooperation of all thy children, regardless of sect or creed, and so may we realize in the future as in the past the results of faith and so may we stand, now, thankful in our hearts, to thee, and in the future, with those, who in the past, through faith, have wrought righteousness, subdued kingdoms, stopped the mouths of lions, quenched the violence of fire, escaped the edge of the sword, out of weakness were made strong, put to flight the armies of the aliens, and we ask it all in his name who died upon the cross to bring forth these precious results of faith and love and sacrifice, even our Lord and Savior, Jesus Christ. Amen.

JAMES CANNON, JR.:

There has been a very carefully planned conspiracy to prevent me from making an address (Laughter) which may work out quite to the contrary in that I may have the chance to make two. (Laughter)

You will remember that on the morning of the day of the Battle of Bunker Hill, that eminent patriot, Sam Adams, foreseeing what would happen, said joyfully to one of his friends "It is a glorious morning." (Applause)

I think it would be fair to say this morning that no matter what kind of weather we had had, we should have said, "This is a glorious morning." (Applause) Glorious, in spite of any reactionary movements that may be detected in high places or low. (Laughter) Glorious, because nothing can prevent the perfect consumption of that for which we have prayed and labored – the victory that is not yet perfect, but is so complete this morning, that without modification or hesitation we can say and sing "Praise God from Whom all

Blessings Flow." (Applause) Do not doubt the final outcome of any good thing and especially do not doubt the triumph of good itself.

Now, before I am aware of it I shall be making a speech and that was not my purpose. What a joy it is to have as the very first speaker this morning in the State of Ohio – the State that contains the town of Hillsboro; the State of Mother Thompson; the State where the Women's Crusade had birth – what a joy it is to have as our first speaker the successor of Frances Willard. (Applause)

Those of you whose ears are quick to hear and whose eyes can see the things that are invisible must have heard this morning – I heard it above the rumble of the railroad train – the song of triumph that is being sung by those women and men who have fought the good fight and finished their course and are already on the planes (sic) of victory.

Frances Willard and Mother Thompson and the great host that no one can know, must be radiantly happy this day – and Anna Gordon.

It is good to salute you and through you the Woman's Christian Temperance Union and all of your sisters, in the name of all those who have fought the good fight and it is good to welcome you here this morning.

ANNA A. GORDON:

Bishop McDowell and friends: we hail a mighty day, a stainless flag floats over our republic this morning, redeemed from the curse of a legalized liquor traffic. (Applause)

The flag, with its red for love, and its white, for law, and its blue, for the hope that our fathers saw of a larger liberty:

> "Praise God from whom all blessings flow,
>   Praise Him all creatures here below,
>   Praise Him above, Ye heavenly Host,
>   Praise Father, Son and Holy Ghost."

I am going to speak just a few moments and it will be a psalm of praise of the Woman's Christian Temperance Union. Our reason for coming here this morning is to thank God. Under the banner of Christ the King and with the stirring slogans for God and home and every land, the path of patriotism is the path of prohibition; bar the barley from the bar and bake it in the bread.

The Woman's Christian Temperance Union, nearly more than half a million in membership, one of the allied temperance forces of our republic, has contributed to this wonderful victory today an intensive program of service and of sacrifice.

Bishop McDowell, we are glad we are in Ohio, where the Crusade first was started in the winter of '73 and '74. Tomorrow we go to Hillsboro to celebrate. (Applause) We might go on to other Ohio towns and we will talk of Mother Thompson and Mrs. McCabb and of Mother Stewart and these wonderful heroines of that Crusade.

We are glad to be in Ohio where forty-five years ago the Woman's Christian Temperance Union was organized, as an outgrowth of the Crusade, and women who love our little talisman have a white ribbon bow always, are praising God for the sacred origin, the inspiring history and the divine mission of the Woman's Christian Temperance Union. Its own organization of Christian women banded together for the protection of the home, for the annihilation of the liquor traffic and for the triumph of Christ's Golden Rule, in custom and in law.

We praise God for Frances E. Willard, this morning; (Applause) one of the Methodists' greatest women, Frances E. Willard, whose mighty grasp of social and spiritual world forces is summed up in two of her immortal epigrams – listen to them: Only the Golden Rule of Christ can bring the Golden Age of Man." (Applause) "The fight for a clear brain is a fight for Christianity – the holiest fight this side Jehovah's throne." For it was Frances E. Willard, who thirty-five years ago founded the World Woman's Christian Temperance Union and sent out the first clarion call to all the governments of the world for the abolition of the liquor traffic and the opium trade, and we thank God for Lillian Stevens, another great leader of our white ribbon host.[26] (Applause)

In that first battle in the old State of Maine, in 1911, when prohibition seemed to hang in the balance in that pivotal state, Mrs. Stevens sent out a proclamation for national constitutional prohibition, closing with these words: "To America, the birthplace of the National and World W.C.T.U., we hereby proclaim that within a decade prohibition shall be placed in the Constitution of the United States and to this end we call to active cooperation all temperance, religious and philanthropic bodies, all patriotic, fraternal and civic associations, and all Americans who love their country."

We praise God for the rank and file of our white ribbon army – that great army, that host in heaven and upon earth, with their tireless energy, their supurb (sic) devotion and their Christ-like consecration – helping so much to bring this wonderful victory today. We don't forget our young people and our precious boys and girls, whose feet kept step to Frances Willard's song, Saloons, saloons, saloons must go and in the public school and the Sunday School and the Loyal Temperance Legion they have been a great force for the coming of this great day.

We praise God for the prohibition heroes in the United States Congress. (Applause) Who blazed the way for this national constitutional prohibition amendment, and we remember that in the legislatures with that great sweep of ratification we practically had a referendum of the electorate of the men and women voters of this nation on this question for those legislators were elected upon this issue "To stand for the ratification of the prohibition amendment."

I wish I had time – I will take a moment to let you look in upon the Nebraska legislature, as they were about to vote for ratification and become the thirty-sixth historic state – the State of William Jennings Bryan. (Applause)

A group of white ribboners up in the gallery of the Senate there, waiting for the Senate to assemble, and one hundred strong, to the tune of the chorus of "Over There" sang:

"Catch the word, catch the word, ratified,
All the states are coming, the air is humming,
With the sound of victory everywhere.
We'll be there, we'll be there on the dates
When the states ratify. (Applause)

"We'll go over, we're going over,
And we won't stop work until the world is dry."
(Applause)

And those splendid men who had come in to the Senate looked up at the choir of women and said, "Sing it again." (Applause)

We praise God for the men in the 65th Congress who gave us war prohibition legislation and more than that, we praise God for the men in the 66th Congress in the special session, assembled in Washington, who are unstampedable, thus far they have not yielded to the extraordinary pressure from high sources, (Applause) and low sources. (Applause and Laughter) And whether demobilization be declared sooner or later, our great land is alight with the coming of national constitutional prohibition, and we are glad that we have had a little part in all this wonderful march, but the Woman's Christian Temperance Union today enters upon a new Crusade July 1, 1919 – a memorable date, and we are deeply stirred by the excelling challenge of a supreme and unfinished task; we exalt in the high purpose of boundless possibilities opening before all the organizations of this reform in this new era for world and for national activity for purity, total abstinence and prohibition and joyfully we sing unto the Lord today a new song with the organizations and forces that have helped to bring this great victory.

We congratulate the Methodist church upon its exalted program in this great era and we as W.C.T.U. will continue our march under the banner of Christ the King. We will do it courageously, we will help heal the heartache of humanity, we will help build anew a world torn asunder by war, we will help in all parts of the world to establish the kingdom of our Lord and Savior, Jesus Christ, remembering that the fight for a clear brain is a fight for Christianity, we will crown him Lord of all, King of Kings, and Lord of Lords, Hallelujah! (Applause)

WILLIAM FRASER MCDOWELL:

Now I have the very great pleasure in presenting Mrs. Ella A. Boole, the Vice President of the National Woman's Christian Temperance Union.

ELLA A. BOOLE:[27]

Mr. Chairman and friends: the marvel of this day is that for the first time in the history of the liquor traffic it has been legally placed on the defensive all over the United States. (Applause)

During all these years of the progress of the temperance reform, we as workers, have been called upon to attack an institution that was legalized. Today it has no legal standing.

It required a great deal of faith on the part of those women who met at Cleveland, Ohio, in 1874, to organize a national society of women whose object was to make public sentiment against the drink habit and the drink traffic. The liquor interests of the nation were not much aroused at that gathering of women. In fact, one of the posters that was used in the Liberty Loan Drive, perhaps, illustrated what they thought. You have seen the poster – the words are these: "And they thought we couldn't fight." (Laughter and Applause) And they didn't think we could, but we knew how to organize and organizing the women of the country in a great society, that touched even the smallest hamlets of this land and reached rural communities where there were not even any churches, as well as the great cities, has helped undermine the power of the legalized liquor traffic, which used to live down at Prohibition Park. They don't call it that now, they call it Westerly, but when it was started it was Prohibition Park, and they had a big tent, something like this, and there were two center poles, something like these, and there were hooks and rings and they put them over the rings over the center poles and fastened the hook to it, and I wondered how they ever got up that big tent. I inquired and they said, "But we fastened ropes to the hooks and then a man stood here and took hold of a rope, another there, and another one there, and there, and there, ten men in all, and then the order was given for every man to pull and one pulled in this direction, another in this, and this, and this, and this, but pulling together the great tent went up in place, the ropes were fastened, and it stood just as this tent is standing today." What does it illustrate? Long years ago the Woman's Christian Temperance Union wanted to raise a great tent and it was the tent of prohibition, and we wanted to extend it all over this land of ours, and there were ropes that were attached to that tent and those ropes were our forty different departments of work, and one woman says, "I believe the way to work is with the children," and we said, "You get hold of that rope." Another said, "I believe the way to do it is to teach the effect of alcohol in the public schools," and we said, "You get hold of the Scientific Temperance Instruction Rope."

Another said, "but the way to do the work is to go to the Sunday Schools." We said, "You get hold of the Sunday School rope."

Another one said, "but the Evangelistic work should be done." We said, "You take hold of the Evangelistic rope, because we know that the grace of the Lord, Jesus Christ, is able to save the worst drunkard in this land," and so some got hold of the Evangelistic rope, and some got hold of a rope of temperance literature, and so on, and so on, and then when the order was given, every one pulled, one pulling in this direction, another in that, and that, and that, and pulling together we helped raise the great tent of prohibition which is to extend all over this United States. (Applause)

On a day like this, when some are to have a part in the program and when there are some phases of this subject to be presented, it is not an easy matter to select from the material gained in almost a lifetime of service the things that need to be presented, but I do know that the prayers of the faithful, earnest women all over this land of ours have counted for something. I do know of our circulation of petitions and how the women have gone around in the rain, in the snow and the sleet and asked men to sign petitions for legislative enactment and in protest against the liquor traffic, because we said a man's name counts so much more than a woman's name. (Laughter)

And lo and behold we have come to a time in the history of the great temperance reform when in some of the states and pretty soon in all of them a woman's name counts as much as a man's. (Applause)

Then we shared in the work in the legislative halls. We couldn't sit in legislative halls. Yes, we had one woman, two women members of the legislative body in New York this year, and one of them wore her white ribbon all the time. Yes, you didn't applaud it much, but it meant a good deal, (Applause) to have a woman in the legislature who considered it the greatest privilege of her life that she could cast her vote for the ratification of the prohibition amendment, and it showed a great march in this great reform.

We have gone on organizing and we have gone on educating and we have been appealing to legislators, and we have gone about it in an orderly way and the eighteenth amendment to the constitution didn't just happen, it came at the end, after a long trail which meant hard work; it came at the end of earnest endeavor; it came when the forces had been organized in such a way to bring pressure to bear at the very point where the liquor traffic seemed to be the strongest.

Simply to illustrate the power of organized womanhood, I was on a lecture trip one time in Northern New York. I had been afraid all that week I was going to be snowed in and if you knew Northern New York as well as some of us know Northern New York you would know that being snowed in was an ordinary occurrence.

I went to my meeting in the afternoon. It was snowing and I said, "I am afraid I will get snowed in," and they said, "Oh, no you won't, it is March now." I went to my meeting in the evening and it was still snowing and I said, "I am afraid I will get snowed in," and they said, "Oh, no, this snow is light."

I awoke in the morning and looked out of the window and it was still snowing and I said, "I am sure I will get snowed in," and they said, "Oh, no, the wind doesn't blow." I was to take a train that morning at 7:42. I went over to the station and asked for my ticket and sat down and waited and waited. I went up to the ticket agent and said, "Has my train come through?" "No," he said, "the train hasn't left Sandy Creek yet." I waited another hour and said, "Is my train coming?" "No, she hasn't left Sandy Creek yet." "But," I said, "why hasn't she left Sandy Creek?" "Why," he said, "lady don't you see this snow?" "But," I said, "snowflakes cannot stop a railroad train." He said, "Lady, one snowflake cannot but these snowflakes are organized." (Applause)

I waited one hour more. My train came along and I got on board. I found I had missed my northern connection and had to go down by way of Syracuse. All went well until we got to Phoenix, a little way out of Syracuse and all of a sudden we stopped and I looked out of the window to see what was the matter.

Lo and behold, we had run up against some more organization. In an hour we got down to Syracuse. I had missed my next train, which was an hour and a quarter late. I waited and waited and finally the next train came along and I said, "Conductor, will you get into Buffalo on time?" He said, "I am afraid not, lady, wind is dead against us and don't you see this snow?"

Well, at ten o'clock we ought to have been at Buffalo and were only at Rochester. At one o'clock we steamed into Buffalo and the city street cars were all stopped. You couldn't have gotten through that storm because the traffic was held up and I had to go to a strange hotel. What was the trouble? Nothing in the world but organized snowflakes, and if organized snowflakes will stop the mighty engine of the railroad trains, what may not organized, what have not organized womanhood and organized manhood have been able to do to undermine the foundations of the liquor traffic and strike it a blow from which it will never recover? (Applause)

Organized womanhood has helped, inspired by a desire to serve God and to honor Him and protect our homes and take out of the way the cause of the shipwreck of human souls. The war didn't do it alone, the war brought men and women the remembrance of the things we have been talking about all these years in order to win the war. We needed men and we needed ships and we needed food and we needed good discipline, and shall I say it was God, brought to the remembrance of the men in charge that alcohol hurt men, that it robbed them of health, that it robbed them of the ability to stand by discipline, that it wasted food, that it hindered labor in the preparation of ships, and because alcohol destroyed everything that was needed to help win the war, alcohol had to go and that is the reason why, today, we are celebrating the beginning of war prohibition. (Applause)

We men and women got the conviction, it helped to bring about ratification of the national prohibition amendment.

I was in Alaska helping a little bit in the campaign to make Alaska dry, and if I had the time I could tell you some wonderful things about a wonderful country, where there are gold mines and copper mines and coal mines and great salmon industries, and where there is a wonderful vegetation in those few months when the day is so much longer than the night. It is a great country and you would be attracted by it and you would want to see those wonderful glaciers, but it has also been a dangerous trip to go up there because there have been some shipwrecks on the line and I tried to find the cause of it, and I found three causes: one old ship the "Dora" – she is the boat that goes out to Una, Alaska, with the Methodist Women's Missionary Workers. They say the "Dora" has hit every rock on the Alaskan Coast and one time she was lost for three months and they didn't worry about her. They said they wouldn't until she had been gone a year, and the summer we were there she was shipwrecked and they patched her up and put on a new coat of paint and sent her out on another trip, but they were going to get a new boat to take the place of the "Dora" and they were going to put other new boats on the line and so get rid of that because of shipwreck. Another cause was uncharted rocks on the coast and one day we were sailing along and I saw a boat balanced on a rock. She had been there for two years, her masts were gone, her rudder was gone, but there she was, and few days afterwards I saw a great government boat, and I said, "What is that?" They said, "That is the United States Geographical Survey." "And what are they doing?" "Charting the uncharted rocks along the coast to get rid of them because of shipwreck." The third cause was drink. Sometimes captains drank and mates and pilots, and the very boat we came down on was on the rocks the year before because the pilot had been drinking, but Alaska voted dry, (Applause) that great missionary territory. There was a clause in the enacting bill that said, "No boat could carry a cargo of rum or maintain a bar," and now the whole nation is going dry and they cannot get the drink from anywhere, and that means getting rid of the third preventable cause of shipwreck.

Oh, friends, do you want to know why we women of the Woman's Christian Temperance Union have been so glad to help in this great fight against the liquor traffic? I will tell you why, it is because we wanted to help remove a preventable cause of the shipwreck of human souls. (Applause)

WILLIAM FRASER MCDOWELL:
Now to a man of my disposition and verbal mental habits, the introduction of the next speaker offers a very great temptation and if you knew the things that I am going to suppress you would wonder at the state of grace I am in. (Laughter)

I will not say then, he has heard them too many times, but I will ask Bishop Cannon to come straight up here beside me and let you look at what, please God, will happen. Bishop Cannon, who is the Chairman of the Temperance Commission of the Methodist Episcopal Church, South, one superfluous word.[28]

JAMES CANNON, JR.:
That time may come, perhaps it is here, when that word will be superfluous. (Applause) Perhaps it has not been up to this time.

If I were to have the time to utter only one sentence, it would be something like this: that the history and irresistible logic of prohibition not only suggests but will compel its world-wide application. (Applause)

Now I am not sure whether I made that as clear as I want to do because all my speech will be an attempt to develop that thought. The history and the invincible logic of prohibition not only suggests but will compel its world-wide application.

Before the Civil War, in many of the Southern states, it was a crime to sell intoxicating liquor to a slave without the consent of his master. The reason for the passage of that law and the consent of the legislatures to pass such a law carries with it the whole prohibition argument, not only for the slave but for the country, the state, the nation, the world.

Why was the slave not allowed to purchase intoxicating liquor? Because intoxicating liquor is that substance or fluid which when taken by a human being, causes that human being to lose control of his powers, therefore, to become less efficient. The masters of the slaves wanted efficient workmen, they wanted men who would not be a menace to the community in which they lived, and I repeat that the adoption of that legislation admitted that intoxicating liquor does destroy efficiency and that intoxicating liquor is a menace to the whole community where it is sold.

Now, fifty years, and a little more since that time, this nation has decreed that what destroyed the efficiency of slaves also destroys the efficiency of strong men and women. Our sons, no matter how intellectual, no matter how noble, they may be, the same thing that was the enemy of the slave is also the enemy of the race, and so we have adopted as the constitutional law of this country that it shall be a crime from this time on for any man to transport, to manufacture, to sell intoxicating liquor, to be used for beverage purposes. That has become the law of our nation and I prophesy here today that the same great underlying principle which has caused this country to put that in the constitution of this nation, that that same great underlying principle will cause all the nations of the world to sweep into line behind America, the most progressive of all the nations of the world. (Applause)

It would be very interesting if we had the time this morning to follow the educative process, to see just how our people gradually went on step by step until they found that the only solution of this question is the solution which we have adopted.

I could trace it better from a southern standpoint because I have been in that southern fight ever since I have been a grown man. Right after the war the law which we had concerning the slave, of course, fell into destitution; the law was still on the statute books, but there were no slaves and so the man who was formerly protected from the assaults of the liquor trade now became its prey and those of us who are from the South remember how, at every cross-road in our agricultural sections, there were located these dens of destruction, these centers of disturbance, and the question arose in a very few years among our people, what should we do with this matter? Here were these men all about us in a large majority in many communities, not trained, childlike somewhat as to their powers of control, having a new found freedom, the right to do as they pleased, and having the appetites which all men have and being subject, as all the native races are, to the attacks the insidious attacks of all kinds of vice.

Now the covetous man in the South seized upon the opportunity to line his pockets and so presently we were faced with the situation that our labor was demoralized, that a man never knew when his team would come back home or whether the work would be performed.

Presently some other things began to happen down there. All during that era before the war our women dwelt in safety in their homes – is it not a tribute to our brethren in black that all during our great war when the battle was waging and when the men were at the front that the women and the children were on the plantations and the masters had no fear but that the colored man in the home would take care of the mistress and of the children? (Applause)

Let me say to you here today there was no doubt some severe masters in the South, as there are all over the world, but let me say to you today that all through the southern country before the war there was a time of genuine affection and love between the masters and the mistresses and the men and women in the cabins on the plantations. (Applause)

The greatest proof of that is the fact that I have asserted that the men of the South did not fear to go from their homes and leave their wives and their children surrounded by a multitude of black men and black women. But after the war, when the cross-roads barroom was located here and there, and the black man became the prey of the liquor traffic, then came the era in our Southern country when no longer could the man, the father, the husband, go from his home and feel absolutely certain as to what might be the state of affairs when he came back. He did not know what fires of passion and lust would be created in men by the devilish liquor traffic which was pouring out its hellish broth to these kindly-hearted people, naturally kindly-hearted, living all about them.

I am simply stating the facts of history here today when I say that in my own Virginia State the time came that we had to pass a law that permitted the women of Virginia to carry pistols and then the men of the State, not only the white men, but the law-abiding Christian colored men said, "The time had come to put an end to this menace that was there in our midst and which demoralized our labor and which made conditions of life intolerable in our midst."

We went to work to restrain this traffic and how did we do it? Well, we went at it by piece-meal, we had not learned our lesson thoroughly, it is an amazing thing how blind the Church of Jesus Christ was to her great responsibility for the existence of the legalized liquor traffic. We were blind, we failed to realize that we were responsible for the things that were in our midst and for the evils that were about us. And so we went at it in the best way we could, perhaps, as we thought – it didn't occur to us then that we could just pass a law to wipe the whole thing out, root and branch; it just simply didn't seem to occur to us that that could be done, and not only to us, but the people all over this nation, except in the State of Maine, and in 1880 in the State of Kansas and a little later on in North Dakota.

Some of the restrictive legislation which was adopted will always be a testimony to the ingenuity of temperance reformers. Take the State of Tennessee as an illustration. Here again the whole question centered around the agricultural life of the people, there was a saloon over there on the crossroads, here was the school house down here, here were the young girls and boys coming by that saloon, that barroom, to get to that school house, and even the drinking men, the men who loved their juleps, the men who loved their toddies, the men who wanted to have their gentlemen friends have drinks on the sideboards, "Oh," they said, "we must protect our child life, of course," and so they went up to the legislature of Tennessee and they said, "we want a law enacted that it shall be unlawful to plant a saloon within four miles of a school house." Well they gave their reasons in a country district and the fathers of Tennessee, the country gentlemen of Tennessee, went to the legislature – they were not the tools of the liquor traffic.

They said, "Gentlemen, we will pass this law," and they passed it, and lo and behold all over Tennessee the demand for school houses began to spread. (Applause) The law also applied to the churches, if I remember correctly, and when a board was to build a new church or a country school board to locate a new school, the whole district was carefully studied to see that that school house was planted where it would protect this neighborhood and that church would take under its shielding wing this neighborhood, and the result was that practically every saloon was swept out of Tennessee, simply by that ingenious law which said there could be no saloon there.

In my own State of Virginia, the judge, who later became the Governor of the State, was a near neighbor of mine and we got together right often – we just lived seven miles apart – and discussed these things, and one day in our conversation we took up the question of the license law, our just license, our saloons, and the question before us was: How can we get a better license law? And in our conversation and working it out, we presented this to the legislature of Virginia, and it has gone down in temperance history as the main law; namely, that no judge could issue a license to a man to sell intoxicating liquor until it was said the applicant was a man of good moral character; (Laughter) until it was said he was suitable to conduct such a dangerous business, and that the place where the saloon was to be located was a suitable, convenient and appropriate place, and that the carrying on of the business would not be detrimental to the moral and the material interests of the community. (Applause)

Well, when that law was propounded, that idea, to the general assembly of Virginia, I might say, metaphorically speaking, they fell back in their chairs and gasped. The idea that any man should propose such qualifications for a dispenser of intoxicating liquor, should limit the granting of licenses to places where they would be detrimental to the moral and material interests of the community, but what legislator could rise up and say I demand that a license to sell a dangerous substance be granted to a man of bad moral character, and what man could rise up and say that there must be a license in a place that is not appropriate, and what man could rise up and say that a license should be granted when it was evident that it was contrary to the moral and material interests of the community? (Applause)

Those gentlemen were cornered and after all sorts of camouflaging and dodging and ducking here and there, that was placed on the statute books of the commonwealth of Virginia. (Applause) That sounded the death knell of the country cross-roads barroom in that State and swept them out by the hundreds. Why? Because there was not a judge with any self-respect who could look that law in the face and say that he was said that the granting of that license would not be contrary to the moral and material interests of the community.

In that sort of legislation which was adopted in our Southern states, in order to curtail as far as possible the evils of this traffic by reducing its scope, every bit of that legislation was simply the forecast of the future. Why? Because the logic of the situation was in it. The stars travel in their course and the heavens do roll, as the Bishop declared here a while ago; in substance, righteousness must prevail on the earth and a righteous cause must triumph, and imbedded in all these local and state laws there ran that thread, the acknowledged thought that the liquor traffic is the enemy of the economic, the social, the moral, the religious life of every community and that it ought to be branded as an outlaw and driven out of society so that it can no longer prey upon men and women under the guise and protection of the law. (Applause)

We found that was not enough. Of course we adopted local option and we voted it out here and there and yonder, but the state-wide principle was obliged to come in and by 1910 there were four more prohibition states – strange to say, unless you thought about it, all those states were Southern states. (Applause)

From that time on this great movement swept the South until every Southern State has been swept into line, with the exception of Louisiana, under state-wide prohibition. (Applause)

Now I am not here to laud the South, I am simply here to speak for the section with which I am well acquainted and to say that our people recognized that whenever there was a menace to their homes, to their children, and that menace could not be controlled or that public nuisance abated by local enactments, that the state must step in and say to the whole of the population, to every county of the state, this is a matter for the state to decide, and state-wide prohibition shall prevail in Richmond, and in Norfolk, and in Petersburg, and in Alexandria, because you are a part of the sovereign State of Virginia and we are responsible for all the deviltry that goes on in your midst. (Applause)

Mr. Cherington (sic) tells me there are thirty-three states now that have passed this state-wide prohibitory law, either constitutional enactment or legislative enactment.[29] Well, why not stop there? How was it that the South, which is so intensely conservative and which advocated to this day the doctrine of the right of the state in matters for its state interests? How could the South come to the point of agreeing that there should be put in the constitution of the United States an amendment, which amendment practically takes charge of the police operation of the state in so far as the liquor traffic is concerned? Not that it destroys the police power, that police power of the state is just as active as it ever was, but it comes in and links itself to that police power and says, "The federal government and the state government will cooperate together here and drive this outlaw to his den and there to destroy him forever."

Why did we do it? Well, there are two reasons which I will simply state in a sentence: the federal government should, by all means, step in and enact a law or adopt a constitutional amendment through the help of the states, by the action of the states, whenever the evil to be abated or the action to be taken is of such a character that the whole nation is affected by the operation of the proposed law.

Now I want to put it in a negative way: whenever the time comes in this country that it is impossible for any state to protect itself against the infringement of its laws and its principles of its declared purpose by the citizens of another state, then the time has come that the federal government must come into play with power, and we must have a constitutional amendment that will enable the states to protect themselves against the malefactors and the evil-doers in other states. (Applause) Now that is why we were ready for the constitutional amendment.

The state of Maryland, right across the line from Virginia, said, "Why, yes, you people of Virginia have passed your state-wide law; what do we care for that; why that just increases our trade. Baltimore will drug you with liquor, Baltimore will pour it down to Virginia by automobile loads; these men will shoot down your constables, kill your deputies, and we have had three brave men martyred in our state within the past twelve months by the liquor outlaws that have swept down in automobiles and on the train from Baltimore to Richmond." What could we do? These men were standing behind the buttress of state's rights, the only thing we could do was to say, "Amend the constitution so that in this matter no man in one state can defy the law of a sister state," and that is why the whole South swept into line, that is why the first state to ratify was Mississippi – the home of Jefferson Davis. (Applause)

That is why the second state to ratify was Virginia, the home of Robert E. Lee. (Applause) That is why the third state to ratify was Kentucky, the home of Henry Clay. (Applause) That is why the fourth state to ratify was South Carolina, the home of John C. Calhoun. (Applause)

That was a witness to the whole world that when a great moral issue rose up the American people did not propose to have any set of evil-doers buttress themselves behind the law of this country but that we proposed to so change that law that the blot, the blur, the disgrace should be removed from the nation – we did it. (Applause)

I have just enough time to say two or three words about the soldiers and the prohibition amendment. I will simply say this much: I was in France in April, 1918. At that time the House and the Senate had both submitted, by overwhelming majorities the constitutional amendment for ratification. There were only three hundred and forty thousand soldiers in France in April, 1918. What becomes of all that slush that the American soldier was cheated out of his rights in that matter. Congress had acted on that matter, and the Congress had been elected a year before we went to war, and by the time the legislatures were elected for the fall of 1918, which ratified the amendment, there were not then as many as a million men by the time the primaries were over. It isn't true and we need not concern ourselves about it any further. (Applause)

In Washington, less than a month ago, what happened? Twelve of the nations of the world assembled and signed the constitution for the world league against alcoholism. (Applause) Finland is dry today – I think the law went into effect June the 1st. Canada is dry; New Zealand and Australia hope to be dry within twelve months; the president of the Czecho-Slovak Republic is an ardent prohibitionist; Belgium, with its minister of justice, Vanderveldy (sic), has passed a prohibition law which will be made much more sweeping; Scotland votes on prohibition in 1920.

Oh, my friends, the leaven which the woman hid in three measures of meal (Applause) is carrying on its work. The ferment – I rejoice in a ferment of that kind (Applause) – and the ferment will proceed until the whole is leaven. (Applause)

W.F. MCDOWELL:

May I introduce the representative Clarence True Wilson, D.D., the corresponding secretary of the Board of Temperance and Public Morals of the Methodist Episcopal Church? This gentleman himself will now speak to you.

CLARENCE TRUE WILSON:[30]

Methodism, founded by John Wesley, a prohibitionist, a hundred and fifty years ahead of his time, put into its general rules a requirement that its members should be total abstainers and that they should not participate in the manufacture and sale of intoxicating liquors. (Applause)

When the general rules of these societies were transplanted to America to be the rules of the Methodist Episcopal Church, that rule was inserted verbatim.

All wars are periods of demoralization and the revolutionary war was no exception. It was followed by a period of drinking and drunkenness, of distilling on the part of good people, even of Sabbath desecration and gambling and of a low order of amusements, and the fearful falling away of membership in the churches. When everything else was going down, that rule was rescinded by our general conference of 1800, and it took thirty-four years of agitation to get it placed where John Wesley had put it as the banner of Methodism. In spite of that lapse in the early day, nine Methodist Episcopal Churches in this country, and the Methodists around the world, have been leaders in the agitation and in the vision which has brought about this day. (Applause)

They have furnished the women – Frances Willard built the Woman's Christian Temperance Union around that consecrated personality. They have furnished the agitators like Samuel Dickey (sic) and John G. Wooly (sic).[31] They have furnished the organizers like Purley A. Baker and James Cannon Jr. (Applause) They have furnished the preachers, like A.B. Leonard and John A.B. Wilson; when the cause was to be blessed with the blood of the martyr, it was the soul of a Methodist preacher, George C. Haddock, from Sioux City, Iowa, that went marching on and leading us to victory. (Applause)

When great movements were to be founded – printing presses and other movements – it was men like Earnest H. Cherington (sic) and William H. Anderson (Applause) who enabled Methodism to secure the men and the money and the inspiration and aggressive leadership. (Applause)

In 1888 the church, deciding that resolutions could not settle the question, organized its Temperance forces into a permanent committee on temperance and in 1904 they organized it into the Temperance Society of the Methodist Episcopal Church, and they did the big thing for that when they selected Bishop William Fraser McDowell as its first president. (Applause)

In 1908 they organized, they gave this society a claim upon the beneficence of the church and asked every minister to take and organize for its support, and two years later the first field officers were elected for the organization – at that time they were without support. They were without backing and being left without funds so long, the society realized that it really had no great mission, when we entered upon our work there with a few things that we resolved upon at the first – we would not do anything that was now being adequately attended to by other organizations. We would not do anything that got into the way of existing agencies.

In the presence of these anti-saloon league men I want to say that sixty-two annual conferences have asked us to give them the right to appoint, under our agency, a field secretary for their conferences, and we could have one for every conference in Methodism in three months from now and we could multiply our income twelve dollars to one, but we refused in a single instance to do it because that was the mode of financing the Anti-Saloon League, indispensable to this reform – that is a sample. (Applause) There has never been a deviation in the ten years in one instance.

We, however, found some opportunities wide open; one of these was a great foreign speaking section of our city not being reached by the human voice or by literature. We organized our foreign speaking department, we published leaflets in a dozen different languages – one of these was a leaflet in the German language, the notable speech by Emperor William[32], in which he said, "In the next year the nation that uses the most alcoholic liquor will be the first to go down." (Applause) "And the nation that uses the least alcoholic liquor will be the victor in the great war." (Applause)

Our country, therefore, when it organized its army to go up against the greatest beer drinkers that the world had, organized the first total abstinence army that ever shook the earth with its tread. (Applause) We put most of the cantonments in dry territory and when it was in "wet" we drew a zone around it and we made it a misdemeanor to sell a drink of alcohol to any man wearing Uncle Sam's uniform. (Applause)

The greatest beer drinkers of the ages with the greatest war machine that the world ever saw and the best organized and with the best equipment, and with the start to victory, came up, for the first time, face to face with the first total abstinence army that the world ever saw, and no man is fool enough on earth today to deny that man for man America's prohibition soldiers were far superior to the beer drinkers of Germany. (Applause)

We saw ten millions of colored people in the United States without a man supported to give his entire time among them in promoting this prohibition question, so eight years ago we selected that splendid leader and eloquent man J.N.C. Cogan (sic)[33] , of Atlanta, Georgia, who sits on the platform here, (Applause) where the fight has been thickest – he has gone without money, without expense charges, in the name of our board to give himself and his resources and the literature of his society and pour his best efforts into deciding the faith of many campaigns. We saw that there was a great need of literature from headquarters and in the providence of God the general conference at the nick of time, when twenty-five state campaigns were coming on in four years, put our board at the capital of Kansas. Every campaign hinged on the success or failure of prohibition in Kansas.

Our board was providential in the capital of Kansas and by the clip-sheet, going to every newspaper in America, and the voice going to forty-two thousand ministers every month, and our speakers going in all state campaigns and many of the conventions and all the Methodist conferences, we told the story of Kansas; that that great state could grow and live and prosper and pay its debts and build its institutions, educate its children, reduce taxation without the help of one tainted dollar of liquor revenue in her treasury for thirty-eight years. (Applause)

We found that in spite of all this, the newspapers of the country were against us in six state campaigns. We only had two daily papers in the entire six states – all the rest were sopping wet. (Applause)

Our board sat down to look that situation over and we said, "Why, it is the influence of the advertising money through the business office of the editorial management that gives the strangle hold on the utterances of the newspapers for the wrong side. Our board will take on itself the work of being the Evangelist to the newspaper world."

We have spent about three thousand dollars in postage writing to them. Our first letter contained this as the first paragraph: "The Methodists of the United States are getting tired of having lying liquor advertisements pervade into their Christian homes recommending beer as a boon and a blessing to old people, to sick people, to babies, and to nursing mothers, that you may blight with the pre-natal damnation of the innocent, the generations yet to be." (Applause)

That was the first paragraph and the warm-up after that. (Applause) We got back the finest assortment of cuss words ever sent to a temperance office. (Applause) But we got back eight pledges from great daily papers, four of them among the greatest papers in America, pledging the Methodists of the United States at our office, never to take another dollar of liquor money or to give another inch of advertising space to the brewers or liquor interests of America. (Applause)

We followed that up until at the end of twelve months from that letter date, we had sixteen hundred and eight so pledged. (Applause) Exactly two years from that date we had three thousand six hundred and eighty-two so pledged. (Applause) On the anniversary of the third year we had eight thousand eight hundred, and then through Congressman Charles H. Randall[34] (Applause) we got a bill offered in Congress making it a crime to advertise intoxicating liquor through the mails of the United States. (Applause)

We communicated with all the newspapers in the country and we laid down on the desk of the Postal Appropriation Committee (Bishop Cannon was present when that was brought in) one thousand two hundred and twenty-four newspapers that had signed the petition for that law, or more than half of all the newspapers in the United States. (Applause)

If our board had never done anything in five years but try to break and succeed in breaking to that extent the strangle hold of the brewers on the newspapers, we would have justified ten times all the money it cost the church. (Applause)

One of the most spectacular things we undertook was this: we found that ten years ago there was a formality in temperance meetings and it had consisted, in many states, of a systematic visit of the churches on Sunday morning talks to the good people and taking collections. We made up our mind never to do it, that we would go to the man on the street and four thousand six hundred street meetings in thirty-eight states, sometimes the same speakers speaking to twelve and one day to seventeen in a day from seven in the morning till one-thirty at night. Not only has it reached hundreds of thousands of people, but it has set a new pace for campaigning in numerous states, so that temperance workers would be ashamed to run a temperance campaign now on the conservative basis of eight years ago. Campaigning with the man on the street where they talk back and ask questions and find out what the other fellow thinks, and in our office it was instinctively felt by all of us that the time had come to stop pussy-footing on this liquor question and to stop handling prohibition with gloves.

We said, "The people are ready for a more radical type of legislation than has ever been conceived," so May 4, 1916, our clip-sheet contained a little editorial that was sent to the states where liquor fights were on. "There were ten of them," we said, "use the term 'alcoholic liquor' and not 'intoxicating liquor' in all legislation." If we had done that with our present amendment, the nervousness and anxiety, trusting to luck for a proper definition of "intoxicating liquor," would not be on us this morning. (Applause)

The seventh advice was "Make your legislation dry, bone-dry," and that was put in big black-face type. It went to eight thousand editors in America and two thousand in Canada that week and in a week the material had caught fire. People said, "What is bone-dry?" They looked at the dictionary – it wasn't there. They asked temperance reformers – no temperance reformer on earth could define it, because there was not on earth any such a law to be defined.

I was campaigning in California, down the whole state in a Reo, sixteen meetings a day, and people asked questions and not having time to read them, said, "What does the Methodist mean by this term, 'Bone-dry'?" I didn't know Methodists had said anything. I wired the office. "What do you mean by 'Bone-dry'?" (Applause) There came a night letter which said, "Stopping manufacture, sale, importation, exportation, transportation, having in possession, carrying on the person, conveying by public or private conveyance, selling or giving away." (Applause)

I got up to Portland, Oregon, in a little group of fellows where we had a dinner, one was Sam Connell, president of the State Anti-Saloon League, the other was Billy Padget, leader of the prohibitionists of the state, the other, our pastor, Doctor Lane. They said, "Wilson, what are we going to do to defeat the liquor dealers' amendment?" I said, "Fellows, nobody at this stage who is not either a fool or a knave will consent to a negative fight. If you fight a negative battle and you win, you haven't nothing more than you had before and if you lose, all is gone." "Well, how can we help it?"

I wrote on the back of an old envelope, Article two, Section seven, of the constitution of the State of Oregon, is hereby amended to read as follows: and I put that whole telegram into the wording and in three days we were out with our automobiles and at the end of three days we had enough names to put it on the official ballot, and the first bone-dry law ever heard of, when the term wasn't in any dictionary of the world and when it had never been mentioned by speaker, lecturer, book, pamphlet, as a scientific term for a definite kind of legislation. Somebody said, "Why I have heard 'as dry as a bone', well that was with reference to sermons." (Applause)

Then Arizona wired, "What can the board of temperance do to help us in our fight; the liquor dealers are trying to amend our prohibition by exempting beer?" We said, "We haven't a man, or a dollar, or a page to give to any state that allows itself drawn in a negative fight, but if you will propose to your people a bone-dry bill similar to the Oregon bill we will send you a thousand dollars to start the campaign fund, I will come in an automobile and speak without a cent of expense to the state and we will give you two pages of literature on bone-dry prohibition and distribute it at every possible office in your state." They wired back, "Terms accepted, send us the law." (Laughter) And we sent a night letter and on the seventh of November, when ten states had a fight on and not an inch of territory or a line of legislation was lost in the United States, when four states, Kansas, Michigan, Nebraska and Montana came over on the Lord's side (Applause), when we defeated in five states every liquor dealer's amendment proposed in the United States, namely, in Oregon, Washington, Idaho, Colorado and Arizona, we lifted another banner to the breezes of heaven – bone-dry prohibition went into the constitutions of Oregon and Arizona.

Now if you could see the letters I got, but I am not mean enough to show them from the Saints, saying "Be very careful, this may be a dreadful reaction." Now, I will tell you the reaction.

In January there were a lot of state meetings, 1917, and before the 30th of January, sixteen states had joined the column with Oregon and Arizona, and we had eight bone-dry states on the last day of January. (Applause)

When the term wasn't but eight months old, and then it swept up to Congress, and in the single month of February five enactments: bone-dry prohibition for Alaska, bone-dry prohibition for Porti (sic) Rico, the dry district of Russia, and a capitol city, and the so-called bone-dry bill which passed by a vote of four to one in the House of Congress. (Applause)

That has been a little outline of the type of things, because we thought we were justified in existence by being a little more radical than organizations of might and of historic fame dared to be on these new things, if they lost we didn't lose so much and if we gained we simply made a contribution to the cause.

Now a word about policies: a hundred years ago Germany was the most powerful Christian nation in Europe, but she adopted a system that disintegrated her Bible, which she called "rationalism." She adopted a materialistic philosophy by which she annihilated the souls of men and blotted God out of existence and called even thought the resultant of physical forces that play in the brain. With no religion there was no place to build a national morality, with no morals she brutalized herself with a national drink called "beer" – that is going out of America forever. (Applause)

If I had my way, having looked at Germany when the temptations of a war came on her and seeing deeds that would make a devil blanch with shame, that outdid the unspeakable Turk in this great war, if I had my way I would have Uncle Sam put his feet in every step by which Germany went to ruin and walk the other way up-stairs. (Applause)

Our board will stand for the total elimination of German beer of all degrees of alcohol. (Applause) It will stand for getting back our American Sabbath on the foundation that our fathers left it before the Hun in our own land trampled it in the mire in our American cities.

It will move forward for the putting of those blessed scriptures that have made us what we are back where they used to be in every public school in the United States. (Applause)

We will stand for American ideals in our home life and for the Americanization of American citizens, and we will build such a civilization on this soil that the gates of Bolshevism and I.W.W., anarchy, and "No Beer, No Work" rebellion shall not prevail against us. (Applause)

One word, and an important word: when the general conference sent our board to Washington D.C., they instructed us to secure a location and to put up a permanent building to commemorate this hundred year fight and this glorious victory. We have the lots facing the very doors of the capitol, just across the street – the capitol grounds will be our Methodist front yard. (Applause)

We have the subscription of the National Woman's Christian Temperance Union for twenty-five thousand dollars. (Applause) In appreciation of that we are going to give them the permanent lease on the center room of the corner looking into the Senate Chamber and right through the capitol. (Applause)

We are going to have a floor for our building. We have twenty thousand dollars subscribed, conditional on raising one hundred thousand by the first day of October. We have one thousand dollars cash in the bank on this subject for this purpose. We have our income guaranteed by the Centenary and if there is any man or woman here who hasn't given the last cent he can and invested the last piece of property he owns in the Centenary, he will come to me within three or four days and say, "Brother Wilson, I want a hand in putting up that temperance, prohibition and public moral center of activity for the new world activity upon which your board now launches with all the rest of the boards and I will give you the glad hand and take it." (Applause)

WILLIAM FRASER MCDOWELL:

It is exactly fifteen minutes past twelve. We have kept mighty close to schedule. I have known a lot of people to go out of meetings before the benediction who are now dead. (Laughter) We cannot afford to lose any of you. There is to be a perfectly tremendous meeting again this afternoon somewhere at the Coliseum they say at two o'clock. (Applause)

It is the subject that draws us together, no matter about the program. Now, Doctor Baker thinks it is pretty late but you want Dr. Baker to speak. (Applause) After Doctor Baker speaks, Mr. Waring is going to give us a bit of music and after that I want Doctor Coggin to pronounce the benediction, but now let us hear from the Rev. Purley A. Baker of the Anti-Saloon League, God bless him.

PURLEY A. BAKER:[35]

A convention of hardware men was being held in New Orleans about five weeks ago. One delegate to that convention evidently did not spend his time in the convention and late in the afternoon was found in the lobby of the St. Charles Hotel in a very happy mood, he was talking fast and loud, and the guests and loafers about the hotel gathered about him and before he was aware of it he was making a speech. He said, "Two hundred years ago our ancestors came to this country and took this United States from the American Indians, took it by force, and we hold it today – so far as I am concerned," said he, "after the first of next July they can give it back." (Laughter and Applause)

It will not be very difficult to get a man of that type of mind and spirit, even though under the influence of liquor, to become obedient to the law. He will accept the dry conditions in a hearty way.

Now I had prepared a few minutes' speech and though I am allowed thirty minutes, I know you will love me better if I will close at the end of twenty.

On the "why" of the Anti-Saloon League: from all I have heard this morning I have felt it might be a wise proposition to change the subject so I will try to move between that and something else.

The eminent speaker who is to talk to us in the Coliseum this afternoon I met some eight years ago aboard a local train running from Rockland, Illinois (Rock Island), to Des Moines, Iowa. It was my privilege to spend the day with him in that train and to take dinner and supper with him. I felt it was a rare opportunity to convince a man who was in the habit, at that time, of running the presidency of the United States, (Laughter) of the merits of the great movement of the Anti-Saloon League. I shall never forget the sage advice he gave me on that journey as to the perils of radicalism and how dangerous it was to get ahead of public sentiment and how we should be conservative and how many other fine things there were that should be enacted into law.

I have taken a great deal of pleasure in throwing it up to him in these late years, but I was reminded of what a Presbyterian preacher said to me many years ago in Birmingham, Alabama. I had spoken in his church and before we got out, for we lingered to the last, it began to rain and we sat down in the church to discuss the southern question, and, of course, the problem of the negro in the South and in the North. Finally, he turned to me and he said, "You northern fellows are constantly," and I will give you his language – it was good Presbyterian language – "you fellows are constantly giving us the very devil for the way we treat the negro, but" he said, "you fellows come down into this country and you are not here more than six months until we have got to watch you to keep you from killing niggers."

I am reminded of that story now, as I sit on the platform, occasionally, and I even listen to Mr. Bryan as he discusses the question, "Has radicalism grown far and away beyond anything we conceived of in those early days?"

All great movements reach their crises, there must be something new, something a little different, something that can grasp the splendid past and mobilize it and hurl it against the proposition in an effective way. Wendell Philips, Lloyd Garrison, Lovejoy, were counted as radicals, that pioneered the way before the great Civil War, but it required Lincoln and Douglas to take their places upon the platform in that memorable series of debates to clear the atmosphere before the shock of arms that was to settle the conflict of three hundred years. So there comes a time when the pioneers must be reinforced.

The Woman's Christian Temperance Union, the mother of all modern effective movements (Applause) against the drink traffic, had practically reached the limit of its power because male civilization had not arisen to the point that she could take her rightful place at the ballot box, consequently her mission was to teach it in the public schools and preach it from the pulpits of the country, that the liquor traffic was wrong and frought (sic) with infinite peril, but it was not possible for them to realize upon their propaganda; the Prohibition Party, which has always been the pickles and pepper of this great movement, had demonstrated the fact most thoroughly that it was not possible to mobilize the natural friends of prohibition under the banner that they bore, bands of hope, total abstinence, societies arose and flourished everywhere, but they could not stay the onward rush of drunkenness and crime.

It was then that a few consecrated men saw the great church of Jesus Christ because of jangling and opposing voices occupying the position of watchful waiting for an opportunity to get into the conflict and the organization yonder at Oberlin, Ohio, of the Anti-Saloon League movement furnished the opportunity for this great mighty moral power of the universe to marshal itself against the common enemy of us all. (Applause)

The Anti-Saloon League and many of my associates do not agree with me on this; strictly speaking, it is not an organization. The Anti-Saloon League is a method of operation. It came into existence with malice toward none, with infinite charity for all, with a single purpose of trying to put the church of Jesus Christ into real action against the liquor traffic. (Applause) That was the purpose of it.

The first of its method was mobilization, to mobilize the church until the church in its thought and in its prayer and in its gift should be brought to bear upon this proposition. It was not a small job to mobilize the church and then it became, secondly, necessary to mobilize the church voter, and that was not an easy job for he was many times mighty nearly a republican before he was a Methodist (Applause), and when we went to him for the appeal not to leave his party we had had the demonstration and example of the impossibility that he would not leave his party – there were too many questions at issue – but our appeal was to leave his party at a given point on a given candidate, when the opposition party had a good man and his party had a bad man. (Applause)

It was not easy. (Applause) It was not easy to marshal the church voter at that point. Many a deacon and class leader would seriously and solemnly shake his head and say, "Well, my brother, I am a temperance man, but I believe the country would be the best served by the triumph of my party ticket and I cannot do it."

Here and there we found a man who had more grace in him than he had politics and he was ready to move over and vote for a good man on the opposite ticket rather than a bad man on his own and, my, but that was a triumph in grace.

Then after the mobilization of the church and after the mobilization of the voter of the church came the mobilization of the legislator, state and national, after he was elected. My friends, it is easier to elect men to a state legislature and to the United States Congress than it is to get them to do teamwork after they are elected. (Applause)

The policy of this organization was to follow the candidate to the furthest political unity either for punishment or protection, whichever he deserved. (Applause) And that wasn't easy and that was not a comfortable job.

The second part was expression. I do not mean expression in oratory. The prohibition party made more orators in this country than any other single organization outside of the church that has ever existed and we have had the opportunity of utilizing many of those eloquent fellows – they didn't require very much reconstruction – the only necessary thing was to get the vision and to recognize that after all the league movement was simply a plan, a method of operation and nothing more.

The Anti-Saloon League has not to its credit the making and development of a single orator, not one, they have been down in the hand-to-hand conflict everywhere, but I will tell you what it has made, it has made an army of magnificent politicians all over the country. (Applause) And some of them are preachers now. It was a serious thing for a preacher to get into politics, but we are coming to feel that the preacher that isn't in politics isn't of much account.

It was a question of expression, these godly women had put instruction into public schools, they had taught it thoroughly, as thoroughly as it was possible under the conditions, they had taught the children the effects of alcohol on the human system, they had taught the parents the menace of the liquor traffic and the peril of the use of strong drink, but they were helpless, they could go no further than that, they could get no expression, they were not allowed to vote. All they could do was to pray and weep and plead and wait, which they nobly did.

Now the question, "What is expression?" Listen, men, I don't want you to forget this, it was the nonpartisan of the Anti-Saloon League, preaching of America, more than any other one thing, that dropped the solvent into party politics that has disintegrated it. There is where you got it first.

I remember in my time in my own state, this state when the man that did not vote the straight party ticket had shut himself out, as they thought, forever from the opportunity of holding public office. It was the indelible brand that was placed upon him; that isn't so now. A man can be thoroughly independent in his voting and we have to be so independent everywhere that we are standing for the man that stands for the right principle rather than for the man that stands upon the given party ticket. (Applause)

The third proposition connected with it was execution. How, by doing trench work, by going back yonder into the primary, yonder into the country district, yonder into the precinct, yonder into the ward, mobilizing the forces, getting a united expression at the ballot box, the bringing in of the fingers of the hand and double over it with the thumb to make a solid proposition by which you could strike a telling blow at a given point for immediate result.

Then it was that we began to get the expression, and with the expression came the execution. To all these organizations be, therefore, lasting honor, commensurate with the work done and the work accomplished, but after we have honored them and crowned them, after all it is upon the brow of the church of Jesus Christ that has furnished the driving force in the mighty conflict that is today giving us a saloon-less America and is to give us a drunkless world. (Applause)

It is no disparagement of other churches that have done magnificently for me to say to you today that the Methodist Episcopal Church, North and South, has sent more men into the field and put more money into the treasury of the Anti-Saloon League than it has been the privilege of any other denomination in this country to do. (Applause)

One thing in conclusion: now, in the execution, wouldn't you make yourself felt yonder at Washington there before the country and the Congress in the code, for the carrying, not only of war-time prohibition, but the 18th Amendment to the Constitution, into full and complete effect? Appeal to your congressmen, appeal to your United States Senator that he lend his influence to an effective code and finally look to the men for tremendous battle, yet to come; look to the men that are going to Congress, look to the men that are to go to the United States Senate, look to the man who is to sit in the presidential chair. (Applause)

The time has come in this country when the temperance people should no longer be compelled to do their work against the moral force and influence of the President of the United States. (Applause)

...Singing by Frank W. Waring...

J.N.C. COGGIN:

The grace of our Lord and Savior, Jesus Christ, the presence of the Father, the benediction of the Holy Ghost rest and remain with us, now, henceforth, and for ever. Amen.

...ADJOURNMENT...

Prohibition Day
Tuesday afternoon, July 1, 1919

...The meeting convened in the Coliseum at 2:30 Bishop Cannon presiding...
...Music by Burke's Band...
...Singing by United Colored Chorus...

HERBERT STANSELL (sic):
After Professor Cartwright has led us in singing, Bishop Cannon will take charge of the meeting.
...Singing of Star Spangled Banner...

JAMES CANNON JR.:
Let us all unite in prayer. We will be led by Bishop Earle Cranston.

EARL CRANSTON:[36]
O God our help in ages past, our hope for years to come, Thou has kept faith with Thy people, Thou has led the march of events toward the glorious consummation of thine own high purpose; Thou has multiplied the little handful of those faithful to his truth as revealed in Christ, of those faithful to the humanity which he died to redeem, until Thou has created a mighty host to carry the message of victory to the ends of the earth. Glory be to the majesty of Thy power, glory be to thine infinite heart of love, glory evermore to thy fidelity in keeping covenant with those who in the spirit of their Lord step forth even to the summit of Calvary to give their testimony in behalf of the life and faith and hope. Thou God of love Thou has had pity on the poor; Thou God of justice, Thou hast heard the cry of the Oppressed; Thou God of Nations by whose power this nation was made a nation and made a mighty power in the world, Thou hast led Thy people in a crusade of freedom to a victory that reaches in its beneficence to all peoples and to all lands.

Now we pray Thee, O God, as Thou hast thus far revealed thyself in conquering leadership, that Thou wilt still lead on as Thou hast given to the American people under the influence of the sacrifices they have made in behalf of mankind, such inspiration and such an uplift of intelligence as has led them to provide in their constitution for the protection of women and children and home, as well as for the protection of the weak and helpless peoples abroad. So now, O God, as Thou hast had Thy will written into our Constitution and made fundamental in our government, will Thou lead our leaders until they shall be able to overcome and overturn all the schemes by which it is sought to thwart Thy will and to destroy that which has been achieved by such glorious conquest. Pour out Thyself upon the world, again O God, in a baptism of freedom that shall in its purpose and aspirations reach to the uttermost of human potentiality in thought and in holiness and to the uttermost of the needs of the masses of mankind everywhere. Spread the blessings of prohibition to the ends of the earth. Save China from the devilish machinations of the traffic that has cursed so many peoples. Save all the nations O God and make the day soon come when that which Thou has got us to contend for and to hope for and to believe in, shall become the heritage in its blessing and promise of all the people for whom our Lord died, the permanent guarantee of the fruition of the redemption that was provided in His precious blood for the glory of Thy name and His name, and by the power of the Holy Spirit let this be wrought, Thy will upon the skies and upon the seas and upon the land and through the valleys till Thy faith shall be known and its glory shine in the face of poor humanity. Amen.

JAMES CANNON, JR.:

This day, the first day of July, 1919, is the new Independence Day of the United States of America. (Applause) As the 4th of July, 1776 stands out as the date of our national declaration of freedom from the stupid and Oppressive tyranny of George III, so the first of July, 1919 will stand out forever in our history as the day when the same country, now grown to be the greatest country in the world, not only proclaimed its Declaration of Independence from the degrading and destructive tyranny of King Alcohol, but also branded the liquor traffic as an outlaw, as the enemy of the economic, social, intellectual and moral life of our people. (Applause) And this new day of Independence is the day which the Lord hath made and let us rejoice and be glad therein.

I count it as a most happy fact that on this day in the providence of God there is assembled to celebrate this day, this great gathering of Christian people and that we will have here today, no doubt the greatest celebration ever held in this country on a matter of this kind.

I take pleasure at this time in introducing the speaker of the hour. I think it but fitting to say that in the pioneer work done in the Southern states, there stand out two figures. There are other figures to whom praise must be given, but Sam Jones[37] and George Stuart[38] (Applause) were two great voices that rang throughout our southern country, and had as much to do as any other two men with the stirring of that powerful sentiment in our southern land which has today swept the liquor traffic from our border. (Applause) Some of us thought that Sam Jones was rather drastic in some of his speeches. I heard him say many times – in fact he said it in every city where I heard him preach – that the man who would sell liquor is an infernal scoundrel and the man who will drink is an infernal fool. (Applause)

In those days some men shook their heads; some men said, "That is too strong, that is too bitter," but Sam Jones always plowed deep and he branded the traffic. He had nothing in his heart against an individual but he put the brand on the traffic wherever he went and he maintained that no man could sell it who had the love of God, or love of man, in his heart; no man could drink it who had full possession of his faculties and who understood what the meaning of life is. Sam Jones is gone from our midst, leaving behind him a great record. George Stuart preached with him, lived with him for 18 years. George Stuart has been, not only for those 18 years, but for years since Sam Jones died, an apostle of prohibition, whose voice has rung throughout our southern country with great power, and it is a great pleasure to me today, as the Chairman of the Commission on Temperance and Social Service of the Methodist Episcopal Church South, to present to this audience George Stewart (sic) of Birmingham, Ala, who will speak to us for thirty minutes.

GEORGE STUART:
My Fellow Countrymen: Down in my country they keep me especially for my beauty and my voice. (Applause) I think you will be able to hear what I have to say if you will keep quiet, and I think I shall not detain you longer than I entertain you, if you have anything to entertain, and if you haven't if you sit right still, nobody will find it out. (Applause)

I want to say that I am glad to be present at this great hour on this great day in this great program. I think it is about fitting that our colored people should sing before I speak for it is among them that I was born and reared. I was bread and buttered down in the south among the colored people, (Applause) and for them I helped to fight this great battle against their worst enemy and the worst enemy of every nation, and for them I have helped to put their enemy down. I am glad to hear your Jubilee Song on this day and I would like to hear you sing after me and we will have a ham sandwich. (Applause)

Oh, yesterday, after the great Peace Congress of the world had signed the greatest international document ever produced since Christ walked Judean hills, and throughout the world Christian people, patriotic people, philanthropic people were praising God, a drunken man at Brest, France, walked up and tore down the national flag and stamped it beneath his feet, telling us that that is what the infamous liquor traffic stands for throughout the world. (Applause)

And that is the picture you have got in the United States, that after our legislative bodies have passed, after our states have acted, after our flag, standing there as an emblem of the strength and power of the nation, the infamous liquor traffic with a lot of petty lawyers and petty politicians would pull down the flag of our constitution and put up beer barrels and whiskey barrels in its place. God forbid that they shall do it. (Applause) They are dead and don't know it.

It reminds me of one of our mountaineers down in the country. When they had saloons he usually went to town, got drunk and came home and wallowed around like a hog. The wife said to him, "Bring me a little asafetida," and she gave him the money. He bought the asafetida, put it in his pocket and got drunk. He got on his horse and went home, but he rolled off his horse in the yard and the stopper came out of the bottle and a little child went out to see about him and looked at him laying there and smelled of him, and went back in and said, "Mamma, Papa is here but he is dead and he don't know it." (Applause)

I want to tell you this infamous, drunken, rotten, debauching, devilish, hell-inspired and hell-doomed traffic is dead and they haven't found it out yet. (Applause) A lot of little, petty lawyers, for the money they can get out of it, are ripping up and down the country with old brewers and distillers following after them, putting up injunctions here and injunctions there, and running over there and putting up another injunction, but I want to tell you that prohibition has come to stay in America. (Applause)

The little lawyers, fooling with these old brewers and distillers, remind me of another scene down in my country. A man went up to an old mountaineer's house, stopped at his gate, and standing there a little while he saw a great pack of hogs, old sows and shoats come tearing by and run up on the hill and stop and stand listening, then they were gone across the hills two or three hundred yards and would stop to listen, and then they would tear down the road and across up on the other hill and stop and listen. Then they would come tearing down the road again and stop and listen. The man said, "Neighbor, what is the matter with your hogs? I never saw hogs do this way before." The fellow said, "Well, you know, two years ago I lost my voice and I had to call the hogs by pecking on the crib, and the corn is all out and I have closed up the crib and the blamed wood peckers are running the hogs to death." (Applause and Laughter)

The whiskey business is dead; the saloons are closed and the little lawyers are running the old brewers and distillers to death. (Applause)

You know I started this thing when it first started, when there wasn't anybody in it but long haired men and short haired women. They laughed at us and made fun of us, and please your life a United States Senator or Congressman or a great politician wouldn't any more run with us than a rat would run with a drove of cats; nobody was with us. We would tell the officers to go out and arrest the saloon keepers who were breaking the law and they wouldn't arrest anybody; they would just smile at us. "Why," I said, "I would as soon put our wax legged hound after an asbestos cat in hell as to put these officers after a saloon keeper in America." (Applause) They paid no attention to us. We would go up to Congress and to talk with Congressmen and they looked at us like blanks, and talked to us as if we were half idiotic. They were sorry for us, but they thought we were weak-minded, and bless your life, we pulled them up to where they have found what fools they were about that time. (Applause)

The world is beginning to see it sometime after we had prohibition down in the south, and I came up north to help you all a little and we have been helping each other, (Applause) we have been helping you fellows and you have been helping us. When you couldn't use the colored man up here, you sold him to us. (Applause) And we helped you out of that hole. Just as we got them to where they didn't work good – you had all your money cut of them – you could see the wrong and we had all our money in them and we couldn't see the wrong. (Applause)

Oh, you came down there and pulled the money off of our eyes and showed us and licked us and we quit, that is to say, we didn't know we had crippled up so many of you as the pension list showed or we wouldn't have quit so soon. (Applause)

But it is all over and we feel good about it and we are glad that the end was that way. (Applause) We are glad you came down to help us. The old sword of our internal strife is sheathed and the guns are stacked and the vine clamors over the mouth of our old cannon, and in America there is the sweetest brotherly love from ocean to ocean and lake to gulf we have ever had since Columbus discovered America. (Applause) We came up to help you all get the money off of your eyes (Applause) and let you see the light. So you have seen the light and so it is done and it is done forever. Some men said to me a short time ago, "Do you think we are done with the saloon? They never have been done with us." I said, "Yes, we are done with lots of things which didn't used to be done with; we are not going back to lots of things; we are not going back to spitting on the sidewalks any more; we are going to prohibit it." (Applause) "And if you can make a man swallow his own spit why can't you keep him from swallowing the spit of some fellow manufacturers?"

Listen, we are not going to have any more diseased meat sold in this country; we have got our government officers there and we are going to prohibit men from selling diseased meat to our people, and we are not going to have any more tubercular milk sold to our people, we are going to prohibit that, and we are not going to let any man, for his own gain, debauch little innocent children by patent medicine and we are not going to let any man with devilish money greed, debauch any worthy man or woman or child in America for money, and we will put the brewer and distiller in their proper places, debauchers of the human body, the human mind and the human soul and destroyers of the welfare of our great nation. (Applause)

You know we have been working on our Constitution a good many years. We have been doctoring it, and it is better today than it ever was when the old constitution dropped out from under the hands of its writers in its early days. It just had seven articles in it and every one of them was as imperialistic as the government of Germany, and there wasn't a single privilege left to the citizen or left to the state except the solitary privilege of electing the President and electing a Congress. You can search it through and that is the only democratic thing in it. And the first time they met they added ten democratic amendments to it, every one of them touching the people and touching the states.

The first amendment they stuck on pulled the bridle off of our religion and turned us loose to worship God as we pleased. They pulled the bridle off of our tongue and turned us loose to speak our honest sentiment in a free country. It took the bridle off our press and allowed us to print the news to the people and it took the bridle off of the people and allowed them to assemble and to honorably petition the Congress of the United States, and the first time they grabbed the bridle on that old imperialistic document they pulled enough harness off of it to get this country free nearly, and then they kept adding to it, and you know we never have made any fuss about it.

Five years ago they added two amendments in one year.[39] You never saw any little lawyers trotting around trying to get up a racket about that; not one in ten of you know how your own state voted on the question. They touched the most vital interests that you can touch in a nation, one of them touched taxation and the other touched the American ballot. Every time you have attempted to touch the ballot, men have risen up and said, "Watch what you do," and every time we begin to touch taxation, they said, "Look out, my stuff is in that," but we passed two amendments on these delicate subjects and nobody raised a question. Why? I will tell you. Because there weren't any organized, monetized, politicized, demonized liquor traffic with its millions to stir up little politicians and pay little subsidized lawyers to raise a fuss against the constitution of the United States of America. (Applause) That is why.

They asked me what caused this big southern temperance wave. I said, "It is not a wave; if it were it would go back." They said, "What caused this great temperance tide?" I said, "It is not a tide." Well," they said, "What is it?" I said, "It is a natural movement, growing out of our present Christian civilization, just as natural as spring grows under the warmth of the sun, and it will no more go back than spring will go back till the glorious harvest time of the liberty and freedom of the people." To tell you the honest truth, the liquor traffic has lived out its day. We are too enlightened, we are too intelligent, we are too humane for that damnable traffic to live any longer in our Christian civilization. (Applause) This is the best age the world ever saw. Oh, how we are moving; we are going so fast it makes my head swim. I used to ride on the old ox wagon and be all day getting nowhere, but now I am no time getting anywhere. I am just afraid I will go by electricity the next time and lose my breath. I don't know what to get on, we are going so fast, but I want to tell you I believe God Almighty is in this movement, and I believe God is in this civilization, and I believe God is in this great convention, and I believe He is in this hour, and I believe His hand pushes the great movement along. It is the movement of God. I feel like that Swede out in Minnesota who got caught in a cyclone which picked him up with his great tent and carried him about three miles and dropped him down in an old farmer's yard. The old farmer went out and pulled the tent off of him and said, "How did you get here?" He said, "The wind blew me." The farmer said, "Are you hurt?" He said, "No, me not hurt." "Well," he said, "the Lord surely was with you." "Well, if the Lord was with me, He were going some." (Laughter and Applause)

I want to tell you that we are going some and God is with us, and I want to tell you another thing. There is power enough in this movement to keep it going. You need not be afraid it is going to stop. I have this to say – when any man, from the White House to the lowest office in America, lifts up a beer keg, he will drop his molasses jug. (Applause) I say that there is power in this thing to keep it going.

Down in our country one of our colored boys had never seen an automobile; he had never heard of one. He came in to Fitchburg, Miss. and a great big automobile whizzed around the corner and ran off down the street. He ran up to the corner and looked after it till it rounded another corner and went away, and he turned to the other fellow and said, "My Lord, dem hosses sho was guine when dey bust loose from that carriage." (Applause and Laughter) Why hadn't anything "bust loose" from that carriage. The power was in that thing to keep it going, and it was going yet. I want to tell you that nothing has "bust loose" in the United States of America. There is an internal power of conscious morality and fear of God and love of man that has power enough in it to put down forever the damnable liquor traffic, and we have done it. (Applause)

When we got our Constitution built and just added on an amendment and another one and another one until we got a good government, it just lacked a little of being done. We wrote our Preamble and the Preamble was written for the last amendment you added. Did you ever study the Preamble? It was written for the last amendment. We put on the head and now we have put on the last and we have it about done. Now listen, what did your Preamble say? "We, the people of the United States, in order to establish justice, (that is the first thing) to promote domestic tranquility, (that is the second thing) and for the common defence, (that is the third thing) and for the common good of all, (that is the fourth thing) and for the liberty of us and our children (that is the fifth thing).

Everything is going along in order. Mr. Bryan came in after I had been going ten years or more. (Mr. Bryan had just come upon the platform) (Applause) This is a wonderful psychological hour. (Laughter)

I was on the Constitution, the Preamble. I said the Preamble of the Constitution had five points in it, first justice, second, domestic tranquility, third the common defence, fourth the common welfare, and fifth the liberty of ourselves and our children, and I say to you that the liquor traffic was against every one of these five principles and when we put this last amendment there we tied up the Preamble, the front end, and the hind end and we buckled her up so she is going to stay and we have got a strap around her and we are going to carry her over the whole world. (Applause)

The liquor traffic is against justice. They are crying now, "Justice, justice, justice." I come up and shoot your whole family down with a pistol and you come up and take my pistol out of my hand and you say, "Now you are unjust, you have got my pistol and you didn't say a word to me about it, you just took it out of my hand." "Well, you scoundrel, you are not fit to do business in this country."

The liquor traffic is the very embodiment of injustice; it is unjust to the man they sell it to because he gives something and gets nothing. The highway robber takes a dollar and leaves nothing; the liquor traffic takes a dollar and leaves a bottle of liquor, and the liquor dealer is as much worse than the highway robber as a bottle of liquor, and a bottle of liquor in an American citizen is worse than nothing. It is unjust to the man who buys it; it is unjust to the woman whose husband buys it. The husband and wife go into partnership and he takes the partnership dollar and goes up to an unjust saloon and unjustly spends that dollar and unjustly pours the whole content into his stomach and unjustly goes home crazy to abuse and bruise and ruin his family. That injustice has been done [in] the homes of America all these years and wherever a home of an American citizen stands, it stands as an appeal to put down the damnable saloon that has been doing it injustice all these years. It is an injustice to our civilization because it throws upon our hands a drunken vagabond for whom we can not find employment and for whom we can find no legitimate business in the world or position in the world. We have tried to find him a position. The banker don't want him; the merchant don't want him; the farmer doesn't want him – doesn't anybody want him, and all the chance he has got on earth is to run for office in some wet district. (Applause)

JAMES CANNON JR.:
There are six thousand people waiting to hear Dr. Stuart at the grandstand so I stopped him short, and his is going over there.

GEORGE STUART:
Just before they sing I want to give you the verse of a little song which you can't sing: "Don't you cry, little beer cart, Oh, little beer cart don't you cry, you'll be a milk wagon in July." (Laughter and Applause)
...Singing by Frank M. Waring...

JAMES CANNON JR.:
It is necessary at this point to make a change in the program owing to the fact that Mr. Bryan is obliged to take an early train. The next address was to have been made by Congressman Rainey who has been one of our great leaders in Congress and who has been especially helpful in reference to the Anti-Drug Laws and who is thoroughly posted on that subject. He has a great message to give to us but owing to the fact that Mr. Bryan must catch this train, there has been a change and Mr. Bryan will speak first; Congressman Rainey will speak right after the song by the Negro Chorus when Mr. Bryan concludes.

I will not take even a minute of time – for Mr. Bryan will need it all – to enter into any eulogistic remarks concerning him. He is well-known in this connection; he is well-known to this audience, and it is a great pleasure to me to present him now to speak on this great occasion.

WILLIAM JENNINGS BRYAN:[40]
Mr. Chairman, Ladies and Gentlemen: This is a great privilege and a great opportunity. I appreciate the honor that the Methodist Centenary Committee has done me in making me a part of the program on this memorable occasion, and I am glad to be on the stage with these representatives of the Temperance forces of this country, for with the Methodist Church so largely represented and the Anti-Saloon League so largely represented and the Woman's Christian Temperance Union represented officially here, we certainly have a great combination of temperance workers, and I wish we might gather on this day the representatives of other churches that have had their part in winning this victory.

Where could we better celebrate the first dry day in a saloonless nation than in the capital of the greatest state that has yet gone dry by popular vote? (Applause) And under what auspices could we celebrate this day more appropriately than under the auspices of this church which, probably more than any other church, has contributed to the victory over the saloon? (Applause)

If I were a preacher and were permitted to take a text – and I think I will take a text, anyhow, even if I am not a preacher – I would take my text from that passage in Matthew that gives the summons that carried Joseph and Mary and the child back to the Holy Land. The words were, "They are dead that sought the young child's life." (Much Applause) When you remember that King Alcohol has slain more children than Herod did, these words are appropriate for this day. (Applause) At times it looked as though we would have to delay the final obsequies until the sixteenth day of January, but I read something Sunday morning that has encouraged me to believe that we have seen the open saloon for the last time in the United States. (Applause) Sunday morning's papers gave us a statement by the President which, I believe, closes the door of hope to those who have been longing for the suppression of war prohibition. The President said that he was satisfied that Attorney-General Palmer[41] was correct in saying that the President had no power to suspend this law or to prevent its going into effect, no power to act until the period of demobilization had been completed. We have over a million men still serving under the emergency law; nearly half of them are in Europe and the chances are a million to one that war prohibition will continue, that demobilization will not be completed until after Constitutional prohibition begins in the United States. (Applause) And every day that this nation goes without a saloon will make the President more reluctant to reopen the grave and call forth John Barleycorn, buried by us July first.

Let me call your attention to some of the causes that have led to our great triumph. First we have had the conscience of the nation on our side, and as that conscience was awakened our cause has grown. This has not been a sudden awakening; it has been gradual; it began a long while ago, but now our churches are awake; the nation's conscious is aroused and it will not go to sleep on this subject.

Second, we have had the benefit of science. Science has aided us wonderfully. The trouble used to be that people had a mistaken idea about intoxicating liquor. They said that it wasn't bad to drink if you didn't drink too much, but as no one could tell how much too much was, a great many good men died of delirium tremens as they sought for an invisible line between moderation and excess.[42] It was like the line of the horizon that was seen as we approach till it is lost in the darkness of the night.

I heard a story that illustrates the difficulty of telling when one has too much. A man was talking to a friend and he said, "I am drinking too much; I know it and I don't want to. It is not my fault, my friends just keep asking me to drink and the first thing I know I get too much." His friend said, "I will tell you how to prevent it. When you get all the ale, all the whiskey you want, don't call for whiskey, call for sarsaparilla." He said, "That is the trouble; when I get all the whiskey I want I can't say sarsaparilla." (Applause)

Now science has shown us that we needn't worry about the invisible line between moderation and excess. There is another line that we ought to look for, a clear-marked line, the line between total abstinence and drinking at all. That is the line that ought to be watched for. Science has shown that no matter what a man is doing he is better off not to have intoxicating liquor in him. If he is shooting at target practice a little alcohol will make him miss more frequently. Let me give you a little illustration? The world now knows a name that has sprung into fame, the name of Alvin York, the greatest soldier, they tell us, measured by individual efficiency, that this world ever knew. (Applause) It is worth something to the temperance cause to know that Alvin York has been a teetotaler ever since he was converted five years ago and became a member of a Christian Church. He had no rum ration within him when he wrote his name above all other soldier's names. It was a clear brain and a steady nerve that enabled him to pick off man after man until he had more deaths to his credit than were ever placed to the credit of a soldier on the battlefield. And my friends, whether a man is striking at the front or working in time of peace, his greatest need is that which no man can have who indulges in any intoxicating liquor – for alcohol is the enemy of a clear brain and a steady nerve.

So here we have an illustration that confirms what science has taught, and science has shown us, and statistics prove, that if a young man starts to drinking at twenty-one, he must deliberately decide to shorten more than four years of his life's expectancy as shown by insurance tables. And more awful than that, science has shown us that there is a poison that travels in the blood, so that if the alcoholic habit is fastened on a man or woman, the evil does not stop with this life but goes on and afflicts a generation yet unborn. Can you think of anything more cruel, more inhuman than that a father or mother should indulge the taste for alcohol, knowing that it may curse a child before it sees the light and bring into the world with no chance in the race for life?

These are things that science has shown and they do not turn back. Business has helped us by showing us that they can't trust a man who befuddles his brain with liquor and patriotism has helped us. Why, my friends, when Europe went into the war they began to get a new light on the evils of alcohol, and the great Premiere of Great Britain, Lloyd George, uttered a sentence that rang around the world. He said they were fighting three enemies, Germany, Austria and drink, and then he added, "As far as I can see, the greatest of these is drink." My friends, he gave the statistics to show that the use of alcohol by those making ammunition cost Great Britain a hundred and fifty thousand men's work a day, and in the interest of efficiency that Britain might have one hundred per cent production in the making of ammunition, he asked for the privilege of closing the saloons, but the liquor men said, "No, let a nation die rather than that we surrender our profits on the stuff." And when we entered the war we found the same thing, the same kind of people in the liquor business here. We found that for what pay they would have they could make drunkards of all our soldiers and leave a nation defenseless before a foreign foe. But we were greater in our strength and better able to defy the liquor traffic than other nations because we had put 28 states dry before we entered the war and had large areas of dry territory in other states not as dry. And, my friends, with the impulse of patriotism added, our Congress wrote the gravest indictment against alcohol ever written up that time. We said the man was a criminal who would sell or give intoxicating liquor to a man wearing a uniform of a soldier and we trained an Army under conditions never known before and that Army amazed the world. They used to think long training was necessary. Some of our boys died within four months of the day they put on the uniform. We showed them that when you took alcohol away from men you could reduce the percentage of preventable disease, and we were able to put on the battlefield men, trained in a few months to be the greatest fighting machines the world ever saw, and our boys (Applause) helped to cut their way to the lines of professional German soldiers and win a victory for the world's democracy.

That was what was possible, my friends. It was a great triumph. If we will not unlearn the lesson we will teach it to other nations, and then it was a very complete victory. We ratified in a little more than one-seventh the time we asked for; we asked for seven years; we ratified in one year; we needed 36 states; we got 45, (Applause) more states than any supporter of the amendment would have dared to guess. It was not sectional. They began to go dry in the south, but the wave swept north until it reached the Canadian line. It began to go dry out west, but the wave swept east until only three states were left on the Atlantic coast that had not ratified. It was not only a national victory in the sense it was not sectional, but it was not a partisan victory – it was the triumph of the conscious of the nation.

My friends, we Democrats and Republicans have been fighting in the arena of politics over every great issue for fifty years, but I thank God that when the greatest issue of war of this generation came, we laid aside our differences on other subjects and the two parties stood together to defend the home against this greatest enemy and shared the glory of getting rid of it. (Applause)

We are going to enforce the law. (Applause) Not everybody is pleased at once. It may take some time to reconcile themselves to the situation. There is some dissatisfaction in Milwaukee, (Applause and Laughter) a little bit in Cincinnati, and there is a Congressman from St. Louis who is trying to get two and three-quarters percent beer. Let him try. The days of trying are not past, but the days of succeeding have gone, never to return. (Applause)

This is no new thing, this attempted distinction in favor of the brewery. It is backed by the brewery and it has been tried and settled; the issue is no longer before the nation. Thirty-three states settled it when they adopted prohibition without making any discrimination in favor of beer; Congress settled it when they submitted prohibition without making a distinction in favor of beer, and the Senate settled it the other day when by a vote of five to one it refused to bring up the question of repealing war prohibition. (Applause) Michigan settled it last April when, by a vote of 207,000 – three times as large a majority as she had cast against prohibition a year ago – decided not to allow wine and beer to come back to Michigan, and only one county in Michigan voted in favor of the proposed amendment. It has been settled, my friends. It ought to be settled. It never will be reopened; it ought not to be reopened. We can't separate beer and wine from whiskey. The brewery and the distillery have been partners in crime for a generation. They have been co-conspirators against everything high and holy, and now as they approach the end of their wicked careers, it would be cruel, cruel to separate these boon companions, the brewer and the distiller. (Applause) And therefore we will not separate them; they shall die together and be buried face foremost in the same grave. (Applause) If anybody tells you it is going to be as hard to enforce prohibition as it used to be, let me give you some reasons why it will be easier.

In the first place, our trouble has been that whenever we got a town, county or state dry, the liquor interests would set up their machinery on some wet spot outside and work against dry territory. They have been the encouragers of lawlessness, but remember that they always had to have a wet spot on which to put their machinery to work against dry territory. Now there is not a wet spot under the American flag and pray God there never will be a spot upon which they can set their machinery. (Applause) They have got to get outside the United States to work against us now, and, my friends, we are going after them when they get out of the United States. (Applause) We will run them out and when they go to curse other lands we will carry a certified copy of the criminal record to show what kind of men they were before they left and why they left. (Applause)

No, they will have no wet spot, and then remember that we have had to fight great combinations of capital. Why, the Anti-Saloon League and the Woman's Christian Temperance Union have been going over the country, collecting a little bit from many people to carry on the fight against the saloon, but a single brewery or a single distillery could put up more money to fight prohibition than either of these organizations could collect from a whole nation in a year. But they are going to be dissolved. We have transformed the business into a crime and now we deal not with combinations of capital, we deal with individual violators of the law, and that is quite different. They can't have a National Association of Bootleggers any more than they can have a National Association of Pick-pockets. Each bootlegger will be running so fast to get away from the officer of the law that he can't stop to cooperate with any other bootlegger running in the same direction.

They used to make money in their breweries and their distilleries day by day, so they had a cooperating fund with which to fight prohibition. But they can't make any more money that way. They have got to convert the buildings to other uses, and they are doing it. Some are being converted into packing houses; some of them are being converted into cold storage plants, and up in Michigan I found a brewery which had been converted into a Methodist church and was used as a social settlement plant, I believe, in conversion. (Applause) But whenever, since the conversion of Saul of Tarsus, has there been such a conversion as there was in Michigan when they converted that brewery into a Methodist church adjunct? The nearest approach to it was in Oregon, and there they converted a brewery into a grape juice factory, and that is some conversion too, my friends. (Applause)

No, my friends, this thing is not going to turn back. We are going to enforce the law; we are going to build up back of this prohibition amendment a wall of sentiment in favor of total abstinence. The work that has been going on through the years is going to continue. It is now nearly fifty years since the Woman's Christian Temperance Union – and I think it is the greatest organization among the women that the world ever knew – began to preach against the use of intoxicating liquor. It is sixteen years since the Anti-Saloon League began its work against the use of intoxicating liquors, and all these churches have been growing in the work they have been doing against the use of intoxicating liquor.

And now we must redouble our energy, for, my friends, we will never hold prohibition unless we carry on our educational work so that each generation will be more hostile than the one before to any use of intoxicating liquors as a beverage.

Then there is the work in the world beyond. We can't be deaf to these Macedonian calls for help from other lands. We have found a great remedy. It is a remedy that the world needs. We have found a remedy for typhoid fever. We now make men immune to the disease, and whereas we lost thousands from our little army in 1898 in the war with Spain, we lost none from typhoid fever on the firing line in France, although we had nearly a million men there – wonderful remedy. We found a remedy for yellow fever. We now destroy the breeding place of the mosquito that carries the germ of the disease, and we have a remedy for alcohol, a dual remedy. By total abstinence we make men immune to alcoholism and by prohibition we destroy the breeding place of the influence that it had over us.

The call comes; we must heed it. We are not only the heir of all the ages when we have received as no other nation ever received from nations roundabout, and we must give as no other nation has ever given. The Bible tells us that the master went about doing good around the shores of the sea of Galilee. He helped the sick and opened the eyes of the blind and cast out devils, and we are commanded to follow in his footsteps, and imitate his example. How can we pay the debt we owe better than to go out in the spirit of the Master to give our remedy to a world that is sick? How can we pay the debt better than to go in the spirit of the Master and open the eyes of the blind that they may see the evil of alcohol and the advantage of the banishment of the saloon? How can we better pay the debt we owe than to go forth in the spirit of the Master and help to cast out this evil spirit that has afflicted mankind throughout the ages. We not only should, we will, and I believe, my friends, we can look forward to an early victory. When, nine years ago I entered the fight in Nebraska, I never expected it in my life time that my state would be dry, much less my nation dry, but our cause has traveled more rapidly than any of us believed it would. We have gained so much, we have moved forward so fast and I have such faith in the power of my nation's example that I believe that with a hundred millions' of people living in a land that is dry from shore to shore, we will shake the world with the testimony we shall give, and I believe that though I am 59 years old I will yet live to see the day when there will not be an open saloon under the flag of any civilized nation on this globe. (Applause)

And now, my friends, before I give way to Congressman Rainey, and I wish he might have been able to speak before me, for I wanted to hear him and I want every one who listens to me to stay and hear him for he has been a tower of strength to every righteous cause in Congress (Applause) and he can help you in the hand-to-hand conflicts that go on day to day – I want you to hear him, I wish I might myself but before I yield to him I want to say one or two words on another subject. It is not very far from the subject I have been talking on – it is the League of Nations. I want to speak of that for a moment. (Applause)

I say it is a subject akin to the one that I have been discussing for the purpose of the League of Nations is to slay the God of War, the only other despot that is a rival to King Alcohol in the world. The purpose of the League of Nations is to furnish a substitute for war machinery by which disputes can be settled without a resort to force, and that League of Nations contains three things that I think make war almost impossible.

First, the League of Nations provides that there shall be investigation of disputes before a resort to war, that no matter what the controversy is, before people go to war, that dispute shall be investigated by an international tribunal, that we may separate fact from fear, fact from quest of honor, that we may have deliberation, time for passions to cool and time for the peace forces to operate.

According to that covenant of the League of Nations, three months' time is to be given to investigate. Our treaties provide for a year, and the idea is taken from the thirty treaties that we have made with three-quarters of the world, but I believe three months, as a rule, will be sufficient. Why, it was 48 hours that Austria gave to Serbia to accept or reject the ultimatum, and in Europe they told me if they had had two weeks they could have prevented war! Our League of Nations gives six times two weeks and besides that it provides also for disarmament, the reduction of armaments, and that is a long step toward peace.

And then it provides for the abolition of secret treaties, and if you didn't know what that meant when it was first suggested, you do know now, for you know much of the time that the Conference was spent in wrangling over the terms of treaties that will be unlawful after this League of Nations is accepted.

And my friends I believe the President never did anything better in his life than when he announced in Paris the other day that this nation would not be bound by the terms of a secret treaty, the existence of which we did not know. (Applause)

I believe that these things make war almost impossible, and I believe the Senate will ratify. I believe that if it doesn't, the American people will elect a Senate that will ratify. (Applause) This nation will not turn back to the old ways of blood and slaughter.

We have our choice between two alternatives. One is to go forward, and take the longest step toward peace taken in a thousand years. The other is to turn back to a system under which wars must recur time after time, and this old earth be reddened again with human blood.

I believe that the American people will go forward; that this League of Nations will become an accomplished fact, and that it will educate through its practical work, and it may, my friends, inaugurate the reign of the Prince of Peace on earth.

Now that the war is over, now that a peace has been agreed upon, the great, supreme duty confronts the Christian Church of the world, and that is to heal the wounds of war, and to bring the nations of the world together in a spirit of brotherhood. For nothing else will make us able to realize the hopes that the League of Nations has put before us. (Applause)

And I believe, my friends, that out of this war is going to come this great good – that the philosophy of Nietzsche has been overthrown – the doctrine of materialism fell when arbitrary power fell, and its contrary spirit, the spirit of the Man of Galilee will blaze forth anew in this old world. And I believe that the Christian Church today has before it this duty of making the love and brotherhood, that the Savior came to preach, a living fact upon this earth, and with it will come the fulfillment of the prophecy that "Swords shall be beaten into plowshares, and people will learn war no more." I thank you. (Prolonged Applause)

...Music by Colored Chorus...

JAMES CANNON, JR.

I now have a great deal of pleasure in introducing Congressman Rainey. Congressman Rainey is the Chairman of the Special Committee appointed by the Treasury Department on the question of narcotic drugs, and he is the man who rewrote the Harrison Drug Law. He is in earnest in his fight to down this great evil. He has a great message to give to us. I take great pleasure in introducing Congressman Rainey.

HENRY T. RAINEY:[43]

Ladies and gentlemen, it is an honor, I assure you, to be permitted to speak from the same platform or just after, the greatest English-speaking orator the world has produced in a hundred years. (Applause)

It is a great honor to speak here on this platform surrounded by these earnest temperance workers who are responsible for this great day in the history of the world. It is an honor, I assure you, to speak here this afternoon on the natal day of a new period in the history of this old earth. It is an honor to speak here the first dry day we have had within the limits of the Continental United States, since Columbus landed with his men on these coasts, because the country is dry. The law has made it dry, and by the Eternal God, the law will be enforced. (Applause) Honors come thick upon me this afternoon.

This old world in its swing through the centuries, has entered a new era. Big things happen in the world today with such bewildering rapidity that we can hardly understand what it all means. Today our khaki-clad warriors are returning from their crusade in Europe, 10,000 of them today, 10,000 of them tomorrow, 10,000 of them every day, until they are all here again.

Today from their convention in a historic old palace in the environs of Paris, earnest representatives of the great nations of the world are returning to their capitols, carrying with them the new world declaration, which when it is ratified by their legislative bodies, will become the organic law upon which a new world, and new world traditions, will grow and develop.

Today somewhere out in mid-Atlantic a great ship is plunging along toward our coasts, bringing back to us the President of the United States, (Applause) fresh from his labors, fresh from his triumphs, as the representative of this great republic.

And today there comes to us with crushing force the realization that we are face to face with a new habit and a new danger, in this world. We have been fighting and we have vanquished an institution which has lasted in the world almost from the dawn of civilization until twelve o'clock last night when it vanished from our boundaries. But we are meeting now a by-product of saloons in the land. We are meeting now a new habit, and a new vice, hardly half a hundred years old.

And I want to talk to you about that seriously because this is a serious convention, and as impersonally as I can so that hundreds of you, I hope, will return to your community impressed with the importance of the message I am going to try to deliver to you this afternoon.

The committee of which I happen to be chairman, and which is composed in the rest of its membership of really competent, scientific men, from our colleges, has completed its labors and has made its report.

I helped draft the original Harrison Act.[44] That Act has simply made it possible to take an inventory in this country of those dealers in drugs who are honest enough to say that they are of those who are addicted to drug habits, who are honest enough to admit it, or who have developed the drug habit to such an extent that they have been compelled to be treated by physicians. The Harrison Act has accomplished that for us in the United States, before the United States Supreme Court declared it unconstitutional. I had the honor of redrafting it, and the redrafted Harrison Act has been on the statute books in the United States for thirty days now, and it meets the objections of the Supreme Court, and is more stringent in its provisions.

There are today in the United States 1,000,000 known addicts. We know who they are. We don't know how many there are who are unknown. You don't know that. You know who gets drunk. They get drunk, and they come out on the street and make an exhibition of their drunkenness. When men and women take drugs, opium in some of its forms, cocoa leaves, its salts or its derivatives, they take that and crawl back into their disordered bedrooms and remain away from the light of day, and you never know how many of them there are. But there are a million, at least – one man out of every one hundred and ten in the United States we know is a drug addict, and needs treatment at the present time.

Those who use heroin, and there are many of them – nothing can be done for them. They will die, every one of them in six years, and there are lots of them in the United States. You don't know it until they die.

At the present time we import $20,000,000 worth of drugs, and the illicit importations into the United States amount to about that much. In other words, $40,000,000 worth of drugs reach the United States legitimately or through underground channels to the great underworld. This estimate as to values is made under our tariff rules and regulations. It means the appraised value of these drugs, not here, but in the country from which they are shipped. As soon as they land here, with the Harrison Act in force, they become at once immensely valuable. They increase in value ten of fifteen times, when they mix them up in milk and sugar and sell them to the ultimate consumers. They represent every year in this country an outlay in money of at least three hundred million dollars.

Yesterday in the United States there were not as many drunkards as there are drug addicts today.

Under the Harrison Act we required dealers to register, and at the present time, not considering the illegitimate dealers in these death-dealing drugs, there are in the United States licensed to sell opium, its salts and derivatives, one dealer for every two school teachers in the United States. There are today more places where you can buy these drugs than there were saloons yesterday. There are today twice as many legitimate dealers in these drugs in the United States as there are clergymen of all denominations in the United States. Today there are four times as many dealers in drugs, who can sell drugs to the public as there are policemen in the United States. There are three times as many dealers in drugs in the United States, recognized by our laws, and admitting that they are dealers as there are of food manufacturers and food distributors in the United States.

In other words, there are today 234,000 licensed dealers in the United States. Now these facts are compelling alone. The saloon keepers and the manufacturers of alcohol liquors didn't stop to think about it themselves until this report made its appearance. Then they began to see their rainbow of hope. And they all said, "Let us sell liquors; let us sell them in the milder form, at any rate, or we will become a nation of drug addicts." That is the danger which confronts the nation. You have your choice, whiskey and beer and wine, or drugs. Which will you take? That is the slogan which saloon keepers are using from one end of this country to the other, and then they say, "We are going to make it illicitly. We will manufacture whiskey anyway and sell it. You can't stop it with laws. We manufacture it now."

And they do in many of our states, but the illicit manufacture of whiskey is absolutely negligible in this country and has been for the last twenty years. Our government agents destroy every year about seven hundred illicit stills, producing, each one of them, only a few gallons of whiskey a year. Why, all the illicit whiskey ever manufactured in the United States in any one year wouldn't supply the city of Cincinnati, Ohio, on an ordinary wet Saturday afternoon for thirty minutes.

There is nothing in that argument. There is nothing in the moonshine argument, or in the material it furnishes, except that it furnishes material for story writers, for our magazines, and that is all. And they all know it. You can't make whiskey – you can't sell whiskey any more in this country because we don't permit them to make it, and if they make it we don't permit them to ship it, and if they do ship it, we don't permit them to sell it. There are penalties all along the line and the trade is ended. And we are not accepting any alternative. It is not whiskey and wine and beer, or opium and cocoa leaves and all their salts and derivatives – we don't have to accept that alternative. Opium never satisfied the appetite of any man for whiskey. It isn't a substitute for whiskey. Whiskey isn't a substitute for opium. There are two separate and distinct appetites. But these addicts, and their blue, shrunken skin and staring, lusterless eyes, who have been found on the streets of our cities – I know one whenever I see one and you will as soon as you commence to study this important question – are the by-products of saloons. I have gone through the opium infested dens of great cities with our earnest, courageous revenue officers, and I found that the boundaries of the red light districts, the boundaries of the saloon districts, the boundaries of the sections which are infested by the dealer in opium who sells to the unfortunates of the underworld, are exactly the same. Saloons have developed harmoniously in this country along with drug addicts. A man who has become brutalized and who has become a beast on account of overindulgence in liquor renders himself liable to the other habit which becomes to assuage the pain, the mental worry and the moral worry which comes to the drunkard. Abolish the saloons and you have destroyed that element which has been most potent in this country for the production of drug addicts.

Now, this is a proposition which is absolutely new to many of you. You heard Dr. Stewart (sic) this afternoon discuss the South. The South, he says, has gone dry. Even Dr. Stewart doesn't know what is going on in the South. Under the law as it stands today, how many of you know, how many of you realize that in any city in this country, in any corner grocery store or drug store in this country, you can sell whiskey, provided you put less than two grains of opium to each fluid ounce? This is Section 6 of the Harrison Act, and in drafting the Harrison Act it was built upon a foundation furnished by a great international opium expert, Dr. Hamilton Wright.[45] Unfortunately, now deceased, under the Harrison Act, this Section 6 makes possible these things. We couldn't keep it out, we were absolutely powerless to keep it out, because no sentiment had grown up in this country against the thing, which I am now going to describe. Such remedies as Bateman's drops, Godfrey's cordial and paregoric contain alcohol. Nearly every little bottle of these remedies contains from 47 to 49 per cent of alcohol by volume, and you can sell those under the law anywhere today in the United States, provided you put the minimum dosage of opium in, that is permitted under Section 6. If you put less than 2 grains of opium to a fluid ounce, if you put less than one eighth grain of heroin to a fluid ounce, you can sell these remedies and people drink them as a substitute for whiskey. The fact that there may be some medical remedies, some medicines mixed up with them, does not destroy the opium they contain. You can become an addict as surely by taking one eighth of a grain of morphine three times a day, as you can by taking three grains of morphine three times a day. That is what is known as the minimum dosage, and it is the most effective way of producing addicts known. The thing you men and women must fight is the drug habit.

Even in my own great state of Illinois, the druggists in their international organization, the physicians in their interstate organization, have denounced the amendments to the Harrison Act. I get thousands of letters and telegrams protesting against depriving the people of such things as Bateman's drops and paregoric and Godfrey's cordial. Why, our investigation showed that a man down in New Jersey sold his little truck farm and took the entire proceeds and bought little bottles of Bateman's drops with them, and when we stopped the manufacture and sale of those kinds of remedies, these peoples who flocked to the South, who have been drinking them, will realize, that without knowing, they have become drug addicts.

Now, may I call your attention – I don't want to take up too much time with any technical discussion of this important subject, because I realize this is not the time for that – may I call your attention, briefly, to conditions in two states? The state of Alabama last year went dry, wasn't it? Was there any other drier section of the United States than Alabama? You know how much of these three alleged remedies they consumed in Alabama last year. They consumed of Godfrey's cordial, Bateman's drops and paregoric 13,572 gallons, and 61,785 bottles in addition to that. Every bottle contained one good drink of whiskey and every fluid ounce of it contained the opiates to which I have been calling intervention.

Now, Illinois wasn't dry last year, was it? Illinois was only dry in spots, and while the spots were large, it was possible from those wet spots to get a plentiful supply brought in. Illinois wasn't dry by any means last year. Illinois contained a population perhaps of 7,000,000 people last year, and consumed of these three alleged remedies to which I have been calling attention, 8,300 gallons and 42,139 bottles, each bottle containing a drink of whiskey and each gallon containing many drinks of whiskey. In other words, Illinois, a wet state, was able to get whiskey! Illinois consumed, with a population three times that of Alabama, with the third largest city in the world within its boundaries, with half of its population living in cities of considerable size, Illinois consumed 33 percent less than Alabama did last year, of just these three remedies to which I have been calling attention.

Now what is the answer to that situation? Why, they can sell, under law, whiskey in Alabama as medicines, and I will only mention three of these alleged medicines which contain opium and cocoa leaves, their salts and derivatives, and there are 982 remedies of this character, not all of them as deadly as they apparently seem, harmless things recognized by the Pharmacopia of Medicine, not all of them dangerous, because not all of them contain a percentage of alcohol to which I have just called attention, and very few of them are drinkable. They drank these alleged medicines in Alabama because they could buy them at any store. They didn't drink them because they contained opium; they drank them because they contained whiskey, they drank them to satisfy an appetite for whiskey – we must stop the sale of these remedies in that state, and, by the eternal God, I propose to lead a fight in the Congress of the United States and everywhere else, to stop it. And, in spite of the prejudice of the doctor, the dentist and the lobbyist, when we stop the sale of these things in the territories that have been dry heretofore, where they have been used as a substitute for liquor, the number of non-drug addicts in the United States will increase by leaps and by bounds. This is as dangerous, as serious a proposition today as the saloon question has ever been, and, having crushed the saloon, of which these habits are a mere by-product, it remains now for us to crush these alleged medicines which go all over this land to the dry sections thereof, and bring about this kind of drug addicts. (Applause)

The drug addiction habit is our habit. We don't get it from other nations, it is ours. And it is ours to stop! Why, in Austria they consume less, and they have accurate methods of arriving at statistics there – more accurate than ours. They consume less than one half of a grain of opiates per capita per year. Do you know how much we consume in the United States per capita per year? We consume sixty-six times that much. We consume thirty-three grains per capita per year. In France they consume three grains per capita per year. We consume nearly twelve times as much as they do in France. The immigrants brought to our coasts, and at whose doors we lay so much of our difficulties and troubles, are not responsible for this. We bring from the South of Europe and from the nations which have been furnishing us with laborers for so many years, no drug addicts. Our population has not been influenced by the men who come here from the Asiatic countries and who use drugs. They don't influence us in any particular; they simply disgust our population. We didn't use drugs in this country before the Civil War. Drug addiction was unknown up to that time, but the wounds, the worry, and the suffering of the Civil War produced drug addicts, until today we are the greatest drug consuming nation among all the white races of the world. It is our national question. We can't blame any other nation for it. We can't stop immigration to these coasts for it, because it is our problem, and the time has come now, after having throttled the saloon, to throttle that by proper laws, that can be enforced, in spite of the drug lobby which extends down to every community in this country. (Applause)

Time may bring strange upheavals in all the nations of the world. There are strange upheavals here. This old world trembles and labors and brings for republics, but in doing that, it brings to the surface these strange new theories and these dangerous factions. The time has come in the world and the time has come in this country for those who have been responsible for the destruction of the saloon to throttle this new vice. The time has come for clear thinking and correct methods of reasoning in this country and throughout the world, and those institutions and those things which contribute to it must be fostered and encouraged. Those things which produce thinking that isn't clear, that isn't correct, disordered; disorganized theories and ideals must be crushed. This drug habit is now the worst of them.

This great convention is attended by earnest thinking men and women from every section of the United States, and I am presenting to many of you for the first time this new danger, and if I have inspired any considerable number of you to go back to the community in which you live to study further this great question and to act, no matter if your local druggist is opposed to these laws – if I have succeeded in doing that, I feel I have accomplished much. (Applause)

JAMES CANNON, JR.
I have an important resolution which will be offered for your action:

"RESOLVED: That the mass meeting of citizens assembled in the Coliseum, at the Methodist Centenary Celebration, in Columbus, Ohio, celebrate the new independence day of the prohibition era and hereby petition the Congress of the United States to enact an adequate law enforcement code to make effective the 18th Amendment to the Constitution of the United States, and it is particularly urged that the definition of "intoxicating liquors" shall include all liquors with more than one half of one percent alcohol by volume." (Applause)

It was intended to present this resolution at a former time in the meeting, but it could not be presented before this time. If you will adopt this resolution, please rise.

It is unanimous and will be sent with the authority of the gathering.

...Singing of the Doxology...

We will now have the benediction by Bishop McDowell.

WILLIAM FRASER MCDOWELL:
May the grace of our Lord, Jesus Christ, and the love of our God, our Father, and the communion of the Holy Spirit rest upon us and remain with us evermore. Amen.

Notes

1. The Woman's Christian Temperance Union originated in small towns throughout Ohio and New York when concerned women met in homes and churches to discuss the perceived destructive influence of alcohol and to determine appropriate methods to close establishments that provided alcoholic beverages. Members of the W.C.T.U. were also interested in other social issues including suffrage, prostitution, and public health. The W.C.T.U. was officially organized in 1874 and continues as a non-sectarian organization today. Methodists Frances Willard and Centenary Celebration speaker Anna Gordon were presidents of the W.C.T.U. For additional information on the history and current work of the organization see: http://www.wctu.org/.

2. The Loyal Temperance Legion was the children's department of the Woman's Christian Temperance Union.

3. Florence D. Richard was President of the Ohio branch of the Woman's Christian Temperance Union. On May 27, 1918, Richard presented a petition to legalize woman's suffrage on the floor of the U.S. Senate. She also published a 5-page pamphlet *The Results of Prohibition* (Westerville, OH: American Issue Publishing Company, 1927).

4. Julia A.P. Bundy Foraker graduated from Ohio Wesleyan University in 1868.

5. "saved" is capitalized in the original transcript.

6. Lily E. Kurzenknabe Andujar was a missionary for the Methodist Episcopal Church in Puerto Rico. At the time of the Centenary exposition she was corresponding secretary for Puerto Rico with the W.C.T.U. *Alumni Record of Drew Theological Seminary, 1867-1905* (Madison, NJ: S.G. Ayres, 1906), 301.

7. The Jones Act of 1917 passed by Congress and signed by U.S. President Woodrow Wilson, granted citizenship to people from Puerto Rico. For additional information on the legislation see Truman R. Clark, *Puerto Rico and the United States, 1917-1933* (Pittsburgh: University of Pittsburgh Press, 1975).

8. Anna Pritchard George was director of the publicity bureau for the W.C.T.U. and later authored the children's play *Prohibition Mother Goose* (New York: Christian Nation Publishing Company, 1921).

9. The Chautauqua Institution was a 19th century educational center founded by Methodist bishop John Heyl Vincent and Lewis Miller. For a historical and religious analysis of the resort see Andrew Chamberlin Rieser, *The Chautauqua Moment: Protestants, Progressives, and the Culture of Modern Liberalism* (New York: Columbia University Press, 2003).

10. Etsu Inagaki Sugimoto (1873-1950). Sugimoto was an author and activist from Japan. She was born in Echigo, Japan and spent a portion of her life in Cincinnati, Ohio, and New York City. She would later teach Japanese language courses at Columbia University. She wrote several books including an autobiography *A Daughter of the Samurai* (Garden City, NY: Doubleday, Doran & Co., 1928) which was translated into several languages. See Setsuko Hirakawa, "Etsu I. Sugimoto's 'A Daughter of the Samurai' in America," *Comparative Literature Studies* 30:4, (East-West Issue 1993): 397-407.

11. Madame Kaji Yajima San was President of the World Woman's Christian Temperance Union and an active prohibitionist in Japan and around the world. Anna Gordon published a pamphlet of a speech by Yajima titled *Madame Kaji Yajima, Peace Pilgrimage to America: A Message from the Women of Japan to the Women of the World* (Evanston, IL: National W.C.T.U. Publishing House, undated).

12. Frances Willard Wong (1897-1970). Wong was an author and social activist in China. She was born Lui-Wang Liming and, at age 12, was one of the first young women to unbind her feet in China. At the age of 18 she joined the Chinese branch of the Woman's Christian Temperance Union and later studied at Northwestern University in Illinois. A year after speaking at the Centenary exposition Wong returned to China to form the Shanghai Woman's Suffrage Association. In 1966, following many years as a social activist she was arrested and imprisoned in Shanghai on charges that she was a secret agent for the Central Intelligence Agency of the United States. She died in prison in 1970. Zheng Wang, *Women in the Chinese Enlightenment: Oral and Textual Histories* (Berkeley and Los Angeles: University of California Press, 1999), 135-143.

13. Oberlin College has admitted both women and men as students since its founding in 1833. For additional history on the college see http://new.oberlin.edu/about/history.dot.

14. Footbinding was the custom of binding the feet of young girls to prevent further physical growth. For additional reading on the historical and cultural politics of footbinding see Wang Ping, *Aching for Beauty: Footbinding in China* (New York: Anchor Books, 2002); and Dorothy Ko, *Cinderella's Sisters: A Revisionist History of Footbinding* (Berkeley: University of California Press, 2005).

15. Maria Augusta Mulligan Oldham served as a missionary to India and Singapore for the Methodist Episcopal Church. At the time of Centenary exposition, Maria and her husband Bishop William Fitzjames Oldham, resided in Buenos Aires, Argentina.

16. "Scientific Temperance" was a movement sparked by the Woman's Christian Temperance Union and other temperance societies to legislate the teaching of temperance in public schools. For a 19th century interpretation of the movement see William Hargreaves, *The Total Abstinence Reader: Alcohol and Man, or the Scientific Basis for Total Abstinence. A Series of Short Lessons designed to teach the Chemical Origin, Properties, and Physiological action of Alcoholic Liquors, Prepared for the use of Temperance Organizations, Families, Schools, and Colleges* (New York: The National Temperance Society and Publication House, 1881).

17. Frances Pride Parks served as President of the West Virginia W.C.T.U. and was National Corresponding Secretary at the time of the Columbus fair. During the 1920s she sponsored a membership campaign to add one million more members to the society. See Elizabeth Putnam Gordon, *Women Torch-Bearers: The Story of the Woman's Christian Temperance Union* (Evanston, IL: National Woman's Christian Temperance Union Publishing House, 1924).

18. Francis Asbury Hall was one of several buildings located on the Ohio State Fairgrounds. The structures were given names that echoed the reach of Methodist missionaries including "The Africa Building" and "The China Building." This practice echoed the naming of pavilions at other contemporary-era World's Fairs. After visiting the Ohio State Fairgrounds in 2005 the author and his father discovered the building is one of three original structures still standing at the contemporary facility in Columbus.

19. Mary Emelia Clarke Barnes was superintendent for the Department of Americanization for the Chautauqua Institution. She co-authored *The New American: A Study of Immigration* (New York: Fleming H. Revell Co., 1913); and wrote several books including *Who is My Neighbor?* (New York: Missionary Education Movement of the

United States and Canada, 1917); and *Neighboring New Americans* (New York: Fleming H. Revell Co., 1920).

20. Catherine Lent Stevenson was president of the Massachusetts W.C.T.U. and served as corresponding secretary for the World Woman's Christian Temperance Union.

21. Hardynia K. Norville was a member of the World Woman's Christian Temperance Union and author of *A Sober South America: Prohibition on our Sister Continent* (Evanston, IL: National Woman's Christian Temperance Union Publishing House, undated).

22. Pedro Flores Valderrama was a minister with the Mexico Annual Conference of the Methodist Episcopal Church, South. He was the first Mexican to serve as head of the Mexican Methodist Institute in Pueblo, Mexico.

23. Aurelia Viera was an educator from Uruguay and a member of the National Anti-Alcohol League of Uruguay. She traveled extensively with Hardynia Norville to discuss educational and social reforms. See National Education Association of the United States, *Addresses and Proceedings of the Fifty-seventh Annual Meeting, held at Milwaukee, Wisconsin, July 28-July 5, 1919* (Washington, DC: National Education Association of the United States, 1919), 21.

24. William Fraser McDowell (1858-1937). McDowell was a bishop and ordained minister with the Methodist Episcopal Church. He was educated at Ohio Wesleyan University and Boston University and received several honorary doctorates. McDowell served churches in the North Ohio Conference and was later appointed Chancellor of the University of Denver. He authored several books including *In the School of Christ* (New York: Eaton & Mains; Cincinnati: Jennings & Graham, 1910); and *This Mind* (New York and Cincinnati: Methodist Book Concern, 1922).

25. Howard Hyde Russell (1855-1946). Russell was a minister in the Congregational Church and founder of the Ohio Anti-Saloon League. He became the first general superintendent of the Anti-Saloon League of America. He was educated at Griswold College (IA) and Oberlin Theological Seminary and served churches in Ohio, Kansas City, and the Armour Mission in Chicago. He practiced law for several years and authored *A Lawyer's Examination of the Bible* (Chicago and New York: Fleming H. Revell, 1893). Russell was a personal friend of John D. Rockefeller resulting in several large donations for the Anti-Saloon League. For additional information on Russell and the Anti-Saloon league see Thomas R. Pegram, *Battling Demon Rum: The Struggle for a Dry America, 1800-1933* (Chicago: Ivan R. Dee, 1998).

26. Lillian Stevens succeeded Frances Willard as president of the Woman's Christian Temperance Union (1898-1914). She was an active temperance advocate in her home state of Maine and served as one of the managers for the 1893 World's Columbian Exposition in Chicago. Mary Elvira Elliot, et al., *Sketches of Representative Women of New England* (Boston: New England Historical Publishing Company, 1904), 19-22.

27. Ella Alexander Boole (1858-1952). Boole was president of the Woman's Christian Temperance Union of the State of New York and president of the World Woman's Christian Temperance Union. She was educated at Wooster College and later became a member of the New York City Woman's Press Club and Woman's Anti-Vice Committee of New York City. In 1920, Boole made an unsuccessful run for the U.S. Senate on the Prohibition Party ticket and later authored *Give Prohibition Its Chance* (Evanston, IL: National Woman's Christian Temperance Union Publication House, 1929). For additional biographical information on Boole see "Mrs. Ella A. Boole, Ph.D.," *The Phrenological Journal* (May 1902): 146-148; and "Boole, Ella Alexander," *Alcohol*

and Temperance in Modern History: A Global Encyclopedia (Santa Barbara, CA: ABC-Clio, Inc., 2003), 109-110.

28. The Commission on Temperance and Social Service for the Methodist Episcopal Church, South, was organized in 1918. Seven members in good standing served on the commission including one bishop, three clergy, and three laypersons. The charge of the commission was to bring awareness concerning temperance to other agencies of the MECS and to outline a program of instruction for membership. *The Doctrines and Discipline of the Methodist Episcopal Church, South* (Nashville: Publishing House of the M.E. Church, South, 1920), 174-175.

29. Ernest Hurst Cherrington (1877-1950) was general secretary of the World League Against Alcoholism. He authored *The Evolution of Prohibition in the United States of America: A Chronological History of the Liquor Problem and the Temperance Reform in the United States from the Earliest Settlements to the Consummation of National Prohibition* (Westerville, OH: American Issue Press, 1920). See "Cherrington, Ernest Hurst," *Alcohol and Temperance in Modern History: A Global Encyclopedia* (Santa Barbara, CA: ABC-Clio, Inc., 2003), 147-148.

30. Clarence True Wilson (1872-1939). Wilson was an ordained minister with the Methodist Episcopal Church. He was educated at St. John's College (MD), the University of Southern California, and Maclay College of Theology (now Claremont School of Theology). He served as general secretary of the Board of Temperance, Prohibition, and Public Morals of the Methodist Episcopal Church and was instrumental in the development of the Methodist Building near Capitol Hill in Washington, D.C.

31. Samuel Dickie was educated at Albion College and was Prohibition Party candidate for governor of Michigan in 1886. He was a layperson with the Methodist Episcopal Church. John Granville Woolley was educated at Ohio Wesleyan University and was a Prohibition Party candidate for U.S. president in 1892.

32. Emperor Wilhelm II (1859-1941) was the Emperor of Germany and King of Prussia from 1888 to 1918. He was the grandson of Queen Victoria and Prince Albert of Great Britain.

33. John Nelson Clark Coggin (1870-1927). Coggin was educated at Clark University and Gammon Theological Seminary. He was an ordained minister in the Upper Mississippi, Savannah, and Atlanta Annual Conferences of the Methodist Episcopal Church and served several churches in Mississippi and Georgia. Coggin was Field Secretary for Colored Work for the Board of Temperance, Prohibition, and Public Morals of the Methodist Episcopal Church. He also edited the song book *Plantation Melodies and Spiritual Songs* (Philadelphia: Press of Hall-Mack Co., 1913). See Frank Lincoln Mather, *Who's Who of the Colored Race* (Chicago: Frank Lincoln Mather, 1915), 71; and A.B. Caldwell, *History of the American Negro* (Atlanta, GA: A.B. Caldwell Publishing, 1922), 30-33.

34. Charles H. Randall (1865-1951) was a member of Congress from California. He was also a member of the Prohibition Party and the only politician from the party to serve in Congress. In 1924 he ran for Vice-President on the American Party ticket. The American Party was heavily sponsored by the Ku Klux Klan. "Randall, Charles Hiram," *Biographical Dictionary of the United States Congress*, accessed January 16, 2012, <http://bioguide.congress.gov/scripts/biodisplay.pl?index=R000036>

35. Purley Albert Baker (1858-1924). Baker was an ordained minister from Ohio with the Methodist Episcopal Church. He joined the Ohio Anti-Saloon League and later became general superintendent of the Anti-Saloon League of America. For additional information on Baker and his historical context within the study of Prohibition see Robert

A. Hohner, *Prohibition and Politics: The Life of Bishop James Cannon, Jr.* (Columbia, SC: University of South Carolina Press, 1999).

36. Earl Cranston (1840-1932). Cranston was educated at Ohio University and served as a Captain for the Ohio Infantry and West Virginia Cavalry during the American Civil War. He was an ordained minister with the Ohio Conference of the Methodist Episcopal Church and served churches in Ohio, Illinois, Indiana, and Colorado. Cranston was elected bishop in 1896 and later published *Breaking Down the Walls: A Contribution to Methodist Unification* (New York: Methodist Book Concern, 1915). He is buried at Arlington National Cemetery in Virginia.

37. Samuel Porter Jones (1847-1906). Jones began his career as a lawyer and later converted to Christianity at a Methodist revival meeting. He was an ordained minister with the North Georgia Conference of the Methodist Episcopal Church, South, and would go on to prominence as a traveling evangelist. He died onboard a train in Arkansas while traveling to a revival meeting and was laid to rest in State at the Georgia State Capitol building.

38. George Rutledge Stuart (1857-1926). Stuart was educated at Emory and Henry College. He was an ordained minister with the Holston Conference of the Methodist Episcopal Church, South, and served churches in Alabama and Tennessee. Stuart worked several years as Chair of the English and Natural Science Department of Centenary College (TN) and published *The Saloon under the Searchlight* (New York: F.H. Revell, 1908); and *What Every Methodist should Know* (Nashville and Dallas, TX: Publishing House of the M.E. Church, South, 1923). For additional information on Stuart see William Washington Pinson, *George R. Stuart: His Life and Work* (Nashville: Cokesbury Press, 1927).

39. Amendments XVI and XVII were added to the U.S. Constitution in 1913. Amendment XVI states, "The Congress shall have the power to lay and collect taxes on incomes, from whatever source derived, without apportionment among the several States, and without regard to any census or renumeration." Amendment XVII states, "The Senate of the United States shall be composed of two Senators from each State, elected by the people thereof, for six years; and each Senator shall have one vote. The electors in each State shall have the qualifications requisite for electors of the most numerous branch of the State legislatures. When vacancies happen in the representation of any State in the Senate, the executive authority of such State shall issue writs of election to fill such vacancies: *Provided*, That the legislature of any State may empower the executive thereof to make temporary appointments until the people fill the vacancies by election as the legislature may direct. This amendment shall not be so construed as to affect the election or term of any Senator chosen before it becomes valid as part of the Constitution." National Archives and Records Administration, "Constitution of the United States, Amendments 11-27," accessed January 16, 2012, http://www.archives.gov/exhibits/charters/constitution_amendments_11-27.html.

40. William Jennings Bryan (1860-1925). Bryan was educated at Illinois College and Union College of Law (now Northwestern University School of Law). He was a U.S. politician and three-time presidential candidate. Bryan was a member of the Democratic Party and served as Secretary of State for President Woodrow Wilson. He was a Presbyterian and strong proponent of Prohibition. Bryan traveled and spoke extensively on the Chautauqua circuit and was a vociferous opponent to Darwinian thought and the teaching of evolution. He is perhaps best known for his debates with Clarence Darrow at the Scopes Trial in Tennessee over the teaching of evolution in public schools. For

additional information on Bryan see Michael Kazin, *A Godly Hero: The Life of William Jennings Bryan* (New York: Knopf, 2006).

41. Alexander Mitchell Palmer (1872-1936). Palmer served as U.S. Attorney General from 1919 to 1921. For more on Palmer see Stanley Coben, *A. Mitchell Palmer: Politician* (New York: Columbia University Press, 1963).

42. Delirium tremens is the medical phrase for withdrawal reactions in the human central nervous system related to the stoppage of the consumption of alcohol. National Center for Biotechnology Information, U.S. National Library of Medicine, "Delirium tremens," *PubMed Health*, accessed January 17, 2012, http://www.ncbi.nlm.nih.gov/pubmedhealth/PMH0001771/.

43. Henry Thomas Rainey (1860-1934). Rainey was educated at Knox College (IL), Amherst College (MA), and Union College of Law (now Northwestern University School of Law). He worked as a lawyer for several years prior to a career in politics. Rainey was a member of the Democratic Party and served in the U.S. Congress for the State of Illinois. He was Speaker of the House of Representatives during the Franklin D. Roosevelt presidency. For additional information on Congressman Rainey see Robert A. Waller, *Rainey of Illinois: A Political Biography, 1903-43* (Urbana: University of Illinois Press, 1977).

44. The Harrison Narcotics Act, passed by the U.S. Congress in 1914, required opiate and cocaine sellers to secure a license in order to sell narcotics. In 1919, the U.S. Supreme Court ratified the Harrison Anti-Narcotic Act which outlawed medical practitioners from prescribing narcotics to known drug addicts. Narcotics could only be prescribed if the doctor was weaning the patient off of a particular drug. The National Alliance of Advocates for Buprenorphine Treatment, "Laws," accessed January 17, 2012, http://www.naabt.org/laws.cfm. For additional information on the history of U.S. drug control and enforcement see David F. Musto, *The American Disease: Origins of Narcotic Control, 3rd Edition* (New York: Oxford University Press, 1999).

45. At the time of the Centenary exposition Dr. Hamilton Wright had served as United States Opium Commissioner during the presidential administrations of Theodore Roosevelt, William Taft, and Woodrow Wilson.

Chapter Five

Methodists, the U.S. Armed Forces, and the American Nation

Introduction

Chapter Five includes speeches that link the work of Methodist domestic missions with the advance of Americanization and Christianity. The chapter is divided into six sections representing various days and events. Speakers included Methodist bishops and ministers, U.S. military leaders, and civil rights advocates. The notion of the "American nation" is a central thread throughout the addresses. Speakers championed the importance of U.S. citizenship to American Indians and also to the many immigrants from Europe and Asia. Several speakers linked American Methodism with the work of the U.S. military and the rebuilding of nations destroyed by the ravages of World War I.

The first section of addresses highlights the "Peace Signing Celebration" at the fairgrounds. Homer Stuntz, James Cannon, Jr., and Wilbur Thirkield reminded expositions audiences of the significance of the end of the Great War and the participation of the American Expeditionary Force in the conflict. Thirkield's address is of particular interest since the Southern bishop highlights the involvement of African American troops in the American Expeditionary Force and also challenges audiences to think more critically upon racial violence as he references the East St. Louis riot of 1917. Racial violence in the forms of lynching, race riots, and discrimination would have been a familiar concern of exposition visitors. Only three weeks after Thirkield's speech a week long race riot took place in Chicago as a component of the "Red Summer" of 1919.

The next collection of addresses was held on "Americanization Day." Chaired by Bishop John M. Moore the session broadcast the concerns of American Methodists toward issues of indigenous peoples (American Indians), immigrant peoples (Europeans), and the revitalization of U.S. cities. Henry Roe Cloud appeared on stage to inform audiences of the Americanization and Christianization of American Indians. Francis J. McConnell spoke on the work of Methodists toward the evangelization of urban centers. The address of Henry

Roe Cloud was a significant moment during the exposition. Cloud, a member of the Winnebago Nation, challenged the audience to think proactively concerning the need for U.S. citizenship for Native Americans. For Methodists in the audience the emphasize upon the Christianization of American Indians was a crucial thrust of the domestic missionary organizations in place in the Methodist Episcopal Church and Methodist Episcopal Church, South.

"Victory Day" at the exposition included addresses by William G. McAdoo and Bishop H. Lester Smith. McAdoo had served as Secretary of the U.S. Treasury in the Woodrow Wilson administration and was a well-known proponent of mass transportation. He would function as an adviser for the United Artist film company and run for U.S. president on the Democratic Party ticket. McAdoo's speech was politically layered as a promotion piece for the newly proposed League of Nations document. The legislation emphasized the involvement of the United States in a treaty with several dozen other nations to prevent future wars. As President Woodrow Wilson made his way back from Europe and began a nation-wide promotional campaign for the League the audience in Columbus would have resonated with McAdoo's push toward global peace.

"Navy Day" celebrated the work of the U.S. Navy in the Great War. Exposition organizers brought in Josephus Daniels, former Secretary of the U.S. Navy, to give the keynote address. Daniels championed the importance of the Navy in transporting soldiers across the Atlantic Ocean. He also celebrated his role in eliminating the consumption of alcohol in the armed forces. Daniels was also careful to point out the connection between American forces and divine intervention. Using language that sounds strikingly familiar to contemporary readers Daniels connected the work of U.S. armed forces with the blessing of God. For Daniels and many Methodists in the audience that day war and divine blessing were intricately interlaced.

"Army Day" included addresses by Bishop James Atkins and General Edwin Glenn. Atkins had served as chair of the Centenary Commission of the Methodist Episcopal Church, South, and introduced Glenn to exposition audiences on July 8. General Edwin Forbes Glenn had served in several military campaigns during the Spanish-American War and had been brought under suspicion of excessive torture (waterboarding) during his time in the Philippines. Glenn had been placed on brief suspension for those actions but would go on to train nearly two hundred thousand U.S. Army recruits at various training facilities throughout the United States. At the exposition Glenn spoke of the realities of the Great War detailing the bombing of France and the use of gas in European trenches. Glenn discussed his role in helping to build morale within the ranks of soldiers. He was careful to point out the importance of literacy among the troops and used the Centenary platform to discuss immigration and citizenship.

The final section of the chapter records the speeches given at a program honoring Lieutenant Commander Albert Cushing Read and Sergeant Alvin C. York. Read and York were two of the most recognizable names in the U.S. military due to their recent experiences in trans-Atlantic flight and the Great

War. Read and several associates had recently completed the first manned flight across the Atlantic in a seaplane. York had returned from the European war theater and had been in high demand as a speaker due to his heroics against the German army. To celebrate the victory of American forces Albert Read and Alvin York informed audiences how Methodists had been the first to volunteer to serve the country and how the United States now needed American Methodists to help with rebuilding efforts overseas. Read gave a full account of the preparation for his flight and the drama that followed until he landed in England. York closed the session with a brief account of how his faith had played a significant role during his time at war. York was an honored war veteran and an American celebrity. To thousands of American Methodists in attendance York embodied a heroic Christian ideal. He believed God had blessed and protected him in the midst of a strenuous campaign to liberate Europe. For audiences at the State Fairgrounds York was a key figure in the interlacing of Christianity, the U.S. military, and Nation-building.

Peace Signing Celebration
Saturday Morning, June 28, 1919

...Reverend Doctor E.C. Hickman introduced Bishop Homer C. Stuntz...

HOMER C. STUNTZ:[1]
(Holding up an extra paper, showing headlines) This is the best news that we have had for nearly five years. The war is over! The war is over! And what I want to do in the few minutes that I shall claim of your attention is to emphasize two facts which this occasion should rivet upon our memories. First, that this is a victory for the church and Jesus Christ, the Prince of Righteousness, which have triumphed in this war. Let no one suppose that the object of the church today is merely to include in her visible membership every person on the face of the earth. I have no hope that this will ever occur, but what I do expect will be that the principles which Jesus enunciated, of brotherhood, of fairness, of right dealing, whether as between nations or individuals, shall prevail as working axioms of national and international life.

These are the principles which the church of Christ has been proclaiming for nearly two thousand years, and when they have triumphed the churches have triumphed through the acceptance of her message.

Second, that the signing of this treaty is another link – possibly the final link – in the chain that winds us forever to world relationships. We entered into world affairs when our navy, under her daring commanders, put an end to Mohammedan piracy in the Caribbean Sea more than a century ago.

But some of our editors, and a few of our Senators have not awakened to the fact that our nationalization, of which they talk so much, is not only a mighty, but a long exploded one. What is the use of our talking about the United States being isolated from the rest of the world? I read this telegram that the German delegates signed the treaty in Paris at 3:12 this afternoon, that Mr. Wilson signed it at 3:14, and Mr. Lloyd George at 3:16.

I am now speaking at 11:20 in the forenoon, and this news has been transmitted across the sea, well out into the American continent, has been set up in type, printed in a newspaper, brought here to these grounds and sold, and it is still five hours before the thing happened. (Laughter)

When this thing happens daily it is folly to talk about our ever being isolated from France or England, the Balkan states, from India, or any other part of the world. They are in our very door yard. We hear them talk in their sleep, their diplomacy, their commerce, their social life – all of it is inextricably interwoven with the fabric of our future, and we ought not to slink from this fact, but on this high day of the signing of this world treaty of peace by our own President yonder in Paris, we will come to the fact that we have finally and forever entered into the main current of world affairs. (Applause) It only remains for us to prove that in the future, as in the past, our impact upon world conditions shall be in the interests of righteousness. (Applause)

JAMES B. CANNON:

Our part in the signing of this treaty of peace was a decisive part. There is no question, I think, but that this treaty of peace that was signed, or as Bishop Stuntz says, will be signed in four hours, of which we have already heard, that this treaty of peace would never have been signed in the way that it was signed today with reluctant, unwilling German representatives dragging their feet to the palace of Versailles and reluctantly putting there (sic) names there. It never would have been signed in that way but for the fact that America went to Europe to make the world free, not for democracy simply, but for righteousness. (Applause)

I was in London the day the great drive began, the 21st of March, 1918. I have seen the British people many times under different circumstances. I never saw them with their backs to the wall as they were the three days that I stayed there after that great drive began. There was no despair among them. There was no break down, no sense of withdrawal, but there was a solemnity all over London that could be felt as they realized that their men, their sons, were being ground to pieces under the awful compact of that last great campaign of the German army. It was my fortune to interview Mr. Asquith, the Premier of England on Saturday morning, the third day of the great drive. I was there to ask him what attitude he would take as the leader of the Liberal Party toward an appeal from our government to the British government that the same regulations as to the sale of strong drink, which we had here in America, should be put into effect in England, and after talking about that, he said, "Well, doctor, really it is hard for me to take and think composedly about anything. My oldest son was killed last year on the battle front. My second son is in the hospital with one of his limbs amputated, and his recovery uncertain, my last son is there in the trenches, and it is hard for me to think about anything but France and my boy and the other boys of England who are over there today."

I went from him to the home of Major Astor, who has become one of the prominent men in English life – not the baron, but his son who married a beautiful Virginia woman, one of the famous 'Longhorn' beauties. I said to her as I was leaving for France that I would never forget what I had seen there of the courage, pluck and tremendous vitality of the English people, and then she turned to me and pointed – we were standing near the great dining hall – she pointed and said, "You see this dining hall. Before the war this was the place of an assemblage of the young life of London. Well, out of from fifty to sixty of the leaders of English social and political life, young men, there have been killed on the battle front thirty-eight of those young men, who will no more assemble around the banquet hall here with us."

The English people suffered quietly, suffered all sorts of privations that the world might be saved for democracy. (Applause) And then I went to France, and I was there on the Good Friday that the Germans bombed the church of St. Gervais. I was sitting in General Lewis' headquarters not over two hundred yards away, and as we sat there discussing the problem that I was discussing that year – immorality and drink – and getting his ideas as to the effect of our laws, and by the way, this testimony is worth while – he said, "When we were on the

Texas Border fighting, or rather guarding, the drink shops and the red light districts had our boys at their mercy. But that great act which Congress passed last spring, which forbade absolutely the sale of liquor to soldiers and sailors in uniform changed the problems of discipline in Texas which was so great and so difficult, and made it such an easy matter that there isn't a General in the army today that would for a moment go back to the old conditions. (Applause) Or who would not declare that we never could have trained as quickly and as efficiently as we did the splendid body of men which we have been sending over to France if we had not had the protection in our camps all over the United States."

We were sitting there talking and suddenly there came this great explosion. Well, I jumped. The General couldn't afford to jump. It was beneath the dignity of a General to jump, but I jumped out of my chair, and said as any ordinary man would have said, "What was that?" And I was shaking considerably. He just pressed a little button very quietly and said as the orderly came in, "Go and see what that was." And presently he returned and reported – saluted in the most orderly fashion and said, "Beg to report, sir, that the big gun has thrown a shell and destroyed the side wall and the roof of the church of St. Gervais, and it is reported that seventy-five to ninety people have been killed."

Every day in the city of Paris, for the time I was there, every thirty minutes that gun sent a bomb into that city. No man knew where it would fall. Every man knew that it would fall with German precision at a certain time, and you might be sitting at the restaurant table and every now and then sometimes I was there, and I would like to look at my watch and wonder where it would fall the next time. Sometimes it fell a mile away, sometimes five hundred feet away. Nobody knew, but that was the sort of strain that even the civilian population of France was under in the city of Paris, during the war.

It is needless for me to say that when America decided to come into that war and fight to save the world for democracy that England and France had done their duty and had done all that those nations could be expected to do. (Applause)

I was there the day that General Pershing issued his statement to General Foch, and said Marshal Foch, "All that we have is yours – our artillery, our men. Take them, use them as you will." That was the time when they brigaded our men here and there and yonder. We did not have that last spring anything like the army that people thought we had in France. About three hundred forty thousand men were all we had there a year ago last May. When I left I saw the official record, but you cannot imagine unless you had been there what it meant to France, to England to have three hundred forty thousand American soldiers on the soil of France, scattered here and there.

That line which they were holding down from Nancy toward the Swiss border, it meant that America, while not there yet in the flesh, was there in the spirit. (Applause) And that that spirit was such that the war could end in only one way. I walked the streets of Paris for a month after the big drive was on. I saw the French people under the tremendous tension as the drive crept closer and closer.

One day the British lines were nearly five miles away, and they had given me passage to go up there to the British front, but the next morning when I awoke to go there I got a message from His Majesty's Service, regretting that it was necessary to withdraw the pass. Why? Because the German drive had swept right up to the British line, and they did not dare to allow any civilians to go up there at that point where we wished to make our investigations.

I was in Paris when forty thousand refugees came pouring down on the railroads from Amiens. The most pitiful sight I ever saw was old men, children, babes in arms, and the things they brought with them. They couldn't bring their furniture, but this man brought a picture, and that woman had some clothes in a bundle, and there was a conglomeration of effects and of people all around the Gar du Norde there, and the question was where to put them to sleep, how to feed them and take care of them.

I have been in the army over there with the YMCA last year, and this year I had a son in the YMCA who did his duty as other men's sons have done their duty to the soldiers in this war. There were the girls in the canteens in the YMCA who worked from morning till night in order that our boys may be comfortable and to give a sweetening touch to the atmosphere in which they moved. The YMCA and the Red Cross and the Salvation Army and the Knights of Columbus, and the other bodies were there trying to alleviate the sufferings of these people, and everywhere I went, and where they recognized me as an American, smiles of gratitude, words of thanks – "Oh, what would we do without America?" – was the thought they all had.

I am not wrong in saying that the greatest event, perhaps, since the coming of St. Paul to Europe was the going of America to Europe – not as a bunch of pleasure seekers, not on a frolick (sic), not to spend money recklessly as we have the reputation of doing, but unselfishly, gloriously, that the world might know that we are not a band of money grubbers and pleasure lovers, but that we are men of high ideals who do not want to fight, but who believe with the apostle Paul that "First pure, then peaceable is God's word," and that it is not only for the life outside, but for the life inside the church of Jesus Christ purity is first, righteousness is first, and there can be no peace to the wicked.

And now, my brethren, we are here rejoicing today. I cannot but feel in my heart that I wish now I was in Paris. I kept hoping that peace treaty would be signed before I left Paris. I was at the peace conference when they had the labor document brought forth and adopted and that was a great day. But I think that this crowd here can have little idea really of what it means to poor, torn, struggling Europe to know that peace has come.

It has cost a great deal. It has cost billions upon billions of substance that might have been used for other and better things. It has cost the devastation of great provinces, and of the destruction of cities. It has brought forth a collection of deviltry that the world did not know really existed in the hearts of man. It has cost the lives of millions, but we, ourselves, have not felt it at all in comparison with England, with France, and with Belgium. We have not felt at all what Italy has felt and those nations in this struggle.

Oh, if we rejoice today surely there is indeed great exultation rolling up over on the other side of the sea, and we can all unite in thanksgiving to Almighty God that peace has come. Oh, shall we not, as Bishop Stuntz has said, stand by the men who were all criticized, and who, as Mr. Lloyd George graphically said, tried to make a peace with stones clattering on the roof and smashing through the windows, and wild men sleuthing through the keyholes to distract them. They have made a peace which, I believe, under all the circumstance is a marvelous document, and which has embedded in it, whether the details be right or not, that golden thread of love, of brotherhood, of a determination that we shall be leagued together as a nation with that nation and with the other nations, that God's spirit of brotherhood which has made of one blood all the races of the earth – that that spirit may go out as the driving wheel of the world from this time on.

I cannot but rejoice myself that the isolation of America has ceased. I do not believe any man, any Christian man, any Methodist especially on this Centenary occasion doesn't know the great commissioning, "Go ye into all the world and preach the gospel to every creature," but rejoice that God has thrown open wide the door for evangelistic effort of the continent of Europe, and that we as a church – both your church and our church – can go in there and bring the pure gospel of Jesus Christ as we have known it in our own lands.

Dr. Hickman who is presiding has secured the colored chorus of fifty voices, who are now going to sing to you, but before they come Bishop Atkins, the pioneer Sunday School editor of the South will address you.

BISHOP ATKINS:[2]

Ladies and gentlemen, first of all I wish to say that I did not expect to speak. I was out under a friendly shade, beginning to enjoy the speech of Bishop Stuntz when I was called on to come to the grand stand. Nevertheless, I have some right to speak. In the first place, I am the hero of two wars myself. (Applause) The first one I did not enter because I was too young to get in. That was the war between the states, and the last one I did not enter because I was too old to get in. (Applause)

But you make the mistake of thinking that the men who were too young to get into the war between the states on both sides, and the men who were too old to get in the war of America in Europe did not have to bear a good part of the sacrifices of the occasion. (Applause)

I have the right to speak, also, because I am from the South. I am glad to see my crowd standing back of me here. (Referring to the Colored Chorus) And whenever they are ready you will have the best part of the day's entertainment, I promise you. I am from the South. I say I am not only from the South, but I am from North Carolina. (Applause)

North Carolina, as you know, is a great liberty loving people. They passed resolutions which amounted to a declaration of independence thirteen months before the Philadelphia specimen was born. (Applause) And when the issue involved came on them, she had the first blood of the Revolutionary War – North Carolina did – and when that war between the states came on them, she had the first blood of that war, and when the war with Spain came on, Raleigh was the first man to lose his life in that war.

Now, when they wanted the force that would certainly break the Hindenburg Line, a New York division, and a North Carolina division were sent to the front and did the work, and made the first break in that line. (Applause) And not only that, but North Carolina was the first state in the union in which the men took the ballots in their hands and went to the ballot box and voted a constitutional arrangement that will forever hold against whiskey. (Applause)

Now, I can't afford to indulge in much more that is autobiographical, because Bishop Cannon, who represents the South, also has given us a most charming autobiography in relation to this war, but I was over there too, but I was over there as a commissioner from Southern Methodism, for I presume most of you are Northern Methodists up here, for the purpose of agreeing upon plans by which we could work together in your principles about Europe. Now, I am a secessionist, all right. You see I am not taking anything back, but I am a unionist now, provided you unite on the conditions that I want to lay down, and we work for the construction of a plan by which the two great Methodisms of America can enter Europe as one, and we will call it, say, the Episcopal Methodist Church of France, of Belgium, and England, and so on throughout the rest of Europe, so I will not make any reference to this.

I did see this – the French Government bestowed upon this Methodist commission a courtesy, I suppose, never bestowed on any other distinctly religious commission in the history of mankind. The French president and General Joffre not only received us, and we got a peep at General Foch with the hallow of his glorious achievements in his countenance – the grandest man as a military man on the face of the earth, or that ever was on the face of the earth. I am profoundly glad, however, today that General Foch's job is ended, and that we have peace, but I was going to say we went over all these battle fields and saw the wreck of one-eighth of the whole domain of France, and we heard from off the ground the stories of those unmentionable outrages that stirred the blood of all the world as nothing else could have done, and we felt all the way through, as you feel today, that Germany has gotten the most generous settlement that ever a set of thieves and murderers and cut-throats and rapists ever got on the face of the earth. (Applause) And I do not think that the end will have probably come until human justice has been vindicated by international punishment of those who are the chief criminals in Germany. Otherwise, what is the use of talking about human justice?

But now there is one thing about our nation entering into this war that I should like to discuss, and that is that we have entered as a matter of principle. We were the one nation in the great fight that didn't have to go in. Now, I know they sunk the *Lusitania* and all that sort of thing, but that was no reason to causa belli (sic)[3] that would justify these tens of thousands of lives and billions of dollars, and we could have gone around, and by the time of their exhaustion settled with them on conditions that would have been very satisfactory in history. We went into it because we had to go into for the principles that have animated us from the beginning of our history.

Now, I come from the mountains, and the mountain people are great people for principles – great on principles, and I will give you an illustration. Up there in Tennessee where I was born and reared and also raised, there was a boy who came in one day with an eye all blacked up, and his friend said, "Bill, what is the matter?" "Well," he said, "I had a fight." "Well, you're pretty well battered up. You got the worst of it, didn't you?" "Yes, but I'm mighty glad I fought him." "Well, what was the matter anyway?" "Why, he insulted my sister." "Insulted your sister?" "Yep!" "What did he do or say?" "Say? Why, he said my sister was cross-eyed." "Well, is your sister cross-eyed?" "Why, no, I ain't got no sister." "Then what was you fighting for?" "Just for the principle of the thing." (Applause & Laughter)

Now, we were just fighting for the principle of the thing. Yes, and when we got into it, it has been perfectly ridiculous all this swash about not staying in, or all this talk about maintaining our isolation, all foolishness. We went into Europe when we went into the war, and we can't get out of Europe till the crack of the doom.[4]

I want to say about the peace treaty – I notice you always cheer when they say anything about the peace treaty and the League of Nations. I want to say this – that the smartest of all – the smartest thing that Woodrow Wilson ever did was holding that league of peace and that treaty of peace together so that they couldn't get it apart, because the mere settlement in the treaty of peace would have amounted to nothing, but when it is settled on the basis of a league of nations to keep the peace throughout all time, it is the greatest document that has ever been formulated by the human mind.

And now I want to make a prophecy. George Elliott (sic), you know, says that the most unjustifiable error in the world is errors men make in prophecies, because they don't have to prophecy. So I don't have to prophecy, but I do predict that the most overwhelming approval that any measure has ever taken in the history of the American people will be America's approval of the League of Nations. (Applause)

Now, gentlemen, I have some other things to say, but I am so sure that you are myself, that you would rather hear these brethren back of me than to hear me – appreciating the compliment bestowed – and I am glad to give way to true southerners. (Applause)

ANNOUNCEMENT:

Now, we have with us here this morning the district superintendents and a number of preachers of the New Orleans area, under the splendid leadership of Bishop Thirkield, and the rest of the show belongs to Bishop Thirkield and his crew.

BISHOP THIRKIELD:[5]

Now, the best message that I can bring you is the message that our colored people often sing in the South, putting into musical form that great utterance of the Scripture that has in it the prophecy of manhood and hope through all the years, and I am going to ask them to sing this message – "Beloved, We are the Sons of God."

...The colored chorus sang the song...

BISHOP THIRKIELD:

This race represented here has done great things across the sea. (Applause) I think the first thing I heard of them – coming right up to the report of others – was that time when that regiment of troops were sorely pressed, and they hadn't the matter of gas masks and all that, and there was a regiment of white troops in the trenches, supported by a group of colored men right behind them. So the colored men went forth and were gassed and the Germans saw them falling back under this devilish treatment, and they rushed forward and just as the white men rushed back to get into their trenches on came this support of a column of colored men, and the Germans began to give way, and finally went back and said, "We don't understand these Americans. Why, you gas them, and they only turn black in the face and keep coming on." (Applause & Laughter)

And they kept coming on and did their part, and we as a nation, related to this twelve million people here represented on this platform should not forget that the only regiment, as I understand it, of Americans, every member of which received from the grateful French nation the Croix de Guerre, was the black regiment.[6]

Now, how are we related to these people? I want to say to you that we should manifest a broader spirit of brotherhood and of kindliness and of sympathy and of helpfulness to this race throughout the North and throughout the South. (Applause) There is some ground for the assertion that if there are as many colored people in the North as there are in the South, our relations would not be as friendly and brotherly as they now are, but I want to say to you that there are discriminations and mistreatments of these people here in this land in the North, as well as South, that in the name of the religion of Jesus Christ, in the name of our nation, in the name of democracy, for which we have fought, should forever be put down. (Applause)

We have been fighting to make this world safe for democracy, and I want to say to you our battle is to make democracy safe for this world. Democracy in America is not safe. It is not safe for the world, when in the town of East St. Louis in the state of Illinois a hundred and seventy-five black people can be butchered and can be treated in ways that are simply unspeakable.[7] Democracy is not safe for this world when one of my district superintendents, just as we are leaving the platform, said to me, "I have got to go home. Down in my town in Mississippi I have got a letter from my wife that a mob has been raging there for nearly a week," and his wife hadn't had her shoes off during that time.

Democracy is not safe for America when in Bogaloosa, Alabama,[8] in my own state – and I speak of this with great interest because the lumber companies are under the control and direction of northern men, the capital is northern, and the leadership there is of northern men – and I want to say to you that our next great battle, my friends, throughout this nation in behalf of the lowly and oppressed black and white is to make this nation safe for the larger democracy that will give every man a chance to develop the best and divinest (sic) that is in him. Now, our churches in this work, and these men here who sing the gospel of Jesus Christ, represent what we as a church have been trying to do upon these religious lines through these years, and I am very glad to report as a final word in connection with our Centenary, that in the New Orleans area, which is composed of two colored conferences – or rather five colored conferences and two white conferences – for purposes of administration, the colored conferences were separated and operated under colored leadership. Those conferences have not only subscribed their quota but as a token of the earnestness with which they are undertaking that work for the Centenary, laid down on Easter Sunday over $90,000 in cash. (Applause)

That includes the West Texas conference, which up to date with the five conferences of the New Orleans area, have brought in almost $100,000. That is their response to the Centenary, and I want to say to these people here represented that that means large things for the kingdom of our God, and my dear Bishop Atkins, I am longing for the day when our churches shall be one in reality. (Applause)

We will not have a Northern Methodism or a Southern Methodism, but one united Methodism throughout the whole nation. And if we could know and so join together in such a brotherhood in Christ Jesus and get our great arms under this race and under these other problems of this nation, we would lift these people up and up and up in the light of the glory of God in the face of Jesus Christ, our Lord. (Applause)

BISHOP ATKINS:

I wish to make this remark – that the people of the South, whether these men come from the North and South of the class that Thirkield belongs to are just as much opposed to all outrageous treatment of the negro as people in any other section of the country. (Applause)

The Bishop has spoken of what the colored people did in the war. I want to say that the marvel of the colored race is its progress in these fifty years between the war between the states and this present war. I dare say that few races in the history of mankind have on all sides experienced such great progress as the negro has done, and especially under the limitations that were put upon him to start with. (Applause)

We are in thorough sympathy – I speak for our Methodist Episcopal Church, South – with every movement for the betterment of all the conditions, home life and religious life and commercial life of the negroes of the South. (Applause)

BISHOP THIRKIELD:

I wish to say that I thank the Lord that I am an optimist. Things are growing better all the time, but I want to say here what I say in Louisiana and Mississippi and all through my area, and what was said in a two column article in the *Times* with reference to a lynching at Monroe only three weeks ago – that the difficulty is that while the decent, law-abiding, religious people of such sections of

Illinois, as represented in East St. Louis, do not stand up and say by all that is holy "The mob must be forever put down." (Applause)

BISHOP ATKINS:

We are saying that, and one difference between us and you is that when a man commits a great outrage we go after the man, and you go after the whole family. (Applause) In other words, I love the negro race. I was reared amongst them. I stand by them. I preached for them. I believe in them, but I think that on occasion of this kind we ought to keep this kind of matter as far out of sight as possible, and I only speak a word because I was afraid somebody, if I kept still, might interpret me as being one of the southerners that didn't stand by the negro race, and all my friends know that I do. (Applause)

...ADJOURNMENT...

Americanization Day Program
Thursday Afternoon, July 3, 1919

The meeting convened in the Coliseum at 2:30p.m., Bishop John M. Moore of Nashville presiding as chairman...
 ...Pageant, 'The City Beautiful'[9]
 ...Music by Gloria Trumpeteers
 ...Singing of 'My Country Tis of Thee'

JOHN M. MOORE:[10]

The last five years have brought strongly to our attention the great problems of our American country. This is a period when our great Republic has been finding itself. It has been finding itself as a great factor in the world's life, but it is also finding itself as the home of the great problems that must be solved for the world's civilization.

This day we come to speak of the things that concern us in making our country the true America, the America of our fathers, and the America of our sons. And there are so many problems that it would be impossible for us even to hint at them at such a time as this.

We are bringing to you especially two of these most interesting problems this afternoon by two speakers that you will be delighted to hear.

The first speaker has every claim to be a real American. He is the descendant of the original American. He is a son of the Winnebago Tribe of American Indians. He is also a man who has had the advantage of the best culture of our country. He is a graduate of Yale University, having the degree of Doctor of Philosophy from that great institution. He has given himself with great loyalty and devotion to the work of leading his own people into a new life, and giving training to the best of the young men for the great service which they must render to their own people and also as citizens in this country.

He is at present the principal of the Training School for the Indian Workers of America. I take great pleasure in introducing to you at this time, Doctor Henry Roe Cloud, who will address you on "The American Indian."

HENRY ROE CLOUD:[11]

In the great Methodist Episcopal Church Centenary plan it is well that the American Indian has been taken into consideration. This fact is in keeping with his own estimation.

An Arapahoe Indian man the other day told me that the first man that was ever created was an Arapahoe Indian, and so I said to him, after I had seen the statue of a man the other day called "The Thinker" – and I asked a white man what he was thinking about and I was told that this was the statue representation of the first man that was ever created, and that he was thinking of woes that he has caused to succeeding generations, and so I said to this Indian that it was a sorry fact that he was an Arapahoe – that this man should have been a Winnebago and we should have had a better time in this world of ours had that been so.

Now in view of the fact that the Indian population of this country is comparatively small – 350,000 souls only – we might well ask the question today whether or not it is worth while to consider the red man in this great working plan of the Methodist Episcopal Church.

I bring to your consideration the following facts as an affirmative answer to this question, "Is it worth while?"

In the first place, it is in keeping with the command of our Lord Christ when he said, "Go ye into all the world and preach the glad tidings to every creature." No individual can be fully blessed in this life if he does not make a glad response to the sense of duty in his heart, to the sense of obligation occasioned by an indwelling Christ. No organization or church can be fully blessed if it does not make a glad response to the sense of duty, to the sense of obligation occasioned by virtue of the indwelling Christ.

So it is in keeping with Christ's command that we should take the Indian man into consideration in the great scheme of the evangelization of the world.

In the second place, we must realize that the red man is our neighbor. He is your nearest neighbor. He sits in need at the very door of the church, and if we neglect him how can we fully serve him who sits far away, however great may be his need. In the third place, whatever we do with the red man in North America bears directly on the great problem in South America. Whatever methods employed with respect to him in the North American Continent to bring him to Christianity, to a modern standard of life that has proved successful, must prove successful in attacking the problem to the south of us in the Latin-Americas and in South America, where there are millions of the same people of the same flesh and blood.

If we succeed in developing a native Christian leadership for the North American Indians, and they in turn win their people to acceptance of Christianity, they can themselves become the pioneer workers in South America, so that it seems to me profoundly important that we should first succeed in solving the Indian problem such as it exists in our midst. Then we can the more successfully and more confidently attack as Christian statesmen the problems that confront us to the south of us in this hemisphere.

And in the next place, America owes a political debt to the American Indian – I mean political freedom. The Indian was free-born. He was as free as the eagle that soars the blue. He never knew what captivity was, or oppression of any sort. By centuries of association with this great country he came to have an undying love for this, his native land.

He raced with the winds; he used the stars of the night for his compass; he walked through the trackless primeval forests, and he roamed the plains where there teemed the buffalo, and he knew the whisperings of nature; he delighted to hear the drippings of the waters from his oar as he silently moved down the streams hunting for his subsistence. And it is no wonder that he fought for his home, for his native land.

This Centenary is held over the ground that has been fought over and over by the Ottawa chief Pontiac. He tried to save that territory to the red man from the white, beginning West of the Alleghenies. He was driven further and further back until he made his last stand on this ground on which we are met today. To the south of us Cornstalk, the Shawnee chief, finally yielded that territory which is now known as Kentucky. And Tecumseh, whom his own people called Shooting Star, made his final stand in that country which is now called Indiana. And Black Hawk made his stand in what is now the State of Illinois. It was here that Keokuk, the great Indian orator, said: "When I look upon these hills and these valleys where my fathers are buried, and some of my children, and every place wrapped in sacred memory, I can not give up these places, my home, my country, without a fight. I will gather my men together as the wind drives the autumn leaves before it I will drive these invaders from my home."[12]

Such was the love of the American Indian for this continent where are gathered every race under the sun, when the Great War came on, 10,000 fighting Indians went. Thank God that they were alive, that they could once more express that love for country centuries old. (Applause)[13]

And they came forward, and I am told that eighty-five percent of them were volunteers. (Applause) When I told an old Indian this fact he said, "If the other Indians had known what all this war was about they would have all volunteered and you would have had a hundred percent."

They went over-seas into France, and the returning soldiers have told me over and over again that they acquitted themselves well. The Indian man who made raid after raid into No Man's Land, when he was finally killed, I was told by members of his band – that when he gave up his life for his country and for humanity, the officers over him, from the Captain on up to the General wept sorely because he was taken away, and I said, "Why did these officers weep over a Creek Indian?" And he said, "Because of his great courage – that he was willing to lead his men into death that thousands of others may live." (Applause)

But even in view of this fact, the most confused legal status of any people in this country today is that of the Indian. We do not know today whether the Indian is a citizen of the great United States or not. And, therefore, I say that it is worth while considering the red man in this program, because this, our country, has not yet given him political freedom. It seems to me that these ten thousand men ought to be given full-fledged citizenship immediately, (Applause) with all the privileges, immunities and responsibilities of citizenship, and that is what we are pleading for today before the authorities in Washington – that this red man should be free in his own home land, for he seems to have demonstrated enough love for his country, enough valor for his country, enough strength of mind, of body and of moral integrity to take care of the sacred responsibilities of citizenship.[14]

Today it seems fitting that I should call you back to the spirit of the fathers. It was not so long ago that pioneer missionaries walked through these trackless forests searching out these roving bands of Indians, and bringing them the glad tidings of the Gospel. Some of them froze to death, some of them died at the stake with a smile upon their lips for the love of Him who died commanding them to go forth and serve him. Others for lack of water took the raindrops from the ears of corn and baptized Huron prisoners.

It was John Wesley who first came to this land out of the motive of bringing Christ to the American Indian. I call you to the spirit of such men as Elliott (sic), of the Mahoo Brothers of Martha's Vineyard, of Brainard (sic) and other such noble, staunch men of vision, of prophetic vision, who laid the pathway for the establishment of a great nation, the first democracy of the earth, and it seems to me that with such spirit dominating us in these later days we can solve not only the North American Indian problem, but we can solve the problem that faces us in such gigantic proportions to the south of us.

In looking to the solution of the world problems, we know that the relationship between peoples and peoples, between nations and nations, must be brought about into a state of more accord and friendship. We realize that it is important to have the best commercial relationships, and we have more sympathy with governments over-seas that are like the form of government which we enjoy. But the fundamental thing in this great question of race accord is that of friendship between peoples, where one people's spirit understands the spirit of another people, and we are convinced today that the open door in China and the happy relationships we bear to some people over-seas are largely due, if not solely due, to the activity of missionaries in the years gone by.

They have gone forth and established friendship with those people such as is permanent and abiding. No such thing can be brought about except through the spirit of the living Christ in our day and generation.

May I be permitted to tell you my personal experience with this thing? I knew nothing about Christianity. I had never heard of Christ until one day a lone missionary came to me way after midnight, and presented to me the call of Christ in terms of his friendship, as a young man to me as a young man, on the reservation to the west of us. Every Sabbath Day we were accustomed as Indians to gather on the highest point to have horse races, gambling, riotous living of every sort. I had in my possession a black pony that won all the quarter mile races for which I got horse prizes, money prizes, and beads and so forth, and after great dancing takes place, the beating of the tom-tom ceases and an Indian usually steps forth and says in the presences of the Gods, "I choose so and so to be my friend today, and in token of this friendship I give him this stick."

This stick represents the best horse that he has, and that chosen one comes out and he says in the presence of the Gods, "I accept this stick for what it stands." It means that these two Indians become friends for life, and they are to defend each other so long as life shall last here on earth, and when they pass into the Great Beyond, into the Land of the Setting Sun, they are to defend each other so long as life shall last there. If you hurt one of them you hurt the other just as much, and he will come to his defense and give his life for his friend.

I had a friend of that character. We stayed together in the night. We stayed together in the day. His mother called him "My Son," because he was my friend in the Indian sense.

And so when this missionary said, "I bring you the friendship of Christ to you, as a young man," I said, "If he has offered his friendship to me first I will accept it this night." And I called to witness the stars that I vow my friendship to him. I understood that I was to defend him so long as I shall live here on this earth and when I passed into the Great Beyond, into the Land of the Setting Sun, that I was to defend him as long as life shall last there, and equally so I expect him to defend me so long as life shall last here, and also in the life beyond. (Applause)

And so I have stood for him on the reservation, the first Christian Indian on the Winnebago Indian Reservation. I won another Indian young man to the same vow of friendship and one day on a dusty road we made our marks side by side that we would be true to our friendship, that we would bring back this message to our people some day. He went to Carlisle, played in their great football games. He was one of these men that when the students returned to the campus with victory in their hands and were shouting for joy each man knew in his heart that it was due to the great work of that young man that victory was possible for his university. So was he. He went back until he gave his life for the cause of his friend on the Winnebago Reservation, notwithstanding the fact that all the priests, medicine men, and every one in the tribe opposed him. He has now passed into the Great Beyond to enjoy that greater friendship begun here on earth. And oftentimes when I feel weary or the burden gets heavy, and I feel that this Indian problem is not solved the way it should be, I think of that silent mark in the earth that has been proved true and square, and I take new courage and take refuge in the fact that there are thousands of other friends of the same Christ whom I can call upon for the solution of this great problem. So I bring you this message of victory in friendship, this vow of loyalty to him and to him alone who has victory in his hand for all these problems that confront us.

If you neglect the American Indian, you will not solve your other problems. If you take the Indian under special consideration, and solve this problem at your door God will come in his richest blessing, and bless all your other activities that reach to the end of the earth. (Applause) And that is the ringing call of the red man to you today, the great Methodist Episcopal Church of America. (Prolonged Applause)

JOHN M. MOORE:

Our next speaker and our next subject will interest every one that is here. He is to speak upon the great subject of "The City in the Work of Americanization" and the speaker is none other than our brother and friend, Bishop Francis J. McConnell, whom I am sure you will hear with pleasure.

FRANCIS J. MCCONNELL:[15]

I think I may be pardoned, first of all, for expressing my very great appreciation of the speech which has just been delivered. I happen to have charge in an official way of the work of the Methodist Episcopal Church in Mexico, and I wish just in a sentence, if I can, to endorse what the speaker has said about the need of our dealing fairly by the Indian in this country as a preparation for dealing fairly with the Indian all the way from the Rio Grande River down to Cape Horn.

Now, passing to my own theme, let me say this, that the Methodist Church always has been known as the church of the frontier. In the early days, as soon as the pioneers began to cross over the Alleghenies and to descend into the great plains of this Central West, the Methodist minister, the circuit rider, went with him, keeping pace with that western movement.

And the Methodist preacher riding as he did out into the West made it possible for the movement westward to be thoroughly Christian, at least in its spirit. If it had not been for that movement of the western circuit rider, keeping pace with the movement of immigration over the crests of the Allegheny Mountains, we do not know what type of civilization we might have had.

There was a time in this country when all the West was looked upon with very grave distrust by the people of the East. Back in the old days, the foundations of our American liberty were laid by the men that dwelt on the eastern seaboard. And the men on the eastern seaboard, the citizens of Boston and of New York and of Philadelphia were very, very jealous of the signs of rising democracy out beyond the crests of the Allegheny Mountains, and when that new type of pioneer, individualistic democracy began to appear, it caused very great disturbance, and certainly very great misgivings on the part of the people in the East. As a matter of fact, some of the people in the East never have gotten over it to this day. But back in the old days it was even more serious. They said, "That wild, rough Western democracy – what will that do to our institutions?" And finally when that wild, western democracy came into the White House in the person of Andrew Jackson there were some persons in the East that experienced great sinking of heart and great foreboding for the safety of the Republic.

Now as a matter of fact, that pioneer contribution to democracy was a very remarkable contribution. It was the old individual type of every man for himself, and too often, of course, "The devil take the hindmost." That was the spirit of the old days, but it was softened, and it was in a measure made American and made Christian by the very fact that the circuit rider went out with the western pioneer, went wherever he did, and tried to hold the pioneer fast to Christ.

That was the significance of the work of men like Peter Cartwright[16] who would have to descend from his pulpit occasionally and walk down into the midst of the audience and by sheer physical violence – well not show some people where to get off, but at least where to sit down. He did that. That was the kind of preaching required in those days. It was a new problem. It was a new experiment.

One of the greatest contributions made by America to the solution of the problems of the world has been just that working out of an individualistic type of democracy to which the Methodist preacher made his contribution.

And then in the after years perhaps the best representative of it was, of course, Abraham Lincoln, and he had been exposed to the religious influences upon the frontier from the beginning. Now that has all passed away.

We have left unsettled and unsolved, of course, this Indian problem. We ought to settle it, and for myself I would give this speaker everything he asks for. (Applause) We have not as yet settled that problem but the old frontier is gone.

For the last thirty years there has not been a frontier in the old sense. I mean by that the sense of a man going out and just taking land as he did in the beginning. That has been made impossible, and ever since 1890. And with the cessation of that rapid movement over the mountains, across the prairies and over the slopes of the mountains toward the Pacific, a new type of problem has come upon us.[17]

The current running so swiftly has come to a stop. It has begun to back up, and now where the frontiers of Methodism in the sense of the place where the great unsolved problems are, are in the city.

That is where we have to work out the new problems. That is the brand new situation. There has been nothing like it since the beginning, and the call is for a type of preaching and for a type of religious work, and for a type of ecclesiastical statesmanship in these days that shall deal adequately with the problem of the city, with the problem of getting hold of these currents and Americanizing them.

Let me give you just a single illustration. We have seated ourselves back in our easy chairs, and we have deplored the coming of a certain type of life and the coming of certain types of thought to our country. We have said, "Oh, these are anarchistic, they are socialistic, they are Bolshevists," and we have rallied out against them and done nothing to search for any solution to these problems. That is not the way to get at the matter.

That is not the way the old-time circuit rider tackled his problem. He tried to find out what the people wanted and how to minister to their deepest needs. That is what we have to do today.

Why you consider socialism. Now I sympathize with the great many things in socialism. Sometimes when I hear the Christian Socialist talk I feel a good deal like a Socialist myself, though I am not, but there are a great many things in their doctrine that I sympathize with, and I certainly sympathize with their spirit of emphasis upon the human values in trying to give the every-day workers a better chance.[18]

But this is the trouble with socialism. It has not yet been given any kind of American statement. That is the trouble. And it has not been fitted into American conditions in any way whatsoever. In England they have done better. They have taken all that was good in socialism and they have worked it out in a certain great movement that has been expressed for example in the movement of the British Labor (sic) Party and in shaping that British Labor Party's deliberations, the Methodist preachers have had a good deal to do, but it has not been so here.

Here political socialism has been a straight out-and-out Prussian movement. That is what it has been. It has been the goose-stepping of the mind. They all had to march alike. It has been stamping free discussion. It has been hindering any kind of adequate discussion of the problem.

Now, there is great good in the movement and the only way we can get hold of it and do anything with it is to go down into the cities and meet it. Meet the men on the street corners. Meet the men in their halls. Try to find out what they want. Try to reason with them as brothers and bring them to a better understanding.

If we don't do that, there is going to be great trouble ahead for us. I went into a meeting under the auspices of the Board of Home Missions – I'll not tell where it was because the men might not like me to say what I am going to say. I was asked this, "Will you go down this afternoon and preach to a meeting of radical, social groups?" "Why," I said, "I will preach to anybody that will sit and listen to me."

And I didn't know what the meeting was to be and when we got there, and to my vast astonishment and a good deal of horror, they began to sing Bolshevist songs, and I heard things there that opened my eyes, and I said to myself, "We'll be lucky if we get through the afternoon here without the police getting us all." I said, "I think maybe I had better say my say and then get out. I had better preach just a straight gospel sermon and then go." They said, "You can't do that. The way we do is this: You preach for thirty minutes and then they ask you questions for thirty minutes, and then they talk and give their views for thirty minutes, and then you get the last thirty minutes to come back at them."

I said, "Two hours of it?" They said, "Certainly – from five to seven o'clock." I got up and I did the very best I could, preaching on Jesus and His relation just to human life as a human life. Then they got up. The first thing they had to get out of their systems was this: How little use they had for bishops – that was the first thing. They said that they were about the poorest kind of men there are. They said, "We had them in England and they always vote on the wrong side, and they are always mixed up with the breweries." Then a man got up and said he came from Russia, and he said the bishops there were a curse in Russia. Well, I didn't get mad about it because I felt a good deal that way myself at times, as far as that is concerned. (Applause) I didn't find anything very heretical about it. I used to say that before I got to be a bishop myself. After I got in I modified it, of course.

Then they told me what they thought of the church, and after a while they gave me a chance to come back at them. Now, the men that were violent in the beginning – the men saying radical and extreme things did what? Every last one of those men came up to me at the close of that service – all those at the beginning who just seemed to me to be waving the red flag and singing the songs of Bolshevism – and said they never had understood the point of view of the church, and they said, "We think maybe you have softened down a good deal, but we wish you, personally, Godspeed," and they went out. (Applause)

Now, I want to tell you this, friends, wherever you are in a city and can do this work at all, you throw open your pulpit or your church on Sunday afternoon, and let them come in to a forum discussion. Let them sing anything they please and don't get shocked about it, and then talk back to them, and after a while you will get a chance for an understanding. Better do that than do nothing. When they are in there they are not talking on the street corner, and talking without any kind of counter-action or correction. That is one way to do. Take this whole problem of the relation of the church to organized labor. Organized labor stands askance and doesn't understand us. There ought to be a plan of the meeting, and there ought to be a place of understanding. We have to grapple these questions seriously if we are going to do anything, and solving some things that may be a menace to us otherwise.

Well, now, you say, "What suggestions have you got?" In the first place, I have got this suggestion, as a matter of policy and dealing with [this] city situation. Friends, we are out here as a Methodist organization, and we are giving ourselves to a great Centenary, and I am not talking about the problem of union in general, but I say this; that when you get down into a city and see the absolute need of bringing to bear every ounce of strength you have got upon the problem, don't let any denomination or pride stand in the way of your coming to some kind of working agreement with the other evangelical church that will enable you to work without friction and without waste of effort. (Applause)

The idea of trying to keep open on one corner and then on the opposite corner two churches, saying precisely the same thing, duplicate ministries, duplicate musical organization, duplicate workers, working in exactly the same area and working on a competitive basis, brethren, Methodism or no Methodism, that kind of thing ought not to be. (Applause)

Now, there is something else. In dealing with this whole problem we must remember that we have got to try to reach all the people, and from the standpoint of Methodism it is an abominable heresy to teach if there is anybody that you can't reach. The old pioneer doctrine of the frontier days used to be this – this was the instruction given in the old days – if you go into a community you look upon everybody in that community as possible who is not tied up actually to something else. And that is just about as good a working doctrine as anything I know – to go into the community and claim everything there for the Lord, Jesus Christ, and for the organization you represent, for the sake of tying that man up to some kind of work in the kingdom of God – and go after the last man.

Now, of course that takes money; that takes a great deal more workers than we have, but that is the way this Centenary movement is run – to get the money and to get the workers to go after this whole city problem as if we had some trace of seriousness about it.

How are you going to solve the city problem by the ministers coming along about ten-thirty Sunday morning and being eloquent, and then going away and coming back at seven-thirty in the evening and being eloquent to six or eight or ten people, then coming Wednesday night and trying to be eloquent to a handful of persons that worship anyhow? That is not the way to deal with the problem. It has to have some more serious effort than that. The attempt must be to reach all the people – reach them everywhere.

And now, the next thing we need in dealing with this problem is simply a reliance upon all the methods we can get; new methods, old methods, any kind of methods that promise anything in the way of a substantial result for the kingdom of God. Go out after men in every way, with any kind of an inducement to bring them to the kingdom of God, or within hearing of the gospel.

Now, brethren, I am afraid some of you will have to get over a good deal of conservatism, but remember this; that John Wesley, the founder of our part of the organized church, said he didn't intend to let the devil monopolize the best tunes; he intending to go and get some of the good tunes for his young people. And I say don't let the devil have all the attractiveness there is in the world for young people. Get just as good a kind of music as you can. Get hold of the picture show and cleanse it of some of its evil associations and make it a mighty instrument of good. We will have to do that! It is here to stay. (Applause) Get hold of any sort of a thing that really makes any human appeal.

Now, it may be heresy from the standpoint of a good many Methodist people, but I want to tell you right now, if you want to get in heresy, remember this; that the clause about the moving picture show had no application in 1607. It wasn't in existence then. (Applause) Now, I go to the picture show, and I'll tell you why I go there. I go to find what sort of thing gets hold of the people – that is why I go. And if you see me at a picture remember this, I am not sneaking in at the back door. I am going right down the front walk; right down there, not because I am particularly crazy about the picture show, because a good deal of it nearly bores the life out of me, but I go in there to find out what it is that gets hold of the people; and I am not making any plea for the picture show, you understand, because I think some of it is absolutely abominable, and I know because I have seen it. I understand that, but nevertheless there is a chance for a popular appeal there that you can get almost nowhere else.[19]

And that kind of thing, in the cities especially, ought to be seized and held fast for the kingdom of God. If we are going to take hold of this thing seriously, and I rejoice, incidentally, in this situation here in the use of the picture show out yonder, in the use of the pageant here as an appeal to the eye. I heard last night some great educational and spiritual lessons taught by the modern method of doing it, and that same method can be of use further.

I remember when I was a pastor years ago in a city church – this may seem ridiculous – but we were to have a watch service on Sunday night, and I was desperately afraid the people wouldn't keep awake till the last of it, and my wife said to me, "Well, maybe we had better serve coffee about eleven o'clock at night." "Oh!" I said, "there is a bishop in that particular congregation. I don't know how that bishop will like it." But I said, "The best way is not to go and consult him, but just go and do it, and after it is an accomplished fact he can adjust himself to it the best way he can." And we did it. The bishop looked a bit surprised, but he came around after a while and said, "It really was very good coffee," and on the whole he approved of it. (Applause)

Well, now, let me tell you one thing about bishops. In working out a city problem don't consult them too much, (Applause) because that embarrasses them before the fact. You know after it is all done, and they are not responsible they are apt to see the good side of it. I think the wisest type of administration for superintendents and for bishops in cities is just this – to get around you the most alert men you can – young men I mean. And I mean by that young men in spirit, not necessarily in years; men willing to try out anything; not that the superintendent, not that the bishop has to do it all himself, but get hold of the men that have the progressive spirit. Let them try out all sorts of things, never check anything that promises good at all. That is the only way we will get anywhere.

That is exactly what the United States Government said to the chemical investigators and to the investigators in physics. "We haven't any desire," they said, "to tell you what to do. But you go out and do the best you can. Try any kind of experiment. Go almost to any kind of expense to find out the way to get this thing done." And what happened? There came long strides ahead in chemistry, as applied to warfare, in chemistry as applied to artcraft; and that is exactly the same way we have to do in dealing with the problems of God in the city today.

I haven't any patent scheme for solving these problems except just fair play, and the desire to understand the people that don't agree with me, and then a desire also to get hold of any man that promises anything in the way of working out the problem, and giving him a free hand to say, "Godspeed." That is one way to say it. The other way is to say, "Go to it and just do the best you can."

Now, there is one thing more, and it is this: We have to have our churches that work all the time – twenty-four hours in the day the church in the city should be ministering in some fashion – I don't say what kind of fashion – seven days in the week the church should be ministering – three hundred and sixty-five days in the year, except in leap year, and then three hundred and sixty-six days, the church should be working in its particular community.

Brethren, it is a perfect scandal for you to accept the tax free situation that obtains in societies, and then have a service on Sunday and close up the doors and not open up until maybe Wednesday, or once or twice a week. Some organizations somewhere should get back to a plan of that kind and run that thing literally all the time.

Now, I believe in the supremacy of virtue to vice, but I do not believe in the ways it sometimes acts. I believe that a vice that works all the time, day in and day out, night in and night out, has the advantage of a virtue that only works spasmodically. You simply have to keep the forces of righteousness applied, and applied constantly.

Now, I was told that this was to be both a city day, and Americanization day, and I was not told but I desired for myself to bring out this idea that into this great open air of the cities, into this great vat – you might say – of the city, into this great melting pot of the city, God has providentially arranged that men shall be thrown not merely for the sake of Christianity as such, but for the sake of that American type of Christianity that we believe in; that American type of service, that American type of helping up the man that is down, that American type of laying stress upon the things that are really fundamental in human nature and bringing them to their best development.

The church is not to think of itself. The church is to think, "Can we in this particular type of environment set the stamp of God upon these lives before us?" I think we can! The city itself is doing some things, and doing them splendidly – has done them. You take this whole Americanization situation. There were two men that I know of that were signally (sic) honored in the last war as private soldiers. One was this man York down in Tennessee. I think it was Foch himself who said of him that he was the greatest single soldier of the war – I mean as a man fighting in the line.

Now, there was another man, a youth of nineteen years. This man also held up a German attack, a party. This man also brought back himself into the American lines a great number of German prisoners. This man also got a document from the chief of staff, and I have read it. It recites what he has done. This man also got a valor medal, which he bears upon his breast. This man was nineteen years of age, and his name isn't a good English name like York – his name is Thomas C. Newbower (sic).

And it means simply this; that the cities of America, no matter what the old folks have thought, have taken the persons we have been suspicious of; have taken our brothers of German and American descent, and they have put the stamp of Americanism upon them so thoroughly that when they were fighting against those of German descent on the other side of the sea they were just as good soldiers as could be found in America. (Applause)

Now, I haven't any patience with these beer brewing Germans that came over here for what they could get out of it. I am not talking about them, but there is another type that came – a type of honest, God-fearing men came, and no matter what the old man thought, or no matter what the mother may have thought, the son came up to be an American citizen.

Theodore Roosevelt said this, "There is no greater outrage done than to fail to recognize the fact that the American cities and the American communities had put the stamp of Americanism upon these men, and they were just as good Americans as you can find anywhere." They fought just as well. I mention them as the most extreme case, but just think, on the other hand, of the Italians, and think of those that had come from Hungary, and think of the Greeks, and think of all the others that had been here long enough to get into our army, and how splendidly they fought!

I was greatly touched – I suppose you were – by seeing an account in a newspaper one time during the war. The scene was down in the east side of New York City. The poor mother was sitting out on the door step. A hot day as hot as this gets awfully hot down on the east side of New York. She was mopping her brow. She had two or three babies around her. They were crawling over her knees, and crawling around in the streets, and it was a discouraging situation. And Tony was off to war. Tony was the boy of nineteen years old, and there she sat at evening time in the midst of the heat. Down comes the younger boy, eight or nine years old, with a newspaper. "Mother," he says, "mother, look at this!" "What?" she says. He said, "Tony! Tony! Tony – he's got the war cross. Tony has got the war cross!" Now, where did Tony come from? Tony came out of the east side of New York, and he fought for the stars and stripes. He fought for the flag that is looked upon as peculiarly as yours and mine, and American patriotism has worked around him and has made him a thoroughgoing defender of the American system. And I say this – what patriotism can do, Christianity can do. What the spirit of devotion to country can do, the spirit of devotion to a Christ can do, if the spirit of Christ can come into our churches, and by working persistently and using all the methods God has sent upon us, we can really get hold of these cities and make them mighty agencies for redemption.

And, friends, remember this – that the real significant prophecy of the New Testament vindicates that after all the final blessings that come upon men are coming to men in great groups – a multitude. The blessings of the Holy Spirit coming at Pentecost came upon a city, upon those dwelling in the upper room, and spreading out to the thousands, and to the number of three thousand in the streets in the city of God.

I suppose we all like the country, but after all, we like to get back to the city. You remember what Mr. Dooley said. Mr. Hennessy once said to Mr. Dooley: "Mr. Dooley, I am going out into the country where all the good things come from." "Are you?" said Dooley. "Well, I am going to stay in the city where all the good things come to." (Applause)

After all, it all comes back to the city. I like to sing that song – "Sweet Fields Beyond the Swelling Flood Stand Dressed in Living Green" – but friends, I don't want to stay out in the sweet fields dressed in living green through all eternity.[20] Once in a while I want to get to town. Once in a while I like to get down to the city; and when I get down into the city nothing can fill my thought of what a city should be rather than those splendid pictures, and the Book of Revelation.

The great city, the pride of Christ let down from God out of Heaven – the gates stand open day and night. No need of an artificial guard of any kind. The lamp of the city, life, and life, and life, everywhere, so that the central part of the city becomes the tree of life whose leaves are for the healing of the nations – a wonderful picture intended to be realized. And this Centenary Movement, if I understand it, has thousands of aims just to take that idea of the city and fulfill the Spirit of God.

Abraham of old went out into the wilderness seeking a city, not because there weren't cities in the land from which he came – there were – but he desired a better city; one that had foundations, whose builder and maker was God. He never saw it. He never found it. He died at the end, disappointed in the promise, and that dream never has adequately been realized, but it is for you and for me to help to realize the dream of Abraham, and the dream of Christ when he looked out over the city and said: "How often would I have gathered thy children together even as a hen gathers the chickens under her wings, but ye would not." His idea, His passion was always for the great city, which was to be the community of God.

It is going to be a great achievement. It is going to be a great redemption. God can redeem the city, and he calls upon you and me to help. (Applause)

...ADJOURNMENT...

Victory Day Program
Friday Afternoon, July 4, 1919

Meeting convened at Grandstand at 1:30p.m. General Carr presiding as Chairman...
...Singing of 'America'...

GENERAL CARR:[21]
Fellow citizens, Ladies and Gentlemen: Before I have the distinguished pleasure of presenting the speaker of this afternoon, I have been requested to read this telegram, "Centenary Exposition, Columbus, Ohio: American Independence has bred such blessings in a century and a half that we may be proud, indeed, to reflect upon its strivings towards progress. Our efforts for the future, it seems to me, must lie in preserving unimpaired our idealism despite our material enrichment and in preserving the fruits of victory lately won by our heroic forces. Signed, Newton D. Baker, Secretary of War."[22] (Applause)

Ladies and Gentlemen: Men and time make events and the greater the men and the greater the time, the greater the event. This has been an epochal making week in this splendid city of Columbus, but this national Independence Day of all red blooded Americans is our red letter day for the reason that we have with us the gentleman who through all the dark days in our nation's life in the great World War guided successfully all of our financial activities and was such a success that when the cry was raised by an anxious public, "Watchmen, watchmen, tell us of the night," the old stars man looked and saw that the guiding hand of Honorable William G. McAdoo was directing the greatest financial institution in this world, and he shouted back, "All is well." Ladies and Gentlemen, it is my delightful pleasure and distinction to present to you Mr. McAdoo.

WILLIAM G. MCADOO:[23] (Greeted with Prolonged Applause)
Mr. Chairman, Ladies and Gentlemen, Fellow countrymen: I wish to express my cordial appreciation of the generous terms in which your presiding officer has introduced me, and I wish also that it was within my power to reach all who are in this great assemblage today and I am quite sure that you will be patient with me if any physical defects of voice are such that I cannot show my proper appreciation of this vast audience by making every man and woman in it hear what I have to say, but after speaking in four national Liberty Loan campaigns and then doing a good deal of talking besides that, I haven't, perhaps, got as much voice left as I would like to have and so I am going to beg you to be as quiet and as patient as possible while I endeavor to reach you with the discussion of one of the most transcendent questions that ever has faced America and the world.[24]

Before I begin the main subject of the day I want to congratulate the American people on their great achievement in their great World War and upon the fact that on this Fourth day of July, 1919, the one hundred and forty-third anniversary –

...at this point Dr. Reisner attempted to bring the audience to better order, and to check movement in the aisles...

This is a Fourth of July crowd and in spite of my friend, Doctor Reisner, I think they are entitled to have all the liberty they want. (Applause) I want to tell you it is the kind of liberty that our boys won for us again in Europe in 1918. (Applause) It is the kind of liberty that we don't intend to let any "red devils" destroy. (Applause) If any of them want to make a demonstration, and I heard something said about their making a demonstration today, I don't suggest that they try it, but if they do try it, my friends, and we have no other safeguard for the republic than the returned soldiers from this great World War, that would be sufficient to take care of America. (Applause) This is a great republic of law and order and any man, or set of men, who think they can successfully substitute the bomb for the ballot in free America have come to the most unhealthy soil they ever set foot upon. (Applause)

Now, ladies and gentlemen, the subject upon which I am to speak is one of such transcendent importance, as I said before, that I have not been willing to trust myself to an extemporaneous speech. I don't like to read a speech, but on this occasion I have felt that I ought to be as exact as I could in submitting the argument to you for your support of this great League of Nations, and I am going to beg you therefore to forgive me for reading a speech on this occasion, a thing I rarely ever do, and whenever I do it, I feel that I ought to apologize for it.

Now, it looks a great deal more formidable than it is. I want to give you that much encouragement in advance, and again must apologize for having to resort to artificiality because I got kind of old in the public service in the six years in which I served. (Applause) I have been assured that while I was in public office I had a good many things to do. I didn't think so myself, because it didn't seem to me that I could do enough in this great war while I was in private life and in safety when millions of our valiant sons were going out to give their very lives upon the battlefield, and so I don't think that anybody who stayed at home, no matter how hard they worked or how much they did, deserves any sympathy or any special praise. (Applause)

This Centenary Celebration of the Methodist Episcopal Church, North and South, marks the beginning of a more intimate and effective cooperation between these two grand divisions of the great Methodist organization. It is an event of commanding importance. The Christian Church represents the greatest spiritual and moral influence in the world, and there never was a time when those forces were so imperatively needed as now. Cooperation between all denominations of the Christian Church is essential for the world's salvation. It will require the mobilized effort of the Church militant to secure the fruits of the great victory for liberty, democracy and world peace which has been won through the blood and valor of America's sons and the blood and valor of the sons of our Allies who fought with us in the titanic struggle just ended.

The Methodist Church has always been a militant influence for good. (Applause) It has stood unswervingly for humanity, for progress and for world peace. Although war is abhorrent to every Christian instinct and principle, the Church has stood for war but only when it was convinced that the Christian objective – world peace – could be obtained by no other means.

We are now facing the most critical situation in which the world has ever found itself, the disposition of our victory. Shall we dispose of it so that human slaughter through war must still be the arbiter of the destiny of nations or shall we so dispose of it that the glorious goal for which humanity has striven through thousands of years of unspeakable misery, torture and sacrifice shall now be realized – namely, the settlement of international disputes by judicial processes and the establishment of world peace through the cooperative effort of the great nations of the earth?

A League of Nations to prevent war would consolidate and organize our victory and make practically certain the peace of the world in the future. A blessing so colossal seems unattainable, and yet it is within our grasp if we have the vision, the courage and the determination to take it. Here is where the Church faces its greatest opportunity and its gravest responsibility.

We must not permit any man or set of men to destroy the League of Nations. (Applause) We must not permit any man or set of men to emasculate it. (Applause) We must not permit any man or set of men to put the peace of the world again in peril. (Applause) The issue is so momentous that the very future of civilization is at stake and humanity from every stricken quarter of the suffering world cries out in agony to Christianity to save it. We are face to face with prodigious events when blind men must not be permitted to lead. (Applause) It is a tragic fact in history that every great step in human progress has been won against the resistance of blind, fatuous and uncomprehending men whose advice and leadership, if followed, would have kept us in the dark ages.

> All the passion and sweet trouble of the Spring is in the air,
> And the remembrance comes that not alone for stem and blade,
> For flower and leaf, but for man also, there are times of mighty
> Vernal movement, seasons when life casts away the body of this death,
> And a great surge of youth breaks on the world. Then are the primal
> Fountains clamorously unsealed; and then, perchance, are dread things
> Born not unforetold by deep parturient pangs. But the light minds that
> Heed no auguries, untaught by all that heretofore hath been, taking
> Their ease on the blind verge of faith, see nothing, and hear nothing,
> Till the hour of some vast advent that makes all things new.[25]

We are celebrating today the 143d anniversary of the Declaration of Independence. The American Colonies planted the seed of freedom and equality in the soil of the Western Hemisphere and then again that irrepressible struggle between democracy and autocracy which culminated in democracy's triumph on the battlefields of France in November, 1918. The signing of the Treaty of Peace with Germany coming so near the day we celebrate gives the added significance and joyousness. Little did the men of 1776 realize that they had launched war against autocracy which required one hundred and forty-two years of struggle to win, and yet they did have the vision to see that the salvation of humanity depended upon freedom and equality of the individual, self-government through democratic institutions and denial of the divine right of kings. As the thirteen feeble American Colonies took the step in 1776 which secured their liberty and independence after six years of desperate war and subsequently consolidated their victory through a Federal Union which brought into existence the greatest Republic of all time, so now that Republic, by combining its strength with the great free democracies of Europe has destroyed the greatest autocratic government on earth and has given the people of Europe the opportunity of establishing self-government by so organizing their victory that the peace of the world may be secured. It rests with us and with them to say whether this shall be a victory of peace or a victory of war.

It is illuminating to recall at this time the events that led up to the formation and adoption of our own Federal Constitution and to outline the character of the fight which was made against the organization of this great Republic, because they present in many respects a striking parallel to the character of fight which is not being made against the ratification of the League of Nations.

The Treaty of Paris of 1783 secured the independence of the American Colonies. Up to that time the common danger had given them cohesion in the war, but no sooner had the victory been won, than the jealousies and rivalries of the several states began to assert themselves. Then, as now, a more critical situation was presented than the war itself had engendered. How to make liberty and independence impregnable and to secure future peace was then as now the great problem. Cooperation between the various states not only ceased, but commercial war between them began. Disputes about territory arose and actual hostilities occurred between Connecticut and Pennsylvania. War was narrowly averted. New York and New Hampshire had a similar territorial dispute which almost eventuated into war. Financial distress prevailed and pervaded every state. There was no reliable medium of exchange, and trade and commerce were hampered everywhere. In Massachusetts and Rhode Island actual rebellion broke out and civil war was threatened. Each state was striving for its own advantage, and selfish interests and bitter antagonism were rapidly producing a condition of anarchy which threatened to destroy all that had been gained by six years of war. The question arose as to whether we would have one nation or thirteen nations on this continent.

In this crisis, the great patriots like Washington, Hamilton, Madison, and Franklin succeeded in bringing about a convention in Philadelphia to consider the formation of a Federal Constitution. The convention met in 1787, in historic Independence Hall, and after four months of earnest and oftentimes acrimonious debate, produced the present Constitution of the United States which was not to become effective unless ratified by nine states. A bitter contest over ratification then ensued. The opponents of the Constitution passionately denounced the present charter of our liberty under which the greatest Republic of all ages has grown up, as a "triple-headed monster" because it had three departments, executive, judicial, and legislative. It was a "triple-headed monster" and they declared it to be "as deep and wicked a conspiracy as ever was invented in the darkest ages against the liberties of a free people." That is the way the opponents of the Constitution under which we have lived for more than one hundred years talked about it at that time. Now, this is strikingly like the kind of denunciation of the League of Nations in which men who, I think, must be the lineal descendents of the short-sighted men who fought the Constitution of the United States, have been engaging. So violent was the fight against the Constitution that it was publicly burned in Albany, New York, and in Carlisle, Pennsylvania. Now, you wouldn't think that was a fact but it is history. Not content with this they burned some of its leading advocates in effigy in public squares. In some states riots occurred with loss of life. The opponents of the Constitution, in their blindness and passion, denounced the venerable Benjamin Franklin as a "dotard" and George Washington as a fool. How similar to the present intemperate assault upon the second great charter of human liberty, the League of Nations, which has been made possible by the wisdom and far-seeing statesmanship of men like those who formulated our own Federal Constitution and gave life and being to this great Republic! (Applause)

With the greatest difficulty the requisite number of states were induced to ratify the Constitution. To show how close the contest was, in Massachusetts the vote was 187 in favor and 168 against, a majority of only 19; in Virginia it was 89 in favor and 79 against, a majority of only 10; in New Hampshire it was 57 in favor and 46 against, a majority of only 11; and in New York it was 30 in favor and 27 against, a majority of only 3. The contest in New York determined the fate of the thirteen colonies, and yet for a long time it was not believed that her approval of the Union could be secured. Governor George Clinton, an irreconcilable opponent, went into the convention at Poughkeepsie with two-thirds of the delegates standing solidly behind him against ratification. But Alexander Hamilton, with only one-third of the delegates behind him conducted for forty days a running debate where the brilliancy of his defense of the Constitution and the sheer force of his intellectual power overcame the opposition, and New York was won over to the cause of liberty and national unity. (Applause) This assured the organization of the United States of America, but it was by a narrow – frightfully narrow – margin. We came that close to having no Federal Union at all. Now, suppose that the unprogressive and uncomprehending opponents of the Federal Union had been successful – my friends, what would have been the fate of America? One cannot picture it, but God ruled, and the Federal Union was won. (Applause)

It brought peace to the distracted thirteen states. It removed all causes of dispute. It brought free intercourse between them and established a cooperation which made them potential, not only for their own protection against external aggression, but enabled them to conquer a vast continent and give it the blessings of liberty under law and self-government from one end of its broad domain to the other.

In 1788 the Constitution of the United States became operative, and George Washington was made the first President in April, 1789. At that time autocratic government was in the saddle throughout the world. The Federal Constitution was the "most gigantic step in constructive statesmanship" that had ever been taken in all history. It marked the beginning not only of a new era, but of a new deal that was to possess the world. Oppressed men of all nations turned eager eyes to the feeble light of liberty which had been lit in the new world, and which gradually grew into the consuming flame which has just gained the final triumph over autocracy.

As the Constitution was the greatest progressive step in liberty and peace for the American colonies, so the League of Nations is now the great progressive step for the maintenance of liberty and democracy, and the preservation of peace between the nations of the world. (Applause) Like the Constitution, it is the "most gigantic step in constructive statesmanship" since the formation of the Federal Union, and yet it is resisted by the same type of uncomprehending men who fought the adoption of the Federal Constitution. They have the same obliquity of vision, the same selfishness of view, the same indifference to humanity, and the same lack of interest in the masses of mankind.

They are opposed to any effective organization to prevent war. They prefer to preserve our imaginary isolation. They regard war as an ineradicable feature of civilized society and they look upon its recurrence with the same indifference that characterized the opponents of the Constitution of the United States. They denounce the League of Nations just as the opponents of the Federal Constitution denounced it, as the most dastardly attempt ever made against the liberties of free people.

The great men who are responsible for the Federal Constitution have emblazoned their names in imperishable letters upon the scroll of fame. All men know them. Who can obscure the fame of Washington, Franklin, Madison, Hamilton and Jefferson? They had the vision, the foresight, and the patriotism to bring into existence this great republic which has not only prospered the American people and protected their liberty, but has had a profound influence upon the destiny of the world.

What of their opponents? Who knows them or has ever heard of them? They have sunk into the blackness of obscurity and are neither known or heard of unless by some student of history who takes the pains to investigate the past and to search out, as a warning to himself and to others, the narrow views and opinions of those whose chief mark of identification is that they were the implacable foes of the Constitution of the United States. (Applause)

The Treaty of Peace with Germany, my friends, has been signed, (Applause) and world peace is now within our grasp. Of course, the terms of the treaty are not satisfactory with Germany. Of course, they are not entirely satisfactory to each and every one of the nations signatory thereto. Such a treaty, of necessity, is the result of compromises and as near an approach as possible to the principles and ideals of those who formulated it.

Germany may regard the terms as harsh, but of one thing the world is certain: That unless the consequences of a breach of world peace by any nation are made so serious and formidable that they will exhaust every conceivable means for the settlement of disputes before resorting to war, the peace of the world cannot be secured in the future. (Applause)

Incorporated in the treaty are the provisions for the League of Nations. What is this League, and what is it to do? Fundamentally, it is a cooperative agreement between thirty-two nations to prevent war by forcing all nations concerned to submit either to arbitration or to conference and discussion international disputes before resorting to war. The machinery by which this is accomplished I shall outline briefly.

First, there is an Assembly or Congress of the nations provided for, in which each nation has three representatives, and in which each nation has one vote. A permanent secretariate, which is the administrative arm of the League, is established, and all positions under, or in connection with, the League are available to men and women alike. (Applause) In this new time, my friends, we men and women must look to the future with genuine vision. Women shall no longer be handicapped by a want of equal civil rights and political liberty with the men of the great republic. (Applause) And this world-wide conference at the peace table where thirty-two nations were assembled has given that recognition to the women of the world. (Applause)

The fundamental purpose of the League is the prevention of war. If it should accomplish nothing else than this, it would confer upon humanity the most inestimable boon with which it has been blessed since civilization began. Ask any mother who lost a son; ask any wife who lost a husband; ask any parent of any heroic American son whose bones rest today in the soil of sacred France if they aren't willing to prevent by every conceivable and honorable means the recurrence of war; ask any soldier who has been there amid shot and shell and hell fire if he isn't willing to go to the extreme to provide the means of preventing war in the future, and they will all tell you yes. (Applause)

It is chiefly those who know that by advocating or standing for war, or leaving the world so unprepared that future wars may and will inevitably occur; it is those who are not soldiers, who have not experienced the bitterness of war and the suffering of war who feel so indifferent to the fate of the nations at this time; and when I say that, my friends, I don't want to say it uncharitably or dogmatically. This is a great and profound question for humanity and for the world. It isn't primarily a materialistic question. It is a question of humanity, and a question of humanity touches the masses of men and women, not the classes of men and women in this world. They are the ones who suffer most when war occurs, and while, as I say, there are, of course, legitimate differences of opinion about the great policy of this kind, and I am not so intolerant nor illiberal as to say that we shouldn't have differences of opinion, and that we shouldn't discuss them frankly and fairly. I do say, however, that the discussion should be lifted upon a plane of non-partisanship. They should be lifted to a plane where as Americans loving our country, loving liberty and loving humanity above mere sordid things, we should earnestly strive by an interchange of views and intelligent discussion of this great question, without bitterness in our hearts and without passion, to find its right solution. We owe that not only to ourselves, but we owe it more to humanity in the future than to anything else.

Now, how is the prevention of war to be accomplished? First of all, it was necessary, my friends, to destroy autocratic government everywhere before any foundation for a League of Nations could be layed (sic). Every effort of the nations in times past to organize for the prevention of war has failed because autocratic and despotic governments were not only unwilling to enter into effective guarantees for the preservation of peace, but they refused to be bound by their agreements after they had entered into them.

These despots held that it was incompatible with the divinity of their right to surrender any portion of their power and that they could violate such agreements at will. Although civilized society has been organized on the basis of law and order within each nation, there has never been any law between nations which made war itself a crime and fixed personal responsibility upon those guilty of provoking it.

Now, I want you to bear this point particularly in mind, because we are on the eve of doing one of the most extraordinary things ever done in the history of the world. We are going to try a despotic monarch who dared to bring the most calamitous war in all the history of the ages upon the human race. Now, what is its value? Why, so long as they could escape the consequences of their actions these despots and autocrats have throughout history precipitated needless wars upon the theory that the king could do no wrong. Think of that, you Democrats and Republicans in this free republic of ours – the king could do no wrong – and untold millions of human beings have been sacrificed for this fictitious doctrine.

We all know now that kings cannot only do wrong, but that they have frequently committed the most colossal wrongs upon mankind. We also know that if the fiction that "kings can do no wrong" had been destroyed centuries ago, millions of human lives would have been saved and untold human suffering would have been avoided, because so long as kings have thought that they could make war with impunity and that the people alone would suffer, they have not hesitated to do so.

By providing in the treaty with Germany for the trial of the Kaiser and the military leaders who with him precipitated this last great war, we have established the principle of personal guilt of the monarch who misuses his power and brings suffering upon humanity. (Applause) We have served notice for all time upon the responsible rulers of the world that they cannot make unprovoked war without standing trial at the bar of an international court and expiating their crime if found guilty. The establishment of the principle of personal guilt of war lords for war is one of the surest guarantees of the peace of the future.

Now, this trial of the Kaiser is not for vengeance. It is for justice (Applause) No one wants to be vindictive with Germany. All humanity is eager that the wounds of this war shall be healed as quickly as possible; that prosperity shall be restored to suffering people everywhere as soon as possible; that the scourge of war shall be prevented for all time, if possible, so that there may never be a repetition of the colossal misery and crime this war has produced.

But unless justice is sternly applied to the guilty, one of the most effective deterrents of future wars will not have been provided. Thus, my friends, abolition of autocracy, the substitution of self-government and democracy therefore, and the establishment of the principle that rulers guilty of causing war shall be punished therefore, has laid the secure groundwork for a League of Nations to preserve peace.

Now, the League of Nations seeks to prevent the recurrence of war by eliminating as far as possible the causes which lead to war through: first, the limitation of armaments; second, guarantees of territorial integrity and political independence; third, the abolition of secret treaties; fourth, compulsory conferences to discuss questions of common interest that may from time to time arise and thereby to bring about cooperation among the nations concerned.

One of the most serious causes of wars in the past has been the creation of vast armaments and great standing armies which have been a constant temptation to aggression by that nation which was possessed of a preponderant force. So long as the policy of any one power was to build up great military and naval establishments, other powers had to enter into competition as a matter of self-defense. The result was that the leading nations of Europe have been for generations past great armed camps ready to spring at each other's throats and precipitate wars upon slight provocation or for causes which no impartial tribunal would, upon investigation, consider adequate.

Now, first – Limitation of Armaments: One of the most important purposes of the League is therefore the reduction of armaments upon an established scale, which will put all the members of the League upon an equality as near as may be in the matter of organized force. Plans for such reductions are to be prepared by the Council and submitted to the several governments concerned, but no plans are to become binding to any nation until adopted by it. Congress is not deprived of any of its prerogatives in this matter, but, on the contrary, retains the sole power to determine what armed forces, military and naval, shall be maintained by the United States.

This League of Nations merely recommends a uniform basis for a reduction of armament. Somebody has got to do that. We have got to have some sort of combined, coordinated study of the problem with respect to all the nations, so we can say how much each nation relatively ought to have, and that is the chief function of this organization – to make a recommendation to prepare a plan and to make a recommendation to each nation concerned.

Now, no nation is bound to accept it, but if they do accept the recommendations of this Council, then if Congress should adopt it for us, for instance, no increase in such armament may be made by any nation without the consent of the League for a period of ten years, at the end of which time the plan will be subject to reconsideration and revision.

Now, we won't go into that unless all the other fellows come in and reduce armaments upon the plan which may be proposed, or upon a plan which we may agree upon after full discussion of the subject. Now, in order to enforce this provision, the Council is to advise how the evil effects of the private manufacture of arms and ammunition can be prevented, with a view to the adoption by governments of the policy of manufacturing for themselves instead of through private interests such war materials as are required for their safety. All members of the League are to interchange full and frank advices, as to military and naval programs, in order that each member of the League may know what the other is doing in respect to armaments. You have got to have a show-down of everybody right on the table, so we will all know what is being done about the observance of the plan which may be agreed upon.

Now, this is the first step, my friends, toward the prevention of war – the limitations of armaments – so that no nation will have a preponderant armed force and be tempted to use it to attack another in the execution of some selfish aim or purpose. The United States is not disadvantaged, but advantaged, by this provision, because it is in line with our historic policy of limited armament and puts all other nations on an equality of armed strength with us.

Now, second – Guaranties of Territorial Integrity and Political Independence. Throughout all history one of the greatest incentives to war has been the lust of ambitious rulers to extend their power and dominion over other peoples and to absorb the territory of other nations. After every great war the map of Europe has been changed and peoples have been transferred from one sovereignty to another without regard to their feelings or interests.

The result of the present war is not different from that of all other wars, so far as changing the map of Europe is concerned, although the motives for such changes are this time quite different from those which have heretofore controlled. We are now trying to restore to the different peoples of the world the territories which of right belong to them, and to set them up once more as politically independent sovereignties with the added right of self-government. The magnitude of this task is exceeded only by its difficulties. There are so many races in Europe and the intermingling of populations along their borders has been so continuous that there are many areas which cannot with accuracy be ethnologically defined.

There are, so to speak, twilight zones of populations which are neither predominantly one nationality or another, and, therefore, the new nations which are to be established under the peace treaty are in some instances given boundaries which must be tested for a reasonable length of time under conditions of stabilized government before the wisdom of such boundaries can be demonstrated. Moreover, some of these nations will be stronger, of necessity, than others. Their peoples are unaccustomed to self-government and must create a political organization and a status for themselves.

Now, this is notably true of restored Poland and Czecho-Slovakia, which will need for some time guarantees against external aggression, which will enable their people to work out their destiny without fear of aggression from their neighbors and under favoring conditions of peace. No less important are these guarantees against external aggression and of political independence to the larger states of Europe than to the smaller. Once it is firmly and clearly established that no nation may commit aggressions upon its neighbors, all may settle down to peaceful pursuits and build up again the prosperity and happiness of their peoples under stable and well ordered government.

Article Ten of the Covenant, therefore, wisely provides that each member of the League shall respect and preserve as against external aggression the territorial integrity and existing political independence of all members of the League. It must be borne in mind that this covenant does not permit the League of Nations to interfere in any uprisings or disturbances within a state itself. The right of revolution against oppressive internal authority remains unaffected and unimpaired, and every people is left to determine for itself what its form of government shall be, and how its internal or domestic affairs shall be conducted.

Mr. Root, in his admirable essay on the first draft of the League of Nations said in support of Article Ten: "I think, however, that this article must be considered not merely with reference to the future, but with reference to the present situation in Europe. Indeed, this whole agreement ought to be considered in that double aspect. The belligerent powers of Germany, Austria, Bulgaria, and Turkey have been destroyed, but that will not lead to future peace without a reconstruction of Eastern Europe and Western Asia. The vast territories of the Hohenzollerns, the Hapsburgs, and the Romanhoffs have lost the rulers who formerly kept the population in order, and are filled with turbulent masses without stable government, unaccustomed to self-control and fighting among themselves like children of the dragon's teeth.

There can be no settled peace until these masses are reduced to order. Since the Bolsheviki have been allowed to consolidate the control which they established with German aid in Russia, the situation is that Great Britain, France, Italy and Belgium with a population of less than 130,000,000 are confronted with the disorganized but vigorous and warlike population of Germany, German Austria, Hungary, Bulgaria, Turkey and Russia, amounting to approximately 280,000,000, fast returning to barbarism and the lawless violence of barbarous races.

Order must be restored. The allied nations in their Council must determine the lines of reconstruction. Their determinations must be enforced. They may make mistakes. Doubtless they will, but there must be decision, and decision must be enforced. Under these conditions the United States cannot quit. It must go on to the performance of its duty and the immediate aspect of Article Ten is an agreement to do that."[26]

Mr. Root suggested an amendment to this article, providing that after the expiration of five years from the signing of the convention, any nation might terminate its obligation under Article Ten by giving one year's notice in writing to the Secretary General of the League. Since Mr. Root's suggestion, a provision has been incorporated in the revised draft of the covenant which is even more favorable to the termination of the obligation than Mr. Root proposed.

Any member of the League may, under the revised draft, withdraw from the League after two years' notice of its intention to do so, provided that all its international obligations and all its obligations under the League covenant shall have been fulfilled at the time of its withdrawal. The effect of the revised covenant, therefore, is to enable any nation to terminate its obligation to respect and preserve the territorial integrity and political independence of the other members of the League after two years' notice of its intention to do so, instead of being bound for five years, as Mr. Root suggested. Certainly, the United States could not do less than join in this guarantee which eliminates one of the most fruitful causes of war and at the same time gives the new nations to be established under the peace treaty the opportunity to organize and erect stable governments, especially when we can relieve ourselves of this obligation at any time after two years' notice.

It is our duty to help these struggling people back to life and to help all the nations of Europe to establish ordered government without fear of external attack.

The argument that this guarantee will involve us in every European quarrel is far-fetched for the following reasons:

> 1. We cannot be drawn into any war unless our Congress first authorizes it.
> 2. After all European armaments are reduced practically to an internal police force basis, any war or attempted war will be a small affair because of the limited armed forces available. Now, isn't that a good thing to bring about?
> 3. The control by governments of the manufacture of war munitions and destruction of great war plants like the Krupps will prevent would-be belligerents from getting the necessary supplies of arms and ammunition, so that they wouldn't have much to fight with if they want to go to war thereafter. (Applause) And I think it would be a grand thing for the world if we could stop this profiteering in war materials and ammunition. (Applause) I would hate to have a fortune, my friends, the foundation of which was furnishing materials to slaughter human beings. (Applause) And we are going to stop that for the future. We are not only going to destroy the Krupps war munitions concern, but the great one in Austria and everywhere else. We are going to take them under control of governments and regulate this thing in such a way that wild people can't get at each other's throats and destroy each other without going through the processes first that are proper.
> 4. In case of conflict in Europe the nearby powers would be called on first to provide the necessary forces, as in the case of conflict on the American continent, the United States would be asked to take matters in hand. But, and I want to repeat it, in no case is the United States bound to go to war or supply an armed force without the authorization of the Congress, which must first consider every case on its merits and act in accordance with the Constitution of the United States. (Applause)

Mr. Root has recently surprised his friends and admirers by urging that Article Ten be stricken from the League Covenant. He has given no explanation for his change of position. He is unable, however, to refute the convincing argument he first made in favor of guarantees of the territorial integrity and the political independence of all members of the League of Nations.

To eliminate this guarantee, my friends, is to extract the red corpuscle from the blood of the League, and render it a weak and anemic institution, incapable of fulfilling the purposes of its creation. Unless the people of each nation can be secured against external aggression, territorial disputes, which have been one of the most fruitful causes of the war, will continue to arise and to jeopardize the peace of the world. I think the fears that this guarantee will involve America in every future European conflict that may arise, and the statement that we are committed to an indefinite engagement to send our sons to fight in unknown and unanticipated European wars are entirely unfounded for the reasons I have already given you.

We can always terminate the engagement by withdrawing from the League upon two years' previous notice. Article Ten will, however, put an end to the menace of war from territorial disputes, but if eliminated from the League, so that these controversies remain a fruitful cause of war, then we shall be involved again in European conflicts, because it is impossible to separate America from the rest of the world and leave her in the imaginary isolation which opponents of the League beguile themselves into believing is a sufficient security for our future peace.

Why, my friends, talking about isolation, do you know that there landed in New York today from Edinburgh, Scotland, a great airship, bringing twenty-three people and sixty-three tons of supplies across the Atlantic Ocean in seventy-two hours?[27] And the other day five gallant men of our own navy made the first crossing of the Atlantic in an airplane.[28] (Applause) They were the pioneers. America first crossed the Atlantic, and they were followed a few days afterward by two gallant Englishmen, who went from Newfoundland to Ireland in about twenty-six hours in an airplane; and yet there are some of these gentlemen who yet can't see that America is no longer isolated from the rest of the world.

In fact, the guarantee of territorial integrity and political independence against external aggression only, as Article Ten provides, will not only prevent war by deterring the signatory powers from attempting it in violation of this Article, but in case of such disputes the League itself supplies the machinery for peaceful settlement, either by arbitration or by inquiry on the part of the Council, and the expressed stipulations of the League are that in case any such disputes shall arise that they will have to be considered either by Council, or they will have to be arbitrated, and if any nation fails to carry out that covenant, I am going to show you a little further on in this paper what will happen to the recalcitrant nation that dares as the Kaiser dared to violate a treaty, because we are going to make nations live up to treatises in the future, and that is one way that we are going to secure the peace of the world. (Applause)

Germany has not accepted the Treaty of Peace voluntarily. I believe I may tell you, in confidence, now that it has been published all over the world, (Laughter) that she will comply with the terms in good faith, but she isn't going to be very happy about complying with them. The other central powers will doubtless sign in the same mood. This makes it essential that the strength of the allied governments remain organized and that their cooperation be continued if Germany and her late allies are to be made to fulfill the obligations of the treaty. How can the power of the allies be more effectively consolidated and applied for these purposes than through a League of Nations? Separate the League of Nations from the treaty and it would be utterly impossible to enforce the treaty not only upon Germany, but upon all the other powers concerned. There would be no means of doing it, except all getting together again and send another great army on the other side of the water, and that is a thing we don't want to do.

Never in all history has it been so necessary that an effective instrumentality for the interpretation of a treaty and for the enforcement of its terms be provided as in the present instance, because never in the history of the world has peace been reestablished after a great war upon such a revolutionary basis. Not only has the form of old governments been changed, but new ones have been established, creating intricate problems which cannot be finally disposed of in terms of peace. Imagine what would happen if there were no League of Nations. Germany would proceed to re-arm herself as promptly as possible in order to renew the struggle and to regain what she has lost. France, England and Italy would also have to begin preparing themselves for the next war by building up their war power to the very limit of their strength. The United States would have to do the same thing. The backs of the people of all nations would bend with the burdens of new taxation for war purposes. They would be ground in poverty and misery to supply out of their labor and production the means by which these wasteful preparations for war would be continued.

Now, secret treaties: Another fruitful cause of war between nations has been secret treaties under which nations attempted to get advantage of their rival, and under which intrigues and private understandings of all kinds have worked for distrust, suspicion and enmity. Article Eighteen of the revised covenant provides that "every convention or international engagement entered into henceforward by any member of the League shall be forthwith registered with the Secretariat and shall as soon as possible be published by it. No such treaty or international engagement shall be binding until so registered." Certainly no nation imbued with good faith toward its neighbors and genuinely interested in preserving the peace of the world can object to this article of the covenant.

When treaties are published, just as are the laws of the United States and of the several states of the Union, so that all may read and understand, the selfish aims and private advantages which have heretofore accrued to nations and to individuals through these pernicious secret treaties will become abortive.

Now, compulsory conferences of the nations: If any one thing has been demonstrated by the great war it is that conference and counsel between the great nations is one of the most certain means of preventing international misunderstandings and of making war impossible. Heretofore such conference could not be held except by the voluntary action of all the parties. In 1914, before Germany precipitated the great war, an urgent effort was made by Sir Edward Gray (sic) to bring about a conference of the powers to consider the dispute between Austria and Servia (sic). Germany refused to enter that conference. She had determined to bring on the war in the execution of long considered plans, and she knew that if she joined a conference of the powers where a full and frank discussion of the issues would be necessary, war would be averted and her ambitions would be thwarted.

One of the most powerful arguments for the League of Nations is the requirement that the assembly, which consists of the representatives of all the members of the League and the Council, shall meet at stated intervals and from time to time as occasion may require, at the seat of the League or at such other place or places as may be decided upon. This provision is mandatory. It provides that the Assembly shall meet at stated intervals, and that the Council shall meet from time to time as occasion may require and at least once a year.

Now, suppose that this League of Nations had been in existence in 1914, and that upon a threat of war a meeting of the Assembly or of the Council had been called. Germany would have been obliged to attend. A discussion of the dispute would have immediately followed, and there is no doubt that the terrible war would have been prevented; that seven million dead men would be alive today, and twenty million wounded men would have been spared; that the horrors and indescribable suffering of the civil populations of all the nations concerned would have not occurred; and that $200,000,000,000 of treasure would not have been wasted in this terrible conflict which has just been ended.

It is a well-known fact, and Germany has admitted it, that Germany expected Great Britain to keep out of the great war, and that if she had known that Great Britain would make common cause with France, Belgium and Russia, she would never have precipitated the disastrous conflict. If even a conference of Great Britain, Germany, Austria, France and Russia had been held in 1914, Great Britain would have made this clear to Germany, and the war would not have occurred.

Now, if the proposed League of Nations accomplishes nothing more than to make certain a conference of the members of the League and of the Council at stated intervals for the purpose of the discussion and conference, it will have a potential influence upon the peace of the world. It will promote international cooperation instead of international antagonism and suspicions, which have been the characteristic evil of the old system of secret treaties and artificial balances of power so long maintained in Europe.

If, however, after limitations of armaments have been secured and guarantees of territorial integrity and political independence have been given and secret treaties have been eliminated and conferences of the powers have been provided for, disputes between nations should arise and take on such an acute form as to threaten war, then the League covenant makes other provisions which almost certainly will result in maintaining the peace of the world.

What are those provisions? They are: First, for arbitration of the dispute, if it is of a character which the contending nations recognize as suitable for submission to arbitration. But if the matter is not suitable for arbitration, then the dispute must be considered by the Council, which shall make such recommendations for its settlement as it thinks just and proper, and which recommendations must be made within six months after the controversy has been submitted. In case either of arbitration or of inquiry by the Council, the parties affected agree that they will not go to war until three months after the award by the arbitrators or the recommendation of the Council.

Now, without going into further details about these admirable provisions of the covenant, it is sufficient to say that they postpone war until there can be a complete discussion of the dispute, either through the medium of arbitration or through the processes of inquiry, and that after award by the arbitrators or a recommendation by the Council which makes the inquiry, neither party shall go to war until three months thereafter, and then they can't go to war with any party to the controversy which accepts the award in arbitration or the decision of the Council. (Applause)

But let us suppose any nation refuses to accept the award of the arbitration or the unanimous recommendation of the Council, which makes the inquiry, and proceeds to make war against the other party to the dispute which has accepted the award or the recommendations of the Council; or suppose any nation goes to war, as Germany did in 1914 without notice to anybody, as the case may be, what then happens?

The offending nation will be deemed to have committed an act of war against all the other members of the League, and thereupon the other members of the League will (1) sever all trade or financial relations between the members of the League and the offending nation; (2) prohibit all intercourse between the citizens of members of the League and the citizens of the offending state; and (3) prevent all financial, commercial and personal intercourse between the citizens of the offending nation and the citizens of any other state or nation throughout the world, whether a member of the League or not. That is what is called an economic boycott. It is a terrible weapon which no sane representatives of any nation would defy with impunity.

Now, let us suppose again that Germany had been faced in July, 1914, with this terrible economic boycott by Great Britain, France, Italy, Russia, Belgium and the United States. Is it conceivable that she would have entered upon the mad career of war with certain defeat staring her in the face at the very outset? No nation is strong enough to resist the combined economic pressure of the greatest powers of the world, and the moral influence and reprehension of the public opinion of the world.

But economic pressure is not the only consequence which a recalcitrant nation would incur because if war should actually result, the League Covenant provides that the Council shall recommend to the several governments concerned what effective military or naval forces the members of the League shall severally contribute to be used against the offending member.

But I repeat that upon such recommendation, if it were recommended, for instance, that the United States should furnish a certain amount of force to join in bringing some recalcitrant or offending nation to terms, we couldn't furnish it until the matter had been submitted to Congress, and the Congress of the United States had expressed its opinion and authorized the use of such force. So we take no risk in doing that. But if arbitration and inquiry fail, if mediation and conciliation prove impotent, if nine months of discussion and conference do not cool the hot passion for war, if every agency and influence of the League are exhausted in vain, then our opponents say that war will happen and that the League Covenant therefore recognizes and sanctions war. It is possible, of course, that war might happen in these circumstances, but it is scarcely conceivable.

If it should happen, how could it be said that the League Covenant sanctions war, because it undertakes to prevent it any more than it can be said that the state sanctions murder because it enacts laws to prevent that crime? In either case the evil is recognized to exist and because every effort is made to destroy it, by no exercise of the imagination can the attempt be distorted into a sanction of the offense if, after all is done, murder is committed or war occurs.

We do not abandon the Monroe Doctrine by entering the League of Nations. That policy is expressly reserved from the operations of the covenant. We cannot be made a mandatory of any foreign colony or territory except with our consent, and no amendments to the League after its adoption will be binding upon the United States unless accepted by it.

In case of attack upon the United States, we can immediately defend ourselves. Nothing in the League Covenant deprives us of that right, notwithstanding the false claim of our opponents to the contrary. The League has nothing to do with immigration, naturalization, or any of our internal or domestic affairs. We shall control these matters just as fully with membership in the League as without it.

Now time forbids a discussion of the admirable provisions of the League of Peace for progressing the solution of great moral and social problems which have long demanded the concerted attention of the civilized nations of the world. I shall merely enumerate them:

1. The endeavor to secure and maintain fair and humane conditions of labor for men and women alike.
2. The general supervision over the execution of agreements with regard to the traffic in women and children, and the traffic in opium and other dangerous drugs.
3. The endeavor to take steps in matters of international concern for the prevention and control of disease.
4. The undertaking to secure just treatment of the native inhabitants under their control.

These great problems appeal to the heart and conscious of humanity everywhere. God grant that their solution may not be prevented by the failure of the Senate of the United States to ratify the League of Nations Covenant. (Applause) Certainly the church, that great moral and spiritual organization, is vitally concerned with holding the ground thus gained in the League of Nations.

Most of the objections to the League of Nations are based upon misconceptions or misrepresentations of its provisions, or upon exaggerated and unfound fears as to its operation. Of course, the instrument does not suit every mind. It is of necessity a compromise of many conflicting views, just as was the constitution of the United States.

I am reminded of what the aged and venerable Benjamin Franklin said when the Constitution was signed at Philadelphia in 1788: "Whatever opinions I have of its errors, I will sacrifice to the public good, and I hope that every member of the Convention who still has objections will on this occasion doubt a little of his own infallibility and for the sake of unanimity put his name to this instrument." (Applause) That is what the great Franklin said. If the opponents of the League of Nations should adopt the advice of this great American patriot and statesman by sacrificing some of their opinions to the public good, and at least they should doubt a little of their own infallibility when they denounce in passionate terms the League of Nations Covenant. (Applause)

Now, when we are urged to reject this League or to amend it, don't you think we have a right to inquire into the judgment and wisdom of the men who urge their advice upon us with such an assurance of infallibility? How can the value of their advice be determined? By our experience with them, and by their records as public men. Some of the men who are now most vehement in urging the rejection of the League of Nations or its emasculation have proven by their records as public men that their advice is not worthy of unquestioned acceptance. I don't say it isn't worthy of acceptance, but it certainly isn't worthy of unquestioned acceptance.

Now, let us take the Federal Reserve Act for illustration.[29] This great measure which has given to the United States an impregnably sound and strong financial system, was denounced by those who are now the leading opponents of the League of Nations as unwise legislation, impregnant with calamity and disaster for the country. That is what they said and you will find it in the Congressional records, my friends. These men voted solidly against this great Federal Reserve system of finance. And yet, without this vital measure of finance preparation the war could not have been won.

Now, the bill for a Merchant Marine and Naval Auxiliary which was introduced in the Congress in September, 1914, was bitterly fought by the very men who are now opposing the League of Nations. It was defeated by a filibuster in March, 1915. This essential measure of preparedness was delayed for two years because of this opposition, so that when we entered the war in April, 1917, we had lost two years of preparation which cost the country millions of dollars in the hasty construction of ships and great delay and excessive cost in the transportation of troops and supplies. Many of these same leaders voted against the Federal Farm Loan System, which has brought such benefits to the farmers of the country.[30]

Have we not a right to question the advice and judgment of these same men when they tell us now that the League of Nations will bring disaster upon our country? If a lawyer gives bad advice to his client and he sustains serious losses or injury therefrom, he promptly chooses another lawyer. If a banker gives wrong advice to a customer about investments or finance, and he loses money thereby, he promptly changes his banker. But in politics we are unfortunately so partisan that a politician may constantly give bad advice. He may constantly vote against measures which are essential to the national welfare, and yet be frequently returned to office and give further opportunity to do grave injury to his country. I think it is time for us to learn to discriminate in our judgments of our public servants, and when I say that, my friends, I say it with respect to every political party – I don't care what label they have on them. (Applause)

I am loath to believe that the discussion of this greatest piece of constructive statesmanship, this League of Nations which concerns the very weal and woe of humanity, can be debased by partisan politics, and yet there are manifestations of partisanship in the discussions, disturbing to every man and woman who loves America and puts country above partisan considerations.

We must not let partisanship nor passion sway us in this momentous hour. Never were wisdom and deliberation on the part of the people and their representatives more needed than now. One cannot be passionate and wise at the same time, even though he be a politician or a statesman. Wisdom is the produce of cool deliberation and judgment. Mistakes are the product of passion and wars are the offspring of the baser instincts of human nature.

A combination of passion and partisan politics will produce inevitable mistakes. God grant that all those upon whom the responsibility rests for deciding the future of the world in this twentieth century may be endowed with the patriotism, the wisdom and the unselfishness of those great Americans of the eighteenth century, who, by their dispassionate judgment, their vision, their self-sacrifice, their devotion to human liberty and to country, formulated the Constitution of the United States and brought into existence this great American Republic.

No amendments of the League of Nations; no reservations in the ratification of the League by the Senate can be effected without imminent peril to the future of the world and without prolonging the state of war. We cannot risk the undoing of all that has been accomplished by forcing another Peace Conference in Paris. Amendment of the Treaty is rejection of the Treaty. Rejection of the Treaty means a new Peace Conference and the indefinite postponement of peace. Let us not misunderstand that. Let us ratify the League of Nations as it is, representing as it does the combined wisdom of all the great men who formulated it. And then let it evolve as our Constitution has evolved, into a more perfect instrument as human wisdom and experience demonstrate that amendments may be necessary.

This is the course we took with our own Constitution. We ratified it first and amended it afterwards. Let us ratify the League of Nations Covenant first and amend it afterwards if necessary. That is the safer plan. The League of Nations Covenant, like our own Constitution, provides the means for its amendment. By this course we shall consolidate and organize the triumph of democracy and liberty and extract from it those superlative blessings for which the human race has striven throughout the centuries.

Let us have peace! Let us have a League of Nations to give the world peace! (Prolonged Applause)

H. LESTER SMITH:[31]

Secretary McAdoo has given us a notable address this afternoon. In this great address we have been challenged by a great moral ideal which has stirred the heart of every man and woman who loves his or her fellowmen. It is not fitting that we should leave this place this afternoon without expressing our judgment upon this address in a resolution which can be given to the country to aid our President and his advisers in the great campaign which is so soon to begin in our country. We ought this afternoon as Christian men and women to help him make public sentiment for the greatest movement of our generation. (Applause)

I wish, therefore, to introduce a resolution pledging this great company of Methodists, North and South, to the support of the ideals for which the President stands, and which has been so ably presented to us by Secretary McAdoo:

"RESOLVED: that we as a group of Christian men and women assembled at the Methodist Centenary Celebration do most heartily and earnestly endorse the effort to secure the League of Nations, which shall serve to preserve peace in the world."

Mr. Chairman, I move the adoption of this resolution.
    ...The motion was promptly seconded...

GENERAL CARR:
All in favor of this resolution say "Aye." Those opposed "No."
...The resolution was unanimously adopted...

    ...ADJOURNMENT...

Navy Day Program
Saturday Afternoon, July 5, 1919

...The meeting convened at three o'clock, Honorable L.C. Laylin, former Secretary of the Interior, presiding...

LEWIS C. LAYLIN:[32]
Ladies and Gentlemen, I have the distinguished honor now to present the Honorable Mr. Daniels, Secretary of the United States Navy, who honors the Centenary by his presence today. (Applause)

JOSEPHUS DANIELS:[33]
During the great war through which we have passed, and which as yet has not been formally named, and about which many people are thinking that it may have a name worthy of its magnitude, I thought to myself that the only fitting name for it should be "The War Against War." (Applause)

During that war the navy of the United States increased from something like seventy thousand to five hundred and twenty-four thousand, and when these young lads, representative of all their associates and comrades, referred to me as "Daddy" of the navy I felt it was a great honor to be regarded by them as one who, when they consider the glory of the new American navy, was worthy to be their daddy. (Applause)

I love them every one as if they were my own blood, and you and all the one hundred ten million Americans who know what they did respect them and honor them. Aye, more, you are grateful to them, whose vast skill and courage carried over the seas the victorious army which won the war. (Applause)

Not long before the armistice, in a great battle in France, our American boys fighting with French and British took a large number of German prisoners, and when they had taken them to the rear and put them under guard, the officers who were assigned to guard them fell to talking with some of the German officers, and among them was a young German officer who had spent part of his youth in America. He could speak English as well as any of our officers, and they exchanged views about some of the campaigns.

He gave them the German theory of why certain marches were made and why certain attacks, and they responded in kind. And so they talked with each other as soldiers always will. One thing which civilians cannot quite understand is that a solder will fight and kill, and when the fight is over they don't hate each other, and I wish to God all men in the world might fight evil without getting hate in their hearts. (Applause)

And they talked with this young chap, and soon discovered that the thing that had astounded him most was to see so many Americans in France. "Why," said he, "gentlemen, when I was home a few weeks ago on a furlough the responsible men of our government told us there were only a handful of Americans in France, and here it looks to me as if the whole face of creation was covered with Yankees." (Applause)

You know the term "Yankee" has come to have a new meaning. There was a time in the early history of this country when only the Down Easterners in Maine were Yankees. But in the process of time we have come to see that it doesn't make any difference where a man lives, if he is an American and goes abroad and fights as our men did they call us Yankees, and I am thankful that our soldiers from North Carolina and Ohio and Maine rejoice to be called Yankee soldiers fighting for American principles. (Applause) But they fight when they come together under the tune of Dixie as well as The Star Spangled Banner. (Applause)

They are all one. This young fellow was troubled about it and was astounded to see so many Americans in France. Why, you know ladies and gentlemen, when this war began the Germans in high authority never took American participation seriously. They said, "Why, the Americans are great lovers of dollars. They lend these allies money, and these Yankee grubbers after money will make a few munitions, but they will never send any soldiers over there." That was their belief. The result showed how false was all German psychology when they came against the American will.

They said, "If they were disposed to send soldiers, they have no trained men. Americans have not been trained to warfare, and if they got over here it would be a mob. They don't know how to fight." They don't think a man can fight unless he is so familiar with the goose step and manual of arms that he can follow on German lines.

Then they said, "But if they had soldiers ready to go, they have no ships." And we had very few, and it troubled us then. They said, "If they get the ships and start across, why, we will sink them all with our submarines." And so they treated us with indifference. No wonder this young fellow, a German officer, was astounded to see so many Americans fighting and winning, and then he asked the question of those American and British and French officers how they won their distinction. The British officer told how he won his Victoria Cross, and the French officer told how he won his Legion of Honor. Then he took out his iron cross and explained how he had won that. He then turned to these officers, representing the three largest allied armies, and he said, "Gentlemen, I can understand all about the Legion of Honor and the Victoria Cross, and the Iron Cross, but pray tell me, gentlemen, how did the Americans get across?" (Laughter and Applause)

You know, I know, and all the world knows they got across because these lads and five hundred thousand more lads were on the job every day. (Applause) When America, in the way it does things, not rashly or hastily, but soberly and with determination, entered this war and four million of our boys went into the army training camps and made ready for the grim business of making this old war over, and that is what it was, ladies and gentlemen, and let nobody ever suppose we entered this war merely to whip Germany. That was an incident. We didn't send our boys to fight and whip one nation and quit. We entered this war as crusaders of chivalry to defeat Germany because it was standing in the way of progress and justice, and we resolved to keep the war up until wars should be no more. (Applause)

There isn't a mother in the sound of my voice, or a father, or one in all America who gave their boys in this crusade – and let us call it nothing less, for it wasn't any war such as the world has seen before, it was as holy a crusade as the misguided crusaders of the early centuries made to free Palestine – the thought in the heart of every parent in America as these boys started across the sea was not fear for them after they had gotten into the midst of battle. They knew the stuff of which they were made – and I use that word "stuff," though I do not know whether it is in the dictionary that way, and it may be that the college of bishops would not use it. This gentleman tells me Shakespeare does. It has been regarded by us until this war (sic) more or less a slang term. But they knew the stuff they were made of, which means physical fiber, moral courage, and mental acuteness.

We knew these boys were made of that stuff, and having given them a gun and the consciousness of a high purpose, why, nothing could withstand them, and it didn't. But the fear in all our hearts – and it was a real fear, it was a genuine danger – was the imminent menace that as they went on the transports and crossed the ocean they might be destroyed by the submarine skulking under the waves. That was a thing that tugged at our hearts and gave us anxiety and trouble.

I shall never forget, if I live a thousand years – and if I could attend Methodist meetings over here all the time I think I'd live that long. I don't mean by that for you to understand I don't attend them every week, but I mean if I could attend a great meeting like this where all America comes together with its youth and enthusiasm and shouting spirit. I remember the first trip that the old *Vaterland* made. We changed its name.[34] We didn't even want our ships' names made in Germany, but we wanted the ship, and we took it over to carry American soldiers to lick German soldiers. (Applause)

This ship had a capacity of ten thousand, but when this ship made its first voyage it carried only eight thousand soldiers because we knew it was risky and dangerous. We knew there was no prize of war that was so valued by the German heads of government as the sinking of their own ships lined with our men. So we didn't dare to put it full. As she went out laden with this precious cargo, the most precious in all the world, our hearts beat rather rapidly lest they should meet the fate of hundreds of thousands of other ships and be sent to the bottom.

I gave word to the Navy Department that no matter what the hour of the night when they heard the first word from this ship I should be called up by telephone, which was stationed at the head of my bed, because I knew that as soon as it had landed safely with its soldiers I'd be fifty years younger. I want to tell you there wasn't a morning or evening during that long voyage that I didn't lift my heart up in prayer to Almighty God for the safety of that ship and those boys. (Applause)

When the news came the telephone rang one morning about four o'clock before day. "Communication wishes to speak with you." My heart almost stood still for fear of the worst. When the young officer said, "The *Leviathan* is safe," I felt like the old Methodist at the camp meeting – I felt like shoutin'.

(Applause) And from then on during the whole war, through the worst infested danger zones ever known in the seas, our ships went day and night, carrying more than two millions of American youths, and never was one lost in all that period. (Applause)

Do you ask me how it was accomplished? I can tell you the human means – the men in the navy, on the ships and in the convoys, in these little destroyers where they slept, where they worked without sleep, and never for ten days dared to sit down to a meal, and caught only a wink of sleep standing on the deck – I tell you it was their courage and sacrifice, their all that man can do; but I shall never doubt so long as I live that because we fought in the righteous cause of God of Battles was with us. (Applause)

I remember in 1917, after the Germans had advanced and advanced, after the British had been driven back here, and the French there, our troops had been unable to make the great record they made afterwards, and the German emperor made a speech at Essen in which he said, "We, the German people, have an open and a valued ally in God Almight (sic), who will surely bring us the victory."

I remember about the same time he was making that speech, the President of the United States – today the greatest statesman in all the world – (Applause) made an address to Congress, and in this address he used these words, "The hand of the Almighty is laid upon the nations, and he will show favor, I verily believe, upon that nation that rises nearest to His goodness and mercy." (Applause)

We had no right to invoke the Divine blessing upon our soldiers unless they were fighting the battle of righteousness. When the German emperor boasted that the God of the universe was an ally of Germany, and the President of the United States, speaking your thought and my thought, and every Christian American's thought, said, "God will show favor to the nation that rises nearest to His conception," there was the contrast between latent impiety and the belief in arms, and the faith that God was on the side of right. (Applause)

And it was because this nation had no selfish purpose in the war; did not enter it to obtain a foot of territory, nor prosecute it to obtain reparation or any gain or glory that should be selfish, but because this whole nation was consecrated and mobilized that right should prevail and the menace of conquest should be over. That was the reason, and at the critical moment the American army was able to throw the decisive strength and win this war against wars. (Applause)

A few weeks ago I had the privilege of standing on the heights of Vallendar, a great plateau in Germany that overlooks the Rhine at the confluence of the Moselle River. It is the place where for generations it has been the custom of the Kaiser at stated periods to review the shock Prussian troops. I stood there reviewing a regiment of twenty-eight thousand men as they passed with their machine guns and the tanks and the instruments of war – sturdy, well set up, splendid young Americans. I believe I felt more than I ever felt in my life proud to be of that blood and that nation.

After the review had passed the general in command said to me, "I wish you'd say a few words to these boys. You are just from home. They have been over a long time; have been through grim warfare, seen their comrades fall beside them. I think they'd like to have a word from home." So we made a little stand and all these boys broke ranks and gathered around. There they sat looking up, heroes of St. Mihiel and the Argonne Forest, who had won a glory that will never fade.

I said, "Boys, what do you want me to talk about?" They replied as if they had drilled it to musical concord, and they sang out in accord as if there was only one voice, "Talk about going home!" That is all they thought about. I said, "Well, the last man I saw before I left Washington was the Secretary of War, and we have made plans so that all the soldiers in Germany and France may be brought home shortly." And they came back again as one voice, "How soon?"

And I had heard that the two French words that all soldiers had learned – I don't know whether I can pronounce them exactly, but I can pronounce it the way the Americans soldiers pronounce it – and I answered to them, "Tout suite." And they said, "Name the day!"

Ladies and gentlemen, every one of those boys represented an American home. They were well housed, billeted in the best houses built in Germany. There they were, comfortable so far as men can be comfortable unless they are at home with their mothers, and can take an occasional walk with a sweetheart. But there they were, having almost forgotten the war. They had forgotten the desire to travel, and the only thought in their minds was getting home; and getting home meant they wanted to come back to America and retake the places they had left, and again enter the battle and conflict to make this old world a better place in which to live. (Applause)

We fought a great war. We have won a great war. We have before us the responsibility of winning a great peace, and sometimes I think that the victories of peace are more difficult of achievement than the victories of war. During the war we were all mobilized and at work. We had a common objective. Men forgot dividends. Men forgot selfishness. Men forgot politics – that is, most of them did. (Laughter) During this great war America rose from partisanship to patriotism. (Applause) May we not hope, may we not pray that the elevation of patriotism that dominated these people will never again sink to the old time partisanship. (Applause)

We have great problems facing us in peace. We met the challenges of war. We met it, and when history writes the story of America's participation in war, it will be a story of such efficiency at home, such consecration in the home, in the factories, and in the field; such courage across the sea, as will lift our nation to a new plane.

Now we come to the problems of peace difficulties. There are natural divisions among us as to what is the best method of preserving what we have done, and making this old country of ours worthy of the men who died to save it for the world. That is our problem, and the men who are going to solve it, and the only men who are capable of solving it are the men in the dominion of America who have any appreciation of the men and women who during the war made sacrifices and consecrated themselves to win the war. (Applause)

If you want to know who is going to rule America the next fifty years, you need only to read history very slightly to know that it is the men who fought across the seas, and the men at home who backed them up with financial support, and everything they could do. They are the men, and no others have a right to voice in the new days that are coming before us.

During the war we found men in great industries thinking more of winning the war than of dividends and profits. We found men in overalls working in the cold of winter and the heat of summer on munitions, thinking more of the product than of the wage. And better than all, we found employee and employer sitting down together and adjusting their differences so from the beginning to the end of the war we had the best labor conditions and capital conditions we had had for fifty years.

And why? Because under the impulse of patriotism men refused to think of themselves, but thought of their country. Let this great gathering of Christian men and women pray and work; because I believe in the old time method, if you want to pray for a thing you have to work for it as hard as though you were not praying, and pray as hard as if you were not going to work; that these conditions of friendship and mutual respect shall prevail in this old world.

There were some men – very few of them – who had an idea that when the war was over we were going back to old conditions, and things were going to be like they were. Let me tell you that in everything except the calendar it is a hundred years since we entered this war. (Applause) And the men who suppose conditions are going to return as they were and that men are going to work for the same low wages they got have got another thing coming to them. (Applause) Men will never again be employed at the same old wage, which was always too low, and we must get together and make it a fair, just living wage for men who labor. (Applause)

And the church of God, getting the spirit of the Master Carpenter, has got to put itself figuratively in overalls and stand by and make men who labor and toil understand that the church of today is the same vital agency, and that its business in the world is to save it for all time. (Applause) There is no place in this world of ours for a church that draws the cloak of self-righteousness about it. There is no place for it unless it stands for justice, and its heart beats first for men who toil.

This great church of ours was born in a college, but it didn't stay in a college long. The atmosphere wasn't favorable to religion in those days, and John Wesley and Whitfield (sic) hurried from the scholastic places to the factories, to the fields, and under the direction of these great Wesleyan leaders the gospel was preached to them and they were made to feel that the church was their place, and it was lifting them to higher planes. (Applause)

We must face these responsibilities of social questions. They have come among us. The church must lead, the church must have the vision; it must stand for justice. I'd like to see the day come when Methodist preachers, if the people do not come to the churches, they will go into the highways and preach to them. (Applause) I do not like to see a preacher preaching in a city church or a country church to a handful of good saints, with thousands of sinners outside. I am not certain but that we have to go back to street preaching.

You know John Wesley was very severe in criticizing Whitfield (sic) for preaching in the streets. He said it did not become the dignity of a clergyman to preach in the streets or else quit preaching. And he had been called to preach. He had a message, and ladies and gentlemen and brethren, the man who has no message, whether he is in the pew or the pulpit, has no place in this new world. (Applause)

We have these problems – social problems, problems of living, problems of care of the child. When I think how long this great nation has permitted women in sweat shops and young children to work without the light and a place to play, it is an indictment against our religion and civilization. The man who makes money out of their labor is sinning against God Almighty as well as the child. (Applause)

The man who makes money in sweat shops, paying women miserable wages, may sit in the pew on Sunday morning and sing, and put his money in the collection plate, but he can never find favor with the just God. The church is no longer to be a cloister; no longer to be a place for men to come into like a fire insurance company and take out a policy to save themselves from eternal burning. That is what many of us have been doing. The church must be the center of a dynamic power. Unless the membership has the spirit of Christ who drove out the money changers, and ate with the Publicans and sinners, unless it comes back to that sort of a church it is a shame, and we need not wonder sometimes that it makes less progress in getting to the hearts of men.

The Centenary Movement came from a new consecration, and a new vision, and a new ideal. I spoke this morning to a million – more or less – of Minute Men. Judging from the numbers they were less. Judging by their zeal and their accomplishments they were more. (Applause) What are we going to do with this great body? They have wrought wonderfully in a great movement. Other great movements are before us. We rejoice that our liberal people, many out of small means, have raised this tremendous fund of a hundred and sixty or seventy million dollars – a very worth while thing if we use the money right. (Applause)

We are sending men to carry the gospel across the sea, and we will send men in greater numbers, and all our churches must see to it in this generation that there isn't a man or woman of any color or creed who does not hear the old story of the gospel. (Applause)

But, beloved, that is the good word of the Scripture. We have a great problem in all our cities which we have only played at. Hundreds of thousands of men have come to our shores from foreign lands, and what have we done to carry them to the gospel and teach them Americanism? When this war began thousands of people who had lived here for twenty and thirty years, and who, we found, had a greater love for some other nation than ours, we truly said to them that they ought not to be in America, and nobody ought to be here unless they love that flag more than anything else on earth. (Applause)

But when they come the church of Christ should be at Ellis Island. It should be at San Francisco. It should go to these ignorant men – ignorant of our institutions and our life – and it should carry to them the knowledge of life that can illumine their path; and I trust that out of this large generosity we shall catch the vision of our duty to newcomers and make them Christians and American citizens. (Applause)

But I must not detain you longer. There once lived in my state an old time, fine old permitted Baptist preacher, and his brother was a United States senator, and he concluded to go to Washington to visit his brother. When he returned he told his congregation of his visit to a Baptist Church there, and among the things he said was, "While I was in Washington I was invited to preach in the First Baptist Church, and I fear, my brethren, the people in Washington can't stand sound doctrine. I fear these city folks lack the spirit. Why, do you know, I hadn't been preaching more than two hours when a half, or two-thirds of that congregation got up and went out." (Applause) "My brethren," said he, "they can't stand sound doctrine."

I do not know, bishop, whether this congregation can stand sound doctrine, but I am going to try them five minutes more. I said in the beginning that when the time came to write the story of the war they would have to give it a name worthy of its achievements, and that name ought to be "The War Against Wars." If it is not that; if we as a people, whom I believe have the largest vision, the greatest righteousness, in my judgment, the nation that compromises, that is able to carry its ideal along with its practical purposes – if we do not rise to the heights of God's justice and wisdom, and make it a war against wars, our young men will have died in vain. (Applause)

I read yesterday that a certain distinguished gentlemen in America, a very able man, a very eloquent man, had said that he would not vote for the League of Nations – which is the only way to make this a war against wars – nothing else can do it. He said that he wouldn't vote for it if Jesus Christ himself came on earth and asked him to do it.

I do not know whether he said it, but I know, and these good bishops know, and every minister and laymen here, and every good Christian knows that is what Christ came to earth to do. He came into this sin-cursed world and war-tossed world for what? That the prophecy sung at Bethlehem, "Peace on earth, and goodwill to men," should be revealed and bless mankind. (Applause)

We are privileged to live in a day when we will see that prophecy fulfilled. We love to think that we have been lifted up by the wonderful and heartening and spiritual day of Pentecost. And these ministers have prayed a thousand times that the spirit of that day might be upon the church in the world. We recall with something of awed surprise and gratitude that when Peter stood up and preached on that day to Galileans and Mesopotamians and Greeks and men of every tongue, they all heard him in their own language. They said to themselves, "Are not these who speak Galileans, and yet we all hear him in the tongue in which he was born."

And Peter standing among them said, "Men and brethren, the prophecy, the promise is to you and to your children, and those who are afar off." The promise of peace, of a covenant, by which the nations of the earth should make war difficult and peace easy has not been fulfilled in these centuries, because men were deaf to this coming of Christ.

It has taken all these years, and this study, and this sacrifice of seven or eight million lives to make men sit down in Paris and discuss for the first time in the world's history how the promise of Christ should come to all men – those afar off as well as those in the kingdom. (Applause)

We shall not fail the seven million men who died that the war might be the last. (Applause) And as a Christian nation, we shall highly resolve, cost what it may, whatever sacrifice is demanded, we shall stand with a great empire, Great Britain, whose men have fought with credit and valor, (Applause) we shall stand with those chivalric men of France, (Applause) for four million of them died, many of them were maimed, who fought with us on all the battlefields – we shall not fail the people of distressed Italy, who after an early fall-back came with courage and power and drove the Huns away from them.

We shall not fail the twenty other nations, great and small, who have ratified this treaty of peace. We shall not, as a nation, have upon our skirts the blood, guile, and destruction of all the future wars that curse mankind if America fails. (Prolonged Applause)

...ADJOURNMENT...

Army Day Exercises
Tuesday morning, July 8, 1919

The meeting convened at the Grand Stand at 11:00AM, Bishop Atkins presiding...
...Music by Rainbow Division Band...

BISHOP ATKINS:
I know that you are all curious to know who these distinguished visitors are, and before introducing the speaker, I wish merely to present these other gentlemen. (Applause)

I have the honor to present Major Dupont of the French Army.

...Audience applauds while the Marseillaise is played...

This is Colonel Bush of the Thirty-Seventh who is in command of these handsome chaps on the left, and Captain Young who is aide-de-camp to General Glenn.

Now, having tried to observe the order of rank in the army with the exception of especial courtesy to the French Army, I desire to reverse the rule and adopt a scripture rule and say to you that I have saved the best of the wine to the last of the feast. I hope the ladies will come forward and I will present them.

Ladies and Gentlemen, this is Mrs. General Glenn whom I have the honor to present, and her friend and my friend, Miss Coltrane from Concord, North Carolina. We are very happy, indeed, to have you with us. (Applause)

Ladies and Gentlemen, I have the honor and the responsibility of introducing the speaker of the hour. If I did not know that you would rather hear him than hear me, I would have some good things to say about him, and the first of these would be that he is a North Carolinian. (Applause) Whenever I find that a man has tar on his heels, I feel sure that he has the sticking qualities that will make a good soldier. (Applause)

Another thing is that the General attained his honors through the excellency of his profession, having taken the course and finished it with honor at our great military academy, the greatest, in some respects, in the world. And then, he has been a soldier in France, which, under all the conditions, entitles a man to special honor, more because of the cause of the contest and the nature of the contest than the endurance which it required.

Now, General Glenn and my military friends, I want to say to you just at this time that you are largely responsible for the very state of things you have before you today – this Centenary. You went and turned the world upside down. We are trying to get it back. (Applause)

There was an old Yorkshire preacher who took for his text on a missionary occasion this passage: "These that have turned the world upside down have come hither also." "Now," he said, "there are just three points in this text. The first: the world is wrongside up. Second: it has to be turned upside down. And third: we are the chaps to do it."

The military and religious order of these modern times have been going together much more closely than many people have observed. The militarians have turned the world upside down and the Christians are busy trying to get it turned rightside up.

One of the largest of Mr. Wilson's many large utterances was one which he made in connection with the declaration of war under the orders of Congress that the object of it all was to make the world safe for democracy. But, a greater task belongs to the Christian church, which is to make democracy safe for the world. (Applause) In other words, it is the great Protestant problem which began under Martin Luther and will continue until the citizenship of the world has become a fit citizenship of Zion.

In order not to detain you, although I should like to say some other things about the General and his achievements, I beg to present to you General Glenn of Greensboro, North Carolina, and of the wide, wide world. (Applause)

GENERAL GLENN:[35]
Mr. Chairman, Ladies and Gentlemen:
...Audience rises and cheers General Glenn...
It is true that I came from the great state of North Carolina. There was a time when I boasted that it was a great state to come from, and one of my friends incidentally remarked, "Yes, provided you leave when you are young enough." (Laughter)

We of the army are perfectly willing to grant that by our efforts in France we have stood the world on its head and that we are responsible, as has been said by the Bishop, for the presence today of this great Centenary. I go further. I believe that we are responsible for creating in the world a broader, a higher, a more intelligent conception of religion and its functions than existed before this war. (Applause)

The subject assigned me today is that the problem of this war and of peace, and the part taken therein by the great state of Ohio. It is broad enough to discuss any and all features of this warfare from any viewpoint, but having expended all of my manhood in the military service of my country, it is quite natural that I should approach it from the military viewpoint.

According to my conception, there were three great problems that presented themselves for solution at the beginning of this war for the United States of America. The first was to organize the resources of men and material of the country to make it available for the prosecution of the war. The second, and it is the first time in history, I think, that this has ever been accomplished, was to organize the men, material and activity of the entire world. The third was to create what I see fit to term imagination, especially among our leaders, of such nature that it would enable them to grasp the magnitude of the undertakings upon which we were embarked.

That we succeeded wonderfully well in the first two and especially in view of our failure, certainly in large part as to the last, there is no sort of question! It is true that in the past Europe with parts of Asia, Africa and America has been engaged in warfare, but never before in the history of the world have we experienced a war in which all of the people of all the nations were called into service and necessarily so for the accomplishment of the purposes had by each of the belligerents. Never before in the history of the world have we been called upon to fight in the air or in the water under the sea, and never before have we been called upon to make use of the new instruments with which we were in no sense familiar. Never in the history of the world has science been so taxed to provide protection for the fighting forces that were engaged in this war.

In illustration of this, let me advise you that we not only had to provide noxious gases but we had to continually provide for new and more deadly poisonous gases as the world progressed. Not only this, but we were forced to utilize such gases that we could provide protection for our own men against their deadly effects.

Another thing in which science was very deeply involved is illustrated by what we call our sound instruments. With these instruments it was possible to locate the submarine and thereby enable our destroyers to make use of the deadly bombs which were also an invention of this war. With the use of these, we were enabled to locate accurately by the means of sound the location of the batteries of the enemy.

I personally saw the result of such location of an enemy battery that was thirteen miles distant from our own battery. After the order had gone forth for this battery of two large guns to be destroyed, our aeroplanes passed over the spot and took a photograph. I personally saw this photograph. The demonstrator proceded (sic) to point out six well-defined shell holes and so accurate was his knowledge of the location of each shot that was fired from our own batteries that he told me this first shot struck here, the second shot struck the enemy gun on our right, the third and fourth shots were misses, the fifth shot destroyed the second gun, and the sixth shot was a miss. (Applause) And, all of these shots were within a radius of about the space covered by two of these partitions.

Another feature of this warfare was the calling into account the effort of what we term generally our welfare workers. We were familiar with the functioning of the Red Cross. We knew from experience at home the magnificent work they had done in floods and fires and similar catastrophes. We knew their ministering to the sick and wounded. We were also familiar with the work of the YMCA and to a more limited extent of the YWCA. Their functions, as you know, were largely limited to the furnishing of amusement and entertainment for the men and the keeping of these men in as close touch as possible with the home. These in all previous wars had been considered desirable but not essential. In this war these were absolutely necessary and essential for the winning of the war. It was absolutely necessary if we were to succeed in this war that we maintain the morale of the men, and we found it to be a fact that men who had been in the trenches subjected to the terrific bombardments that were so common in this war, must necessarily be removed from these surroundings after a limited experience, and after being removed therefrom, they must be entertained and diverted and made to forget what their experiences had been.

Without morale it is impossible for an army to fight, and this morale could not be maintained in any other way. For the first time in the history of the world, the American stage as well as the stage of our allies did their bit towards furnishing this entertainment. You could not go into a single camp where you did not find special entertainment provided practically every night of the week.

The stage of all the allied countries could not possibly furnish sufficient entertainment to meet these ends, it was manifest, and, therefore, it was the custom in all armies to designate certain men who were capable of furnishing this amusement and entertainment, requiring them to devote themselves exclusively to that work.

Just previous to this war the people of the United States had indicated in the most positive terms that they did not wish war and yet when our president and congress decided in their wisdom that war was necessary and further decided that conscription should be applied in this country for the first time, the people of this country, and especially between the ages of twenty-one and thirty-one responded to the call practically unanimously. It was not difficult, therefore, to secure either men or money which constitute the sinews of war. But, it was difficult to know how to organize, train and equip a million of men when we knew that we must train and equip many million if we were to be successful.

We had not a single man in this country who had ever had experience in commanding large bodies of troops in the field. We had neither clothing nor other supplies such as the equipment required for the soldier in sufficient quantities to equip our own army. We knew also from having studied the operations of war previous to this time that our people who were actually engaged in the warfare must employ not only new weapons but new methods of warfare.

To illustrated the point I am trying to make, let me take the infantry soldier familiarly known throughout our army as the doughboy and generally recognized in all armies not only as the backbone of the army but as the one responsible for winning this war. Previous to this war his function was limited practically to being efficient in the use of the rifle and bayonet, but in this war he had to use what is generally known as the bomb or hand grenade, the rifle grenade, the automatic rifle, the machine gun, and what is known as the thirty-seven millimeter gun. In addition to these and in order to function with the other arms he must be familiar with the use of the trench mortar, the field artillery, the heavy artillery, the tank or the aeroplane and he must understand the various forms of signals for communicating with them and for general communication. This was extending or reaching down in military education to the infantry soldier that was never conceived of in all previous history.

Referring to my own experience in the training of these men, I found myself at the beginning of the war placed in charge of the first reserve officers training camp where we had more than six thousand young officers or would-be officers. It was my good fortune not only to carry these officers through until they had secured their commissions but to follow them throughout the entire war practically. They were men principally from this great state of Ohio.

It was these men who were to receive organized training and discipline, what we call the conscript army, who reported in the first part of September, but so great was our lack of preparedness that it was months, at least weeks, after the men were there before we could get even the rifles and the other elements such as hand grenades, and so forth, were manifestly impossible.

The greatest trouble was the transportation of our armies abroad. When I was in France in March 1916, after a careful study had been made as far as practicable, up to that time it was determined that it was impossible for us to transport across the ocean and deliver upon the firing line or in the training camps of France to exceed ninety thousand men per month. And yet, I found on my return that we exceeded this number during that month, that we very greatly exceeded it during the following months and that within seven months or at the time of the armistice, this country had actually transported to France more than two million of men in khaki uniform, in addition to the welfare workers and their necessary equipment. (Applause)

You know such a feat as this has never been accomplished before in the history of the world and this feat required not only an accurate knowledge of the location of all the supplies of the world, including the raw material, but it required a similar knowledge of all the transportation facilities whether of shipping railroad or otherwise that existed throughout the world.

It required further that these various facilities should be organized and made available for the use of these armies. It meant not only that these men and these supplies for the army should be transported across but it meant that the civil population of Europe and Great Britain which were dependent upon receiving supplies from abroad should not suffer materially. This work was accomplished through American business methods. It can be safely asserted that there was no great suffering among the civil population of France, Italy or Great Britain, and it is a well established fact that all of the armies and especially the American army had full rations practically every day of the entire service.

Now, under these conditions, this lack of officers and men competent to perform the functions of an army and the necessity for securing these things by intensive, short, quick methods, it is perfectly natural that great mistakes should have been made. Blunders have been made, errors of judgment that have cost much in money as well as in lives. All of this is deplorable and it is believed that it should be and will be investigated. It is hoped that it will be investigated thoroughly and that the results will be made known to our people, not for the purpose of party political advantage but for the purpose of enabling us to avoid similar mistakes in the future. (Applause)

In my own personal experience I have had pass directly under my control for training more than two hundred thousand men and I have been brought more or less into personal contact with a great majority of them. I saw them, as I stated, from the commencement of the training to secure officers until sometime after the armistice – still in France. I have been associated with these same men since their return because I have been in charge of one of the greatest demobilization camps in this country at Camp Sherman.

The psychological viewpoint in considering these men under these conditions certainly presents a great field for study. From the commencement of the war up to the time of the armistice, every individual man composing these armies was, as we express it, on his toes. He expended every ounce of energy and all of his nervous force to equip himself so that he would be prepared and efficient in meeting the Hun.

Just as soon or almost immediately after the armistice was signed, or certainly just as soon as he realized or believed that the war was over, he expended an equal amount of nerve force and energy to get out of the army. He wanted to see no more war. He doesn't want to see any more war today. He wants to discard it and in this frame of mind lies, what I believe, a real danger.

The present longing for peace, we admit, is a perfectly natural result and conforms to all history. It is probably one of the strongest factors in support of the proposed League of Nations. It must not be forgotten, however, that no peace settlement of the past has succeeded in bringing about permanent peace or in doing away with war. That we shall have wars in the future can be confidantly (sic) asserted and is recognized even by the great men who have formulated this great League of Nations, and it is an absolutely necessary conclusion if we are to believe in past history. It is confirmed by the fact that we have from fifteen to thirty wars in Europe today and we must recollect that the inherent quality of the human race whether considered alone or in the aggregate, considering the jealousies, the ambitions, the ideals which must necessarily conflict under different forms of government are bound to produce contests of one sort or another, and these under any previous arrangement or any previous form of government have not prevented resulting wars.

It seems, therefore, that ordinary prudence dictates that a nation should not permit its desire for peace to induce it to forget to take the necessary precaution for self-protection. Until we can safely leave our valuables openly exposed, until our banks can do away with safety vaults and municipalities can dismiss their police forces, nations must be prepared for defence (sic) and through this preparation secure the greatest assurance and security against foreign aggression. (Applause)

We must, therefore, equip ourselves now that war has ceased, supposedly, for the great national problems that confront us and one of these can be safely asserted to be the problem of securing the most efficient and the least expensive system of national defence. (sic)

Another problem that confronts us is to do away with, and I believe we can do it, the alleged conflict between capital and labor. (Applause) I believe firmly that when capital and labor have studied in an intelligent, comprehensive way the necessary relation that must exist between the two, we in this United States will find a solution for the present strikes and resulting disorders that have upset the economic conditions in this great country.

But, in order to accomplish this, the great, and I believe controlling, problem presents itself for solution in this country. I refer to the question of illiteracy. I do not believe that our people at large understand the extent to which illiteracy exists all over the United States. Our census of 1910 showed that we had eight million five hundred thousand people over ten years of age who were classed as illiterate, who could not read a newspaper or a letter sent to them from home.

These figures are appalling enough, God knows, but they do not tell the whole story. In taking the census the census takers contented themselves with simply asking the question. There was no verification so that we actually put men to the test as we did in reaching out for and securing our soldiers for this war through the conscription act. We actually found that in thirteen camps where twenty-five percent of the men between twenty-one and thirty-one years of age were passed, thirty and eight-tenths percent of these men could not read an English newspaper or write a letter. Gentlemen the figures are astounding! In the county of Ross where Camp Sherman is located, eleven hundred men between twenty-one and thirty-one years of age were actually rejected upon this test of illiteracy. And, it is as fair to assume that these conditions exist everywhere.

There is a rift in the cloud. These illiterates are composed not only of the native white and black but of the immigrant and this has been gradually decreasing insofar as the native white and black are concerned at a reasonably satisfactory rate during the past thirty-five years.

On the other hand, the rate of increase of illiteracy among our foreign born or immigrants is rapidly increasing, and it is manifestly so to anyone who will consider this subject, that it is impossible for any man or any woman to become one hundred percent American citizen when they cannot read a newspaper, when they cannot read the Christian Bible or when they cannot understand the fundamentals of our own government. (Applause)

This government demands a high order of citizenship in order that we may continue to live. This citizenship cannot be French or German or Italian or English, if you please, although our American citizenship is a blend of practically all of the nations who have migrated to this country. It differs from all, thank God it does, but in its essence it is American and must continue so for all time. (Applause)

It is American. It must be American in spirit, and it does not permit or contemplate that we shall have or observe in this country any holidays or birthdays except those of our own people. (Applause)

There is no place in this country but for one flag and that is Old Glory. (Applause) It is not only the greatest flag that the sun has ever shown upon but it is the oldest flag now flying of any civilized nation on the face of the earth. (Applause)

Now, I confidently make the assertion if the people of this United States will take hold of the question of illiteracy with the same intensity of purpose that we took hold of the question of stamping out the Hunism or the threat to our institutions by the German confederation, it will be but a very short time until illiteracy will be wiped out and cease to be a disgrace as well as a menace to the well-being of this great country. (Applause)

There has been much talk of Bolshevism. It is a sort of by-product of this war. Russia with her one hundred and eighty million people has sort of crumpled up, as we might express it. I am one of those who do not believe that that great nation, speaking practically one language is going to be wiped off the face of the earth. I believe she will come back and I am also one of those who do not believe and absolutely refuse to believe that Bolshevism is going to be or is, in fact, a menace in this country. Let me tell you why.

You realize that the total wealth of this country amounts to two hundred and fifty billions of dollars. You realize that we have twelve million depositors in our savings banks with an aggregate deposit of six billion five hundred millions of dollars. Did you realize that we have more than six million five hundred farms valued at forty-one billions of dollars and yielding an annual income of eight billions of dollars? We have nearly two hundred seventy thousand miles of railways over which is transported everywhere more than one billion of people and more than two billion two hundred five million tons of freight. We have schools at which there is an average attendance of twenty million children. We have twenty-one millions of people occupying more than eighteen millions of homes, most of them owned by themselves.

Now, it must be frankly admitted when we consider this question of illiteracy in this question that our schools, in spite of the fact that they have laws requiring the attendance of every child up to a certain age, varying from twelve to fifteen or sixteen years, are not functioning as the American people demand or will demand when they know the fact that they should function. I personally think that we have neglected our schools largely in our failure to pay the school teacher, be it man or woman, what his services are honestly worth. (Applause) But, it has been demonstrated beyond the peradventure of a doubt not only in Maryland but in Kentucky that by proper methods illiteracy can be wiped out in the county and that these methods will be pursued if they are brought to the notice of the other counties by all of these other counties. And, in the county in Maryland to which I refer and where this experiment was put into effect before the declaration of war, there wasn't a single county in the whole United States that was more patriotic, that had more patriotic organizations or did more in proportion to their ability than this particular county of practically general illiteracy before the experiment was tried.

Is it worth the while? Now, I could point out to you how this illiteracy is a menace not only to the country but is a menace to the individual himself. As one example, for instance, this great state that is producing such enormous quantities of coal – everyone knows that there are lurking dangers in all mining work and especially coal mining when you take foreigners and employ them largely in these coal mines. Of what avail is it to post a danger sign in the English language when the man – the great bulk of workers can't even read the sign and couldn't read it, many of them, in their own language.

Common decency, the religion that is supposed to be inherent in us, in fact, everything that goes to promote civilization, in my judgment, should compel us as a nation to take a hold of this terrible situation and correct it and correct it at once! (Applause)

Now, as to Ohio's part in this great war and in this peace. I want to say first as to the peace: I happen to know that there is being organized in this country what is known as the American Legion, composed of those men, whether soldiers or sailors, who took active part in this war. I happen to know that this organization proclaims, and up to date has lived up to its profession that it will forever bar out partisan politics, but that it is going to take an active part in formulating the policies of this country and to that extent engage in politics I shall forever pray. I believe in it. And, I wish to say to you after association for more than two years with the men, particularly the young men (and I have come in contact with at least one hundred thousand of them from the state of Ohio) that I have been with them not only in times of ease but I have been with them in times of trouble and while they were undergoing hardships of all kinds. I have seen them called upon for the performance of all classes of duty in connection with this war. They have accomplished marvelous results. As a matter of fact, they have accomplished everything that has been assigned to them to perform. (Applause) As soldiers I have never met any men anywhere more responsive to discipline, who were more willing to make sacrifices of all kinds, including the supreme sacrifice, the extreme sacrifice of necessity, or who displayed more intelligence and diligence in the performance of that which was assigned to them for performance.

I have an abiding faith that these men, not only insofar as the state of Ohio is concerned but insofar as our great nation is concerned, have come back to you with a broadened intelligence and a higher conception of statesmanship. I unhesitatingly say to you, therefore, that these men can be trusted and must be trusted to take charge of and carry out the great policies of this great commonwealth.

That you can trust them I pledge my honor and my absolute faith! (Applause)

I thank you. (Applause)

...Playing of "America" by Rainbow Division Band...

...ADJOURNMENT...

Program Honoring Lieutenant Commander A.C. Read & Sergeant Alvin C. York
Saturday Morning, July 12, 1919

...The meeting convened at 10:30 o'clock, Mr. Alonzo B. Wilson presiding...
...Singing of "The Star Spangled Banner"

ALONZO B. WILSON:[36]
Let us have it as quiet as possible so that our great guest may speak. We have another guest coming in a few moments. Before introducing one of America's greatest citizens, and possibly for the benefit of our guest who is a stranger and has been busy elsewhere, may I be permitted to say that the Great Centenary Movement of the Methodist Episcopal Church and the Methodist Episcopal Church South is a celebration of one hundred years of missionary effort, and that as a culmination of this campaign which resulted in raising one hundred and sixty-five million dollars for foreign and home work and war reconstruction by these two great denominations this is a celebration of that event, and a million people have gathered here in three weeks or a little more in rejoicing of this the greatest Christian event in the history of any church in the world. (Applause)

We have been making history in these last days and years. We have been adding to the beacon lights of history. In ancient times they had their Abraham and Moses, David, Solomon, and the Christ, and then later Luther and Wesley, and in secular events of achievement we have such men as Stevenson, Fulton, Edison, and Burbank, and so we have been adding others in these days too numerous to mention. But there is one man who has blazed the way for quick achievement in reaching from shore to shore, and laughs at oceans and seas and makes it possible, in emergencies particularly, to get foreign missionaries to other lands – India and China and South America – in a few days, and we hope, thank God, that in these great ships there will not be room like in the present ships to carry missionaries and New England rum at the same time. (Applause) This has been the shame of our America, and we hope it is at an end never to happen again. (Applause)

We have with us today the son of a Baptist preacher who takes naturally to water, and who is not afraid of it. (Applause) He is indirectly with the Methodist Church, his mother-in-law being a devout member of the Methodist Church. (Applause) Adding the influence of fire with that of water you get good, large results. (Applause)

Furthermore, he is a Yankee, a New Englander, a native of New Hampshire. For sixteen years he has been in the United States navy, a busy man, and was selected to achieve one of the great world events, and we are very happy to have him here today as the guest of this Centenary Celebration and Exposition of two Methodisms, that we might welcome him and his wife, and show him, at least, a little honor and expression of our love as American citizens. And so it is my privilege to introduce to you this New Englander, this man from New Hampshire, this man of the American navy whose name will go down in history, and whose name will be honored by our children and our grandchildren for ages to come as the man who blazed the way from shore to shore across the ocean, the first man to go from America over to Europe in an airship – the NC-4.

He will now speak to you. He is not an orator, but a man of the navy, a man of achievement – Lieutenant Commander A.C. Read of the United States Navy. (Applause)

A.C. READ:[37]
Officials of the exposition, I would like first to express the honor that I feel at being a guest in Columbus at the exposition. Ladies and gentlemen, it is not only an honor, that I feel, but it is a great pleasure. One of my relatives was born in Columbus, William Barker Curthing (sic) of the Albermarle fame. (Applause)

I hope that you are not expecting much of an address today, and am glad that you are warned. While my father was a Baptist minister, I did not inherit his gifts or his familiarity with the pulpit. I might tell you in a few words the main features of the first trans-Atlantic flight. (Applause) It was entirely a Navy Department project, and all of the features of the flight were worked out with great care, mostly by others than myself. I had some small part in the preparation and fortunately had a little larger part in the execution.

We had originally intended to have four planes make the trip. This number was reduced to three because one was wrecked early in the period of preparation. The Navy Department hoped to get three across. They thought they would probably get two across. They knew they would get one across! (Applause) We used some battleships. We used most of the destroyer force. We used the entire organization of the Navy Department in making preparations.

Every one gave us the most cordial support, without which the trip would have been impossible. Early in the preparation period we adopted a symbol – "T.A." – for trans-Atlantic. The letters "T.A." were enclosed in a red circle. That symbol we put on all correspondence. Whenever that was seen the officer whose duty it was to carry out the provisions of the letter would put all work aside and give the "T.A." project a clear gangway. In that way the trip was made possible on the date which had been set several months before.

The three of us left Rockaway on the eighth of May. I am sorry to say only one of us landed in Lisbon on the twenty-seventh of May. The NC-4 which finally got across did so after a beginning that brought us the sympathy of all concerned. A few days before we started a fire nearly burned up the machine. The day before we started one of the four propellers cut off the left hand of our leading technician. He was forced to stay behind. A few hours after we started the NC-4 was forced to land eighty miles at sea off Cape Cod with a sick engine. That was about three o'clock in the afternoon. All that afternoon and all the evening following through the night we came in over the water with our two good motors, and we made Chatham at daylight. After getting the plane fixed up with the help of personnel at the Chatham Naval Air Station a northeast gale set in. This was most discouraging.

The other two planes had gone on to Halifax; the day following they had gone on to Newfoundland. But finally the weather cleared and we joined them at Newfoundland. The day after we got in Trepassy (sic) Bay the start of the three planes was made for the Azores. When only a few hundred miles from our objective in the Azores one of the worst fogs that I have ever encountered sprang up. The NC-1 got lost and landed, hoping to find themselves, but found the sea too rough to get off again. They were picked up by a tramp steamer a few hours later. The NC-1 sank a few minutes later.

The NC-3 also got lost. They landed, but they finally, after nearly sixty hours of battling a thirty-foot sea and a fifty-mile gale, sailed stern first two hundred miles and made Ponta del Gada in the Azores under their own power. This was one of the most remarkable feats of seamanship that has ever been accomplished. (Applause)

The last of the three – the NC-4 – finally made Lisbon on the Twenty-seventh of May. The last hop from Lisbon to Plymouth was a very simple affair. We didn't care whether we saw the destroyers or not, we knew that the European continent was off to the right, and we could make it somewhere and get ashore somehow if we had to.

We were received with a remarkable welcome. I have often been asked if the trip was not a great nervous strain, and have always said it was, but the greatest strain was after the real trip was over. They put us through a series of receptions, dinners and luncheons the like of which I have never seen in my life and never expect to see again. (Applause)

In Lisbon we were impressed with the great friendliness that the Portuguese people have for the Americans. In England we were impressed with the sportsmanship of the British people. In France we were impressed with the great enthusiasm that the French have for all things concerned with the art of flying. In England they also have that enthusiasm.

I am sorry to say that on my return to this country I find that the same enthusiasm is lacking. Everybody seems to be afraid of aviation. I cannot blame them much. The papers all feature the few fatalities that occur and every one has the idea that to ride ten minutes in an airplane they are risking their life, and they have something to talk about for the rest of their lives. In a few years a ten minute ride you may pay a few cents for, and think only of the reduction in time to get to where you wish to go.

The British nation has appropriated about five or six times as much for aviation as we are appropriating. This is not the fault of Congress. They generally do what the people back home want them to do. It is the fault, or rather it is a misfortune, of the people at large. They don't know the future of aviation, and they are afraid of it. But we hope that in a few years you will no longer be afraid of it, for it is one of the coming things, and there is a greater field open for aviation than anything else I know of in the line of science.

I hope you will forgive me for this little propaganda. There are so many people here that I couldn't resist the temptation. (Prolonged Applause)

...Three cheers were given for Commander Read...
...Singing of "America"...
...Singing of "The Star Spangled Banner"...
...Sergeant York entered the coliseum amid wild cheering and applause...

THE CHAIRMAN:
In the war that has been fought on the other side of the world one dominant feature has characterized the United States of America – that is, we have today a country that is united from the Great Lakes to the Gulf, and from the Atlantic to the Pacific, in one great democratic ideal. (Applause) And the South has contributed so much to the success of the war – (Applause) – that it is only fitting to have a man of the South to introduce Sergeant York. (Applause) Therefore, we have brought a man from the South – Dr. W.B. Beauchamp, the chairman of our Centenary Program Committee – to introduce a tall man from the South – so tall that he outstripped the Tennessee mountains. (Applause) It is now my privilege to introduce Dr. Beauchamp, who will introduce the tall man.

W.B. BEAUCHAMP:[38]
Whatever might be believed concerning apostolic succession, I am very certain that this magnificent audience will agree that I am in the line of Dr. Fisher. (Applause) It is a distinguished honor to stand just for a moment before this audience to introduce to them formally the most famous single soldier of the great war which has just closed. (Applause)

I am sure after what Dr. Fisher has said, which is voiced absolutely in the South, that we are one country without any sort of distinction; that no section of this country would take exception to the very great pride which we have in the South in regard to the soldiers which we have produced from the time of George Washington until now. (Applause)

I feel somewhat disturbed that Sergeant York isn't from Virginia, (Applause) but he is very close to it, and many of the great Tennesseans went from Virginia, so we are close kin to him. I asked Sergeant York coming out if he would mind telling me just a little of that hot spot where the wonderful thing took place. (Applause) Now I have found that Sergeant York's heroism is only equaled by his modesty. (Applause) And it was very difficult to get all I wanted, and I didn't get it. I have this much from him, which was published as you may remember in the Saturday Evening Post of April 26th, that in that hot spot in the Argonne Forest when this adventure closed there were twenty-five Germans on the field left dead, thirty-five machine guns captured, and a hundred and thirty-two German prisoners. (Applause)

Now, somebody from New York said today: "If we just could have found nineteen other Yorks that would have been all that was necessary to send across the sea." (Applause) There is a note, which you will find immediately when Sergeant York speaks for a little while, as long as he will – for nobody can get him to talk as long as they want him to talk – that the first note and the last note of what he says is a great personal religious faith. (Applause)

It seems a rather striking conjunction of these events that the greatest religious missionary occasion that the world has ever seen, which Methodism has been putting forth here in Columbus, should have as one of their honored guests today the most distinguished soldier that comes back to us from across the seas, and the most distinguished soldier, perhaps, in all the world. (Applause) I take pleasure, therefore, in introducing to you Sergeant Alvin C. York, also Colonel on the staff of Governor Roberts of Tennessee. (Great Applause)

ALVIN C. YORK:[39]
Ladies and gentlemen, I feel it a high honor to me to have the privilege of standing before this audience this morning. Had it not been for the invitation that I received to come to Columbus, I might have never met many of you who are here today. So I feel that I am highly honored and I would be glad – more than glad – if I could deliver unto you a speech or some kind of an address that would interest you this morning, as I am not a speaker, but just a country boy from the mountains of Tennessee. (Applause) But I can say that being a country boy I do live and practice a full salvation. (Applause)

In regard to fighting in foreign countries, I have but very little to say about that; (Applause) for I feel that what we have to say about the fighting is in honor to God, for God was with the American army, and without the hand of God we could not have accomplished what we did. (Applause)

I further want to say that I have learned by self-experience that if we will be true followers of Jesus Christ and be soldiers for him that we can be far better soldiers for our country. (Applause) If we go into any kind of business, if we want to make a success we have to have some kind of an organization to back us up that is able to push us through, and I am most sure when we go into the soldier warfare for Jesus Christ that we have a backing that will shove us through, if we will stand true. (Applause)

I started out in this Christian warfare some number of years before I went to the army, and when I went to the army I practiced this full salvation just the same as I did when I was in civilian clothes. When I was on the battlefield I was continuously in prayer to God to protect me and to help me that I might return to America without one scratch from the Germans. I didn't get it! (Prolonged Applause)

So therefore you cannot make me doubt anything regarding the full salvation and answer to prayer, for God is the God who will answer prayer and who will hold us up if we will only look to Him and Him alone. (Applause)

Now, as a great many have been asking me what I am most interested in – some may think I am most interested in moving pictures or vaudeville or something like that – well, I am not! (Applause) The thing I am most interested in is Christianity, and what can I do for to help those who have drifted away from God and need help to come back unto him. (Applause) I think that is one of the greatest works that any man or any woman can get into – to help spread the gospel, and to help lift up the fallen.

You may think sometimes that people get down so low that they cannot be lifted, but God can lift any one, and I want to say as I said just a moment ago that I am more than glad to be here today, and I am sorry that I cannot stay longer than today, but owing to the fact that my wife has been sick I will have to return tonight. I would be glad to stay longer but I cannot under those circumstances. So I thank you all. (Prolonged Applause)

...The audience stood and sang "The Battle Hymn of the Republic"...

...ADJOURNMENT...

Notes

1. Homer Clyde Stuntz (1858-1924). Stuntz was an ordained minister with the Upper Iowa Conference of the Methodist Episcopal Church. He transferred to the South India Conference and worked as a missionary and editor of the *Bombay Guardian* and *Indian Witness*. He later served in the Philippines. In 1912, he was elected bishop and assigned to South America. During World War One Stuntz served as Administrator of War Work for the Methodist Episcopal Church. He authored *The Philippines and the Far East* (Cincinnati: Jennings and Pye; New York: Eaton and Mains, 1904); and *South American Neighbors* (New York and Cincinnati: Methodist Book Concern, 1916).

2. James Atkins (1850-1923). Atkins was educated at Emory and Henry College. He was an ordained minister with the Methodist Episcopal Church, South. Atkins served as president of the Asheville Female College and Emory and Henry College. He was elected bishop in 1906 and chaired the Centenary Commission of the MECS. Atkins was an advocate for Christian education, edited Sunday School materials, and authored several books and hymnals including *The Kingdom in the Cradle* (Nashville: Publishing House of the M.E. Church, South, 1905); and *The Young People's Hymnal, No. 3: Adapted to the use of Sunday Schools, Epworth Leagues, Prayer Meetings, and Revivals* (Nashville and Dallas: Publishing House of the M.E. Church, South, 1911).

3. "case belli" can be translated "case for war."

4. Bishop Atkins may have stated "crack of the door" instead of "crack of the doom."

5. Wilbur Patterson Thirkield (1854-1936). Thirkield was educated at Ohio Wesleyan University and Boston University School of Theology. He was an ordained minister with the Methodist Episcopal Church and served as Dean of the Gammon Theological School. Thirkield later became general secretary of the Freedmen's Aid Society and was elected bishop in 1912. He authored several books including *Service and Prayers for Church and Home* (New York: Methodist Book Concern, 1920); and *The English-speaking Peoples: Will they Fail in their Mission to the World?* (New York and Cincinnati: The Abingdon Press, 1926).

6. Thirkield appears to reference the 369th Brigade of the U.S. Army. The 369th was the first unit of African American soldiers to fight for the U.S. Army in World War One. For additional information see Stephen L. Harris, *Harlem's Hell Fighters: The African-American 369th Infantry in World War One* (Washington, DC: Brassey's, Inc., 2003).

7. Thirkield references the 1917 East St. Louis Riot. The riot was one of the worst race-related riots in U.S. history. See Harper Barnes, *Never Been a Time: The 1917 Race Riot that sparked the Civil Rights Movement* (New York: Walker & Company, 2008).

8. Bogalusa, Louisiana

9. Participants with the 'City Beautiful' movement attempted to revitalize urban development by cleaning up public parks, starting new building projects, and creating spaces of leisure. The City Beautiful pageant at the exposition evidenced the work of American Methodists toward urban development and also attended to concerns related to the religious revitalization of American cities. For contextual information on 'City Beautiful' see Joaquin Miller, *The Building of City Beautiful* (Trenton, NJ: Albert Brandt, 1905). For further analysis of the movement see William Henry Wilson, *The City Beautiful Movement* (Baltimore, MD: Johns Hopkins University Press, 1989).

10. John Monroe Moore (1867-1948). Moore was educated at Lebanon University (OH) and Yale University. He received several honorary doctorates from schools throughout the United States. He was an ordained minister with the Methodist Episcopal Church, South, and served churches in Missouri and Texas. Moore was elected bishop in 1918 and assigned to Brazil, South America for several years. He also worked as editor of the *Nashville Christian Advocate* and served on the Joint Committee on Unification. He authored several books including *The South To-day* (New York: Methodist Book Concern, 1916); and *Making the World Christian: Essential Objectives in Missionary Endeavor* (New York: George H. Doran Co., 1922).

11. Henry Roe Cloud (1884-1950). Cloud was educated at Yale University, Oberlin College, and Auburn Theological Seminary. He was Winnebago and a minister in the Presbyterian tradition. Cloud was the first Native American to receive a Bachelor's degree from Yale and later founded the American Indian Institute in Wichita, Kansas. For additional information see Joel Pfister, *The Yale Indian: The Education of Henry Roe Cloud* (Durham, NC: Duke University Press, 2009); and David W. Messer, *Henry Roe Cloud: A Biography* (Lanham, MD: Hamilton Books, 2010).

12. For biographical sketches of Native American leaders see Bruce E. Johansen and Donald A. Grinde, eds., *The Encyclopedia of Native American Biography: Six hundred Life Stories of Important People from Powhatan to Wilma Mankiller* (New York: H. Holt, 1997).

13. For additional information on Native Americans and the Great War see Thomas A. Britten, *American Indians in World War I: At Home and at War* (Albuquerque: University of New Mexico Press, 1997).

14. The American Indian Citizenship Act, passed by the U.S. Congress on June 2, 1924, granted citizenship to all Native Americans born in the United States. For additional information on early 20th century Native Americans, citizenship, and the "Indian problem" see Lucy Maddox, *Citizen Indians: Native American Intellectuals, Race, and Reform* (Ithaca, NY: Cornell University Press, 2005).

15. Francis John McConnell (1871-1953). McConnell was educated at Ohio Wesleyan University and Boston University. He was an elder in the New England Annual Conference of the Methodist Episcopal Church and the Methodist Church. McConnell served as President of the Federal Council of the Churches of Christ in America and was an active participant in the Methodist Federation for Social Action.

16. Peter Cartwright (1785-1872). Cartwright was self-educated and converted to Methodism at a camp meeting in 1801. He was an ordained minister with the Methodist Episcopal Church and served churches and circuits in Indiana, Kentucky, Ohio, and Tennessee. In 1846, Cartwright ran for the Illinois State Legislature and lost the seat to future U.S. President Abraham Lincoln. See Robert Bray, *Peter Cartwright: Legendary Frontier Preacher* (Urbana: University of Illinois Press, 2005).

17. Frederick Jackson Turner was a professor at the University of Wisconsin and Harvard University. His controversial "Frontier Thesis" examined how the "frontier" had shaped American history and society. See Frederick Jackson Turner and John Mack Faragher, *Rereading Frederick Jackson Turner: The Significance of the Frontier in American History, and other Essays* (New Haven, CT: Yale University Press, 1998).

18. Christian Socialism is a contested ideology that combats capitalism through the use of biblical texts and societal application. McConnell's address identifies his intellectual warmth for the movement while at the same time he is careful to distance himself from actual practice. For Methodist audiences that day McConnell's attendance at socialist meetings would have been somewhat controversial. Seminal 19th and early 20th century authors included Fredrick Denison Maurice, *The Kingdom of Christ* (New York: D. Appleton and Co., 1843); and Adin Ballou, *Practical Christian Socialism: A Conversational Exposition of the True* (Fowlers and Wells, 1854).

19. For further examination regarding Methodists and early film see Christopher J. Anderson, "To 'Elevate Unfortunate Humanity' Onscreen: Linking World War I and Protestant Missions through Silent Film," *Journal of Religion and Film* 12:2 (October 2008) <http://www.unomaha.edu/jrf/vol12no2/Anderson_SilentFilm.htm>.

20. The title of the hymn is "There is a Land of Pure Delight" from George Dawson ed., *Psalms and Hymns* (London: E. Theobald, Paternoster Row, 1853), 472-473.

21. Julian Shakespeare Carr (1845-1924). Carr was educated at the University of North Carolina-Chapel Hill and was a member of the Methodist Episcopal Church, South. He fought for the Confederate States of America during the Civil War and was later given the title "General" by the North Carolina branch of the United Confederate Veterans. Carr was instrumental as a benefactor for Duke University. See Mena Webb, *Jule Carr: General without an Army* (University of North Carolina Press, 1987).

22. Newton Diehl Baker, Jr. (1871-1937). Baker was Secretary of War during the Woodrow Wilson administration.

23. William Gibbs McAdoo (1863-1941). McAdoo was educated at the University of Tennessee-Knoxville and practiced law in Tennessee, New York, and California. He was instrumental in the development of the mass-transit tunnel system into New York now used by Amtrak, New Jersey Transit, and the Long Island Railroad. McAdoo would later serve as Secretary of the Treasury during the U.S. presidency of Woodrow Wilson. He published an autobiography *Crowded Years: The Reminiscences of William G. McAdoo* (Boston and New York: Houghton Mifflin, 1931).

24. A portion of this speech was published in 1919. See William McAdoo, *A League to Prevent War: With a Review of the Fight against the Formation of the United States* (New York: League to Enforce Peace, 1919); and "The League of Nations," *New Outlook* 122:9 (July 2, 1919): 367-372.

25. Excerpt from the William Watson poem "To the Invincible Republic." See William Watson, *New Poems by William Watson* (New York: John Lane Company, 1909), 26-28.

26. Elihu Root, *League of Nations: Letters of the Honorable Elihu Root relative to the League of Nations* (Washington, DC: Government Printing Office, 1919), 14.

27. The British airship R-34 commanded by Major George Herbert Scott left Edinburgh, Scotland on July 2, 1919. The ship landed on Long Island, New York on July 6. "Giant Airship Starts for New York," *New York Times*, July 2, 1919, 1.

28. The NC-4 U.S. Navy Curtiss flying boat was the first airplane to cross the Atlantic Ocean. The trip began at Rockaway, New York, and continued until May 31, 1919 with a landing in Plymouth, England. The plane was piloted by Albert C. Read.

Read addressed exposition audiences concerning the flight later in this chapter. The Newfoundland to Ireland flight mentioned in the address took place in June, 1919, by two British pilots flying a Vickers Vimy bomber. This flight was the first non-stop flight over the Atlantic in an airplane. See National Archives and Record Administration, Photographs of Flying Boat NC-4 and of Airship C-2, 1919-1919 accessed January 23, 2012, http://research.archives.gov/description/535426.

29. The Federal Reserve Act, enacted by the U.S. Congress on December 23, 1913, established a central banking system in the United States. The Act was signed by U.S. President Woodrow Wilson. See Gerard P. Walsh, *Federal Reserve Act of 1913: With Amendments and Laws related to Banking* (Washington, DC: U.S.G.P.O., 1981).

30. The Federal Farm Loan Act, enacted by the U.S. Congress on July 17, 1916, provided credit loans to U.S. farmers and their families. The Act was signed into law by U.S. President Woodrow Wilson. See Stuart W. Shulman, "The Origin of the Federal Farm Loan Act: Issue emergence and agenda setting in the Progressive Era Print," in *Fighting for the Farm: Rural America Transformed*, Jane Adams, ed., (Philadelphia: University of Pennsylvania Press, 2003), 113-128.

31. Harry Lester Smith (1876-1951). Smith was educated at Allegheny College, Drew Theological Seminary, and Columbia University. He was an ordained minister with the Pittsburgh Annual Conference of the Methodist Episcopal Church and served several churches in Michigan, New Jersey, New York, and Pennsylvania. He was elected bishop in 1920 and assigned to India and later several annual conferences in the United States.

32. Lewis Cass Laylin (1848-1923). Laylin was a lawyer and Speaker of the House of Representatives for the State of Ohio. He was elected later as Secretary of State for Ohio. *The Ohio Hundred Year Book: A Handbook of the Public Men and Public Institutions of Ohio from the formation of the North-west Territory (1787) to July 1, 1901* (Columbus, OH: Fred J. Heer, State printer, 1901), 422.

33. Josephus Daniels (1862-1948). Daniels was an editor, author, Secretary of the U.S. Navy, and U.S. Ambassador to Mexico. He was educated at the University of North Carolina Law School and received several honorary doctorates. Daniels was editor of the *Raleigh News and Observer* and was active in the Prohibition movement as a Democrat. He was appointed Secretary of the U.S. Navy upon the election of his close friend Woodrow Wilson to the presidency. As Secretary he abolished the consumption of alcohol by officers and soldiers. In 1933 he was appointed Ambassador to Mexico by Franklin D. Roosevelt.

34. In 1917 the *SS Vaterland* was renamed the *SS Leviathan*.

35. Edwin Forbes Glenn (1857-1926). Glenn was educated at the United States Military Academy and earned a law degree in 1891. He served the U.S. Army in the Philippines and during World War I. He attained the rank of Major General in 1917. The "Glenn Highway" is a part of U.S. 1 in Alaska. A section of U.S. 1was named after Glenn as a result of his Alaskan expeditionary work in 1898. In 1902, Glenn was brought under charges for using water cure torture (today known as waterboarding) in the Philippines during the Spanish-American War. He received a one month suspension of military duties. See Leon Friedman, *The Law of War: A Documentary History, Volume One* (New York: Random House, 1972), 814ff.; and University of Alaska-Anchorage and Alaska Pacific University Consortium Library, *Guide to Edwin F. Glenn Papers*, 1889-1917, accessed January 23, 2012, http://consortiumlibrary.org/archives/FindingAids/hmc-0116.html.

36. Alonzo E. Wilson was a member of the National Prohibition Party and served as president of the Lincoln Chautauqua Circuit. He edited *The American Prohibition Year Book* and also compiled a 400-page record of the Centenary exposition, *Methodist Centenary Celebration, State Fair Grounds, Columbus, Ohio, June 20-July 13, 1919, Official Reports and Records* (S.l.: The author, 1919).

37. Lieutenant Commander Albert C. Read was Commanding Officer and Navigator for the U.S. Navy NC-4 seaplane. For additional information on Read and an account of the NC program and transatlantic flight see G.C. Westervelt, H.C. Richardson, and A.C. Read, *The Triumph of the N.C's* (Garden City, New York, and London: Doubleday, Page & Company, 1920).

38. William Benjamin Beauchamp (1869-1931). Beauchamp was educated at Randolph-Macon College and Vanderbilt University. He was an ordained minister with the Methodist Episcopal Church, South, and served in several churches in Kentucky and Virginia. Beauchamp was general secretary of the Laymen's Missionary Movement and director of the Centenary Fund capital campaign for the MECS. He was elected bishop in 1922 and assigned to Belgium, Czechoslovakia, Mexico, and Poland.

39. Alvin Cullum York (1887-1964). York served in the 82nd Infantry Division of the U.S. Army. In 1918, he received the Medal of Honor and became one of the most memorable figures of World War One. He was a member of the Church of Christ in Christian Union. For an autobiographical sketch see Alvin Cullum York and Thomas John Skeyhill, *Sergeant York: His Own Life Story and War Diary* (Garden City, NY: Doubleday, Doran, and Company, Inc., 1928).

Appendix:

Images and Photos of Participants in the 1919 Methodist Missionary Fair, A Centenary Celebration of American Methodist Missions

288 *Appendix*

**Image of front cover from
Centenary Exposition Souvenir Program**

Methodist Library Collection,
Drew University, Madison, New Jersey, USA

**View from Airplane of Centenary Exposition,
Columbus, Ohio, USA**

Easterbrook Collection, Methodist Library,
Drew University, Madison, New Jersey, USA

Kraal Exhibit in Africa Building, Centenary Exposition, Columbus, Ohio, USA

Easterbrook Collection, Methodist Library,
Drew University, Madison, New Jersey, USA

Appendix 291

**View of crowds at Centenary Exposition,
Columbus, Ohio, USA**

Mission Albums Collection,
General Commission on Archives and History,
The United Methodist Church, Madison, New Jersey, USA

Sketch of Entrance Archway for the Centenary Exposition, Columbus, Ohio, USA

Easterbrook Collection, Methodist Library, Drew University, Madison, New Jersey, USA

Appendix 293

**View of storefront exhibit in China Building,
Centenary Exposition,
Columbus, Ohio, USA**

Mission Albums Collection,
General Commission on Archives and History,
The United Methodist Church, Madison, New Jersey, USA

**Image of motion picture and lantern screen,
Centenary Exposition, Columbus, Ohio, USA**

Easterbrook Collection, Methodist Library,
Drew University, Madison, New Jersey, USA

Appendix 295

Parade on grounds of the Centenary Exposition, Columbus, Ohio, USA

Mission Albums Collection,
General Commission on Archives and History,
The United Methodist Church, Madison, New Jersey, USA

**Woman's Christian Temperance Union exhibit,
Centenary Exposition, Columbus, Ohio, USA**

Mission Albums Collection,
General Commission on Archives and History,
The United Methodist Church, Madison, New Jersey, USA

Appendix 297

**Image of Japanese child at Centenary Exposition,
Columbus, Ohio, USA**

Easterbrook Collection, Methodist Library,
Drew University, Madison, New Jersey, USA

Image of Native Americans and missionaries at Centenary Exposition, Columbus, Ohio, USA

Mission Albums Collection,
General Commission on Archives and History,
The United Methodist Church, Madison, New Jersey, USA

**Stage at Coliseum of Centenary Exposition,
Columbus, Ohio, USA**

Mission Albums Collection,
General Commission on Archives and History,
The United Methodist Church, Madison, New Jersey, USA

Bishop Joseph Crane Hartzell

Mission Albums Collection, Portraits #1,
General Commission on Archives and History,
The United Methodist Church, Madison, New Jersey, USA

Bishop Alexander Priestly Camphor

Mission Albums Collection, Portraits #1,
General Commission on Archives and History,
The United Methodist Church, Madison, New Jersey, USA

Reverend Edwin Field Frease

Mission Albums Collection, Portraits #2,
General Commission on Archives and History,
The United Methodist Church, Madison, New Jersey, USA

Bishop Isaiah Benjamin Scott

Mission Albums Collection, Portraits #1,
General Commission on Archives and History,
The United Methodist Church, Madison, New Jersey, USA

Reverend Charles Albert Tindley

Mission Albums Collection,
General Commission on Archives and History,
The United Methodist Church, Madison, New Jersey, USA

Bishop Robert Elijah Jones

Methodist Library Image Collection,
Drew University, Madison, New Jersey, USA

Reverend Irving Garland Penn

Mission Albums Collection, Portraits #3,
General Commission on Archives and History,
The United Methodist Church, Madison, New Jersey, USA

Bishop Randall Albert Carter

Methodist Library Image Collection,
Drew University, Madison, New Jersey, USA

Belle H. Bennett

Mission Albums Collection, Portraits #1,
General Commission on Archives and History,
The United Methodist Church, Madison, New Jersey, USA

Appendix 309

Madame Kaji Yajima

Mission Albums Collection, Portraits #3,
General Commission on Archives and History,
The United Methodist Church, Madison, New Jersey, USA

Martha E. Drummer

Mission Albums Collection,
General Commission on Archives and History,
The United Methodist Church, Madison, New Jersey, USA

Anna Adams Gordon

Mission Albums Collection, Portraits #3,
General Commission on Archives and History,
The United Methodist Church, Madison, New Jersey, USA

Reverend Clarence True Wilson

Mission Albums Collection, Portraits #3,
General Commission on Archives and History,
The United Methodist Church, Madison, New Jersey, USA

Appendix 313

S. Earl Taylor

Mission Albums Collection, Portraits #2,
General Commission on Archives and History,
The United Methodist Church, Madison, New Jersey, USA

Reverend William Washington Pinson

Mission Albums Collection, Portraits #3,
General Commission on Archives and History,
The United Methodist Church, Madison, New Jersey, USA

Reverend Harry Lester Smith

Mission Albums Collection, Portraits #4,
General Commission on Archives and History,
The United Methodist Church, Madison, New Jersey, USA

William Jennings Bryan

Mission Albums Collection, Portraits #4,
General Commission on Archives and History,
The United Methodist Church, Madison, New Jersey, USA

Bishop James Cannon, Jr.

Methodist Library Image Collection,
Drew University, Madison, New Jersey, USA

318 *Appendix*

Reverend John Monroe Moore

Mission Albums Collection, Portraits #4,
General Commission on Archives and History,
The United Methodist Church, Madison, New Jersey, USA

Reverend Homer Clyde Stuntz

Mission Albums Collection, Portraits #3,
General Commission on Archives and History,
The United Methodist Church, Madison, New Jersey, USA

Reverend Wilbur Patterson Thirkield

Mission Albums Collection, Portraits #4,
General Commission on Archives and History,
The United Methodist Church, Madison, New Jersey, USA

Josephus Daniels, Secretary of the U.S. Navy

Mission Albums Collection, Portraits #2,
General Commission on Archives and History,
The United Methodist Church, Madison, New Jersey, USA

Reverend William Benjamin Beauchamp

Mission Albums Collection, Portraits #2,
General Commission on Archives and History,
The United Methodist Church, Madison, New Jersey, USA

**Lieutenant Commander Albert C. Read and
Sergeant Alvin C. York**

Methodist Library Collection,
Drew University, Madison, New Jersey, USA

Index

Abbott, Lyman 55
Abt, Martha E. 71, 93-99
Abuse 33, 193
Adams, Samuel 164
Addison, Joseph 61
Africa
 Algeria, 24-25, 28; Angola 88; Carthage 24; Constantine City 25; Congo (Belgian) 13, 18, 20-23; Egypt 24, 27, 56, 149; Ethiopia 16; Gold Coast 17-18; Liberia 17-20, 88, 116; Libya (Tripoli) 24-25; Madeira Island 18, 149; Morocco 24-25; Rhodesia 17, 23; Sahara Desert 25-26; Tunisia 25, 28
African Americans
 "Black Mammy" 62; Church Leadership 14, 50-54; Citizenship 34-35, 37, 45-49, 62-63; Colonization to Africa 44, 54, 66; Discrimination 49, 62, 67, 213, 223; Emancipation 14, 56, 66; Illiteracy 45, 56, 274; Interracial Marriage 38; Lynching 4, 14, 37, 45-50, 58, 66-67, 213, 224; Military 45-46, 54, 57-60, 80, 223-224, 282; Music 15, 41, 121, 187, 201, 220, 222-223; Representation 55-58; Slavery 14, 42, 56-57, 146, 171-172
African Methodist Episcopal Church 2
Airplane/Airship
 NC-1 279; NC-3 279; NC-4 278-279; 284
Alabama 50, 64, 67, 183, 204-205, 211, 223
Alaska 22, 83, 170-171, 181

Alaska Pacific University 285
Albert of Prussia, Frederick William Victor (Kaiser) 35, 246, 251, 262
Albion College 134, 210
Alcohol (Alcoholism) 4, 9, 57, 72, 96-97, 139, 141-143, 149-150, 153-154, 158-161, 163, 168, 170, 176, 178, 180-181, 185, 194-196, 199, 203-207, 212, 214, 285
Alienists 98
Allegheny College 285
Allegheny Mountains 231
Allen University 68
American Baptist Churches, USA 5
American Federation of Labor 14, 50, 67
American Indian Citizenship Act 227-228; 283
American Indian Institute 283
American Missionary Association 68
American Party (Political) 210
American Red Cross 78, 90, 96, 99, 219, 270
American Revolutionary War 177, 220
American Social Health Association 140
Americanization 9, 84, 95, 136, 151, 156-158, 182, 208, 213, 226, 236
Amherst College 212
Amusements
 Billiard Table 126; Bowling Alley 126-127, 130; Dancing 127
Anarchy 182, 232, 242
Anderson, William H. 177
Andujar, Lily E. Kurzenknabe 149, 207
Angel Island 66
Anti-Saloon League 73, 142-143, 177-180, 182-186, 194, 198

325

Anthony, Susan B. 100
Antietam, Battle of 35
Appalachia, People of 82, 189-190, 222
Appomattox Court House 35
Argentina 142, 156, 160, 208
Arizona 100, 180-181
Arkansas 65, 108, 211
Armenia 24, 129
Armour Mission (Chicago) 209
Ashville Female College 282
Asquith, Henry Herbert 217
Association Men 8
Astor, John Jacob 217
Athlete, Christian 8
Atkins, James 214, 220-222, 224-225, 268-269, 282
Atkinson, Virginia M. 89, 137
Atkinson Academy for Boys 137
Atlanta Annual Conference (MEC) 210
Atlantic Ocean 24, 74, 192, 196, 209-210, 246, 273, 275, 279, 281
Attucks, Crispus 35, 46, 66
Auburn Theological Seminary 283
Australia 104, 145, 149, 176
Austria 191, 195, 200, 244-245, 247-248
Autocracy 54, 149, 236-241
Automobile 5, 24, 126, 176, 180-181, 192
Baker, Newton Diehl Jr. 239, 284
Baker, Purley Albert 142, 177, 182-186, 210-211
Baker University 138
Baldwin, Francis Everett 112, 119, 139
Baldwin-Wallace College 135
Baltimore and Richmond Christian Advocate 139
Bantu People 56
Baptists 5, 60-61, 108, 266, 277-278
Barbary Wars 28, 65
Barge, Carrie 90-91, 137
Barnes, Mary Emelia Clarke 151, 208-209
Basuto People 63
Bateman's Drops 204
Baumwell, Maria Regina 160
Bay of Bengal 29
Beauchamp, William B. 280-281, 286
Belgium 22, 171, 214, 216, 244, 248-249, 281
Bell Telephone Company 56

Bennett, Belle H. 73, 75-77, 81, 85-86, 88-90, 134
Bennett College 63, 66
Bennett College Quintet 121
Berber Peoples 24-25
Berlin, Irving 129, 140
Bible
    Abraham 238, 277; Book of Revelation 238; David 26, 45, 277; Devil 43, 126-127, 164, 183, 199, 231, 235; Goliath 26; Herod, King 88, 194; Moses 277; St. Paul 73-74, 219; Saul of Tarsus 198; Sermon on the Mount 108, 115; Solomon 277; Ten Commandments 108; Virgin Birth 74
Biblical Seminary of New York 65
Birmingham-Southern College 138
Birth of a Nation 66, 129, 140
Bitzer, Johann G. W. "Billy" 140
Black Hawk, Chief 228
Blackstone College for Girls 42, 66, 139
Blake, Edgar 109-111, 139
Bolshevism 36, 47, 50, 177, 227-228, 244, 269-270
Bombay Guardian 282
Boole, Ella A. 167-171, 209-210
Boston Common 35, 46
Boston Massacre 35
Boston University 10, 134, 138, 280
Boston University School of Theology 66, 134, 139, 279
Brady, William A. 129, 140
Bragg, Braxton 148
Brainerd, David 229
Brazil 134, 283
Brewer, Isaac W. 57
Brewster, William N. 5, 10
Bridge Whist Club (New York) 127
Brigham Young University 136
British Women's Temperance Association 157
Browning Industrial Home 136
Brum, Baltazar 159
Bryan, William Jennings 2, 9, 141-143, 166, 183, 193-201, 211-212
Bulgaria 46, 244
Bulkley, Daisy McLain 71, 85-87, 136
Burma (Republic of the Union of Myanmar) 29, 81, 149

Butler, Clementina 89, 136
Calhoun, John C. 176
California 33, 122, 124, 135, 140, 180, 210, 284
Camphor, Alexander Priestly 8, 13, 17-21, 64
Canada 13, 22-23, 64, 104, 136, 149, 176, 180, 251, 279, 285
Cannon, James Jr. 2, 9, 72, 111-112, 139, 163-165, 171-177, 179, 187-189, 194, 201, 206, 213, 217-221
Caribbean Sea 216
Carr, Julian S. 62, 239, 258, 284
Carter, Randall Albert 8, 14, 55-58
Cartwright, Peter 231, 283
Centenary Celebration of American Methodist Missions
    African Day 8, 13, 16; African Desert 8; Americanization Day 213, 226, 236; Army Day 214, 268; Minute Men Convention 72, 121; Minute Men Day 71-72, 105; National Woman's Party Meeting 100; Navy Day 214, 259; Negro Day 8, 13-14, 31, 33, 39, 41-42; Peace Signing Celebration 213, 216; Prohibition Day 142, 187; Southern Day 13-14, 59, 61; Temperance Rally 163; Victory Day 214, 239; Woman's Christian Temperance Union Program 141, 144; Woman's Day 9, 71-73, 93, 134, 141, 148
Centenary College (TN) 211
Centenary Fund 4, 6, 286
Central Alabama Institute 64
Central College (Missouri) 64
Central Illinois Annual Conference (MEC) 64
Central Intelligence Agency 208
Central Tennessee College 63
Character
    Individual 57, 71, 87-88, 158, 161, 174; Nation 87, 114, 162
Chatham Air Naval Station 279
Chautauqua Institution 151, 156-157, 207-208, 211, 286
Cherrington, Ernest H. 175, 177, 210
Chicago Political Equality League 125, 137

Chicago Preachers' Meeting 125
China 17, 46, 77-78, 81-84, 89, 113, 118, 130-132, 136-138, 141-142, 148-151, 153-156, 183, 188, 203, 224, 229, 272, 277
Christian, William Asbury 14, 42-45, 66
Christian Americanization 84, 136
Christian Civilization 1, 5, 24, 192, 241
Christian Church (Disciples of Christ) 5
Christianization 9, 213-214
Church Missionary Society 3
Church of Christ in Christian Union 195, 286
City Beautiful Movement 226, 283
Civil Rights 2, 52, 213, 245
Civil War (War Between the States) 50, 102-103, 113, 117, 171, 183, 206, 220-221, 224, 242
Clair, Matthew 63
Clark, Elmer T. 72, 105-108, 129-133, 138-139
Clark University 136, 210
Clay, Henry 176
Clemenceau, Georges Benjamin 29, 65
Clinton, George 243
Cloud, Henry Roe 9, 213-214, 226-230, 283
Coggin, John Nelson Clark 182, 186, 210
College of West Africa (Monrovia Seminary) 64-65
Colonization 3, 64-66
Colonial Exhibition 3, 7
Colorado 49, 138, 181, 211
Colored (Christian) Methodist Episcopal Church 14, 55, 68
Columbia University 207, 285
Community Centers 93, 127
Confederate States of America 284
Congregational Church 209
Congress (U.S.)
    65th Congress 150, 167; 66th Congress 167
Conneaut, Duchess of 80
Connecticut 65, 242
Constitution (U.S.) 28, 47, 100, 117,

166, 169, 172, 175-176, 186-187, 189, 191-193, 195, 206, 211, 242-244, 250, 255, 257
Cornelia, Statue of 148
Cornstalk (Hokoleskwa) 228
Cox, Melville B. 64
Cranston, Earl 187-188, 211
Crawford, Daniel 56
Croix de Guerre 62, 223
Cushing, William Barker 278
Czechoslovakia 171, 243, 281
Daniels, Josephus 9, 72, 110, 112-120, 139-140, 214, 259-267, 285
Darrow, Clarence 97, 211
Darwin, Charles 211
Davis, A.B. 97
Davis, Jefferson 176
Decatur, Steven Jr. 28, 65
Declaration of Independence 188, 220, 241
Delaware Annual Conference (MEC) 64, 66
Delirium Tremens 195, 212
Democracy
  Christian 46, 269; Doctrine of 5, 34, 40, 46-49, 52-53, 59-60, 62, 87, 154, 191, 196, 217-218, 223, 229, 231, 240-244, 246, 257, 269, 280; "Make the World Safe for" 49, 59, 223, 269
Democratic Party 101, 104, 211-212, 214
Denmark 144
Department of Public Welfare 72, 93
DePauw University 139
Dickey, J.H. 108
Diffendorfer, Ralph E. 4, 10
Disabilities 71, 98-99, 138
District of Columbia (Washington) 9, 75, 77, 100-103, 107, 138, 146, 148, 150, 167, 176, 182, 186, 210, 228, 263, 266
Douglas, Stephen 183
Douglass, Frederick 14, 56
Doyle, James 13, 22-23
Drew Theological Seminary 5, 134, 280
Drug Trafficking 143, 202-203, 210
Drummer, Martha E. 83-84, 131
Duke University 279
Dunbar, Paul L. 14, 56

East Calvary (Tindley Temple) Methodist Episcopal Church 14, 32
East St. Louis Race Riot 49, 208, 218-220, 277
Edison, Thomas 141, 272
Eggleston, Edward 110
Eighteenth Amendment 143, 164, 181, 201
Electoral College (U.S.) 95
Eliot, George 110, 134, 217
Eliot, John 224
Elk Club 122
Ellis Island 84, 132, 260
Emancipation 14
Emerson College of Oratory 130
Emory and Henry College 206, 277
Empire 2, 35, 265
England 3, 53, 86, 134, 138, 144, 153, 210-214, 216-217, 227-228, 247, 274, 279, 285
Epworth League (MEC) 133
Evangelical Methodist Church of France 25, 65, 221
Evangelist (Evangelism) 21, 112, 115, 132, 168, 179, 211, 220
Evangelization 19, 23, 27, 72, 75, 213, 227
Evans, Alice Stewart 40
Fakir 8
Federal Council of the Churches of Christ in America 10, 280
Federal Farm Loan System 253, 282
Federal Reserve Act 253, 282
Federalism, British 53-54
Female College of the Methodist Episcopal Church 14, 42
Finland 149, 176
Fisher, Lena Leonard 2, 9, 68, 74-78, 132, 277
Flanders 58, 77
Florida 125
Flynn, John C. 137
Foch, Ferdinand 113, 215, 218, 233
Foraker, Julia A.P. Bundy 144, 204
France 19, 22, 24-25, 27-29, 58, 65, 67, 78, 80-81, 91, 97, 115, 149, 176, 189, 199-201, 205, 214, 216-219, 221, 228, 241-242, 245, 249, 252-254, 257, 259-260, 263, 267-269, 272, 279;

Franklin, Benjamin 31, 239-241, 252
Frease, Edwin Field 23-26, 70
Freedman's Aid Society 14, 59, 61, 64-65, 68, 282
Gage, Charles A. 163
Galloway, Charles Betts 47, 67
Games
  Baseball 86; Boxball 127
Gammon Theological Seminary 63-65, 210, 282
Garfield, James A. 36
Garrett-Evangelical Theological Seminary 64
Garrison, William Lloyd 183
George, Anna Pritchard 150-152, 207
George, Lloyd 115-116, 196, 216, 220
George, William Frederick III 188-189
George Peabody College for Teachers 140
George R. Smith College 65
Georgia 50, 59, 61, 68, 108, 118, 122, 136, 139, 178, 210
Georgia Annual Conference (CMEC) 68
German-Americans 237
Germany 19, 22, 27, 50, 60, 91, 178, 181, 191, 196, 210, 221, 241, 244, 246, 249, 251-254, 260-263;
Gettysburg, Battle of 35
Glenn, Edwin Forbes 214, 268-276, 285
Godfrey's Cordial 204-205
Gordon, Anna Adams 9, 89-90, 137, 141-142, 144-153, 155-157, 159, 165, 207-208
Grant, Ulysses S. 113
Great Lakes Band 105, 280
Grey, Edward 252
Griffith, David W. 8, 11, 66, 126, 140
Griswold College 209
Haddock, George C. 177
Hadley Concert Company 121
Haig, Douglas 79, 91, 116
Hamberg, A.P. 129
Hamilton, Alexander 242-244
Hampton University 67
Hardy, W.H. 120
Harrison Anti-Narcotic Act of 1919 212
Harrison Narcotic Act of 1914 143, 201-204, 212
Hartford Theological Seminary 65
Hartzell, Jennie Culver 77
Hartzell, Joseph Crane 8, 13, 16-18, 20, 22-26, 28, 64
Harvard University 284
Hawai'I 83, 85
Hayes, Lucy 135
Heck, Barbara 76
Heihachiro, Togo 28, 65
Helms, Mary 77
Hendrix College 138
Hester, Everett Knight 93, 137
Hickens, Ben 108
Hickman, E.C. 216, 220
Hill, James J. 22
Hollywood 8
Holston Annual Conference (MECS) 211
Hooker, Joseph 148
Hoover, Herbert 94-95, 135
Hope Academy and College 65
Hospital 5, 13, 21, 28, 78, 80, 94, 98-99, 136-137, 217
Hughes, Jennie 82-83, 136
Hugo, Victor 76-77
Hungary 237, 249
Hymns 2, 19, 29, 64, 75, 112, 114, 123, 137, 163, 282, 284
Iceland 149
Idaho 181
Illinois 6, 34, 64, 93-99, 106, 115, 122-123, 125, 137, 142, 183, 204-205, 208-209, 211-213, 223, 225, 228, 283
Illinois College 211
Illinois Wesleyan College 64
Illiteracy 45, 56, 84, 273-275
Immigration (Immigrant) 22, 33, 66, 84, 135-137, 205-206, 213-214, 231, 255, 274
India 17, 25-29, 75, 113, 118, 130-131, 144, 203, 211, 272, 280
Indian Ocean 298
Indian Witness 282
Indiana 122-124, 228, 282
Industrial homes 82, 136
Industrial Workers of the World (I.W.W.) 50-51, 182
Interchurch World Movement 127, 139

Internationalism 51-54
Iowa 63, 123-124, 176-177, 182-183, 281
Ireland 149, 157, 251, 285
Italian-Americans 84-85
Italy 86, 146, 219, 249, 252, 254, 267, 272
Jackson, Andrew 231
Japan 22, 28, 46, 70, 78, 80, 144-148, 202
Java (Indonesia) 29
Jefferson, Thomas 28, 244
Jim Crow 37, 66
Joffre, Joseph 221
John Barleycorn 146, 195
John Bull 27
Johnson, Eben Samuel 17, 63
Johnson, Elijah 64
Joint Commission on Unification 134, 283
Jones, Bob 112
Jones, Robert Elijah 2, 8, 13-14, 16-17, 45-49, 63, 66-67
Jones, Samuel Porter 188-189, 211
Jones Act of 1917 149, 207
Jordan River 54
Kabyle People 25
Kaffir "Red" People 17, 63-64
Kansas 100, 127, 172, 177, 180
Kansas Annual Conference (MEC) 138
Kentucky 61, 108, 134, 139, 175, 227, 274, 283, 286
Kentucky Annual Conference (MECS) 134
Khoikhoi People 63
King, Martin Luther Jr. 14
Kipling, Rudyard 29
Knights of Columbus 219
Knox College 212
Korea 7
Kraft, William J. 58
Ku Klux Klan 66, 210
Labour Party (U.K.) 232
LaGrange Female College 137
Lane College 68
Lantern Slides 4
Lasal Seminary 137
Latin America 7, 82, 135, 158-162
Latitudinarianism 115
Laylin, Lewis Cass 259, 285
Laymen's Missionary Movement 110, 133, 286
League of Nations 4, 9, 27, 49, 54, 67, 72, 87, 118-119, 131, 143, 149, 199-201, 214, 222, 240-258, 266, 273, 284
Lebanon University 282
Ledbetter, J.M. 108
Lee, Robert E. 175
Legion of Honor 255
Leonard, A.B. 72, 172
Leviathan 256
Lewis, H.W. 116
Lexington Annual Conference (MEC) 65
Liberal Party (U.K.) 217
Livingstone, David 16, 63, 88, 111
Logan, W.H. 31
Long, Fred 106
Louisiana 14, 45, 51, 75, 77, 175, 182, 222, 224, 282
Louisiana Annual Conference (MEC) 51, 64
Louisville Annual Conference (MECS) 139
Lovejoy, Elijah Parish 183
Loyal Temperance Legion 145, 166, 207
Lunacy Commission 98
Lusitania 221
Lynching 4, 14, 37, 45-50, 58, 66-67, 213, 224
McAdoo, William 9, 129, 214, 239, 257-258, 282
McConnell, Eva T. 10
McConnell, Francis J. 1, 3, 10, 14, 49, 211, 228, 281-282
McDowell, Clotilda Lyon 73, 132-133
McDowell, William Fraser 161, 163, 165, 169, 174-175, 180, 204-205, 207
McKinley, William 36
Maclay College of Theology 208
Madison, James 240, 242
Maine 157, 166, 173, 209, 260
Malaysia 26-29
Maryland 4, 44, 66, 107, 134-135, 175-176, 275
Mason-Dixon Line 61, 116, 130
Massachusetts 4, 10, 35, 46, 66, 76, 79,

81, 95, 107, 110, 112, 122, 124, 134, 136, 152, 155, 157-158, 164, 228, 242-243, 293
Mathews, Alma 89, 137
Mecca 28
Medal of Honor 286
Medical Missions 13, 21, 63-64, 89, 153
Mediterranean Sea 24, 28
Methodist Brotherhood 72
Methodist Building (Washington, DC) 210
Methodist Church
   Central Jurisdiction 14, 66; Woman's Division of Christian Service 135
Methodist Episcopal Church
   Board of Bishops 298; Board of Foreign Missions 4-5; Board of Home Missions and Church Extension 4, 233; Board of Sunday Schools 139; Board of Temperance, Prohibition, and Public Morals 142, 163, 176, 180, 210; Church Union 52; Colored Conferences 52, 71, 224; League of Intercession 131; Temperance Society 142, 175; Woman's Foreign Missionary Society 9, 11, 75, 77, 79-83, 89-91, 133-137; Woman's Home Missionary Society 71, 77, 82-83, 87, 133-137; Young Peoples' Work 136
Methodist Episcopal Church, South
   Board of Missions 138; Church Union 52; Commission on Temperance and Social Service 188, 209; Woman's Missionary Council 72, 133, 136; Woman's Parsonage and Home Society 134
Methodist Federation for Social Action 10, 282
Methodist Protestant Church
   Woman's Foreign Missionary Society 133; Woman's Home Missionary Society 133
Mexico 35, 50, 138, 141, 157, 229, 284-285
Mexico Annual Conference (MECS) 208

Mexican Methodist Institute 208
Michigan 65, 106, 124, 134, 181, 197-198, 282
Midland College 137
Military, U.S.
   Camp Sherman 271-273; Eighty-Second Infantry 285; First Division 95; Secretary of the Navy 71, 116, 119, 139, 213, 258, 285; Secretary of War 117, 239, 263, 284; Sixth Brigade (Marines) 96; Thirty-Third Division 97; Three Hundred Sixty-Ninth Infantry 62, 68, 282
Miller, Lewis 207
Minnesota 135, 150, 192
Minute Men 9, 71-72, 105-114, 117, 119, 121-125, 127-133, 265
Missionary Education Movement 4, 136
Missionary Exposition
   Baltimore 4; Boston 4, 10; Chicago 4; Church Mission to the Jews 3; Cincinnati 4
Missionary Review of the World 4
Missionary Society of the Methodist Episcopal Church 6, 14, 68, 135
Mississippi 51, 67, 176, 192, 220-221
Mississippi Annual Conference (MECS) 51, 67, 210
Missouri 49, 65, 67, 106, 127, 134, 138-139, 197, 209, 219, 223, 280, 282
Mob Violence 14, 45-46, 60, 118, 223, 225
Monroe Doctrine 255
Montana 181
Moore, John Monroe 213, 226, 230, 283
Moore, Watson 106, 119
Morningside College 63
Morris, Dinah 115, 140
The Moslem World 13, 23, 26, 65
Mother's Day 84
Motion Pictures (Film) 4, 8, 66, 72, 126-129, 138, 140, 284
Mott, John R. 109
Mount Holyoke College 137
Muhammad (Prophet) 27-28
Mumpower, Daniel Leeper 13, 20-22,

332 Index

64
Munsey's Magazine 19
Murray, Virginia May 100
Mutual Film Company 129
Nashville Christian Advocate 283
National American Woman Suffrage Association 134, 138
National Anti-Alcohol League of Uruguay 142, 209
National Association of Motion Picture Producers 140
National Council of Women 137
National Exchange Club 125
National Geographic 4
National Temperance League 161-162
National Travelers Aid Society 100
National Woman's Party 9, 71-72, 100, 104, 138
Native American (Indian)
Arapahoe 226; Creek 228; Huron 228; Ottawa 227; Shawnee 228; Winnebago 137, 214, 226, 230, 283; Wyandot 14, 20, 40, 77, 68
Nebraska 124, 166, 181, 199
Neihardt, John 65
Netherlands 22
New Brunswick Theological Seminary 65
New England Annual Conference (MEC) 10, 283
New Hampshire 139, 242-243, 277-278
New Hampshire Annual Conference (MEC) 139
New Jersey 64, 66, 138, 204, 284-285
New Orleans Christian Advocate 14, 67
New Orleans University 63-64
New York 34, 47, 66, 73, 76-77, 80, 84, 86, 96, 101, 106, 112, 123, 125, 128-130, 135, 139-140, 156-157, 169-170, 207, 209, 221, 231, 237, 242-243, 251, 278, 280, 284-285
New York Age 65
New York Annual Conference (MEC) 138
New York Elevated Railroad (New York City Subway) 56
New Zealand 104, 176
Newark Annual Conference (MEC) 136
Nietzsche, Friedrich 200

Nineteenth Amendment 9, 100, 103, 138, 141, 166
North Carolina 63, 135, 220-221, 260, 268-269, 284-285
North Carolina Annual Conference (MEC) 63
North Dakota 173
North Georgia Conference (MECS) 211
North Ohio Conference (MEC) 209
Northwest Iowa Annual Conference (MEC) 63
Northwestern University 64, 67, 208, 211-212
Norville, Hardynia K. 141-142, 155-156, 158-162, 209
Norway 104, 149;
Nullification, Doctrine of 117, 140
Nyack Missionary Training Institute (Nyack College) 65
Oberlin College 153, 208, 283
Oberlin Theological Seminary 209
Ohio 1-2, 4, 6-10, 14, 34, 39, 41, 49-50, 55, 68, 75, 86, 93, 97, 99, 104, 106, 119, 121-123, 135, 137-140, 142, 144-149, 152-153, 165, 168, 184, 190, 197, 201, 203, 206-210, 214, 219, 239, 260, 269, 271, 275-276, 278, 281-283, 285
Ohio State Fairgrounds
Africa Building 7, 88, 208; Asbury Building 150, 156, 208; The Big Tent 93, 112, 121, 142, 163, 168; China Building 7, 208; Coliseum 2, 14, 16, 31, 41, 72-73, 112, 142, 182-183, 187, 206, 226, 280; Grandstands 4, 194, 239; Motion Picture Screen 140
Ohio Wesleyan University 134, 207, 209-210, 282-283
Oldham, Maria Augusta Mulligan 155-156, 208
Oldham, William Fitzjames 208
Oregon 100, 180-181, 198
Oxenham, John 136
Pageantry 4, 8, 72, 101, 110, 129, 140, 226, 235, 283
Paine College 67-68
Paine, Robert 68
Palmer, Alexander Mitchell 195, 212
Palmer's Kaffir Boys Choir 17, 63-64

Pankhurst, Christabel 138
Pankhurst, Emmeline 138
Parades 4, 72, 98, 101, 109-110, 126, 129, 138, 140
Paramount Film Company 129
Paris Peace Conference 67, 115, 216, 219, 257, 267
Parker, Lois Lee 89, 136
Parks, Frances Pride 150-151, 156, 208
Patriotism 4, 35, 71, 78-80, 114, 165-166, 189, 196, 237, 244, 257, 263-264, 275
Paul, Alice 2, 9, 71-72, 100-103, 138
Penn, Irving Garland 14, 31, 40-42, 45, 49, 55, 58-59, 61, 65, 68
Pennsylvania 6, 8, 14, 31-32, 34, 64, 66, 104, 123-124, 220, 230-231, 242-243, 255, 285
Pentecost 238, 266
Perry, Matthew C. 35, 120
Pershing, John J. 116, 218
Petty, Russell 97
Philander Smith College 65
Philanthropy 18, 51, 79, 166, 189
Philippines 209, 277, 280
Philips, Wendell 183
Pilgrimage 6, 17
Pinson, William Washington 105-106, 139
Piracy 216
Pittsburgh Annual Conference (MEC) 285
Poland 91, 95, 248
Portugal 22, 28
Prairie View A&M University 60
Presbyterians 183, 211, 283
Princeton Theological Seminary 65, 139
Princeton University 139
Prohibition 9, 73, 77, 90, 113, 116-117, 120, 139, 141, 143, 147-151, 156, 160, 165-171, 175-182, 184, 186-190, 195-199, 206, 208, 211, 285
Prohibition Party 139, 209-210, 286
Propaganda 23, 47, 97, 184, 279
Puerto Rico 136, 149, 207
Pullman Company 107
Quaker (Society of Friends) 138
Race

Amalgamation 45-52;
Discrimination 49, 62, 67, 213, 223, 256; Riots 4, 66-67, 213, 282
Railroad 6, 56, 165, 170, 219, 272, 284
Rainbow Division Band 268, 276
Rainey, Henry Thomas 142-143, 194, 199, 201, 212
Raleigh News and Observer 139, 285
Randall, Charles H. 179, 210
Randolph-Macon College 66, 139, 286
Read, Albert C. 9, 214-215, 277-278, 280, 284-286
Red Sea 28
"Red Summer" of 1919 213
Reformed Church in America 65
Reisner, Christian F. 9, 72, 105-107, 109-113, 119-121, 124-125, 128, 130, 138, 140, 240
Religions
  Buddhism 83-85; Hinduism 8, 46; Islam (Mohammedans) 17, 19, 21, 23-30, 216; Judaism 3, 84, 129; Mormonism 83, 85, 122; Roman Catholicism 82, 85
Republic of Macedonia 118, 199
Republican Party 104, 197, 246
Rhine River 80, 262
Richard, Florence D. 145-146, 150, 156, 207
Richmond Planet 65
Rio Grande River 77, 229
Roberts, Albert H. 280
Roberts, Brigham Henry 85
Rockefeller, John D. 206
Roosevelt, Franklin D. 209, 282
Roosevelt, Theodore 209, 234
Rotary Club 72, 125
Russell, Howard Hyde 160, 206
Russia 28, 86, 176, 228, 244, 248-249, 269
Russian Revolution of 1917 47-48, 67
Russo-Japanese War 28
Rust College 65
St. Gervais Church 214-215
St. Louis Annual Conference (MECS) 138
Sabbath Observance 86, 177, 181, 229
Saloon 9, 72, 77, 117, 123, 126-127,

141, 147-148, 163, 166, 173-174, 177, 186, 189-191, 193-196, 199, 201-206
Salvation Army 219
San, Suiga 85
San Juan Hill, Battle of 35, 46
Savannah Annual Conference (MEC) 210
Scarritt College for Christian Workers 134
Scientific Temperance 156, 161, 168, 208
Scopes Trial 211
Scotland 63, 149, 158, 176, 251, 284
Scott, George Herbert 284
Scott, Isaiah Benjamin 8, 17, 41, 63
Sea of Galilee 199
Second Regiment Band 41
Sectionalism 46, 116
Serbia 200
Seventeenth Amendment 211
Shanghai Woman's Suffrage Association 208
Shaw, Anna Howard 73, 115, 134
Shellabear, William Girdlestone 65
Sherrill, Joseph C. 31, 65
Shinn, Asa 134
Simpson, Matthew 148
Singapore 28, 203
Sixteenth Amendment (U.S.) 211
Skidmore, Harriet 77
Slavery
    African 14, 42, 56-57, 146, 171-172; White 24
Smith, Alfred E. 159
Smith, Fred B. 8
Smith, Harry Lester 214, 257, 285
Smoot, Reed 85, 136
Snethen, Nicholas 134
Social Equality 14, 38-39, 148
Social Services 71, 93, 99
Socialism (Christian) 232-233, 284
Society for the Colonization of Free People of Color in America 66
South Carolina 48, 59, 68, 136, 176
South Carolina Annual Conference (MEC) 136
South India Annual Conference (MEC) 282
Southwestern Christian Advocate 45, 63-64

Spain 22, 28, 199, 221
Spanish-American War 35
Spilman, Lucy Lee Mahan 73, 134
Springer, Helen Emily 23, 64
Springer, John McKendree 23, 64
Stansell, Herbert 187
State Militia 50
Stevens, Lillian 166, 209
Stevenson, Catherine Lent 157-158, 209
Stewardship (Tithing) 21, 110-111, 131
Stewart, John 14, 20, 40, 55, 68, 86
Stock, Arthur 106
Stock, Eugene 3
Stowe, Harriet Beecher 146
Stuart, George Rutledge 62, 188-189, 194, 211
Stubbs, Harriet 77
Stuntz, Homer Clyde 213, 216-217, 220, 282
Sue Bennett Memorial School 134
Suffrage 4, 9, 71-72, 77, 100-103, 134, 138, 141, 148, 169, 207
Sugimoto, Etsu Inagaki 151-152, 207
Suicide 38-40
Sunday School 25, 90, 118, 166, 168, 220
Swain, Clara 135
Swarthmore College 138
Sweden 149
Syria 144
Tanner, Henry O. 56
Taxation 47, 94, 178, 191, 252
Taylor, S. Earl 4-5, 10, 110-111, 139-140
Taylor University 65
Tecumseh 228
Temple University 138
Tennessee 31, 41, 50, 60, 63, 108, 123, 139, 173-174, 211, 222, 226, 236, 280-281, 283-284
Tertullian 26
Texas 31, 60, 122, 139, 218, 283
Texas Annual Conference (MEC) 63
Thirkield, Mary Haven 75-76, 135
Thirkield, Wilbur 213, 222-224, 282
Tindley, Charles Albert 2, 8, 14, 32, 65-66
Tobias, Charles Henry 15, 61, 68
Training School for Deaconesses (Boston, MA) 136

Training School for the Indian Workers of America 226
Treaty of Paris of 1783 242
Trepassey Bay 279
Tuberculosis 57
Tulane University 67
Turkey 27, 244
Turner, Frederick Jackson 284
Tuskegee Institute of Alabama 67
Union College of Law 211-212
Unionism 50-51
United Artists Film Company 129, 214
United Church of Canada 2
United Confederate Veterans 284
United Methodist Church 68
United Quartette 31
United States Geographical Survey 171
United States Medical Reserve Corps 57
United States Military Academy 268, 285
University of Alaska-Anchorage 285
University of Denver 209
University of Georgia 139
University of Glasgow 63
University of Mississippi 67
University of North Carolina-Chapel Hill 284
University of North Carolina Law School 139, 285
University of Pennsylvania 37
University of Southern California 135, 210
University of Tennessee-Knoxville 284
University of Wisconsin 284
Upper Iowa University 139
Upper Mississippi Annual Conference (MEC) 210
Uruguay 142, 158-162, 209
Utah 85, 122, 136
Valderrama, Pedro Flores 158, 209
Vanderbilt University 64, 66, 286
Vandervelde, Emile 176
Vasquez, Isabel Gonzales 160
Vaterland 261, 285
Verdun 285
Vermont 122
Versailles 217
Victoria Cross 260
Viera, Aurelia 158-160, 209

Vincent, John Heyl 207
Vinton, S.R. 140
Virginia 42-43, 46, 59, 66, 173-176, 211, 217, 243, 280, 286
Virginia Annual Conference (MECS) 66, 139
Virginia Union University 67
Vitagraph Film Company 129
Volstead Act 150
War of 1812 46, 65
Waring, Frank W. 182, 186, 194
Washington (State) 181
Washington, Booker T. 14, 46, 51, 56, 67
Washington, George 28, 35, 48, 79, 242-243
Waterboarding 214, 285
Webb's School (TN) 139
Wesley, John 1, 26, 105, 113, 115, 118, 127, 140, 164, 177, 229, 234, 264-265, 277
Wesley, Susanna 115, 140
Wesleyan Methodist Church 116
Wesleyan University 139
West Texas Annual Conference (MEC) 224
White House (Washington, DC) 35, 60, 101, 103, 148, 192, 231
Whitefield, George 115, 264-265
Wiley College 63, 65
Williams, Daniel H. 56
Wilson, Alonzo E. 277, 286
Wilson, Clarence True 9, 141-142, 176-178, 180, 182, 210
Wilson, John A.B. 171
Wilson, Woodrow 4, 9, 38, 48, 51, 67, 72, 101, 102, 104, 138, 143, 148, 158, 207, 211- 214, 216, 222, 269, 284-285
Wisconsin 197
Woman's Anti-Vice Committee 209
Woman's Christian Temperance Union Polyglot Petition 150
Woman's Club 99, 127
Woman's Press Club 209
Women's Medical College of Philadelphia 64
Wong, Frances Willard 141-142, 153, 208
Woodruff, May Leonard 81, 136

Woods, Granville T. 156
Woolley, John Granville 210
Wooster College 209
World League Against Alcoholism
    137, 139, 176, 210
World Outlook 139
World Parish 139
World War I
    African American Soldiers 45-46,
    54, 57-62, 80, 223-224, 282;
    Burma 81; Chateau Thierry 96;
    Croix de Guerre 62, 223; Draft
    Board 59; "Flanders Fields" 58,
    80; Gas, Use of 98-99, 214, 223,
    270; Liberty Loan Drive 168, 239;
    Native American Soldiers 228,
    283; Peace Treaty 54, 219, 222,
    248-249; Sexually Transmitted
    Disease 117-118; Submarine
    Warfare 19, 117, 260-261, 270;
    Training Facilities 57, 214, 260,
    271-272; Trench Warfare (No
    Man's Land) 5, 24, 29, 37, 58-59,
    91, 214, 217, 223, 228, 270-271;
    War Council 93; Western Front
    46, 48, 54, 62, 78, 80-81, 196,
    217, 219, 221
World Woman's Christian Temperance
    Union 141, 153, 166, 208-209
World's Fair
    Atlanta 14, 59; Chicago 2; San
    Francisco 2
Wright, Hamilton 204, 212
Wyandot Indian Mission 68, 77
Wyandot Nation 14, 20, 40, 68
Yajima, Madame Kaji 152-153, 208
Yale Conservatory of Music 58
Yale University 25, 64, 226, 283
Yasumori, Katsutaro 83
York, Alvin C. 29, 195, 214-215, 237,
    277, 280-281, 286
Young Men's Christian Association 8,
    219, 270
Young People's Missionary Movement
    4
Zion's Herald 6
Zulu People 63
Zwemer, Samuel 13, 23, 26, 45

www.ingramcontent.com/pod-product-compliance
Lightning Source LLC
Chambersburg PA
CBHW021818300426
44114CB00009BA/222